57⁵⁰

D0915405

Marine Electrical Practice
– 5th edition

Marine Engineering Series

MARINE AUXILIARY MACHINERY — 5th edition
Ernest Souchotte, C.Eng., F.I.Mech.E., M.I.Mar.E. and
David W. Smith, C.Eng., M.I.Mar.E.

MARINE DIESEL ENGINES — 5th edition
C.C. Pounder

MARINE ELECTRICAL PRACTICE — 5th edition
G.O. Watson, F.I.E.E., F.A.I.E.E., M.I.Mar.E.

MARINE AND OFFSHORE PUMPING AND PIPING SYSTEMS
J. Crawford, C. Eng., F.I.Mar.E.

MARINE STEAM BOILERS — 4th edition
J.H. Milton, C.Eng., M.I.Mar.E.
Roy M. Leach, C.Eng., M.I.Mech.E., M.I.Mar.E.

MARINE STEAM ENGINES AND TURBINES — 4th edition
S.C. McBirnie, C.Eng., M.I.Mech.E.

Marine Electrical Practice – 5th edition

G.O. Watson, CEng, FIEE, FelIEEE, FIMarE

Specialist contributors

G.A. Bowie
M. Carlisle
T. Morgan
A. Robson
S.L. Richards
N. Townson

Butterworths
London Boston Sydney Wellington Durban Toronto

First published in 1957 by George Newnes Ltd
Second edition 1962
    Reprinted 1965
Third edition 1967
Fourth edition 1971
    Reprinted 1975, 1976, 1978, 1979
Fifth edition, 1981

© Butterworth & Co (Publishers) Ltd, 1971
© Chapter 15, Brown Brothers & Co. Ltd and
Muirhead Vatric Components Ltd, 1981

British Library Cataloguing in Publication Data

Watson, George Oliphant
    Marine electrical practice. — 5th ed.
    1. Electricity on ships
    I. Title
    623.85'03   VM471   79—41640

ISBN 0-408-00498 3

Typeset by Scribe Design, Gillingham, Kent
Printed by Fletcher & Son Ltd, Norwich

Preface

This fifth edition has been thoroughly revised and many of the chapters have been rewritten to take account of the drastic and revolutionary changes in marine electrical practice over the past two decades. One of the most important changes has been the almost complete elimination of d.c in favour of a.c, although the former is still used in very small ships. In view of this the chapter on d.c generators has been considerably shortened and the space used to include revised and expanded material on a.c generators, switchgear, and distribution systems. The revised chapter on d.c generators will however, still be of interest in relation to older installations, small ships, and for main propulsion (electric) systems.

The subject of electro-magnetic compatibility (i.e. interference) has been receiving ever-increasing attention and this is applicable to marine electrical installations as well as to those which are shore-based. A separate chapter has now been added on this subject which covers possible cases of interference and how to avoid these by careful planning of the installation.

Many developments have taken place in the manufacture of cables for marine purposes. Rubber- and lead-sheathed cables have now been almost eliminated in favour of new types of covering using elastomeric compounds. In consequence of this the chapter on cable installation has been completely re-written to include up-to-date information on cabling.

Recent years have seen the advent of the so-called unmanned engine room and also the introduction of super-tankers. In view of these changes, the tanker section has been completely re-written by Mike Carlisle of Shell Tankers who is a well-known expert on this subject. This chapter now reflects the current thinking on electrical equipment installed in tankers from the important safety aspect.

I would like to express my thanks to the contributors of the various chapters and also to the many firms and organisations who have supplied material and illustrations.

G.O. Watson

v

Specialist contributors

George A. Bowie, DFH, CEng, FIEE
Independent Consulting Engineer

D.M. Carlisle, FIEE, MIMarE
Senior Electrical Engineer, Shell International Marine

T. Morgan
Ministry of Defence (Navy)

A. Robson, CEng, MIEE
Chief Electrical Engineer, NEI Clarke Chapman Eng. Ltd.,
Clarke Chapman Marine

S.L. Richards, BA, AssocIEE
Design Engineer, GEC Large machines, Rugby

N. Townson, DipEE, CEng, MIEE
Formerly with Y-ard Ltd, Glasgow.

Contents

1 Introduction

It is now generally accepted by those with experience in marine work that electrical apparatus made primarily for land use is not as a general rule suitable for installation in ships. Climatic conditions, vibration, the continual motion of the ship, temperature and conditions of usage are all contributory factors. Usually (although admittedly not in every case) apparatus ashore is not operated at a constant load, day and night, for long periods, in industry there are peak loads and off-peak load periods and these factors have considerable effect on the life of equipment. Factories may be remodelled as new production lines are introduced or new machine tools become available, but in ships the electrical equipment is expected to last the lifetime of the ship. During this time maximum reliability is important, particularly in regard to those services which are vital for propulsion and safety.

Requirements and regulations

Practically every ocean-going ship is registered with a Classification Society and is therefore required to comply with the Rules of the relevant Society. These differ slightly in technical and also in survey requirements, and for the benefit of those wishing to study the regulations of the various Societies a list of them is included in Chapter 23. The International Electrotechnical Commission (IEC) has issued Publication No. 92, *Recommendations for electrical installations in ships,* for the guidance of national bodies and Classification Societies in removing these technical differences and achieving international standardisation.

In addition to classification requirements there are statutory international requirements, namely the Convention on Safety of Life at Sea 1960 (sometimes referred to as SOLAS) which is administered by National Governments. Subject to compliance with specified conditions it will in due course by superseded by SOLAS 1974.

1

Ships having British Registry are required to comply with Department of Trade (Marine Division) regulations. References to appropriate regulations will be found in Chapter 23.

There are two outstanding considerations in the selection and installation of marine electrical equipment. Firstly, outstanding reliability and freedom from breakdown for those services which are essential for navigation (steering, navigation lights, radio services, etc.), and propulsion. Secondly, freedom from fire risks. Both these conditions demand a well-found installation with first-class materials and, above all, good workmanship and maintenance. In the following chapters, some of the factors which contribute to these requirements will be dealt with more fully, and a better understanding of the installation by seagoing engineers and electricians will, it is hoped, lead to efficient maintenance and operation.

Some factors are common throughout and to save repetition may be summarised here. All materials should as far as possible be non-flammable, but some insulating materials cannot all be made to meet this requirement and the nearest approach is that they should be flame-retardant, i.e. will not continue to burn when the flame is removed.

The standard requirement, now universally accepted, requires propulsion and auxiliary machinery fitted in the ship to be capable of operating when the ship is upright and when inclined at any angle of list up to and including 15° either way under static conditions and 22½° under dynamic conditions (rolling) either way and when simultaneously inclined dynamically (pitching) 7½° by bow or stern. Classification Rules require also that emergency generating sets shall be capable of functioning when the ship is inclined 22½° from upright and/or is inclined 10° by bow or stern.

One of the main factors concerned with these inclinations is that of lubrication and another is that of the functioning of contactors, switchgear and relays having unsymmetrical or unbalanced magnet systems where the magnetic pull required to operate increases with tilt. Any apparatus containing oil, such as transformers or switches, would also be affected.

Temperature requirements

The performance of electrical items is affected in practically every instance by temperature. Temperature not only affects performance but determines the effective life of the electrical apparatus. For instance on all devices which are dependent on electromagnetic operation by shunt coils the resistance of the coil increases with temperature, thus reducing the ampere turns. A contactor or relay may fail to function if allowed to become overheated. In a generator the voltage will decrease as the machine heats up and in a d.c. motor the speed may increase.

The important factor is the total temperature, and this is determined partly by the ambient air temperature and partly by the heating effect of the current in the windings. Under the same conditions of loading and operation the latter effect for all practical purposes will always be the same and the resultant temperature change is always referred to as the 'temperature rise'. Other things being equal, the temperature rise is virtually always the same. It follows that the total temperature (which is what determines the life of the insulation and the performance of the device) will be at its maximum when the ambient is at its maximum — usually in the tropics. For design purposes Lloyd's Register of Shipping specifies a cooling air temperature of 45°C as the basis for machines in ships classed for unrestricted service; for restricted service and vessels intended solely for use in northern or southern waters outside the tropical belt, the basis is 40°C. When water-cooled heat exchangers are used for cooling the ventilating air the maximum temperature of the sea water is to be taken as 30°C and 25°C respectively.

Adequate ventilation and the avoidance of hot pockets in which electrical apparatus may have to operate are of prime importance.

Machines should be installed with their axes of rotation either vertical or in a fore and aft direction. If they unavoidably have to be placed athwartships care must be taken to reduce end-play and to provide suitable thrust bearings to prevent any hammering action when the ship rolls. Special attention must also be paid to lubrication of ring lubricated sleeve bearings.

The usual cause of overheating in electrical joints is loose connections and to counter this, particularly in view of the ever-present vibration problem, not only should all screws and nuts be effectually locked but periodically they should be examined and tightened up if necessary. This applies not only to heavy current circuits but also to control and shunt circuits, any of which if allowed to become slack may cause erratic operation or complete failure.

A.C. installations

A word of warning may not be out of place in regard to a.c. installations. Today almost all installations are a.c., but there may still be a few operating on d.c. The standard supplies for d.c. are 100 and

220 V and although under certain conditions these can be lethal, generally speaking the danger of shock is not nearly so great as with high-voltage a.c. supplies. Ships are now equipped with 380 and 440 V a.c. and shock from these voltages may be fatal. One of the effects of a.c., apart from other considerations, is that it causes a tightening of the grip which often means that the unfortunate victim cannot let go. A case is on record of death as a result of shock at 60 V a.c. and Regulations require special precautions to be taken where the supply voltage to earth exceeds 55 V.

2 Insulation and temperature ratings of machines

For easy reference insulating materials are grouped in classes according to their nature and the working temperature for which they are suitable.

Classes O, A, B and C have been in general use for many years, but Class O is now known as Y and three new classes E, F and H have recently been added to legislate for some of the new materials and processes in this field.

Further information on this subject can be found in BS 2757: 1956 and IEC Publication No. 85 but for convenience the descriptions pertaining to these classes have been abstracted and are given below.

Class Y insulation consists of materials or combinations of materials such as cotton, silk and paper without impregnation. Other materials or combinations of materials may be included in this class if by experience or accepted tests they can be shown to be capable of operation at the Class Y temperature.

Class A insulation consists of materials such as cotton, silk and paper when suitably impregnated or coated or when immersed in a dielectric liquid such as oil. Other materials or combinations of materials may be included in this class if by experience or tests they can be shown to be capable of operation at the Class A temperature.

Class E insulation consists of materials or combinations of materials which by experience or tests can be shown to be capable of operation at the Class E temperature (materials possessing a degree of thermal stability allowing them to be operated at a temperature 15°C higher than Class A materials).

Class B insulation consists of materials or combinations of materials such as mica, glass fibre, asbestos, etc., with suitable bonding, impregnating or coating substances. Other materials or combinations of materials, not necessarily inorganic, may be included in this class, if by experience or tests they can be shown to be capable of operation at the Class B temperature.

Class F insulation consists of materials or combinations of materials such as mica, glass fibre, asbestos, etc., with suitable bonding, impregnating or coating substances. This class also includes other materials or combinations of materials, not necessarily inorganic, which by experience or tests can be shown to be capable of operation at the Class F temperature (materials possessing a degree of thermal stability allowing them to be operated at a temperature 25°C higher than Class B materials).

Class H insulation consists of materials such as silicone elastomer and combinations of materials such as mica, glass fibre, asbestos, etc., with suitable bonding, impregnating or coating substances such as appropriate silicone resins. Other materials or combinations of materials may be included in this class if by experience or tests they can be shown to be capable of operation at the Class H temperature.

Class C insulation consists of materials or combinations of materials such as mica, porcelain, glass, quartz, and asbestos without or with an inorganic binder. Other materials or combinations of materials may be included in this class, if by experience or tests they can be shown to be capable of operation at temperatures above the Class H limit. Specific materials or combinations of materials in this class will have a temperature limit which is dependent upon their physical, chemical and electrical properties.

In each class, a proportion of materials of a lower temperature class may be included for structural purposes only, provided that adequate electrical and mechanical properties are maintained during the application of the maximum permitted temperature.

An insulating material is considered to be 'suitably impregnated' when a suitable substance such as varnish penetrates the interstices between fibres, films, etc., to a sufficient degree adequately to bond components of the insulation structure and to provide a surface film which adequately excludes moisture, dirt and other contaminants.

For some applications, compounds and resins without solvents may be used which may substantially replace all the air in the interstices. In other applications, varnishes or other materials containing solvents may be used which provide reasonably continuous surface films and partial filling of the interstices with some degree of bonding between components of the insulation structure.

An insulating material is considered to be 'suitably coated' when it is covered with a suitable substance such as varnish which excludes moisture, dirt and other contaminants to a degree sufficient to provide adequate performance in service.

It will be seen that the new Class E is intermediate between Classes A and B, and Class F covers Class B materials with bonding substances which make them suitable for an additional 25°C. Generally speaking Class C is not appropriate for machines.

The endurance of insulation is affected by many factors such as temperature, electrical and mechanical stresses, vibration, exposure to deleterious atmospheres and chemicals, moisture and dirt. For example, some varnishes tend to harden with age to such an extent that cracks are formed and moisture is then admitted.

The majority of marine apparatus hitherto has been insulated with Class A materials and to a lesser extent with Class B, but it is anticipated that Class E will enter this field more and more in the future. Class O (now Y), being without impregnation, is hygroscopic and therefore unsuited to marine conditions.

Hot-spot temperatures

When considering suitable operating temperatures it is the temperature at the hottest point that is important, and this is referred to as the 'hot-spot' temperature. In a field coil, for instance, the hot-spot is somewhere near the centre of the winding and there is a temperature gradient from there to the surface, so that the temperature is not uniform throughout the coil. For research purposes the temperature of this spot can be measured by embodying a thermo-couple in the winding but this is not practicable in production machines except in the slots of large alternator stators. The only means available in practice therefore is to determine the temperature either by the change in resistance of the winding, or by measuring the surface temperature by thermometer. The surface temperature will obviously be less than the hot-spot, and to a certain extent the difference will depend on the depth of winding. From previous research and experience, values of surface temperature corresponding to specified hot-spot temperatures have been determined and are now universally accepted. If the resistance method is used, it is evident that as there is a temperature gradient the resistance must lie somewhere between what it would be if the whole coil was at hot-spot temperature, and what it would be at surface temperature. The temperature determined by resistance is therefore higher than the surface temperature, and the accepted difference will be noted in the standard tables.

For Classes A and B hot-spot temperatures of 105°C and 130°C respectively have been universally accepted for very many years.

These figures correspond roughly to about twenty years' working life under average industrial conditions. It must be remembered however that in industry there are usually peak periods of loading interspersed with off-load or reduced load periods for meal-breaks, and these periods of rest have considerable influence on the life of machines. Under marine conditions some machines may run for days at a constant load, and experience has shown that under these conditions the life may be reduced to about fifteen years. No hard and fast rule can be made because conditions vary, but taking into account also the necessity for utmost reliability in marine installations the need for a more conservative approach to this problem is indicated. It is generally accepted that insulation life is approximately halved for each 10 per cent increase above the accepted hot-spot temperature limits for Class A and Class B materials.

Temperature rise

A continuously-rated machine will eventually reach a steady temperature at which the heat in the windings and magnetised cores and the heat arising from frictional losses will be dissipated at the same rate as they are generated. The difference between this steady temperature and that of the incoming cooling air is the temperature rise. For all practical purposes, other things being equal, this rise is always the same regardless of the temperature of the cooling air. Accordingly if a machine is tested in an ambient or cooling air temperature of 20°C and a machine temperature of 55°C is recorded, the rise is 35°C; when the same machine is in the tropics and the cooling air is at 45°C the rise will still be 35°C, giving a total machine temperature of 80°C.

Having determined the appropriate hot-spot temperature for a given class of insulation, and from that the surface temperature, the permissible temperature rise is arrived at by deducting the maximum ambient air temperature under which the machine will be called upon to operate. When carrying out temperature tests on machines it is important to remember that the surface temperature of windings is affected by windage and the temperatures recorded while the machine is rotating must not be taken as the maximum for determining temperature rise. After the machine has come to rest a further rise will occur and the thermometers must be observed for several seconds after stopping, until the temperature reaches its maximum. Thermometer bulbs should be shielded with a pad of felt, cotton wool or other non-conducting material approximately 3 mm thick, extending at least 20 mm in every direction from the bulb, in order to prevent loss of heat by radiation and convection from the bulb.

Ambient air temperatures

Certain types of ship such as coasters, harbour craft, train ferries, etc., built primarily for service in temperate climates will normally never be required to operate in the tropics. The ambient air temperature for such ships can be based on temperate conditions, bearing in mind that temperatures in the machinery spaces will be higher than outside temperatures. But for ocean-going ships it is required that temperature rises should be based on tropical conditions. Notwithstanding the intentions of the first owner such ships sometimes change hands and must therefore be suitable for service in any part of the world.

Temperatures recorded in various positions in many types of ships have been tabulated and studied. It has been shown for instance that certain parts of engine-rooms are almost invariably warmer than other parts of the same engine-room and it is logical therefore to accept lower temperatures for switchboards, for instance, than for generators and motors.

Basis of machine ratings

In the past there have been two methods of assessing the ratings of motors and generators:

(*a*) continuous rating permitting overloads (abbreviated to c.r.p.o.);

(*b*) continuous maximum rating (c.m.r.).

When BS 2949 was issued c.r.p.o. ratings were no longer standard and c.m.r. only is recognised standard. Temperature rises have been revised accordingly. This is in line with the practice on land as it is now accepted that the sustained overload previously included in the rating was seldom if ever called upon in service.

Momentary overloads (for which, for test purposes, 15 s is recognised) of 50% in current for generators and of varying amounts in torque for motors according to type, size and duty are recognised. CMR does not mean that machines are incapable of carrying moderate overloads of reasonable duration but that the makers are not called upon to state either the magnitude or duration or to submit machines to an overload test. In actual fact electric motors

Table 2.1 Limits of permissible temperature rise of a.c. machines of continuous maximum rating or short-time rating based on 50°C. cooling-air temperature (from BS 2949)

Part of machine	Machines other than totally enclosed			Totally enclosed machines		
	Class A	Class E	Class B	Class A	Class E	Class B
	deg. C.	deg. C.	deg. C.	deg. C.	deg. C.	deg. C.
1. Stator windings, rated voltage below 1,000 volts. Rotor windings (other than Item 3) connected to sliprings or commutators	40*	50*	60*	45*	55*	65*
2. Stator windings, rated 1,000 volts and upwards:						
(a) Outputs below 5,000 h.p. or kVA having core length less than a metre	(50)	(60)	(70)	(50)	(60)	(70)
(b) Outputs below 5,000 h.p. or kVA having core length of a metre of more.	Note 2	60†	70†	Note 2	60†	70†
(c) Outputs 5,000 h.p. or kVA and above irrespective of core length	Note 2	60†	70†	Note 2	60†	70†
3. Salient-pole field windings, stationary or rotating:						
(a) Single layer windings with exposed bare surface	55 (55)	70 (70)	80 (80)	55 (55)	70 (70)	80 (80)
(b) All other salient pole field windings	40 (50)	50 (60)	60 (70)	45 (50)	55 (65)	65 (75)
4. Non-salient pole field windings, for turbine-type generators	(55)	(70)	(80)	(55)	(70)	(80)
5. Permanently short-circuited windings, insulated	55	70	80	55	70	80
6. Sliprings*	50	60	60	50	60	60
7. Commutators≠	45	55	55	45	55	55
8. Iron cores and other parts in contact with insulator windings	45	55	65	45	55	65

9. Permanently short-circuited windings uninsulated	The temperature rise shall in no case reach such a value that there is risk of injury to any insulating material on adjacent parts.
10. Iron cores and other parts not in contact with insulated windings	
11. D.C. machines used for excitation	See Table 2.2

Notes for Table 2.1

*When the windings of a machine are not readily accessible to thermometers, the resistance method may be used. In such a case the limits of temperature rise shall be in accordance with Item *2a*.

†Embedded temperature detector.

Temperature rises shown in brackets are by resistance. Others except those marked † are by thermometer.

≠Where the windings and the commutators or sliprings to which they are connected are insulated with different classes of insulating material, the temperature rise associated with the lower class applies to the commutator or sliprings.

Note 1. The embedded temperature detector (e.t.d.) method may be used for Item *2a* instead of the resistance method with the same limits of temperature rise.

Note 2. Class A insulation is not recommended for stator windings in this category.

Table 2.2 Limits of permissible temperature rise of d.c. machines of continuous maximum rating or short-time rating, based on 50°C. cooling-air temperature (*from BS 2949*)

Part of machine	Machines other than totally enclosed			Totally enclosed machines		
	Class A	Class E	Class B	Class A	Class E	Class B
	deg. C.	deg. C.	deg. C.	deg. C.	deg. C.	deg. C.
1. Armature windings	40	50	60	45	55	65
2. Field windings						
a. Single layer windings with exposed bare surface	55	70	80	55	70	80
b. Series and commutating pole windings of more than one layer and all compensating windings.	50	65	75	50	65	75
c. Shunt windings and all field windings other than 2a and 2b	40 (50)	50 (60)	60 (70)	45 (50)	55 (60)	65 (70)
3. Commutators*	45	55	55	45	55	55
4. Sliprings*	50	60	60	50	60	60
5. Iron cores and other parts in contact with insulated windings	45	55	65	45	55	65
6. Iron cores and other parts *not* in contact with insulated windings	The temperature rise shall in no case reach such a value that there is risk of injury to any insulating material on adjacent parts.					

*Where the windings and the commutators or slip rings to which they are connected are insulated with different classes of insulating material, the temperature rise associated with the lower class shall apply to the commutator or sliprings.

and generators have an inherent capacity sufficient for average requirements.

For exceptional applications where overloads are anticipated in normal service the purchaser should seek the advice of the manufacturer or select a standard motor of higher rating. Such cases might arise with motors coupled to oil pumps where the load may be increased for short periods while pumping cold oil.

Class E insulation has been introduced to enable full advantage to be taken of the new synthetic resin enamels and similar materials now in use, which are suitable for higher working temperatures than the oleo-resin enamels which were currently available when the present limits for Class A were established.

Method of measurement of temperature rise by resistance

When converting temperature *rises,* 5°C is equal to 9°F.

If it is desired to measure temperature rise by resistance it is important to obtain a reliable reading of the cold resistance and corresponding temperature. The machine should have been standing at atmospheric temperature for some time so that it is at a uniform temperature. The initial resistance and the temperature at which this is read, as measured by a thermometer on the winding, should be recorded simultaneously.

The hot temperature is determined from the following formula:

$$t_2 = \frac{R_2}{R_1}(t_1 + 234.5) - 234.5$$

R_1 = resistance of winding cold
R_2 = resistance of winding hot
t_1 = temperature of winding cold °C.
t_2 = temperature of winding hot °C.

Since the increase in resistance of copper per degree centigrade is about 0.4% special care must be taken to use calibrated instruments and accurate recording and rapid measurement after shutting down.

A rapid estimation of temperature rise can be made on the basis of 0.4% increase in resistance per degree centigrade. For instance if a 20% increase in resistance is recorded the temperature rise is approximately 20 ÷ 0.4 = 50°C.

When it is intended to use embedded temperature detectors (e.t.d.) they must be built into the machine during construction. They may take the form either of thermocouples or resistance thermometers. This method is generally used for large alternators to record the temperature of stator windings, in which case at least six detectors are suitably distributed around the stator and placed where it is expected the highest temperatures are likely to occur. They are usually placed between upper and lower coil sides within the slots and midway between radial ducts, if any.

Measurement of ambient air temperature

The cooling air temperature should be measured at different points around and half-way up the machine and at distances of from 1–2 m away from it. The thermometers should indicate the temperature of the air flowing towards the machine and should be protected from heat radiation and stray draughts.

The value to be adopted to determine temperature rise is the average of these temperatures from readings taken at the beginning and end of the last half-hour of the test. If the conditions are such that parts of a machine are in a position in which ventilation may be impeded, e.g. in a pit, the air temperature in such a restricted area is deemed to be the ambient temperature. If the air is admitted into a machine through a definite inlet opening or openings, the temperature of the cooling air should be measured in the current of air near its entrance into the machine.

3 D.C. generators

Auxiliary generators for supplying the ship's services are usually either (*a*) compound-wound; (*b*) stabilised shunt; or (*c*) three-wire. Compound-wound generators are by far the most commonly used and (*b*) and (*c*) are almost entirely confined to American-built ships. Shunt-wound generators are only very occasionally encountered, and then usually in small installations of not more than about 30 to 40 kW and in association with batteries. Their chief asset is that the voltage can be varied over a wide range for battery charging purposes. They do not give rise to any special operational problems. They may also be used in conjunction with an a.v.r. (automatic voltage regulator) designed to maintain constant voltage.

Field regulators and the effect of tropical temperatures

Field rheostats are necessary with all types of generator in order to adjust the voltage for various conditions of running. They are chiefly used to compensate for changes in the shunt field resistance between cold and hot and for changes due to varying cooling air temperature. Unless due allowance is made when designing the machine it may be found that when the ship is in the tropics and air temperatures are in

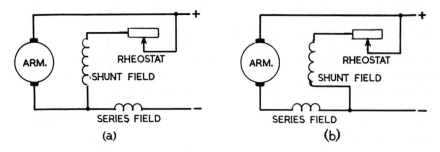

Figure 3.1 Compound wound generator
(a) short shunt connected
(b) long shunt connected

14

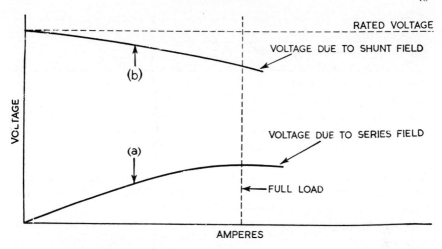

RATED VOLTAGE

VOLTAGE DUE TO SHUNT FIELD

(b)

VOLTAGE

VOLTAGE DUE TO SERIES FIELD

(a)

←—FULL LOAD

AMPERES

Figure 3.2 Characteristics of a compound wound generator
            (a) as series generator
            (b) as shunt generator

the region of 45°C the field resistance becomes so high that the
correct field current is not maintained and the busbar voltage drops.
This fault will not reveal itself when the machine is tested at the
maker's works, where the air temperature will most likely be nearer
15°C. The effect can be calculated, however, and when tested in an
ambient of 15°C the voltage across the field regulators should be not
less than 14% of the machine voltage, which still leaves a slight
margin in hand under tropical conditions.

Although some operators continually adjust field rheostats in
order to keep constant voltage at the busbars this should not be
necessary with properly compounded machines, once they have
attained constant temperature, and provided that the cooling air
temperature remains the same.

COMPOUND-WOUND GENERATORS

The compound-wound generator, as already stated, is the type most
commonly used and it is desirable to understand the factors affecting
its voltage characteristics and operating requirements.

It has a series and a shunt field (Figure 3.1) and its terminal
voltage is a combination of the characteristics of a shunt and a series
generator.

Standard practice is to connect the series field to the negative
pole; the generator manufacturer and the maker of the switchgear are
both concerned and uniformity is therefore essential.

Figure 3.2 shows typical voltage characteristics, curve (*a*) representing the voltage due to the series field and curve (*b*) the voltage due to the shunt field.

The effect of the series field is to produce additional ampere turns proportional to the load and thus offset the drooping characteristic as a shunt machine. The resultant voltage as a compound generator is nearly, but not quite, the sum of the ordinates of the two separate curves, the difference being due to the fact that as a compound machine the excitation voltage of the shunt winding is very nearly constant.

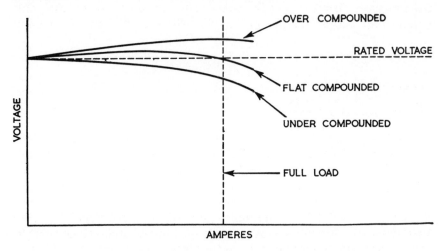

Figure 3.3 Various compound characteristics

Various effects can be obtained depending on the strength of the series winding, such as under-compounding, flat compounding or over compounding (Figure 3.3). The arrangement usually adopted is flat compounding as required by Lloyd's Register.

It will be observed that neither curve is straight and the slight increase in voltage at intermediate loads on a flat compounded machine is referred to as the 'hump'. In extreme cases, particularly in small machines, the hump may be as much as 6—7% of rated voltage, but in normal cases it will usually be about 2—3%.

Adjustment of compounding effect

There are various ways in which the voltage characteristic can be modified. A method adopted at maker's works is adjustment of the air gap by inserting or removing shims between the poles and the yoke. Other methods are the use of a diverter resistance connected in parallel with the series winding in order to modify the effect of this winding, or by adjustment of the brush position. The shunt field may be connected in what is termed 'short shunt' (Figure 3.1a), or 'long shunt' (Figure 3.1b). The method adopted has very little practical effect on the characteristic, but machines should always be operated as originally built.

Commutating poles

Commutating poles (or inter-poles) are necessary to ensure good commutation at all loads with fixed brush position. They are usually

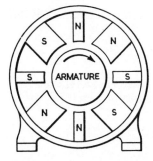

Figure 3.4 Polarity of commutating poles for a generator

not shown on wiring diagrams, being taken for granted as complementary to the armature. Each commutating pole for a generator must have the same polarity as the main pole immediately following, according to the direction of rotation (Figure 3.4).

Shaft currents

In large generators, i.e. where the current exceeds about 1000 A, it is generally necessary to take steps to avoid magnetising the shaft as this would lead to the generation of stray voltages at the bearings sufficient to puncture the oil film with consequent pitting of bearing and journal surfaces.

It will be appreciated that as the compounding coils are connected all in series this in effect constitutes one complete turn around the shaft and the main current thus creates ampere-turns numerically equal to its magnitude in amperes. The commutating poles are similarly connected in series and contribute exactly the same number of ampere turns. The usual arrangement therefore is for the current in the two sets of connections to flow in opposite directions around the shaft so that they neutralise each other (Figure 3.5).

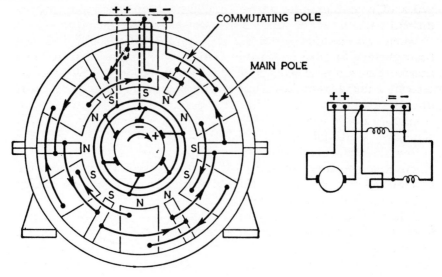

Figure 3.5 Series and commutating pole connections of a compound wound generator arranged so as to obviate magnetisation of the shaft. (The shunt field winding is omitted) Note that the current in the series field connections flows clockwise and counter-clockwise in the commutating pole connections

PARALLEL OPERATION

In small installations the generators may be arranged to run independently, i.e. not in parallel, but more usually and almost invariably in larger installations parallel operation using flat compounded generators is the general rule. The only advantage of running independently is that the switchgear is simpler and fuses can be used for the generators instead of circuit breakers, but on the other hand the disadvantage is that if a generator goes out of service, for example due to engine stoppage, all the services connected to that set are also interrupted.

In order that proper load-sharing may take place with parallel-connected generators careful attention to voltage characteristics and the provision of equaliser connections is necessary. Even if the generators are identical in design and rating there are bound to be differences in magnetic and electrical properties. Also it is frequently necessary to operate with machines of different ratings or of different makes. No two engines have identical governor characteristics or speed of response to load changes.

Steam turbines have totally different speed/load characteristics compared with diesel engines. So parallel operation with different types of engine or different sizes of generator sometimes presents difficulties.

When two machines are operating in parallel a change in load will bring the engine governor into action, causing a change of speed and therefore of terminal voltage. If there is no equaliser connection the set which is then running at the higher speed will grab more than its due proportion of load, which in turn will increase its series field strength, causing it to grab still more load until eventually the other generator sheds all its load. The process will continue until the current in the second generator reverses; its series field now being reversed, it becomes a differentially compounded motor. In practice this all takes place very suddenly and unless the circuit is very quickly interrupted serious damage may occur.

A usual after-effect of such an occurrence is a reversal of polarity and this should therefore be carefully checked before again attempting to put the set on the bars. The remedy is to lift all the brushes from the commutator and then close the main switch so that the shunt field is excited from the busbars. Turn the field rheostat to full field and then, before opening the main switch, return it to the minimum field position (this is most important). It is also of the utmost importance that the switch or circuit-breaker used to open the field circuit be so manipulated that it opens very slowly, drawing a long arc as it does so. Otherwise pilot lamps may be blown and the insulation of the field winding may be permanently injured by the induced voltage. The generator should be stationary and excitation for a few seconds is all that is necessary. Replace the brushes and the machine should now generate with correct polarity.

The only correct way to run compound machines in parallel is to connect the series fields in parallel, the paralleling connections being known as equalisers. Any increase in the voltage of a generator in relation to others with which it is working in parallel will tend to increase its share of current. This will increase the voltage drop across its series field and line connections, causing some of the current to be diverted to the series fields of the other generators and thereby restoring equilibrium to the system. If the generators are of different size or the resistances of the connections to the busbars are unequal the current will divide in inverse proportion to the combined resistance of series field plus connections. It is by the correct proportioning of these resistances that machines of dissimilar size or of varying distance from the switchboard are made to carry their correct proportion of load. Within certain limits, say 10%, a slight departure from the true values can be tolerated.

Unsatisfactory load-sharing may be due to two main causes:

(a) Discrepancies in the shape of the voltage curve so that the amount of hump in the curves is widely different.

(b) Wide differences in the voltage drop across the series field plus the connection to the busbars.

Comparison of characteristics of parallel-operated generators

If cause (a) is suspected a check can be made by plotting the curves together on the same graph. Voltages may be plotted either as actual values or as percentages, but if the machines are of different kW. ratings then the load axis should be plotted as percentages. What is aimed at eventually is that at each load percentage each machine should have the same voltage and therefore take its share, within a reasonable limit, in the ratio of the generator ratings. Typical results might be as shown in Figure 3.6.

The peak of the hump usually occurs at about half-load. With such a set working at a load below the hump an increase in load will cause a rise in voltage, and if the other set has a fairly level characteristic or has already passed the hump the first set will take over more than its correct share and may even motor the other set. Similar effects may occur with decreasing loads after load-sharing has been correctly adjusted at full load.

An actual example will demonstrate this. Assume two machines, one rated at 150 kW and the other at 70 kW 220 V, with curves as in Figure 3.6 working in parallel without equalisers. Governors and field regulator settings ensure correct load-sharing with full load on each generator. If a reduction in total load occurs which results in 40% load on the 150 kW (No. 1) set its voltage will rise to 222.7. But this voltage is attained on the 70 kW (No. 2) set at 82% load. As the hump for machine No. 1 is at about 48% load any further reduction in load on this machine will cause its voltage to fall whereas the

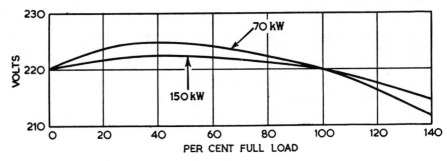

Figure 3.6 Typical characteristics of two generators

voltage of machine No. 2 will rise. Eventually with further reduction in total load machine No. 2 will motor machine No. 1. The reversal of current in the series field of No. 1 will cause an increase in its speed with the possibility of mechanical damage.

Equalisers will modify these effects, but if there is too great a disparity it may be impossible to effect a remedy. Should this prove to be the case it can only be properly overcome by a change of design of one of the machines so that it works on a different point on the saturation curve. It is well therefore when ordering machines to see that the suppliers are given full details of any other machines which may be worked in parallel. With modern machines difficulties of this nature are rare as nowadays characteristics are usually fairly flat, but manufacturers are usually willing to collaborate if necessary.

Reverse power

With steam turbine sets it is important to note that when one set motors another the losses in the set with full vacuum will be extremely light. As little as 3% of the full-load rating is sufficient to motor them at full speed, so very little additional reverse power will be required to cause overspeeding. It is for this reason that Lloyd's require the overspeed trip on turbine sets to be fitted with contacts to trip the circuit breakers. Overspeeding would occur, for instance, if a set were being motored and the field current of that machine were reduced by altering the setting of the field rheostat.

Voltage drop in field and line connections

The second cause of faulty load-sharing already referred to may arise because of differences in the voltage drop across the series field and the line connection. We have seen already in the previous example that the voltages of all machines running in parallel must be as nearly identical as possible, but in actual fact the point at which they are paralleled is at the busbars.

If the voltage drop across the series field and the connections to the busbars is widely different then obviously operation in parallel will be unsatisfactory. This may be caused by unequal distances from the generators to the busbars or, as in the case of generators of unequal sizes, due to different resistances of the series winding.

4 D.C. switchgear

Switchboards are either (a) main switchboards, to which the main generators are connected; (b) emergency switchboard, to which the emergency generator or emergency battery is connected; (c) section boards (or sub-boards); or (d) distribution boards.

They may be the open type in which all the essential switchgear is exposed on the front of the panel, or 'dead-front' in which all the live parts are concealed behind sheet steel panels and only the operating handles and instruments appear on the front.

Types of construction

Open type construction is generally favoured by marine constructors in the UK whereas foreign constructors, including USA, prefer the dead-front type; either type can be entirely reliable and satisfactory: With open construction all parts, front and back, are readily accessible for maintenance and adjustment, a very important point when it is remembered that these operations have to be performed on a live board. Dead-front boards can also be made readily accessible, but there is sometimes a tendency to crowd too much into a small space so that maintenance becomes difficult and hazardous. In some cases this objection is met by providing hinged doors on the front and in others by providing draw-out gear. The whole of the ship's electrical services are dependent on the main switchboard, and an important consideration affecting reliability and freedom from breakdown is the periodical cleaning of insulation and seeing that there are no slack connections. Inaccessible items are apt to become neglected.

In small equipments, particularly in small cargo ships, most of the motors can be fed directly from the main switchboard but as the size and multiplicity of services increase it becomes necessary to curtail the number of outgoing circuits on the main board. This is done by grouping some services on one or more local section boards (sometimes referred to as sub-boards) supplied by a feeder from the main board. Further splitting up, particularly in the case of lighting and heating, is usually necessary and this takes the form of distribution boards of smaller capacity which may be fed either direct from the main board or from a section board. These usually consist of a group of fuses, with or without switches, in ironclad boxes or arranged in cupboards in alleyways or other suitable locations.

Switchgear for parallel operated generators

The generator switchgear for parallel operation for an insulated two-wire system comprises a double-pole circuit breaker and an inter-locked equaliser switch as described in Chapter 3, or alternatively the equaliser switch may be combined by using a triple-pole circuit breaker, (Figure 4.1).

Reverse current protection

Overload protection must be provided on both poles and reverse current protection in the positive pole, i.e. the pole opposite to that to which the series field is connected. Reverse current protection prevents motoring of the generator, which would otherwise occur if

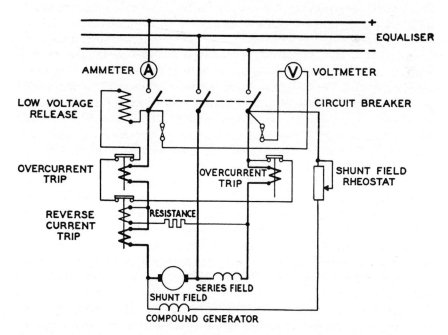

Figure 4.1 Typical connections for compound wound generators for parallel operation

its excitation were reduced to too low a value or if the prime mover were to lose power.

The reverse current device comprises a shunt coil excited by the generator voltage (in some cases this is replaced by a permanent magnet) and a series coil. Change of polarity (due to reversal of current) of the series coil in relation to the shunt coil causes the relay to trip the breaker.

Instruments

For paralleling purposes it is necessary to know the busbar voltage and the voltage of the incoming generator. If there are only two generators a voltmeter for each generator will supply the necessary information. For more than two sets it is usual to provide one voltmeter permanently connected to the busbars, and either a voltmeter for each generators or one voltmeter and a voltmeter switch or plug enabling it to be connected to any generator.

An ammeter connected in the positive pole is necessary for each machine; an ammeter in the negative pole would not be suitable as owing to the action of the equaliser connections it would not always record the true output of the generator.

Preferential tripping

It is essential that precautions be taken to prevent interruption of services necessary to maintain propulsion and navigation. These must be safeguarded even if other services such as domestic supplies are temporarily sacrificed. In practice essential services are safeguarded in two ways, firstly through a requirement of classification societies that there must be at least two generators, the rating of which must be such that essential services can be maintained if one set is out of commission. Secondly, protection must be provided so that if the total sea load is too much for one generator a system of preferential selection will operate.

Putting this requirement into practice, however, involves borderline cases where the nature and extent of the non-essential loads make it uneconomic or impracticable to provide preferential selection, and each case is considered on its merits. In some cases the non-essential load is relatively too small to warrant the additional switchgear.

It is generally in the larger installations that this form of protection becomes necessary. The controlling factor is whether two or more generators are necessary to carry the sea load since, should loads such as heating, lighting, galleys, etc, not under the complete control of the engineers be switched on to such extent that the generators become overloaded, a generator may trip out throwing all the load on to the remaining set or sets causing them in turn to trip and resulting in a complete shut-down. Similar effects might be produced if a prime mover should inadvertently stop.

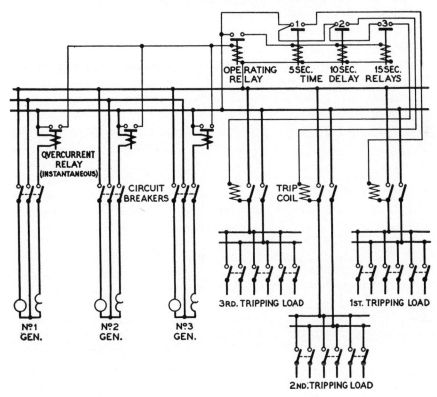

Figure 4.2 Typical diagram of preferential tripping circuits

To give effect to this requirement the non-essential services must be fed through one or more circuit breakers fitted with either shunt-retaining coils or shunt-tripping coils. Over-current relays with time lags are provided for each generator. When a generator becomes over-loaded for certain predetermined periods of time the appropriate relays operate and trip out the non-essential services. Some of the latter are more important than others, so in a large equipment they may be subdivided into degrees of preference and tripped out at different intervals of time according to the extent and duration of the overloading. (Figure 4.2).

The usual settings recommended are 150% load (i.e. 50% overload) with a time delay in accordance with the nature of the load for the generator overload protection, and the following times coming into operation when any generator load reaches 110%:

First tripping circuit — 5 s
Second tripping circuit — 10 s
Third tripping circuit — 15 s

Where electrically-driven machinery essential for cargo refrigeration is involved it should be included in the last group to be disconnected. Whether the non-essential loads are tripped in one, two or three batches depends on the nature of the loads.

Dashpots

The usual form of time delay is an oil dashpot having an inverse time current characteristic (Figure 4.3), but fixed time delays such as the clockwork escapement type are also used. Careful consideration

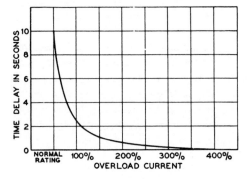

Figure 4.3 Curve showing typical time/current characteristics of an oil dashpot having inverse time delay

requires to be given to the combined effect, i.e. generator overload trips and preferential trips, to ensure proper discrimination. Otherwise a severe overload which would trip all three non-essential groups might also trip the generator.

It is important to note that as the viscosity of oil varies with temperature, so will the operating times of oil dash-pots vary, and Figure 4.4, taken from actual tests, is typical. Makers will generally supply dash-pot oil suitable for their circuit breakers and relays. The recommended oils are usually selected on the basis of least variation in viscosity over the working range, coupled with viscosities which will give the time delay marked on the calibration plate. These special oils should therefore invariably be used. The time delays are usually calibrated at 15°C. unless otherwise stated by the maker and are only correct at this temperature.

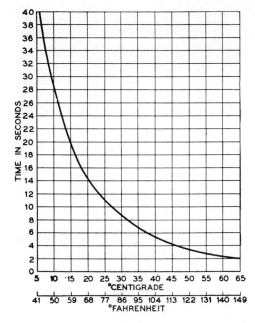

Figure 4.4 Typical time/temperature correction for oil dashpot

It is important to remember that according to British Standards over-current protective devices fitted with oil dashpot time lags do not function at the current marked on the calibration scale but at a current 25% greater with the appropriate time delay. The current marked on the scale is the value at which they would operate without time delay. Some makers supply an instruction plate indicating the exact current at which the relay will operate with a given time setting.

Earth indication

The method most commonly used for indicating the state of insulation of the system consists of two lamps, each not exceeding 30 W and each suitable for the full voltage of the system, connected in series and with the mid-point earthed. If the insulation of the system is healthy each lamp will be on half-voltage and correspondingly dimmed, but should there be a direct fault to earth on one pole the lamp on that pole will be short-circuited and the opposite lamp will attain full brilliance. Low-resistance faults will cause one to glow brighter than the other. To enable small differences to be identified the lamps should be placed not more than 150 mm apart. The weakness of this method is that if there is a low-resistance earth fault of approximately equal value on each pole the effect cannot be observed on the lamps. If switches are connected on the line side of each lamp, then by switching off one at a time low-resistance faults will cause the other lamp to glow, but the method still lacks sensitivity.

A variation of this method, but more expensive, is to use small voltmeters in place of the lamps. The reading on the meter is more positive than comparison of the brilliancy of lamps, but the drawback when there are approximately equal faults on each pole still exists.

A more exact method, largely used in Europe, consists of an ohmmeter with a switch enabling it to be connected to either pole. The insulation to earth can be read directly.

Pilot lamps

A pilot lamp for each generator is usually fitted, enabling the generators on load to be identified at a glance and from a distance.

Protection against short-circuit

Protection against short-circuit is provided by circuit breakers or fuses and the breaking-capacity rating of every protective device must be not less than the peak value of the short-circuit current which can flow at the instant of contact separation in the case of circuit breakers and at the end of the pre-arcing period in the case of fuses.

In the case of circuit breakers which may be closed on a short-circuit the making capacity rating must be not less than the maximum prospective short-circuit current at the instant of making. Motors which may be connected to the system when a short-circuit occurs will act as generators and will augment the short-circuit current from the main generators. In the absence of exact data it can be assumed that the short-circuit current from d.c. generators (including spare) is ten times full load current and the contribution from motors six times the full load current of motors simultaneously in service.

For the protection of distribution circuits the impedance of cables can be taken into account and this can usually be calculated or in an existing installation can be checked by a simple test. Arrange for a suitable load to be connected at the point at which information is required and connect an accurately calibrated ammeter and voltmeter in the circuit. Measure the voltage, then switch on the load and again measure the voltage and also the amps. These readings must be accurately observed as an error of a fraction of a volt will make a considerable difference to the result. Assuming for example that the reading on open-circuit is 220 V and the readings on load are 98.5 A, 218 V then the prospective short-circuit current at that point will be:

$$\frac{220 \times 98.5}{220 - 218} = 10{,}885 \text{ A}$$

The use of a circuit breaker of breaking capacity less than that calculated for the point where it is to be installed is permitted provided it is preceded on the generator side by fuses or by a circuit breaker having at least the necessary breaking capacity and relative operating time, i.e. its contacts must separate before those of the breaker which it is safeguarding. This is known as 'back-up' protection. The generator circuit breakers must not be used for this purpose. It is always advisable to prove the efficacy of back-up protection by an actual test. After a short-circuit has been broken the circuit breaker on the load side should be capable of further service but it is admissible that it may require servicing after it has been closed on a short-circuit.

Fuses

Fuses also have their limitations of breaking capacity. Suitable filling powders used in cartridge fuses have the property of quenching the arc. The time/current fusing characteristics of reliable makes of cartridge fuse are very consistent, making them accurate, and non-deteriorating in service (Figure 4.5).

Fuse carriers which will protect persons handling them from shock or burns are required, or alternatively detachable handles or insulated tongs are acceptable. Figure 4.5 gives typical fusing characteristics for cartridge fuses but should not be taken as applying to all makes.

The rating of a fuse is the current which it will carry continuously, e.g. for a circuit rated at 30 A continuously a 30 A fuse would be appropriate, unless it were a motor circuit in which case a higher-rated fuse would be acceptable. Fuses (and circuit breakers) on switchboards and distribution boards are intended primarily for the protection of the cables and not for the protection of apparatus. Overload protection for motors is usually provided in the motor starter.

The fusing factor of a fuse is the ratio, greater than unity, of the minimum fusing current to the current rating:

$$\text{Fusing factor} = \frac{\text{minimum fusing current}}{\text{current rating}}$$

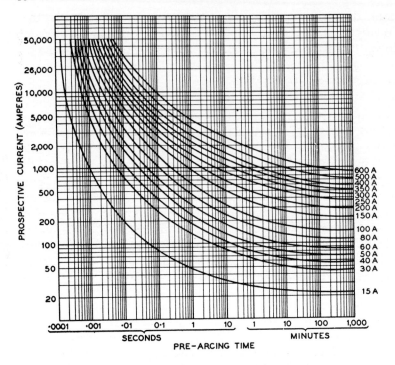

Figure 4.5 Typical time/current characteristics of cartridge fuses

The minimum fusing current is the minimum current at which a fuse-element will melt.

Discrimination

Discrimination is a complex subject and can only be briefly dealt with. It will be appreciated that a circuit connected to a distribution board may be fed through three, if not four, fuses or circuit breakers in series. For example a heating circuit may connect to a 15 A fuse in a fuse-box fed from a section board through a 100 A fuse, and the section board may be fed in turn from a 500 A circuit breaker on the main board. Discrimination occurs when the fuse or fuses nearest to a fault operate, leaving all other fuses or protective devices in the circuit intact.

Discrimination may be required between fuse and fuse, or between the fuse and another over-current protective device such as a circuit breaker. In this connection pre-arcing time is important, this being the time between the commencement of a current large enough to melt a fuse element and the instant when the arc is initiated. It will be obvious that after the arc has been initiated, even though the circuit is interrupted elsewhere, the particular fuse in question will have blown. Total operating time for a fuse is the sum of the pre-arcing time and the arcing-time, and for the purpose of studying discrimination we must therefore compare the time/current characteristics of the fuses concerned solely on the basis of pre-arcing times.

In motor circuits the breaking capacity of motor starters is usually very limited and does not as a rule greatly exceed the starting current of the motor unless, as is sometimes the case, contactor-type circuit breakers are included in the starting panel. The fuse should therefore be just large enough to carry the starting current for the time necessary to start the motor plus a suitable margin. If correctly chosen this will ensure that the fuse can never operate except under electrical or maximum mechanical fault or overload conditions, and at the same time give protection should the fault current be in excess of what the motor starter can handle; in other words, back-up protection for the motor starter.

The performance of fuses is affected if they are enclosed in containing cases because their temperature is increased and their fusing time for any given current is therefore reduced. Unless they are supplied by the manufacturer in enclosing cases it is therefore important to consult the supplier before adopting any form of enclosures which does not provide adequate ventilation.

Busbars

Busbars and busbar connections are required to be of copper, except that under certain conditions Classification Societies will accept copper-clad aluminium. To ensure reliability of joints these should be either dip-tinned or coated with petroleum jelly (Vaseline).

Clamps should be of rigid and robust construction so as to give a uniform pressure over the entire contact surface. They have the advantage that drilling for bolts is unnecessary, and they leave a certain degree of latitude for lining up both for through connections and for teeing off to circuit breakers, etc.

Bolted joints on the other hand are more compact and a higher joint pressure is possible. Care must be taken to remove burrs after drilling or punching the bolt-holes, so that there is no obstruction in the joint faces. In fact with both clamped and bolted joints the contact surfaces must be flat, smooth, and clean. Draw filing will remove any high spots and a medium grade emery cloth will remove any oxide, etc., immediately before making the joint.

The clamping bolts for either method should be substantial and not too small so that an adequate clamping pressure can be obtained, using standard spanners, without stressing the bolts anywhere near the elastic limit. The ratio of co-efficient of expansion of copper to steel is 17 to 12, and when the copper is heated to the permissible limit of 90°C after bolts have been overstressed when hardened up at say 10°C they may be given a permanent set and on cooling off the contact pressure will be reduced. Oxidation may then set in causing a hot joint, softening of the copper and finally complete failure. In a new ship, especially one having heavy current busbars, it is recommended practice to make a periodical inspection during the first year for possible slackened joints. It is good practice to use large plain washers of adequate thickness under the bolt heads and nuts in order to increase the area under pressure. All nuts should be locked; in this connection it is worthy of note that for small currents where a washer can be dispensed with, a hexagon steel nut without chamfered corners used direct on copper requires no further locking device.

The co-efficient of linear expansion of copper is usually taken as 17×10^{-6} per degree C and this corresponds to approximately 0.008 inch per foot length for a temperature rise of 40°C or about 5 mm on 7 m. This is hardly sufficient to warrant an expansion joint on the length of board met with in average practice, provided the bars are free to move longitudinally, but freedom to slide in the supports is necessary.

British Standards for busbars and busbar connections permit a temperature rise not exceeding 50°C based on an ambient temperature having a peak value not exceeding 40°C and an average value not exceeding 35°C over a 24-hour period. Above about 90°C the rate of oxidation and softening of copper in air increases rapidly and excessive heating at joints and contacts may take place. In land practice busbars may be mounted in busbars chambers and compound filled but this practice has not yet extended to ships.

Instrument and meter shunts may cause a local excess temperature and this is permitted.

Busbar cooling

Busbars are cooled mainly by convection and radiation, generally in the ratio of two-thirds dissipation by convection and one-third by radiation; cooling by conduction is negligible, due to the poor heat conductivity of the insulated supports. With small conductors the ratio of convection to radiation increases, and conversely as the size increases more heat is dissipated by radiation. The amount of exposed surface is the determining factor, hence the standard practice of using rectangular sections usually not exceeding 6 mm thick. Mechanical strength is also important as will be seen later. It will be apparent that adequate ventilation is necessary.

To obtain the maximum cooling effect the bars should be mounted vertically on edge. If mounted with the wide face horizontal the heating will increase by 18—25% compared with vertical mounting. Long vertical runs as opposed to the usual horizontal runs will also affect the heating. The sections commonly used do not exceed 100 mm × 6 mm and when the current exceeds the capacity of one bar of this section, two or more in parallel are used with 6 mm spacing between bars. As an example of the economy effected by adopting a laminated structure instead of one solid bar, a 100 mm × 12 mm bar although having twice the section of a 100 mm × 6 mm bar will carry only 45% more current; two 100 mm × 6 mm bars spaced 6 mm apart would carry 84% more current than a single bar, or 92% more if 9 mm spacing were adopted. It will also be apparent that very wide spacing between adjacent bars does not appreciably increase the carrying capacity.

Temperature is materially affected by the nature of the surface finish. A dull black finish will appreciably increase radiation as compared with the bright surface of hard drawn copper bar. For bars with ordinary black paint finish the current rating is 8 to 10 per cent less than with a good dull black finish, and for bright finished hard drawn sections the rating is 20—25% less.

D.C. busbar ratings

Researches carried out have confirmed the accuracy of the following formulae for the maximum direct current for bars in a normally tarnished condition for a 50°C rise above an ambient temperature of 30°C.

For flat bars with major axis vertical
$I = 185\ A^{0.5} \times p^{0.39}$ (in cm. units)
or $I = 678\ A^{0.5} \times p^{0.39}$ (in inch units)
  For round bars (solid or hollow)
$I = 193\ A^{0.5} \times p^{0.36}$ (in cm. units)
 or $I = 685\ A^{0.5} \times p^{0.36}$ (in inch units)
where I = current.
  p = perimeter of bar.
  A = sectional area of bar.

Other experiments have shown that a double layer of Empire tape was more efficacious than dull black paint as a means of increasing heat dissipation.

When bars are connected in parallel to obtain greater current-carrying capacity, the ratings per bar are reduced due to the restricted flow of air which reduces the dissipation of heat by convection, and also due to the screening of the inner surfaces reducing the dissipation by radiation. The usual arrangement is to interleave the bars at joints and tee branches so that the spacing between bars becomes the same as the bar thickness. For the usual 4 mm thick bar with two bars in parallel and 6 mm spacing the reduction in combined rating is 16%, and for additional bars the rating of each bar is reduced by 32%.

The considerations for a.c. are quite different and will be found in Chapter 8.

It is important to note that figures in Table 4.1 for current ratings are for average conditions and do not apply to every condition of service, and that the ultimate criterion is the temperature as originally stated.

For other temperature rises the watts dissipated can be taken as proportional to $t^{1.25}$, t being the total temperature in °C. If the current rating for a given temperature rise is known, the temperature rise for a different current or alternatively the current for a different temperature rise can be calculated.

Electromagnetic effects on busbars

Busbars must be rigidly supported at appropriate intervals so that they can resist the electromagnetic effects when subject to short-circuit. As is well known every conductor carrying current creates a magnetic field, and when two conductors are run parallel to each other carrying currents in the same direction they are attracted together and when the currents are in opposite directions they repel each other.

Under normal conditions of load the electromagnetic forces are small but under short-circuit conditions they can become considerable. With d.c. the forces are unidirectional and come into operation very suddenly.

The electromagnetic force between two straight parallel bars (or cables) of *circular* cross-section may be calculated from the following formula:

$$F = \frac{4.5 \times I^2 \times l \times 10^{-8}}{d}$$

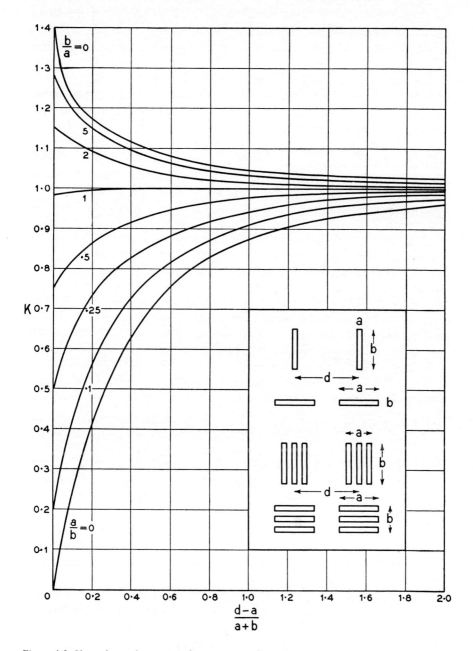

Figure 4.6 Shape factor for rectangular copper conductors

Table 4.1 D.C. ampere ratings for horizontal bare rectangular copper bars mounted vertically on edge and freely exposed in still air. 45°C rise above ambient air temperature of 45°C

Thickness mm	Width mm						
	25	31.5	40	50	63	80	100
2.5	260	320	390	480	590	–	–
4	340	410	510	610	750	920	1120
6.3	440	530	650	780	950	1170	1420
10	–	–	–	1010	1220	1500	1810

*Calculated from the expression:

Ide = 6.976 $A^{0.5}$ $p^{0.39}$ amps (and rounded off)

where A = cross sectional area (mm) and
    p = perimeter (mm)

where F = the force of attraction or repulsion in lbs.
    I = short-circuit current in amperes.
    l = length of conductors in inches.
    d = distance between conductors in inches.

Where the bars are very rigidly supported or where resonance due to mechanical vibration may occur a greater force may be produced.

It will be noted that the formula applies to circular conductors but it will be found sufficient for all practical purposes if applied to rectangular busbars. Strictly speaking it is also only correct for bars of infinite length, and for comparatively short bars the forces calculated from this formula may be too high. According to Dunton* the correct value can be obtained if

$$\sqrt{\left(\frac{L}{d}\right)^2 + 1} - 1$$

is substituted for l/d and the formula then becomes

$$F = 4.5 \times I^2 \times \left\{ \sqrt{\left(\frac{L}{d}\right)^2 + 1} - 1 \right\} \times 10^{-8}$$

*Dunton, W.F., "Electromagnetic Forces in Current Carrying Conductors." *Jour. Sci. Instr.*, Vol. 4 (1927), pp. 440–6.

where L = total length of the bars in inches, and not the distance between supports, and F is the total force on the whole length of the bar. It will also be seen that when the ratio L/d is very large $\sqrt{\left(\dfrac{L}{d}\right)^2 + 1} - 1$ becomes practically equal to L/d, so the original

formula is near enough for practical purposes and no serious discrepancy will occur where L/d is greater than, say, 20.

If a more accurate estimation is required for rectangular bars a correction can be applied*, so that

$$F = 4.5 \times I^2 \times \frac{l}{d} \times k \times 10^{-8}$$

Values of k are given in the curves in Figure 4.6. The ratio $\dfrac{d - a}{a + b}$, has first to be calculated and then k may be read from the curve for the correct ratio of a/b; d, a, and b are measured as indicated in the sketch.

As in the case of fuses, there is difficulty where d.c. generators are concerned in estimating the probable maximum short-circuit amperes owing to the uncertain behaviour of the generators under these conditions. For the purpose of these calculations, however, in the absence of precise information a maximum short-circuit value of say ten times the aggregate full load currents of the generators might be assumed.

For complete data on busbar calculations the Copper Development Association handbook on "Copper for Busbars" is recommended.

*Dwight, H.B., "Repulsion between strip conductors." *Elec. World*, Vol. 70 (1917), pp. 522–4.

5 Rotary amplifiers

Rotary amplifiers are probably better known under their proprietary names such as Amplidyne, Magnavolt, Magnicon, Metadyne, Rototrol, etc, and although not in very common use in merchant ships up to the present, they may be found in special applications and are included here in view of their rather unusual characteristics. They are known generically as rotary amplifiers because by control of comparatively very small field currents large amplification in effect is obtained. Moreover this amplification is obtained with remarkable speed and with great accuracy. The rotary amplifiers whose trade names are given above differ radically in construction and do not all have the same characteristics, but the basic principles are similar.

Consider first of all a straight-forward two-pole d.c. generator. When the field coils are energised, a flux between the poles is induced in the well-known manner, and when load is applied to the armature the load current in the latter produces a flux at right angles to the normal excitation. This is commonly known as the armature reaction flux. In a normal generator this distorting flux is troublesome and steps are taken to counteract it, but in the rotary amplifier it plays a very important part.

If the brushes of a normal shunt-wound generator are connected together, or in other words the machine is short-circuited, it will be

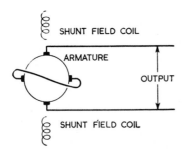

Figure 5.1 Rotary amplifier on open circuit

apparent that a very small field flux is necessary to induce a large armature current and armature reaction flux. If now we place brushes on the commutator at right angles to the normal brushes, as shown in Figure 5.1, a voltage will appear at this new position. We now have a rotary amplifier. A load can be connected across these brushes, and this in turn will result in an armature reaction flux, but this time in opposition to the field flux produced by the field coils, as illustrated in Figure 5.2.

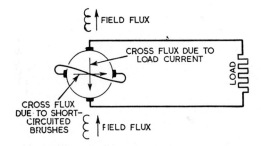

Figure 5.2 Rotary amplifier with applied load

A very small field flux will produce a short-circuit current sufficient to generate the maximum voltage of the machine at the secondary brushes, and the resultant cross-flux effect almost cancels the field flux. In this way the load current is almost directly proportional to the excitation. With fixed excitation the output is practically a constant current. A comparison between a normal shunt generator characteristic and a rotary amplifier is shown in Figure 5.3.

That is a description of the machine in its simplest form. Modification may take various forms, usually by adding other field

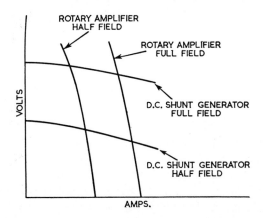

Figure 5.3 Comparison of characteristics, shunt generator and rotary amplifier

windings to the primary exciting system to obtain variations in the
output characteristics.

There is for instance the Amplidyne construction shown in Figure
5.4 in which a field winding in series with the load modifies the
effect of the load armature-flux. The effect on the characteristic can
be varied very widely according to the number of ampere-turns
in this compensating winding. This arrangement also embodies a field
in series with the short-circuiting connection to increase the short-
circuit armature flux, thus permitting a reduction in the armature
current and a saving in armature copper.

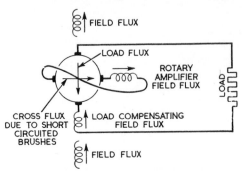

Figure 5.4 *Rotary amplifier with
series compensating windings*

This description has been simplified in order to obtain a clear
picture of the principles involved. In practice the physical construction of the machine is not so simple, as the poles are sometimes
split and other physical changes introduced.

It will be appreciated from this very brief description that the
distribution of current round the armature is not uniform and that
the performance of the armature differs materially from that of a
normal generator. Consequently the armature will be slightly bigger
than for a generator of the same output, and the machine itself will
be anything up to 25% larger than a normal generator. Commutating
poles may also be added with certain designs.

As already indicated a relatively small field current is necessary to
obtain these results. The amplification ratio is expressed as:

output watts
―――――――
control watts

and depending on various factors may be between 5000 and 10 000.
As this ratio increases the speed of response decreases. The control
watts are almost independent of the output, from which it follows
that the greater the amplification the larger the machine. The speed
of response is improved by designing for a low time constant, that is

to say, by winding the field coils with a high resistance to reactance ratio.

In outward appearance these machines are the same as ordinary generators and maintenance is the same, with the usual attention to brushes and commutators.

6 A.C. generators

Synchronous a.c. generators for auxiliary supplies are usually of the type having a rotating field and with the armature windings on the stationary frame. Inverted constructions are also available and in this type the armature is rotating. Limitations in the size and complexity of the sliprings and brushgear limit the inverted construction to about 150 kVA. Unless specifically mentioned in this chapter the information in this chapter relates to the rotating field type.

Construction

On generators used for marine installations the field system may be of the salient-pole type in which the fieldpoles will be similar to those of a d.c. generator and projecting towards the air gap. Alternatively generators of the non-salient or cylindrical construction with distributed field windings embedded in slots may be used. The cylindrical type is generally used in high speed turbo-generators but some manufacturers now prefer them for all speeds.

Power factor

The physical size of the machine is influenced by the power factor of the system, and it is usual to base the rating on a power factor of 0.8 lagging which represents average operating conditions. The kVA rating is proportionately higher than the kW rating, and the increased current at this power factor means higher watts to be dissipated in the stator windings (usually referred to as the 'copper losses'). Extra excitation is also involved which in turn increases the excitation losses (Figure 6.1) and these affect the physical dimensions of the rotor.

The power factor (p.f.) of the system is dependent on the type of load. Filament lighting, heating and cooking will be at unity power factor but induction motors, fluorescent lighting and transformers will take less than unity. Motors running at less than their full load rating will generally have a lower power factor than at full load, so the load current is not strictly proportional to the output. As it is desirable to keep the p.f. as high as possible it is therefore important not to install over-size motors. Cage type induction motors also have a very poor power factor which may be as low as 0.3–0.4, when starting, when the current is 4 to 6 times the full load current.

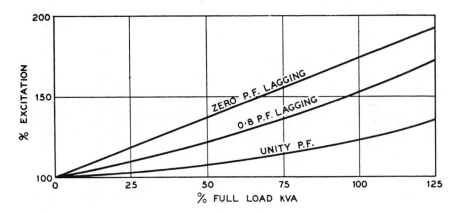

Figure 6.1 Variation of excitation for constant voltage

Load-voltage characteristics (regulation)

The characteristic load-voltage curve of an a.c. generator is very similar to that of a shunt wound d.c. generator, although the cause of the voltage drop as load is applied is very different. At unity power factor the voltage drop is caused by stator resistance and by distortion of the flux path. With lagging power factors there is a further loss of voltage caused by stator leakage reactance, and by the fact that a component of the stator m.m.f. has a directly demagnetising action. The lower the p.f. the greater will these effects become.

In machines of normal design the drop between no load and full load with 0.8 power factor will be of the order of 25–35%, assuming constant excitation. Figure 6.2 shows typical characteristics under various p.f. conditions. The effect of lagging p.f. is clearly shown; in practice the voltage is restored to normal by increasing the excitation, and it will be seen that as the p.f. gets worse more and more excitation is required, thus increasing the amount of heat dissipated in the field windings.

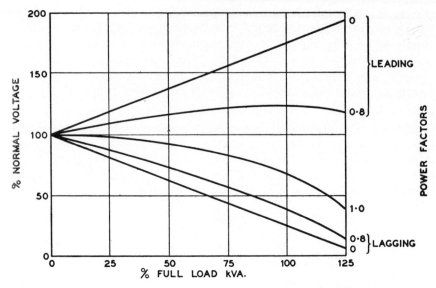

Figure 6.2 Variation of voltage at various power factors with constant excitation

Sub-transient and transient reactance

The behaviour of an a.c. generator when subject to transcent loading, e.g. starting comparatively large induction motors or when subject to short-circuit, is somewhat complicated. A variable wholly reactive impedance becomes apparent in three fairly distinct stages. The first, known as the sub-transient reactance is the reactance of air-leakage paths of the stator windings, and in the type of machine used in ships is of the order of 10%. It is this value which is used in short-circuit calculations.

This is followed after about one cycle by an intermediate stage where a higher but varying reactance known as the transient reactance takes control over a longer period. In the final stage this reactance stabilises into the synchronous reactance of the machine. These phases can be distinguished on a short-circuit oscillogram (see Figure 6.3). There is first an instantaneous current peak of about

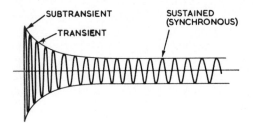

Figure 6.3 Symmetrical short circuit current characteristic of a typical generator

ten times full load current as determined by the sub-transient reactance. This peak decays rapidly to a lower value and then at a slower rate determined by the varying transient reactance until a steady state is reached, determined by the synchronous reactance.

Voltage drop (dip) is similarly determined during transient loading, i.e. there is an instantaneous voltage dip followed by recovery to a final steady state condition. The effect of power factor of the transient loading on the transient as well as the steady state voltage regulation is important and it is necessary to take these conditions into account in the design of the machines. It is important to note that the magnitude of the effects of sub-transient and transient reactance is not controllable by a.v.r.

Voltage dip

One of the inherent advantages arising from the adoption of a.c. is the facility to switch motors direct-on-line, i.e. without resort to star-delta starters or auto-transformers. The factor limiting the size of motor which can be so started is the sub-transient reactance of the generators. The current peaks of induction motors during starting are at a low power factor, usually of the order of 0.3 to 0.4, with a large wattless component. Although the generator windings and connecting cables are subject to these loadings the mechanical load on the prime mover is not correspondingly increased but the governor and flywheel should be capable of keeping the speed within prescribed limits when subjected to these sudden mechanical load changes.

The effect of the current peaks at low p.f. or of any other large load suddenly switched on to a relatively small power installation will be an instantaneous dip in the generator voltage. This cannot be obviated either in a self-regulating machine or in a generator with an a.v.r. as it is due to the sub-transient reactance of the machine. The dip occurs in two stages, the first being practically instantaneous (within ½ cycle) causing an immediate voltage change followed by a comparatively slower change occupying several cycles. The amount of dip is independent of the load already carried by the generators, particularly with mixed loads, i.e. partly heating and lighting and partly power. Too great a dip with too long a recovery time will cause objectionable flicker of lighting and may have adverse effects on the running of other motors and voltage sensitive equipment such as radar (if operated direct from the supply system) and on the starters for fluorescent lighting.

British Standard specifications require contactors to operate satisfactorily at 85% of normal voltage but although when closed they will generally hold in at much lower voltages, there is a danger of the contact pressure being so reduced that contact welding occurs. Furthermore Lloyd's Register of Shipping and BS limit the stalling torque of induction motors to not less than 1.6 × full load torque and as this is reduced as the square of the voltage a motor running at full load could theoretically be on the point of stalling at 79%. However this is not likely to be critical as usually there will be sufficient inertia to overcome the temporary dip especially with centrifugal loads which shed load as the slip increases. Starting torque also falls as the square of the voltage, but will be restored as soon as the voltage recovers.

An a.v.r. or the automatic regulation of statically-excited machines cannot control the amount of dip but can influence the speed of recovery. Recovery time is also affected by the time constant of the generator and exciter and the voltage ceiling of the latter. With static excitation, where the time constant of the system can be ignored, the response time is determined by the available excitation surplus i.e. field forcing.

BS. 2949 prescribes a standard condition for generator performance based on the starting kVA of the largest motor or of a group of motors starting simultaneously not being in excess of 60 per cent of the capacity of the generator. It is specified that the voltage shall not fall below 85 per cent nor rise above 120% of rated voltage when such a load at a p.f. between zero and 0.4 is thrown on and then off. The voltage must be restored to within 3% of rated voltage within 1.5 s (see Figure 6.4). For emergency sets these values may be increased to 4% and 5 s.

Special agreement between customer and manufacturer is necessary when:

(a) The transient load exceeds 60%. When the exact magnitude is not specified, 100% is assumed.
(b) The generator is required to supply a.c. multi-speed cargo winches.
(c) The generator is intended to supply a special load such as a cargo-pump motor.

Under steady short-circuit conditions the generator together with its excitation system should be capable of maintaining a current of at least three times the rated value for two seconds unless selectivity requirements allow a shorter duration and safety of the installation is assured.

Unfortunately low transient dip and low short-circuit currents involve opposing conditions on the designer. The advantages of improving performance to meet either of these conditions has to be balanced against possible increase of machine size, weight and cost. A low dip requires low sub-transient reactance but too low a reactance may involve short-circuit currents in excess of available protective gear. Specifications must take both of these factors into account. It has been known for a voltage dip to be specified so low that the machine reactance to achieve this had to be lower than that required to meet the specified fault current limitation.

Recovery time involves the excitation system. The requirements for excitation voltage and current vary over a very wide range, not only to meet the normal load and p.f. changes (see Figure 6.1) but also upward and downward field forcing. The more rapidly the output voltage can be changed so more rapidly can the generator voltage be restored and this must be achieved without sacrificing stability. A sufficiently fast response may be difficult to achieve with a rotating exciter although there are many applications for which such an exciter is suitable. Static systems can produce very fast response but do not necessarily do so unless so designed. Compounded generators using current transformers correctly designed are capable of providing a high instantaneous forcing voltage giving the best potential transient performance and as they do not operate on a closed loop system there is no risk of instability. The need to avoid a

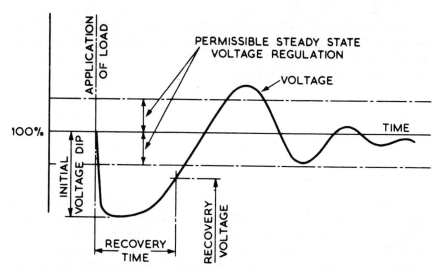

Figure 6.4 Typical voltage response characteristic

total collapse of generator voltage under short circuit conditions is fundamental to the maintenance of protective and discriminatory systems.

These limitations have led to the development of self-excited compounded generators in which not only is the dip much less but the recovery time is also considerably improved. The rapid spread in the development of this type of machine is considered sufficiently important to merit the inclusion in this chapter of an examination of schemes which have been evolved. In these systems the load change itself has an immediate effect on the excitation without any delay arising from a.v.r.'s or exciters.

Generator time-constant is another factor and is the ratio of inductance to resistance in its field circuit, including cables and rheostat, if any.

Parallel operation

For a.c. generators to operate in parallel three primary conditions arise:

1. Sharing of kW power load will depend entirely on the speed regulation of the prime movers.
2. Division of the kVAr wattless load between the generators depends entirely on the voltage regulation of the generator.
3. An oscillating driving torque e.g. by a diesel engine can cause fluctuations, (see also Chapter 9).

The p.f. of a single generator supplying a load is determined by the load impedance but when two or more generators are connected in parallel they form a closed circuit in which power or wattless kVAr can circulate while bypassing the load. The p.f. of each machine is therefore not a function of load impedance alone. For a given driving torque the kVAr output of each generator depends on its excitation and therefore on its a.v.r. When an extra generator has been synchronised and connected to the system it does not commence to share the load until its speed has been suitably adjusted. Voltage regulation by adjustment of the a.v.r. affects only the distribution of the wattless load.

Sharing of the power load at all speeds between no load and full load depends on the speed characteristics of the prime movers being identical at all points. If the ratings of the machines are unequal the proportional load sharing distribution will depend on the speed/load characteristics being identical. When generators are required to operate in parallel the manufacturer should be informed of this condition at the time of enquiry and confirmed when ordering. Generators should have an excitation/voltage regulation system which will enable them to share the steady state reactive load such that no machine exceeds its proportional share of reactive load by more than 10% of the rated reactive load of the largest generator.

When the machines are appreciably different in size special consideration is necessary as the foregoing condition could lead to a generator exceeding its rated kVA. The governors of prime movers should enable them to share the kW power load and maintain kW power load swings within acceptable limits as such power sharing is primarily the function of the prime mover and not of the generator.

Effect of unbalanced loading

Care must be taken to ensure that as far as possible the current is the same in each phase. Where lighting and heating loads are involved a certain amount of unbalancing is inevitable, but if it appears consistently the cause should be investigated and circuits rearranged. A large single-phase load on a three-phase network with limited generator capacity will result in excessive heating in the stator and rotor of the generator.

GENERATORS

Self-excited a.c. generators

It has long been recognised that self-excited generators were feasable but the practical development of sizes suitable for ship's generators was delayed until the advent of the silicon semi-conductor rectifier. The copper oxide rectifier was not commercially available until 1925 and was unsuitable because of its size. The better performance and efficiency of the silicon-junction rectifier made the use of self-excited a.c. generators a practical and acceptable proposition.

Many of these generators are also compounded and therefore come into the category of voltage regulating schemes described as 'functional'. This term embraces systems of voltage control which operate by measuring or sensing changes in loading conditions and endeavour to maintain the normal voltage by the use of components built into the system. They differ from 'error-operated' systems in which a change of voltage takes place and is then restored to normal.

It follows that functional systems will generally respond faster than error-operated systems. Nevertheless most functional systems, because of practical difficulties in maintaining normal voltage within very narrow limits, use an a.v.r for trimming purposes. All the methods normally supplied will maintain the a.c. voltage within ± 2½% but some work much closer and ± 1½% is attainable with standard equipment.

The systems adopted by manufacturers differ slightly from one another but the following examples demonstrate the general principles in use.

A common denominator is the use of terminal a.c. voltage for establishing the no-load voltage and using the load current as a means for providing the extra excitation needed to balance such things as armature reaction and leakage reactance. Where systems differ (and no two systems are alike) is in the trimming necessary to take care of loading conditions, variation of field resistance between cold and hot, and power factor.

Self-excited a.c. generators with 'error operated' voltage control systems draw the full excitation power from the machine terminals. This dispenses with the current transformers, reactors and capacitors necessary for accurate compounding, but renders the excitation system vulnerable to variations in its output voltage. If a severe voltage dip occurs, this voltage reduction affects the a.v.r. just at the time when it must produce its maximum output in order to restore the voltage quickly to normal. An extreme case of this occurs if the generator suffers a short-circuit, in which case all excitation power would be lost. For this reason 'error-operated' systems normally include current transformers, which provide an alternative source of excitation power during short-circuit conditions.

Components, generally speaking, are entirely static, e.g. transformers, reactors, capacitors and rectifiers, so that there are no moving contacts, electronic valves, etc requiring maintenance as was the case with earlier schemes. There are usually no fuses in the regulating system (as distinct from the excitation rectifier) and therefore there is no risk of excessive excitation or excess voltage as was experienced with the earlier vibrating contact systems with d.c. exciters.

Where machines are intended to operate in parallel it is important to ensure that phase connections in the control systems are identical. Transformers, etc must be in identical phases so that the phase sequence is not changes; current transformers must be in the same phase and their polarity according to the diagram.

SEPARATELY-EXCITED A.C. GENERATORS

There are certain advantages in providing a supply of excitation current entirely independent of the generator output. These include:

(i) Current compounding or short-circuit maintenance transformers and other components are unnecessary since an 'error-operated' system can be used which is guaranteed a constant supply voltage at all times.
(ii) Voltage build-up difficulties which sometimes occur in separately excited generators are entirely avoided.
(iii) There is less risk of radio interference, since the excitation thyristers are not connected to the generator output circuit.

The separate excitation supply is usually derived from a shaft-mounted permanent magnet a.c. pilot exciter, though the system could be designed to work with any suitable electrical supply. A pilot exciter carries the possible disadvantage of a small increase in overall length.

Thyristors

High current thyristors have proved to be ideally suitable as power control elements for use in automatic voltage regulators (AVR's). They are completely static, fast in response and, for a given power output, small in size and relatively inexpensive. Designs using thyristors as the control element of the AVR are now almost universally used and generator output voltage can be controlled to within ± 1%. The regulators have negligible wattage loss and are unaffected by normal variations in ambient conditions.

Excitation systems

Systems of a.c. excitation available for a.c. generators can be divided into three categories:

(a) Direct self-excitation (Figure 6.5).
(b) Indirect self-excitation (Figure 6.6).
(c) Separately excited (Figure 6.7).

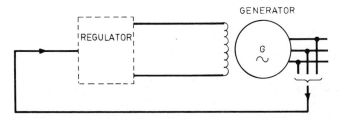

Figure 6.5 Static self-excitation

Direct self-excitation. Excitation is provided from the output side of the a.c. generator through a regulator. Correct field voltage depending on the load is supplied via a controlled rectifier. A fast response time results, e.g. for a 50% load change a response within 0.2 second is obtainable. This method is in general use for generators of the order of 100 kVA and is advantageous where space is limited i.e. for machines of limited length. It is sometimes specified for higher ratings when fast response times are essential.

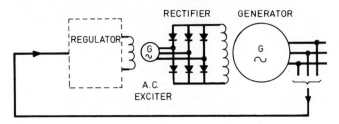

Figure 6.6 Self-excitation (indirect)

Indirect self-excitation. As shown in Figure 6.6 this is similar to direct self-excitation but the excitation is provided by a rotary a.c. exciter and a rectifier. The field of the exciter is controlled by a regulator. With brushless machines the rectifier will be mounted on the generator shaft and will therefore be rotating. This system will mainly be applicable to generators in excess of about 100 kVA (see Figure 6.8).

The response times are approximately 0.5 s for the size of generator usually met with being a shade slower that with the direct systems due to the inherent response time of the rotary exciter.

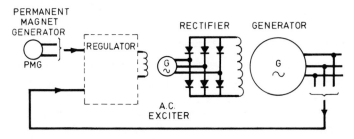

Figure 6.7 Separate excitation

Separate excitation. In the system shown in Figure 6.7 the excitation supply is derived from a constant voltage (permanent magnet) pilot exciter (Figure 6.7) or from an external source. The pilot exciter is mounted on, or driven by, the shaft of the main generator. The main

Figure 6.8 Rotating rectifier assembly (GEC Machines Ltd.)

exciters are similar to those used in indirect self-excitation systems. With these methods the main generator output voltage will build up whether or not there is any residual magnetism in either of the machines. Also maintenance of excitation under short-circuit conditions is inherent because of this external source and also from compounded schemes.

Thyristor automatic voltage regulators (a.v.r.)

As previously stated the systems adopted by various manufacturers differ slightly, mainly in methods of building up generated voltages from standstill and for dealing with power-factor variations but generally speaking the basic elements will be as shown in Figures 6.9, 6.10 and 6.11. They will comprise:

(a) A voltage sensing circuit containing a rectifier, smoothing elements, and probably an input transformer.
(b) A voltage reference bridge containing zener diodes for establishing a standard reference voltage and comparing it with the generated voltage.
(c) An amplifier.

(d) A thyristor firing circuit (or other signal generator if the output circuit does not employ thyristors).

(e) An output circuit containing one or more thyristors and diodes capable of handling at least a substantial portion of the excitation power (or some other control element, e.g. saturable reactor or power transistor.

(f) A potentiometer for varying the output voltage of the generator.

(g) A quardrature droop compounding circuit consisting of a light-current current transformer (not to be confused with the heavy-current compounding or short-circuit excitation current-transformer) with an adjustable output.

It will be seen that Figures 6.9 and 6.10 contain the heavy-current current-transformers referred to, which feed directly into the output circuit. These transformers supply the current for compounding

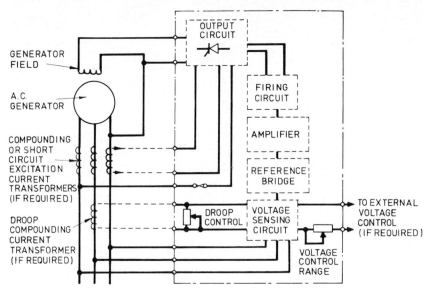

Figure 6.9 Direct self-excitation

purposes (in a 'function al' scheme) or for short-circuit excitation (in an 'error-operated' scheme. Figure 6.11 contains instead a permanent magnet pilot exciter. However it is to be understood that the system could be designed to utilise any suitable a.c. or d.c. source of supply.

The exciters shown in Figures 6.10 and 6.11 have been represented as brushless a.c. exciters since this is the most common type now supplied. Possible alternatives are the traditional d.c. exciter and the induction frequency changer.

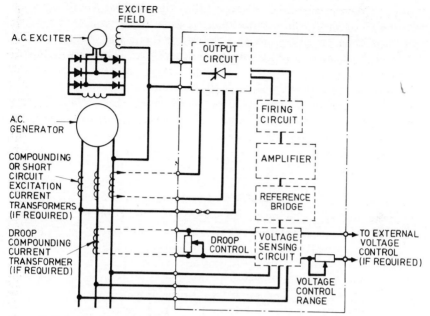

Figure 6.10 Indirect self-excitation

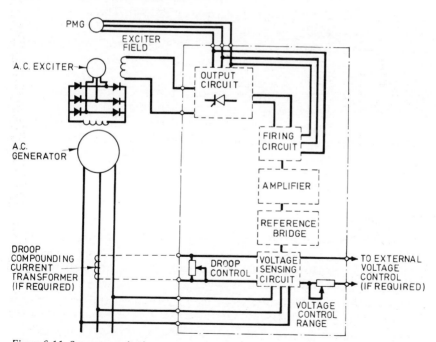

Figure 6.11 Separate excitation

Supply to the regulator can be from the generator output as in Figure 6.9 or from an external source such as a permanent magnet generator. The supply from the generator feeds the voltage sensing circuit and is then stepped down and rectified. The resultant d.c. voltage is then taken to the reference bridge and compared with a reference voltage. If the voltage differs from the reference voltage a voltage is produced which, after amplication is applied to the thyristor firing circuit which in turn controls the point in the positive half-cycle at which the thyristor is fired and in so doing controls the machine excitation.

Thus a sudden load change or other change in generator output voltage will vary the thyristor firing angle and correct the field voltage in the required direction. In practice various firing circuits are made use of such as phase-control saturable reactor, blocking oscillator or transister switch type.

The accuracy of regulation normally obtainable is ± 1% but under normal running conditions ± ½% can be achieved.

When generators are running in parallel the kW output is determined by the speed governor of the prime mover and reactive kVA is determined by the excitation. To ensure stable operation and correct sharing of reactive kVA the generator voltage should droop slightly with increasing lagging reactive kVA load. The usual method is by quadrature droop compounding (see Figures 7.7 and 7.8) by connecting a current transformer in the generator output to feed a load current dependent signal into the sensing circuit of the regulator. This signal is arranged to make the droop zero at unity power factor and a maximum at zero power factor lagging. The droop of each of the generators working in parallel should be the same if equal sharing is to be achieved. Other methods of achieving reactive load sharing are also in use.

For fault discrimination protection it may be necessary particularly in marine applications, to maintain excitation for a limited period in the event of a generator short-circuit. Clearly there is no problem with a separately excited generator, since the normal excitation supply voltage is still available. The voltage reference circuit detects zero generator output voltage and demands ceiling excitation current in an effort to restore the voltage to normal. This excitation current enables the generator to feed a large current into the short-circuit. With a 'functional' control system there is usually equally no difficulty. The normally constant portion of the excitation current disappears, but the large short-circuit current of the first few cycles (which is dependent on the flux existing at the instant of short-circuit) results in a large load-dependent component of excitation current. There is thus a positive feedback condition — the greater the short-circuit current, the greater the excitation — and the fault current settles down to a value governed by saturation in the excitation circuit. It is only in the case of a self-excited generator with an 'error-operated' control system that a problem arises, since the short-circuit deprives the excitation circuit of its sole supply. The normal technique is to provide one or more current transformers (so that the system looks at first sight as if it were of the 'functional type') which supply the field winding in parallel with the AVR output. Where operation differs from the 'functional' scheme is that no attempt is made to add this extra component of excitation current vectorically. Under normal operating conditions this can sometimes prove an embarrassment at unity power factor, since it is possible for the extra unwanted component of excitation current to exceed the total requirement. The AVR then loses control and the system voltage rises, unless there are other generators in parallel capable of supplying current at leading power factor. Under short circuit conditions the circuit behaves exactly as already described for 'functional' systems.

Because of their suitability for operation under high ambient temperature conditions all the semi-conductor components are of silicon rather than germanium.

Self-excited generators require an automatic feature to be provided which will enable them to build up their voltage from the normal residual value when the set is started. Various methods have been adopted for this.

Rotating rectifiers

Brushless generators such as those used in marine installations will usually have a rectifier assembly mounted on, and rotating with, the shaft (see Figure 6.8). Its purpose is to convert the a.c. output from the exciter into a d.c. supply for the generator field winding. The most usual arrangement is the three-phase bridge connection, although other arrangements e.g. three-phase star or six-phase star are sometimes used.

Some designs use thyristors but it is more common for all the devices to be silicon diodes. Diodes are available in either polarity so it is essential when fitting replacements to maintain correct polarity. Alternatively some diodes are of a double-sided construction in which case it is essential to fit them the correct way round. Not all diodes are clearly marked but by using an Avometer or similar instrument the conducting direction can be determined.

Rectifier assemblies will usually have all diodes of the same polarity or half the diodes of each polarity.

In a three-phase bridge rectifier each diode conducts for just over one third of each cycle and blocks for the remainder of the time. It follows that a diode which fails in the short-circuit condition will have a much more deleterious effect on the rectifier than one which fails in open-circuit. In the former case it is usually necessary to take the generator out of service immediately whereas with one open-circuited diode it is usually permissible to run for a period of several hours. For this reason, some manufacturers fit a fuse in each diode circuit which automatically converts any fault into an open-circuit. On the other hand other manufacturers omit the fuses on the basis that a fuse is less reliable than the diode it protects. It certainly is a fact that diode failures are very uncommon in properly designed equipment.

However it would be unwise to continue indefinitely under open-circuit conditions and a means is available for detecting a faulty diode. A ripple is induced in the exciter field current due to the unbalanced loading on the a.c. exciter and if a single diode has failed the predominant component of unbalance is the half-wave d.c. drawn by the good diode in the faulty phase. A d.c. field sets up in the rotating armature which induces a ripple in the exciter field of about the same frequency as that of the exciter output. The magnitude of the ripple is about 50% of the d.c. component and therefore easy to detect. In the ripple detector developed by Brush Co. Ltd. a small current transformer has its primary in series with the exciter field. The secondary has a large number of turns and is loaded by a high resistance across which a neon lamp or other suitable warning device is connected. The fault ripple is at a much higher level than that normally present in the exciter field current and therefore easily discernable.

A short-circuited diode also induces a ripple in the exciter field circuit at fundamental exciter frequency but of much greater magnitude. This can be detected in the same way as an open-circuit diode though it is quite likely that the generator would be tripped out by the under-voltage protection relay. This depends on the degree of AVR field forcing and whether or not the set is paralleled. Failure to trip could result in serious damage to the exciter if it is not rated for fault condition.

Disconnecting the generator and switching off the AVR is not always sufficient to protect the exciter since it is possible under certain circumstances for the exciter to suffer from self-excitation. This is a hazard which can occur on any a.c. generator (in this case

Figure 6.12 Diode failure detector, Type FV 223, for brushless a.c. machines (GEC Industrial Controls Ltd.)

the exciter) whose armature and field circuits are connected to rectifiers. The mechanism responsible for self-excitation is as follows. The failed diode in the armature circuit causes an a.c. voltage to be generated in the field circuit. If the field is still connected to the output circuit of the AVR containing rectifying elements this induced a.c. voltage will cause a half-wave rectified direct current to flow in the field circuit. The magnitude of this induced field current depends on the magnitude of the armature current and it has been known for the excitation to build up to a dangerously high level even with the AVR supplying no normal field current. This situation can be prevented by arranging for the prime-mover to be stopped, or by incorporating a diode failure protection relay which inserts a resistor into the exciter field circuit in the event of diode failure or disconnects the exciter field from the AVR.

One of the hazards of the rotating rectifier is the reverse voltages which might be impressed across it by the field winding during abnormal running conditions, e.g. faulty synchronising or pole slipping. To guard against this some manufacturers connect a permanent resistor (sometimes non-linear) across the rectifier output. For the same reason it is prudent to short-circuit all diodes or thyristors before making insulation tests on any part of the rotor.

Power factor

The physical size of an a.c. generator is determined largely by its kVA rating and by its speed. The kW rating has little influence except on such machines which have to provide the driving torque. The power factor at which the generator operates is determined by the load which it supplies e.g. induction motors, fluorescent lighting, etc. Filament lighting, heating and cooking are virtually at unity power factor but help to improve the general overall result.

Induction motors take about 0.8 lagging power factor but when started direct-on-line can take as low as 0.3 or 0.4 lagging. Thyristor-fed d.c. motors may take current at virtually any power factor between zero lagging and almost unity depending on the firing angle of the thyristors. Synchronous motors may be designed to operate at virtually any power factor but more usually operate at about unity.

Electrical systems on ships generally average out at between 0.8 lagging and unity and generators are nearly always based on 0.8 lagging. Operating at leading power factors can cause loss of stability, resulting in pole-slipping or loss of control by some types of voltage regulators but is most unlikely to occur in marine installations except under certain (rare) fault conditions.

SHAFT-DRIVE GENERATORS

Many ships are now being fitted with shaft-driven generators, especially those sailing for long periods at a constant ship speed. The reasons for this trend are largely economic and concern particularly diesel-engined ships. An investigation taking into account all aspects, (not only running and maintenance costs) but also the extra outlay for the plant involved as against capital savings in other directions has shown annual reductions in generating costs per kWh of up to 50%.

Such a saving is based on the considerable advantages in cost of fuel for propulsion diesel engines compared with that of auxiliary diesel generators. Other potential advantages include:

(a) Saving in maintenance and repair costs due to reduction in running hours of auxiliary diesels.
(b) Saving in lubricating oil costs.
(c) Possible capital savings by reducing the number and rating of auxiliary diesels.
(d) A reduction in space and weight.
(e) Reduction in noise.

Nevertheless the effect on the power available for propulsive effort cannot be neglected. Unless the size of the main engines is increased to take care of this additional load, with consequent increase in capital cost, a reduction in ship speed must be taken into account. In a specific case this reduction was evaluated at as much as two knots.

The saving in fuel costs relates mainly to diesel-propelled ships and not, in general, to steam propulsion with steam driven auxiliary sets.

Availability of sources of supply for electrical power is of prime importance for essential services and to a large extent these are dependent on the reliability of the prime mover. Of particular importance is the problem of maintaining electrical supply during emergency manoeuvring astern. It would be good housekeeping to run a diesel generator in parallel with a shaft generator in bad weather or in congested waters.

The general problem is that of overcoming the conflicting demands for constant voltage and frequency for the ships' system versus propulsion requirements for variable ship and propeller speeds. It is a generally accepted principle to design the system in such a way that full generator capacity is available at speeds between 60% and 100% of normal even during fast speed changes caused by the propeller abruptly leaving and re-entering the water in very heavy seas.

With d.c. auxiliaries power can be taken direct from the propulsion system by either a chain or a belt drive, using an AVR to maintain constant voltage. An auxiliary drive can be taken from the main gear box.

For a.c. systems more elaborate means are necessary in order to obtain constant frequency and a number of methods are available:

(a) A d.c. generator with an a.v.r. supplying a d.c/a.c. motor alternator set.
(b) An a.c. generator and rectifier supplying a d.c/a.c. motor alternator set.
(c) An a.c. generator supplying a static inverter system.
(d) An induction generator and a motor/alternator set.
(e) An alternator with excitation poles mounted directly on the propeller shaft.

The methods of drive available for the above are:

(i) Belt or chain drive.
(ii) A direct coupling engaging the propeller shafting.

(iii) Power taken direct from the main gearbox.

(iv) Power taken from the free end of the main engine.

Method (ii) is restricted by the maximum diameter of the stator which can be accommodated and the number of poles that can be fitted on the shaft for an acceptable machine design of the required rating.

Method (iii) enables the optimum design of alternator to be chosen when selecting the gear ratio. On the other hand either a separate gearbox is required or an additional pinion and possibly a clutch must be included in the gearbox.

Method (iv) is preferred by some operators as it may dispense with the need for a gearbox or an additional pinion. It is a convenient solution for medium speed engines.

With system (a) the motor/alternator set must run at synchronous speed and the overall efficiency of such a system would be 65—75%. A practical limit for such a system would be about 750 kW because of physical size. At least one installation has been based on system (b) for an output of one MW. It is feasible to share the rectifier output between two motor/alternator sets.

European manufacturers have fitted a number of ships with the rectifier/static inverter system. This system is handicapped by the limitations of high-power electronics and by the space required. The latter comprises a synchronous compensator, chokes, and capacitors. These installations are about one MW per shaft and give an overall efficiency of about 85%.

The induction generator system has not found the same favour. The frequency is controlled by the speed of the motor/alternator which also provides excitation for the induction generator. There are a number of variations of this method.

All these systems are suitable for use with fixed pitch propellers. The generator is usually designed to deliver its rated output between 75% and 100% shaft speed but with progressive reductions in output down to 50% at about half speed. Below this the auxiliary diesel sets take over.

For ships with controllable pitch propellers an extension of the range of ship operable conditions is available. Inclusion of a d.c. element would enable transients due to weather and sea conditions to be alleviated. However the d.c. element can be eliminated by using a synchronous generator if the speed can be maintained reasonably constant over the range.

Alternative systems would comprise control solely by pitch control or by a combination of pitch control and engine speed. The controllable pitch control makes possible an extension of the useful range of the shaft generator, so keeping the frame size and consequently the cost to a minimum.

With the static inverter system an undesirable feature may occur namely, the presence of notches or dips in the wave-form due to commutation of the thyristors. Large filters might be necessary if steps are taken to eliminate these, making the system uneconomic. However it is not on record that interference from this source has actually occurred. Radio interference from other causes has been recorded and has been remedied by changing the radio frequency equipment concerned.

Voltage and frequency are dependent on a number of factors. A fast response with static excitation on the shaft generator and also on the synchronous compensator and its AVR may be obtained to cope with transient loads. Frequency control depends on the time constants of the shaft generator and its AVR and the inertia of the compensator.

In an a.c. generator static inverter system the short-circuit characteristic differs from that of a conventional auxiliary generator. The output of the inverter is either restricted or switched off for the duration of the fault and the fault requiremer¹s are provided by the synchronous compensator which will then slow down since it has no prime-mover. This system cannot function in the same manner as a conventional generator as it is not capable of sustained output under short-circuit conditions and steps must be taken to ensure ample discrimination.

A d.c. link static inverter can operate in parallel with a diesel generator if the correct functions are included in the control system. It is usually necessary to parallel the diesels and the shaft generators temporarily when starting or transferring supplies or when shutting down. With controllable pitch propellers in conjunction with a synchronous machine appropriate measures are necessary to deal with the different characteristics of the respective prime movers.

Lloyd's Register would only enable a shaft generator to be regarded as a service generator if the main engine is intended to operate at constant speed e.g. in conjunction with a C.P. propeller. If the main engine does not operate at constant speed, e.g. when manoeuvring, the shaft generator would be disregarded as a service generator and at least two other independent generators would be required.

7 Automatic voltage regulators

An a.c. generator supplied with constant excitation current produces a voltage which exhibits a pronounced droop with the application of normal ships' loads (i.e. at power factors between unity and zero lagging). This variation was shown in Figure 6.2. The way in which the excitation current must be varied in order to maintain constant terminal voltage was shown in Figure 6.1.

With the aid of certain simplifying assumptions it can be shown that this excitation current is approximately proportional to the sum of two components. The first is constant and in phase with the terminal voltage (this is the no-load excitation current). The second component is proportional to the load current, and leads it by 90 electrical degrees. When the excitation current is obtained from a circuit which performs this vector addition, the generator is said to be 'compounded'.

By means of a carefully designed compounding circuit, the voltage variation may be reduced to perhaps ±2½% with no further control of the excitation current. However even this accuracy is not easy to achieve, and further improvement is rendered impossible by a number of effects which are neglected by the simple theory. Among the most serious of these are magnetic saturation in the generator, and the asymmetry between 'direct' (polar) and 'quadrature' (inter-polar) axes in salient pole generators and exciters. Furthermore, there is often some complication involved in the parallel operation of compounded generators, since the compounding effect will tend to increase the excitation of the generator which is carrying the largest reactive load, thereby transferring a still larger share of this load to that particular generator.

For these and other reasons, it has become almost universal practice to equip a.c. generators with automatic voltage regulators (a.v.r.'s). The accuracy of voltage control may then be improved to perhaps ±½% in the steady state. It also becomes possible to incorporate other modes of control which may sometimes be desirable, such as constant voltage per Hertz.

Component parts

Although automatic voltage regulators are usually built on one chassis, it is convenient for the purpose of explanation to divide the circuit into a number of blocks, each of which performs a distinct function. Following this approach, the a.v.r. may be considered to consist of:

(i)   A voltage comparison circuit for the detection of any discrepancy between the generated voltage and its required value.

(ii) An amplifier and conditioning circuit which converts the information received from the voltage comparison circuit into a control signal suitable for actuating the control element.

(iii) A control element which varies the excitation current in the manner demanded by the amplifier.

(iv) Various other circuits which, while not essential to the basic operating principle of the a.v.r., nevertheless improve its performance.

These parts will be considered in more detail later.

Operating principles

The way in which an a.v.r. controls the excitation of a generator or exciter varies from one model to another, but all schemes fall under one of the following two descriptions:

(i)   *Excitation supply a.v.r.* In this arrangement, the a.v.r. supplies the whole of the required excitation current (at least under normal operating conditions).

(ii) *Compounding control a.v.r.* In this arrangement, the generator is compounded to produce an excessive excitation current at all times. The function of the a.v.r. is to trim this current down to the correct value.

The advantages of the former arrangement are that a particular a.v.r. can be used with a wide range of generators, little or no adjustment being necessary to cope with varying generator characteristics, while good sharing of reactive load is facilitated by the absence of a current-dependent component of excitation.

The latter arrangement has the advantages that an AVR with smaller current-carrying components may be employed (provided that the compounding circuit is accurately matched to the generator under control) and that a high forcing voltage is assured by the characteristics of the compounding current transformers. Furthermore, if the a.v.r. should fail to operate, the voltage will remain between limits governed by the degree of compounding.

Both types of a.v.r. are produced by various manufacturers, and either type is capable of giving fast voltage recovery times, good voltage stability, and accurate sharing of reactive load.

Sources of excitation supply

With a compounding control a.v.r, the constant part of the excitation current is normally taken from the generator terminals (via a transformer if it is necessary to change the voltage), while the current-dependent part is derived from one or more current transformers connected into the power output circuit of the generator.

With an excitation supply AVR, the excitation current may be either

(a) taken from the generator terminals as above,
(b) derived from a shaft-mounted pilot exciter (usually a permanent magnet a.c. generator), or
(c) taken from an entirely separate supply.

If the first method is employed, it will be necessary to arrange for a separate excitation supply during generator short circuit conditions. The second method entails an increase in the length of the generator, while the third method carries the disadvantage that the generating set becomes dependent on external supplies. However this is often the most satisfactory system if the generator has to operate over an appreciable voltage range (e.g. constant voltage per Hertz for a.c. propulsion duties).

Voltage comparison circuit

The voltage reference element in all modern AVRs is the zener diode. This device will be described in more detail in Chapter 13. At this stage it is sufficient to say that a zener diode is a semi-conductor diode of special design which is connected into the circuit in such a way that it is subjected to a higher reverse voltage than it can withstand. So long as reverse current is flowing, the voltage appearing across the zener diode is almost independent of the current flowing and of the temperature. This voltage forms the 'standard' with which a known fraction of the generated voltage is compared by the AVR.

Arrangements will obviously differ in detail, but the circuit of Figure 7.1 will illustrate the general principle. The generator terminal voltage, transformed if necessary, is rectified by the diode bridge rectifier D. The d.c. output is smoothed by inductor L and capacitor C and applied to the voltage reference bridge consisting of zener diodes Z_1 and Z_2 and resistors R_1 and R_2. This bridge is arranged to be balanced when the generator is producing its correct voltage.

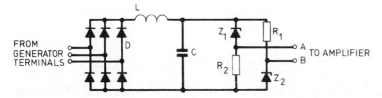

Figure 7.1 Detection of voltage error

There is then no output signal to the amplifier. If the generator voltage should fall, then the current flowing through the arms of the bridge will also fall, and so too will the voltages across R_1 and R_2. The voltages across Z_1 and Z_2 will however remain unaltered, and terminal A will become negative with respect to terminal B. A rise in generator voltage would produce the opposite effect.

Amplifier and conditioning circuit

The error voltage produced by the voltage comparison circuit is amplified by a transistor amplifier (which may consist of a single transistor only) and converted, if necessary, into a form suitable for the excitation control element. If this is a thyristor (the most common case) the output would normally consist of a train of pulses, synchronised with the excitation supply voltage, and bearing to it a phase relationship which is controlled by the amplifier. If the excitation control element is a saturable reactor or transformer, then the output would consist of a direct current of variable magnitude.

Feedback is normally applied across the amplifier to prevent the possibility of instability due to the time delays in the generator and exciter. The amount of feedback can often be varied to give the optimum voltage response to a sudden change in load. Too little feedback will cause the voltage to overshoot, and perhaps to oscillate several times before settling to its steady value. Too much feedback will cause an unnecessarily slow voltage recovery.

Amplifier designs vary from one manufacturer to another, and from model to model in the range of a particular manufacturer, but the function is similar on all types.

Excitation control element

The final stage of the a.v.r. which controls the excitation current may have to handle a current of a few amperes if the controlled field winding is that of a rotating exciter. Alternatively, if it controls the main generator field winding, the current may be a few hundred amperes.

The most common control element is a thyristor (or silicon-controlled rectifier) and is described in detail in Chapter 13. Basically it blocks the flow of current in both directions until a small current is applied to the 'gate' or control terminal. If this occurs when the voltage across the thyristor is in the forward direction, the thyristor will begin to conduct, and will continue to do so until the forward current falls to a very low value. It will then revert to the blocking state.

It can be seen that while it is very easy to turn a thyristor on, it can only be turned off by events occurring in the external circuit. The simplest application of a thyristor is therefore producing direct current from an alternating source. As the voltage goes into the negative half-cycle, the current dies away, and the thyristor regains its blocking state. The magnitude of the current is controlled by varying the point in the positive half-cycle at which the thyristor is turned on.

Alternative control elements sometimes encountered are the power transistor (see Chapter 13), and the saturable transformer or reactor. This is an iron-cored device carrying the normal a.c. windings and an additional control winding. The magnitude of the direct current applied to the control winding governs the degree of

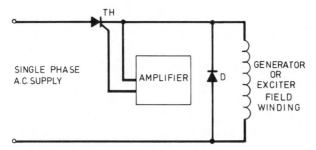

Figure 7.2 Power circuit of excitation supply a.v.r

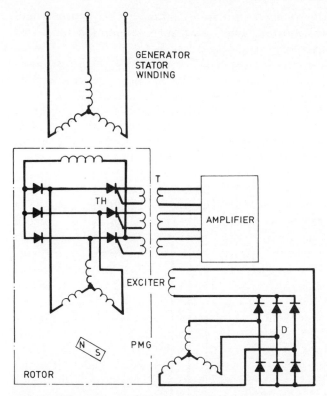

Figure 7.3 Brushless control of generator field current

saturation in the iron core, and hence the magnitude of the alternating current.

The circuits in Figures 7.2 to 7.4 all show thyristors in use as the control elements.

Power circuits

Figure 7.2 shows the power circuit of an excitation supply a.v.r. The field current can be varied from zero when the thyristor TH is off all the time, to a value depending on the supply voltage and field resistance when the thyristor is on for each complete positive half-cycle. The diode D is termed a 'free-wheeling diode' Its function is to allow the current through the thyristor to die away at the end of the positive half-cycle. If it were not for this diode, the very con-siderable inductance of the field winding would cause positive current to continue to flow through the thyristor during at least part of the negative half-cycle.

The diagram shows a single thyristor producing a single-phase half-wave rectified field current. Obviously single-phase full-wave and three-phase versions of the circuit are possible.

An interesting variation of the basic circuit of Figure 7.2 is shown in Figure 7.3. Here the AVR controls the main generator field current in a brushless arrangement. A permanent magnet a.c.

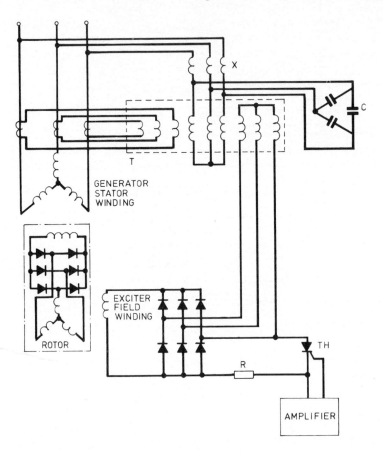

Figure 7.4 Power circuit of compounding control a.v.r

generator (PMG) acts as a pilot exciter to supply the exciter field with constant current through the diode bridge rectifier D. If no further control were exercised, the generator would be permanently at its ceiling excitation. However, half the diodes of the conventional rotating rectifier bridge are replaced by thyristors TH, which receive their control signals from the amplifier through the special transformers T.

These transformers are of unusual design in that their primary windings are stationary while their secondary windings rotate with the rotor. This arrangement is capable of faster response times than the conventional brushless arrangement, since the exciter with its time constant has been removed from the control loop.

Figure 7.4 shows one version of the power circuit of a compounding control a.v.r., including the method of compounding. The figure is drawn for the case of a brushless generator. T is a three-winding, three-phase transformer whose function is to add together two components of current. The current obtained from the generator terminals is constant (for constant terminal voltage), and logs the generated voltage by 90° due to the effect of the reactor X. The component obtained from the current transformers is proportional to and in phase with the load current.

It has been shown in Chapter 6 that the vector addition of these two currents in the correct proportions will give approximately the correct excitation current under all operating conditions. The output winding of the transformer T feeds a three-phase rectifier, which in turn supplies the generator or exciter field winding. The circuit is designed to produce an excitation current which is always in excess of requirements. Thyristor TH is connected so as to divert a portion of the current produced by one phase of the transformer T. The magnitude of the diverted current is controlled by the amplifier, while R limits this current to a safe value.

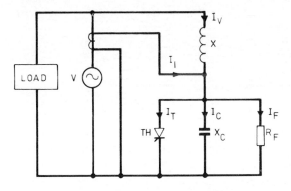

Figure 7.5 Analysis of compounding circuit

The three-phase capacitor C is not essential to the operation of the circuit, but is fitted by some manufacturers to prevent the variation of field resistance with temperature from affecting the compounded current. The effect of the capacitor can be explained by reference to Figure 7.5, which shows a much simplified single-phase version of the circuit of Figure 7.4. In this diagram, X_c is the reactance of the capacitor, and R_f is the resistance of the field winding transferred to the a.c. side of the rectifier.

Inspection of the circuit shows that:

$$I_v = \frac{V - I_f R_f}{jX} \quad \text{and} \quad I_c = \frac{I_f R_f}{-jX_c}$$

now $I_v + I_i = I_f + I_c + I_t$

i.e.

$$\frac{V - I_f R_f}{jX} + I_i = I_f + j\frac{R_f}{X_c}I_f + I_t$$

i.e.

$$I_f \left[1 + j\frac{R_f}{X}\left(\frac{X}{X_c} - 1\right)\right] = \frac{V}{jX} + Ii - It$$

Now, if Xc is made equal to X,

$$I_f = \frac{V}{jX} + I_i - I_t$$

and it can be seen that the field current is independent of the field resistance

Load sharing

When a single generator is supplying an isolated load, the a.v.r. circuits as described so far are satisfactory. But as soon as two or more generators are connected in parallel, the problem arises of ensuring that each generator supplies its fair share of the total load.

This implies that each generator is supplying the same fraction of its rated kVA, and that all are operating at the same power factor, which must be the power factor dictated by the load. If the governor of one of the prime movers causes it to develop more than its share of the kW load, then the governors of the other prime movers will cause them to reduce their kW outputs to prevent the system frequency from rising. If the a.v.r. of one generator causes it to develop more than its share of the kVAR load, its power factor will fall to a lower lagging value than that of the load.

The a.v.r.'s of the other generators will cause them to reduce their lagging kVAR outputs to prevent the system voltage from rising and the power factors of these generators will rise to a higher lagging value, or possibly change to a leading value. It should be appreciated that kW load sharing is controlled by the governor of the prime mover, whereas reactive load sharing is controlled by the a.v.r, and the two functions are entirely independent.

Because of the impossibility of manufacturing two identical pieces of equipment, generators whose a.v.rs give rise to constant terminal voltage will not naturally share reactive load. This is illustrated in Figure 7.6, which shows the characteristics of two generators whose a.v.rs are producing very slightly different terminal

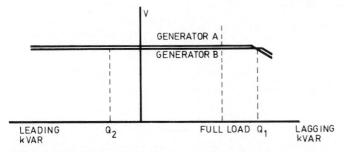

Figure 7.6 Principle of quadrature droop compounding. Two generators are producing slightly different terminal voltages

voltages. When the machines are paralleled, they are forced to operate at the same voltage, which results in generator A supplying Q, lagging kVAR, considerably in excess of its full rating, while generator B supplies Q_2 leading kVAR, just sufficient to keep generator A operating at Q_1.

The normal solution to this problem is the technique of 'quadrature droop compounding', whereby the voltage is caused to droop by an amount proportional to the component of current which lags the voltage by 90°. Figure 7.7 shows the same two generators with AVRs modified to operate in this mode. In this example, generators A and

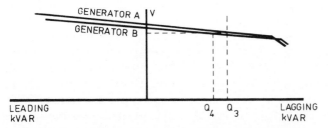

Figure 7.7 Diagrammatic solution to the problem in Figure 7.6

B are supplying respectively Q_3 and Q_4 lagging kVAR, and it can be seen that the load sharing is much improved. It is generally considered satisfactory if the reactive load on any generator deviates from its correct share of the load by no more than 10% of the kVAR rating of the largest generator. The amount of droop is usually variable up to about 5% of rated voltage for rated current at zero lagging power factor. All generators which have to run in parallel should be set to have the same amount of droop. Most a.v.r's incorporate a switch, so that the droop can be eliminated when the generator is running on its own.

One simple method of achieving quadrature droop is shown in Figure 7.8. The voltage for the voltage comparison circuit is obtained through a star/delta transformer to produce a 30° phase change (i.e. V_Y is at 30° to V_{BC} etc.). A current transformer T is connected

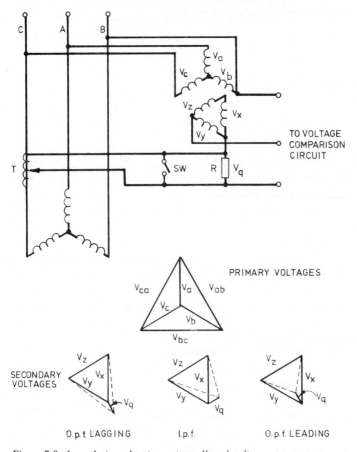

Figure 7.8 A quadrature droop compounding circuit

to one of the outgoing lines and loaded on to a resistor R. The voltage V_q thus developed across the resistor is added to the secondary voltage of the star/delta transformer as shown in the vector diagrams. The relative magnitude of V_q has been greatly exaggerated for clarity. It can be seen that the resultant vector triangle has been increased in size for lagging current, little changed in size for current at unity power factor, and reduced in size for leading current. For the normal case of lagging current therefore, the voltage applied to the voltage comparison circuit has been

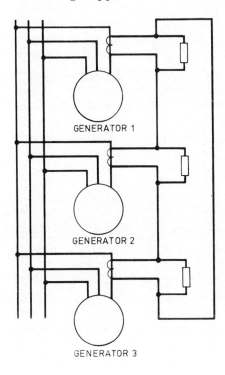

GENERATOR 1

GENERATOR 2

GENERATOR 3

Figure 7.9 Astatic compounding

artificially increased in size. The circuit interprets this as excessive generator voltage and reduces the excitation current, thus producing the voltage droop. The transformer T is usually supplied with a variable topping position to enable the amount of droop to be selected, while closing switch SW inhibits the droop.

An objection to quadrature droop compounding is that a small amount of droop occurs at the normal operating power factor of about 0.8 lagging. This can be overcome by incorporating in addition a similar circuit which gives a voltage rise which is proportional to the component of current which is in phase with the voltage. The two circuits can be balanced against each other to give a level voltage characteristic at any required power factor.

An alternative method occasionally used is depicted in Figure 7.9. This is known as 'astatic compounding' and the circuit functions as follows. Each compounding current transformer is connected to its droop resistor as in Figure 7.8. The transformer tappings and resistors must be selected so that the secondary currents of all the transformers are equal when the generators are sharing load equally. The secondary windings of the current transformers of all the generators which are operating in parallel are connected in series to form a ring. Provided that the load sharing is correct, the same current flows in all the transformer secondary windings and bypasses the droop resistors. If one generator should take an increased share of the load, the excess current produced by its transformer cannot flow round the ring, but flows through the droop resistor of that particular generator, and thereby causes a reduction in its excitation. This system has not found much practical application due to the extra complication of switching the current transformers as generators are paralleled or shut down.

Excitation during short circuit

It is a normal requirement that if a generator suffers a short circuit, its excitation system shall be capable of maintaining the current in the short-circuited lines at about three times its rated value. This is to enable the circuit breaker or fuse protecting the faulty part of the circuit to isolate the fault rapidly.

Compounding control a.v.rs and excitation supply a.v.rs with pilot exciter or separate supplies will normally provide this facility naturally. However an excitation supply AVR which draws its supply from the generator terminals will clearly lose that supply if a short circuit occurs on the generator output. This problem is usually overcome by providing extra current transformers in one or more of the generator lines. These feed a rectifier, whose output supplies the field in parallel with the normal a.v.r. output. This gives rise to an extra component of excitation current which is proportional to the load current, and may be looked upon as a form of compounding.

However, since the current addition is performed on the d.c. side of the rectifier and a.v.r., it is insensitive to power factor, and could result in over-excitation during operation near to unity power factor. If this occurs, a contactor can be installed to short out the output of the excitation current transformers until a short circuit takes place.

Additional features

In addition to maintaining a constant generated voltage, modern a.v.r's are called upon to perform various additional tasks.

For a.c. propulsion duties, a different operating mode is required. Here the generator is run over a wide speed range, while the synchronous or induction propulsion motors require a voltage which varies in proportion to the frequency. A modification ot the a.v.r. voltage comparison circuit enables it to provide this facility. a.v.r's for ships' service generators often incorporate a similar feature, which maintains constant voltage down to a pre-set minimum frequency, and voltage proportional to frequency below that point. This prevents overloading of the a.v.r. and exciter if prolonged low speed running should occur.

Many a.v.r's incorporate an over-voltage/under-voltage relay, which will trip the generator circuit breaker in the event of a malfunction in the excitation system. The generator terminal voltage cannot be used as a reference for this relay, unless the generator is operating on its own. When two or more generators are running in parallel, an excitation fault in one of them will have little effect on the bus-bar voltage, since the a.v.r's of the healthy generating sets will compensate for any deficiency or excess in the supply of reactive volt-amperes. Instead, the relay senses the voltage applied to the voltage comparison circuit including the effects of quadrature droop compounding. Apart from transient excursions, this voltage should remain within close limits at all times.

A protective circuit which is sometimes incorporated in a.v.r's gives indication of the failure of any of the rotating diodes of brushless generators. If one diode should fail to the open-circuit condition, the increase in excitation current will probably be small enough to escape notice. The diode failure protection circuit monitors the exciter field current. If a diode fails to either the open-circuit or the short-circuit condition, the unbalanced exciter armature currents induce a ripple in the exciter field current at fundamental exciter frequency. This ripple is detected by the diode failure protection circuit, which may be arranged to give a warning, or to shut down the generator, as required.

8 A.C. switchgear

While d.c. switchboards may employ open type panels, metalclad dead-front equipment is mandatory on a.c. systems unless the voltage between poles and earth is 55 V or less. A.C. systems require additional apparatus to be switchboard mounted; this includes frequency meters, synchroscopes, wattmeters, voltage and current transformers, ammeter switches, voltage regulators and means for adjusting the speed of the prime mover.

With an a.c. system the duty of fault interruption is made easier than on d.c. When an a.c. fault occurs the fault current, after the first few cycles, will pass through a current zero every half cycle. Thus the arc initially drawn between the contacts of the opening circuit breaker will have a natural tendency to extinguish at each current zero. Conversely a d.c. breaker can only interrupt the fault current by continually increasing the resistance of the arc until the latter can no longer maintain itself. Consequently, for a given type of circuit breaker, it is usually possible to obtain a higher interrupting capacity on a.c. than on d.c.

While there are several different types of a.c. switchgear only air-break and moulded case circuit breakers are in common use on marine systems. The voltages usually adopted for auxiliary power are either 440 V or 380 V with perhaps 3.3 kV being used in larger vessels. For system voltages at 3.3 kV and above the air-break circuit breaker finds almost universal application although it is probable that the vacuum circuit breaker will soon become a serious contender due to the minimal maintenance required. However at present the application of vacuum breakers is limited due to the low fault ratings which are available. (This limitation does not apply to vacuum contactors which are backed-up by fuses and these are discussed in Chapter 12.)

CIRCUIT BREAKER RATINGS

When a circuit breaker is selected for a particular application the principal factors which must be considered are system voltage, rated load current and the fault level at the point of installation.

Voltage rating

It may seem that selection of equipment with the correct voltage rating should be straightforward. Indeed on medium voltage systems i.e. exceeding 250 V but not exceeding this is so. However at higher voltages the method of earthing must also be considered. For example, on a 3.3 kV insulated neutral system the phase to neutral voltage is 1.9 kV and, in the absence of a fault, the phase to earth voltage will also be approximately 1.9 kV. If an earth fault develops on one phase, the potential of the two healthy phases with respect to earth will rise to 3.3 kV. A marine system may be required to operate in this manner for a considerable time.

When such a duty is possible some manufacturers may wish to offer a circuit breaker designed for a nominal system voltage of 6.6 kV in order to ensure that the insulation is not subject to excessive stress. Also, on an insulated neutral system, high overvoltages may be caused by arcing faults (see Chapter 9). On medium voltage switchgear the insulation is usually quite adequate to withstand such voltages but the margin of safety is much less at 3.3 kV and above. Consequently, when the voltage rating of a circuit breaker is to be determined on a high voltage system, both the system voltage and the method of earthing must be considered. If necessary, the manufacturer should be consulted.

Current rating

The current rating of a circuit breaker is determined by three factors:-

(a)   The maximum permissible continuous operating temperature of the circuit breaker copperwork and contacts. This may be set by either the particular National Standard to which the breaker is designed or by the limiting operating temperature of adjacent insulation.
(b)   The ambient temperature.
(c)   The temperature rise of the copperwork due to the load current, this being determined principally by its cross sectional area.

All circuit breakers are therefore assigned a current rating at a particular ambient temperature. For industrial use this is generally 35°C. If the same circuit breaker is to be used in a marine environment, in order to prevent the maximum operating temperature from being exceeded, it must be derated for use at the particular ambient temperature envisaged. This is normally 40°C or 45°C, these being the figures applicable to Lloyd's 'restricted' and 'unrestricted' use respectively.

Manufacturers ratings should be interpreted with care. For example, the rating quoted for a particular circuit breaker may be a 'free air' value. When switchboard mounted the breaker will have to be derated by an amount which will be dependent upon several factors; these include the degree of ventilation provided, the number of circuits breakers in each tier and the arrangement of the busbars. The final switchboard rating could be only 80% or 90% of the free air rating. Direct acting series trip devices, if fitted, may also influence the current rating. If in doubt the advice of the manufacturer should be sought.

Fault rating

While the circuit breaker is normally used as a convenient switching device it must be remembered that its primary function is to isolate any fault which may develop on the electrical system. To do this the breaker must be capable of interrupting the maximum fault current which could occur at its point of application within the system. In addition it must be possible to close the circuit breaker onto a faulty circuit. Four fault ratings are important:

(a) The symmetrical breaking current (the r.m.s. value of the ac component of the breaking current).

(b) The asymmetrical breaking current (the r.m.s. value of the total breaking current, which includes both the a.c. and the d.c. components).

(c) The making current (the peak value of the maximum current loop, including the d.c. component, in any pole during the first cycle of current when the circuit is closed).

(d) The short time rating (the r.m.s. value of the current that a circuit breaker is capable of carrying for the stated time).

A pre-requisite to the selection of switchgear is a fault level study. However, before discussing the calculation techniques used, it is useful to have a knowledge of the characteristics of fault current.

When a fault occurs at the main busbars the current magnitude will be limited predominantly by the impedance of the generator, this being mainly reactive. Consequently the fault current will tend to lag the generator internal e.m.f. by almost 90°. If a fault occurs on an unloaded generator when the system voltage is at or near its peak value the fault current will be a normal sinusoid, symmetrical about the zero axis. The peak value of this current, which is equivalent to the making current, will be $\sqrt{2}$ times the r.m.s. value of the symmetrical current. Consider now a fault which occurs at the instant the system voltage passes through zero. The fault current must lag by $90°$ and therefore, at the instant of fault inception, must be at its peak value. However, an instantaneous current change, from

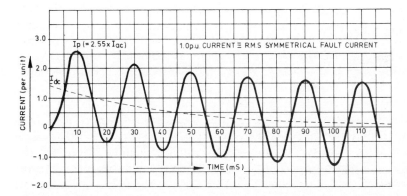

Figure 8.1 Asymmetric current wave (50 Hz system with 0.07 fault power factor)

zero to peak, is impossible in an inductive circuit. The fault current must still rise from a zero value. These two apparently irreconcilable requirements are resolved by the fault current becoming asymmetric to the zero axis. This is illustrated in Figure 8.1. It will be seen that this asymmetric current can be assumed to comprise an alternating component, I_{ac}, which is symmetrical about a direct component, I_{dc}. Note that the peak current, I_p, occurs one half cycle after fault inception. For convenience each of the two components can be discussed separately.

A.C. component

The reactance which a generator presents to the fault current is not constant but increases from an initial minimum value, designated the sub-transient reactance (see also Chapter 6). It is this reactance value which is used to determine the initial r.m.s. symmetrical fault current, I_{ac}. The reactance of machines is usually expressed as a percentage, and is the reactance voltage drop per phase when normal full load current is flowing, expressed as a percentage of the line-to-neutral voltage. A typical value for a marine generator might be of the order of 10%, which means that, as a first approximation, the r.m.s. symmetrical fault current at the terminals of the machine would be ten times the full load current.

If preliminiary calculations indicate that the fault current could be close to the rating of the switchgear it becomes prudent to reassess the problem in more detail. A useful guide is IEC Publication 363, *Short circuit current evaluation with special regard to rated short-circuit capacity of circuit breakers in installation in ships.*

D.C. component

The magnitude of the d.c. component is obviously important in determining both the peak current and asymmetric breaking current. From an initial magnitude which is equivalent to the peak value of the r.m.s. symmetrical current the dc component will decay at a rate determined by the X/R ratio of the fault circuit (where X is the inductive reactance and R is the resistance of the fault circuit).

For the two academic examples of zero and unity power factor the d.c. component would either persist indefinately or be completely absent. On a marine power system the fault power factor at the busbars is often assumed to be 0.07 which represents an X/R ratio of 14 and a d.c. time constant of about 45 ms, at 50 Hz. A power factor of 0.07 has been used in the construction of Figure 8.1.

Making current

The rated making current of the circuit breaker which is selected must be greater than the peak fault current. As previously described the latter can be assumed to occur at a time equivalent to one half cycle after fault inception, i.e. 10 ms and 8.3 ms at 50 Hz and 60 Hz respectively. In order to calculate the peak fault current the d.c. component at 10 ms must be added to the peak value of the a.c. component. To simplify the calculation it is often assumed that the decay in the a.c. component is negligibly small.

For a fault power factor of zero, (i.e. no d.c. decrement) the peak current would be given by $I_{dc} + \sqrt{2} I_{ac}$, i.e. $2.83 I_{ac}$. This would be an extremely onerous duty and in practice, unless a more rigorous calculation is made, the making duty for a marine system can be based upon a fault power factor of 0.07. With this assumption the dc component at 10 ms will have decayed to 80% of its initial value of $\sqrt{2} I_{ac}$. If the a.c. component remains constant over this period

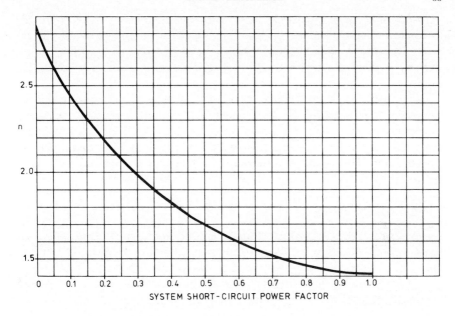

Figure 8.2 Multiplying factor n (IP/Iac) related to system short circuit power factor

the peak current will be equivalent to 2.55 I_{ac} as shown in Figure 8.1.

For a particular system a more accurate assessment of the peak fault current, I_p, can be made by first calculating the power factor of the fault circuit and then referring to Figure 8.2 to find the appropriate multiplying factor, n. Thus, if a fault power factor is 0.2 the peak current will be 2.2 I_{ac}. The curve in Figure 8.2 assumes negligible decrement of the a.c. component over the first half cycle.

Asymmetrical breaking current

If it is assumed that the decay in the a.c. component is negligible, then the magnitude of the asymmetrical breaking current is determined by two factors, the fault circuit power factor and the minimum opening time of the circuit breaker. The d.c. component time constant is determined by the first factor and its actual percentage by the second. Thus, if the power factor is 0.07 (time constant 45 ms at 50 Hz) the dc component will have decayed to about 50% of its initial value at an opening time of 30 ms. The r.m.s. symmetrical breaking current will then be:

$$I_{asym} = \left[I^2{}_{ac} + I^2{}_{dc} \right]$$

$$= \left[I_{ac}{}^2 + (0.5 \sqrt{2} I_{ac})^2 \right]$$

and

$$I_{asym} = 1.225 I_{ac}$$

However, if either the fault power factor is high or the opening time is relatively long the asymmetric breaking duty required will not differ appreciably from the symmetrical breaking duty.

The short time rating

Often circuit breakers must remain closed for a short time when a fault occurs in order to allow other devices which may be closer to the fault to trip first. A breaker must therefore be capable of carrying its rated breaking current for a specified time. The most common short time rating is one second.

Motor fault contribution

Induction motors which may be running at the moment of short-circuit will augment the contribution of the generators to the short-circuit current. The initial r.m.s. symmetrical current from a motor may be assumed to be equal to its direct-on-line starting current but this will rapidly decay. In the absence of exact data IEC 363 recommends that the following values be used, I_m being the sum of the rated currents of motors simultaneously in service:

At fault inception	$6.25\,I_m$
One cycle after fault inception	$2.5\,I_m$
Two cycles after fault inception	I_m

The motors will also make a significant contribution to the peak current and this should be allowed for when considering the making duty of circuit breakers. IEC 363 suggests that a peak current contribution of $8\,I_m$ should be assumed. This should be added to the peak current supplied by the generators.

The IEC recommended figures for motor contribution are based upon an average rating of 20 kW and allow for cable impedance. They can be applied to motors with ratings between about 5 and 50 kW. Larger motors can have significantly longer time constants and should be treated individually.

SPECIFICATIONS

Air-break circuit breakers for use above 1000 V were originally covered by BS 3659 : 1963 but this was superseded in 1976 by BS 5311. There are numerous differences between the standard ratings in these specifications although both adopt a fault power factor of 0.07 for the basis of making and breaking current duties. The relationship between the a.c. component and the peak making current is therefore 2.55 in each specification. Concerning the asymmetric breaking duty the older specification required that the circuit breaker must interrupt an asymmetric current containing a 50% d.c. component. In the new specification a definite value of d.c. component is not stated but is related to the opening time of the circuit breaker.

Circuit breakers designed to either specification should be suitable provided that:

   (a)   The a.c. component of the fault current does not exceed the rated symmetrical breaking current, and

   (b)   The fault circuit power factor is not less than 0.07.

The later specification permits a higher conductor temperature than BS 3659. Consequently, a circuit breaker which is assigned a certain rated normal current to BS 3659 could, to BS 5311, be allotted a higher rated normal current. This should be taken into consideration when comparing circuit breakers designed to different specifications.

For medium voltage circuit breakers the situation is more complex. Until 1971 air-break circuit breakers were covered by BS 3659 : 1963 but in that year BS 4752 : 1971 was introduced. This was superseded again in 1977 by BS 4752 : 1977 in which the scope of the specification was enlarged to include moulded case circuit breakers, previously covered by BS 3871 : Part 2 : 1966. The new specification now corresponds to IEC 157–1 and 1 A. Again many of the standard ratings were changed and in particular the familiar breaking capacity rating of 31 MVA at 415/440 V (43.3 kA) was no longer quoted. In the new specification the breaking duty at a particular voltage is given in terms of current alone. At 415/440 V the recommended breaking current ratings are 16, 20, 25, 31.5, 40 and 50 kA. Each value of breaking current is now associated with a particular power factor and, consequently, with a particular making peak multiplying factor. These are listed in Table 8.1.

It will be noted that for marine use the standard power factors are rather high. This does not necessarily imply that circuit breakers to this standard are not suitable for marine use, rather that they should be selected with more care. For example, if the symmetrical fault

Table 8.1 Ratio between make and break current

I_{ac} short-circuit breaking current kA	Standard power factor	Ratio, n, between minimum required making capacity and break current
$I_{ac} \leqslant 1.5$	0.95	1.41
$1.5 < I_{ac} \leqslant 3.0$	0.9	1.42
$3.0 < I_{ac} \leqslant 4.5$	0.8	1.47
$4.5 < I_{ac} \leqslant 6.0$	0.7	1.53
$6.0 < I_{ac} \leqslant 10.0$	0.5	1.7
$10.0 < I_{ac} \leqslant 20.0$	0.3	2.0
$20.0 < I_{ac} \leqslant 50.0$	0.25	2.1
$50.0 < I_{ac}$	0.2	2.2

current on a system is 40 kA at a power factor of 0.07, the peak current could be 102 kA (see Figure 8.2). A standard breaker to BS 4752 might have a breaking current of 40 kA but it would only be rated to make 40 × 2.1, i.e. 84 kA. Consequently a circuit breaker with a breaking current rating of 50 kA should be selected in order to match the required making current. A supplementary short-circuit test at 40 kA and 0.07 power factor should confirm the suitability of this circuit breaker. Further information on the selection of circuit breakers for marine duty is given in IEC 363.

For circuit breakers which comply with both BS 4752 and also the earlier BS 3659 it may be noted that the normal rated currents quoted against the earlier specification are lower. This is again because of the higher operating temperatures which are now permitted by the later specifications.

CONSTRUCTION

For small installations, particularly those which do not include paralleling of the generators, simple metalclad switchgear will suffice and may consist of standard self-contained switches or switch fuses assembled together to form a combined unit. With these units it is usual to interlock the switches with the lid or door so that the door cannot be opened while the switch is in the closed position and conversely the switch cannot be closed when the door is open. However, in most installations draw-out type switchgear is now normally used and this greatly simplifies routine maintenance.

Draw-out type switchgear

Draw-out type switchgear has been standard for many years in industry. The circuit breaker manufacturer normally supplies the breaker complete with its housing to the switchboard builder. The housing will contain slide rails for horizontal isolation of the circuit breaker and adaptors for the main copperwork and the auxiliary circuits. Safety shutters are often provided to cover the fixed contacts. The housing itself may be of either open angle iron or sheet steel construction. The switchboard builder then assembles the switchboard about these units. The individual units are often known as sub-cubicles or cassettes. The front panel of the cubicle is often part of the circuit breaker itself. In other designs the front panel of the cubicle is a door which must be opened before the breaker can be withdrawn.

Figure 8.3 3.3 kV air circuit breaker (Whipp & Bourne (1975) Ltd.)

Figure 8.4 3.3 kV air circuit breaker in maintenance position (Whipp & Bourne (1975) Ltd.)

It is possible to mount the cubicles on top of each other to give a two or three tier panel, however, the circuit breaker in the top tier will then be operating at a higher temperature. It is sometimes necessary to limit the total current which can be carried by all the circuit breakers in a multi-tier panel in order to avoid an excessive temperature rise. The circuit breaker manufacturer will give advice on this point.

For use at 3.3 kV it is usual to mount the circuit breaker on a transportation truck such that when withdrawn the breaker runs on the deck. A typical 3.3 kV air circuit breaker is shown in Figures 8.3 and 8.4, the arc chutes being in the maintenance position in the latter illustration.

The demand for such industrial equipment far exceeds that for ships and as there will be a strong tendancy to use existing standards it is advisable to consider features which may require modification.

Industrial switchgear is mounted on a floor which is always level, usually of concrete, and free of vibration. None of these conditions applies to ships. Provision must therefore be made so that when the gear is released for withdrawal it is at all times under control and firmly held when fully withdrawn. The construction frequently involves loosely fitting links and levers for interlocking purposes, etc and these are apt to rattle when subject to vibration. As with all marine gear, special attention must be given to the prevention of corrosion. The effect of the higher ambient temperature of marine environments should also be considered in relation to equipment ratings and protective device characteristics. It should be noted that BS 4752, which is based upon industrial practice, states that it '. . . does not include the additional requirements which may be necessary for circuit breakers used on board ships'.

When a switchboard is being assessed, particular attention should be paid to the degree of segregation employed both between adjacent switching devices and also between each switching device and the busbar chamber. If there are no internal barriers between the various units there is a much greater possibility that a single fault will cause the loss of the whole switchboard. This aspect of construction is covered in detail in BS 5486 : Part 1 : 1977 *Factory-built assemblies of switchgear and control gear for voltages up to and including 1000 V a.c. and 1200 V d.c.*

Closing

The circuit breaker must be closed against powerful 'throw-off' springs which are later used to open the contacts in the tripping operation. In addition, if the circuit breaker is closed onto a fault, the electromagnetic effect of the fault current will attempt to open the contacts and will therefore act in opposition to the closing force. For safe operation when closing against a fault the contacts should fully close before opening. Consequently, as the fault rating of the circuit breaker increases the closing force must also be increased. For high fault level equipment an operator may be unable to produce the force necessary to ensure correct closure and all modern designs of air circuit breakers now use either springs or solenoids.

Spring closing may be by either an independent manual spring (i.m.s) or a motor-charged spring. In an i.m.s mechanism the breaker is closed by using an operating lever to charge the springs and, at the end of the closing stroke, the springs are released. The force of the actual closing operation is therefore always consistent and independent of the operator. With a motor-wound mechanism a small motor charges or compresses the springs, usually using a ratchet arrangement, until they automatically latch. This method is employed on the circuit breaker shown in Figure 8.5. Closing is initiated by releasing the latch either electrically or mechanically. When the circuit breaker is closed the springs can be recharged so as to give a 'reserve' closing operation. It will then be possible to close the breaker immediately after a tripping operation. Typical spring

Figure 8.5 Air-break a.c. circuit breaker with motor-wound spring closing mechanism (GEC Switchgear Ltd.)

charging times using a motor are between 10 and 20 s. In the event of a failure of the motor or its supply an emergency manual charging method should be available. This may have to be ordered separately. If required the manufacturer can usually supply a spring charging mechanism without a motor, all charging being completed manually. This is called a hand charged spring circuit breaker.

When a solenoid is used to close a circuit breaker it will usually require a power of several kW and it is necessary to employ direct current. (Vacuum circuit breakers are an exception here because of the small mass of their contacts.) Until recently this implied that either a large lead acid battery or metal rectifier stacks in a separate cubicle would be required. With the advent of the silicon rectifier it has become possible to mount the rectifier within the cubicle and many such designs are now available. The closing supply is derived from the incoming side of the circuit breaker via suitable fuses. The solenoid will be short-time rated and therefore it will be necessary to provide circuitry to prevent unduly long periods of energisation. The same circuit is used to prevent 'pumping' of the circuit breaker (repeated closing and opening operations).

Isolation

The circuit breaker is usually equipped with both main and auxiliary isolating plugs. These enable isolation to be achieved by withdrawal of the circuit breaker from its frame. Normally two withdrawal

Figure 8.6(a) 440 V circuit breaker in 'fully-withdrawn' position for maintenance (Whipp and Bourne (1975) Ltd.)

Figure 8.6(b) 440 V circuit breaker in 'isolated' position (Whipp and Bourne (1975) Ltd.)

positions are provided. In the first position the circuit breaker is isolated from the busbars although many designs permit the auxiliary contacts to remain made, if this is specified. This feature has the advantage that testing is facilitated but greater care will be required. In order to effect isolation only a small degree of withdrawal is required. In fact, if the breaker is behind a door it may be possible to

close the door with the breaker in this position. In the second
position the breaker is withdrawn further to permit maintenance.

In Figures 8.6(a) and 8.6(b) a 440 V circuit breaker is shown in
each of the two positions. When the circuit breaker is removed completely from the switchboard a handling truck will normally be
necessary.

Most designs now provide for automatic shutters to cover the
fixed contacts when the breaker is withdrawn. When the breaker is
fully withdrawn it is advisable to padlock the shutters closed if this
facility is available.

Interlocks

Isolating contacts are not designed to make or break load current and
certainly not fault currents. Safety can only be ensured if certain
circuit breaker operations are carried out in the correct sequence.
For example, the breaker should not be moved from the isolated
position onto the busbars if the contacts are closed. Similarly the
door should not be opened if the circuit breaker is on the busbars.

Even an experienced operator can sometimes attempt to carry out
these operations in an incorrect manner and interlocks can be
provided to prevent this. If a hand or motor wound spring
mechanism is employed interlocks will prevent the release of the
springs if the breaker is closed or if the springs have not been fully
charged.

Earthing

On some circuit breaker designs, particularly those intended for
operation at 3.3 kV and above, it is possible to earth either the
feeder or busbar sides of the circuit breaker. This could be a feature
of the circuit breaker itself or may be achieved by a separate earthing
device which is fitted to the breaker. The circuit breaker protection
should be 'arranged to be operative during the earthing operation.

Indication

Local and remote electrical indication will often be employed to
show the state of a circuit breaker. However, whether or not
electrical indication is provided, mechanical indicators should be
included in the circuit breaker design. These are used to show
whether the circuit breaker is open, closed or isolated.

This function is sometimes provided by mimic diagrams on the front panel of the circuit breaker, an arrangement which is preferred by many engineers. These diagrams are single line schematic type showing the particular circuit with 'windows' at the breaker position. A mechanical indicator behind the window shows the state of the circuit. When a spring charging mechanism is used the state of the spring should be indicated; either 'charged' or 'free'.

Insulation

Medium voltage circuit breakers are usually assembled on a back panel of insulating material such as phenolic laminated wood. This panel also provides the mechanical strength necessary to support the operating mechanism.

At higher voltages a more compact arrangement is usually obtained by using a steel framework with the various conductors passing through bushings. However, a more recent technique is to support and insulate the whole assembly on an epoxy resin casting.

MAINTENANCE

After a ship enters service it is exceptional for the main busbars to be made dead; electrical supply of some sort is always needed, even if it consists only of lighting. It therefore follows that the busbars are continuously alive practically throughout the life of the ship as, even in dry dock, a shore supply will usually be taken.

This means that, as far as the main switchboard is concerned, routine maintenance work must be carried out with live busbars and some thought should be given to this in the design and layout stage. In land practice necessary provision is sometimes made by using duplicate busbars, but space does not permit of this in ships. However this equipment has been used in certain offshore drilling rigs.

On a single busbar system a limited solution can be achieved by using isolators to sectionalise the switchboard; splitting of the lighting feeders can also help. However, in large installations draw-out type switchgear undoubtedly offers the best solution.

A.C. is much more lethal than d.c. at similar voltages and on no account should work of even the simplest nature be undertaken on live a.c. apparatus without the operator being fully protected. For work on medium voltage installations rubber gloves are sometimes used but these must be specially made for the purpose and comply with BS 697, *Rubber gloves for electrical purposes*. They should be periodically tested in the prescribed manner to ensure that they are effective.

Precautions must be observed not only to isolate the apparatus but to verify that it is isolated and to ensure that it cannot inadvertently be made alive. Where interlock circuits, pilot lights or control circuits are involved there is always a risk that although the main circuits may be isolated these auxiliary circuits may still be energised from a separate source. Fatalities have resulted from this cause. Where switches can be locked 'off' it must be seen that this safeguard is used and the keys are removed. Where there are main fuses in the circuit, these might be removed as an additional precaution. Before commencing work it should be verified that the apparatus is actually dead by using a live-line detector. This test should be conducted not only between phases but also between phases and earth.

Portable handlamps used to facilitate the work should be fully insulated with non-metallic guards, so that there is no risk of shock or short circuit being caused should they inadvertently come into contact with live parts. When closing any switch by hand, whether in normal operations or when testing, it is a golden rule to do so in one clear positive movement without hestiation.

The necessity for cleanliness of all electrical apparatus has previously been emphasised. When apparatus is dismantled for maintenance it should therefore be kept clean and dry. Porcelain insulation should be examined for 'tracking' and blistering in the vicinity of exposed live metal. If the material is of the bonded laminated type examine for splits along the laminae.

Overheating may be caused by loose connections, poor contact pressure (particularly at fuse contacts), or poor alignment of contacts. On air circuit breakers the condition and alignment of the contacts can be checked by removing the arc chutes to expose the contact assembly. On some high voltage designs the arc chutes tilt forward to provide access. This inspection should be made annually and the mechanism should be lubricated at the same time. Copper contacts may be dressed by using a fine file or fine glass paper but emery or carborundum paper should not be employed. Silver or silver plated contacts seldom require attention. Their black appearance is due to oxidation but the oxide is a good conductor. If cleaning is required metal polish may be used.

A slight smear of petroleum jelly, particularly on contacts which are frequently operated, helps not only to preserve good contact but also reduces mechanical abrasion. Excessive application must be avoided as this may cause burning and pitting of contacts.

Oil levels in dashpots should be checked. Particular care should be taken, when topping up or replenishing, to use the correct grade of oil as proper functioning of the switchgear is entirely dependent on this (see Chapter 4).

Whenever the opportunity occurs direct-acting overcurrent trips and relays should be tested by current injection. Primary injection is always to be preferred to secondary injection (i.e. injection into the primary copperwork rather than current transformer secondary circuits). Injection testing is performed to verify not only operation but also the time current characteristics. This should be compared with the manufacturers operating curves.

In this brief description of switchgear maintenance it has not been possible to cover the subject in the depth which it describes. For further information the reader is referred to BS 5405 : 1976 *Code of practice for the maintenance of electrical switchgear.*

A.C. BUSBAR RATINGS

General remarks on busbar construction and factors affecting dissipation of heat are given in Chapter 4. With heavy alternating currents two additional factors, skin effect and proximity effect, decrease the d.c. current ratings and require special consideration.

Skin effect

The alternating current carried by a conductor sets up magnetic flux and the corresponding lines of force cut through the conductor. The linkages are not uniform across the conductor cross-section but are proportionately greater at the centre. Consequently a higher back e.m.f. is set up at the centre and the resulting effect on the current distribution across the conductor is that the current tends to concentrate where the back e.m.f. is at a minimum, i.e. at the skin of a round rod or at the corner of a flat strip. This is generally known as the 'skin effect'.

There is an apparent increase in resistance compared with the value when carrying d.c. because the whole of the copper is not carrying an equal share of the current; this also increases the losses. The ratio of a.c. resistance to d.c. resistance, the 'skin effect ratio', is dependent upon frequency, conductor shape and the operating temperature.

Rods and tubes of a size likely to be affected by skin effect are unlikely to be used in modern ship's installations and attention can be confined to flat copper bars. Skin effect causes concentration of current at the edges (not the sides) of the section and the effect will always be less than in a circular rod unless the bar section is square rather than rectangular. In fact, for larger cross-sectional areas the skin effect is greatly dependent upon the ratio of width to thickness.

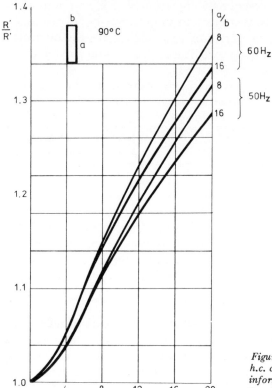

Figure 8.7 Skin effect in rectangular h.c. copper bars at 90°C (based on information supplied by the Copper Development Association)

The curves in Figure 8.7 are based upon figures derived by H.B. Dwight[1] and, together with other data in this chapter, are published by courtesy of the Copper Development Association. In these curves R' is the a.c. resistance of the conductor and R is the corresponding d.c. resistance. The approximate a.c. current rating can be obtained from the d.c. rating by:

$$I_{ac} = I_{dc} / \sqrt{R'/R}$$

The curves of Figure 8.7 are drawn for high conductivity copper bars at an operating temperature of 90°C. The curves may still be used at other operating temperatures by multiplying the cross-sectional area by the factor 2.20/ρ, and using this corrected value of c.s.a. to determine the skin effect ratio. The resistivity of copper per cm. per cm² section at 90°C is 2.20 microhms. The new resistivity, ρ, must be determined at the operating temperature required.

Table 8.1 60 Hz a.c. ampere ratings for horizontal bare rectangular copper bar mounted vertically on edge and freely exposed in still air. 45°C rise above ambient temperature of 45°C.

Thickness mm	Width mm						
	25	31.5	40	50	63	80	100
2.5	260	320	390	480	580	–	–
4	340	410	500	600	740	900	1090
6.3	440	530	640	770	930	1130	1350
10	–	–	–	970	1160	1390	1660

As an example of this effect a 100 mm × 6.3 mm bar on edge in still air would have a d.c. rating of 1416 A when operating at 90°C in an ambient of 45°C. The corresponding 60 Hz a.c. rating would be 1346 A. It will be seen that under these operating conditions skin effect is not significant for flat bars less than about 6 cm² in cross sectional areas, the derating factor being 5% or less. However, it becomes of greater importance as the cross sectional area increases or the operating temperature decreases.

The effect can be ameliorated to some degree by placing the conducting material where it will be least affected, for instance by using tubular conductors or by placing reactangular conductors so that they occupy the four sides of a hollow square. However, the busbar ratings employed on modern ships are unlikely to be of such a magnitude as to warrant these devices. Table 8.1 gives, as a guide, current ratings for flat horizontal copper bars in free air. In practice the proximity effect and the degree of ventilation provided will reduce these ratings.

Proximity effect

The discussion on skin effect has assumed that only one conductor has been used in each phase and that the other phases are sufficiently far away so as to have a negligible effect. When the busbars are laminated the currents in the bars will, of course, be in the same direction in any one phase and consequently there will be an increase of flux linkages about the centre laminations. The higher back e.m.f.

set up at the centre results in the outer laminations carrying a greater proportion of the current.

When the phase conductors are close together, as they can be in medium voltage installations, at any instant in time adjacent phases can be carrying current in opposite directions. This has the effect of causing the current to concentrate towards parts of the conductors which are in the closest proximity. Again the effect is to increase the a.c. resistance.

The distortion of the current distribution due to proximity effect can be reduced by spacing the conductors in the different phases as far apart as practicable. For currents of 3000 to 4000 A the phase centres would have to be placed at least 450 mm apart if serious proximity effect is to be avoided. Usually, in order to provide a compact busbar arrangement, it is necessary to accept that the copperwork must be derated to allow for the proximity effect. Table 8.1 makes no allowance for this effect but further guidance may be found in references 2 and 3 at the end of this chapter.

Magnetic materials can considerably influence the field around busbars and consequently their use is not recommended in the close proximity of heavy busbars.

Short-circuit rating

The busbars must be rated to withstand both the electromagnetic and the thermal effects of the fault current. Electromagnetic effects on d.c. busbars have been dealt with in Chapter 4 but, as in the case of current ratings, the determining factors with a.c. bars are different. If a fault occurs between the poles of a d.c. system the forces are uni-directional; with a.c. the type of fault must also be considered.

On an unearthed three-phase system the short-circuit can occur either across two phases only or across all three. For a solid fault across two phases the current in each of the faulted phases will have a phase displacement of 180°, i.e. the current in each of the phases will always be flowing in opposite directions. (Current in the third phase may be neglected.) This results in a pulsating repulsive force between the two phases and represents the worst condition likely to be met in practice. For a solid three-phase fault the forces developed between the bars will alternate between repulsion and attraction and there will be a degree of neutralisation. An extremely severe condition which can occur on generator busbars would be that due to an attempt to parallel two generators 180° out-of-phase.

Theoretically the maximum force which can be developed is that due to the maximum peak value of the fault current and this is the value which is used in calculations. However, the period of application is very short and, provided the bars are not too rigid, the subsequent flexing of the bars will absorb some of the force. Nevertheless, considerable mechanical support is required. It must be remembered that the short-circuit current may be completely asymmetrical (Figure 8.1) and the peak current may accordingly be 1.8 times that of the symmetrical wave (i.e. 2.55 times the r.m.s. value).

The formulae for calculating the forces involved for faults in single phase circuits or phase-to-phase faults in three-phase circuits, are the same as for d.c. and are given in Chapter 4. The busbars must be designed to withstand the phase-to-phase fault rather than the three-phase fault, the former representing the most onerous condition.

Before attempting to calculate the short-circuit forces which may act on busbars it is necessary to formulate an estimate of the probable peak fault current. The maximum force attributed to the peak current is applied within the first half-cycle after the fault occurs and, in some marine installations, has been estimated to be of the order of four tons.

The busbars must be capable of carrying the fault current for the operating time of the protecting circuit breaker without suffering thermal damage. Thus, the short-time rating of the busbars must equal or exceed that of the circuit breaker.

In this brief review it has only been possible to indicate the various factors which must be considered when heavy alternating current busbar systems are designed. In particular the type of enclosure used and the degree of ventilation provided will significantly affect the rating of the busbars and this can only be confirmed by tests. The reader should consult the references at the end of this chapter for further information[2,3].

GENERATOR PROTECTION

When a ship's generator is subjected to an overload either a supporting generator must be paralleled or non-essential load dropped. If the overload is allowed to trip a generator circuit breaker an even greater overload will be thrown onto any paralleled machines and cascade tripping will occur resulting in a complete loss of supply.

Preference tripping

If the overload builds up so quickly that an additional machine cannot be connected then a generator overcurrent trip can be prevented by using a preference trip relay. This operates after a fixed time delay causing non-essential loads to be shed. One such relay will be associated with each generator. If necessary multi-stage relays can be used in order to continue the shedding of load if the overload persists.

The operating current of the relay should be set to a value between the generator full load current and the minimum operating current of the generator overcurrent trip. A setting of 110% of the generator full load current is often used. Such a relay can be usefully supplemented by an overload alarm set to operate at 100% of the generator rating. This alarm can be initiated by either current or power using a contact ammeter or wattmeter. A wattmeter is preferable as it is less likely to give an alarm when motors are started.

It will be obvious that the preference trip relay cannot be allowed to operate instantaneously at its current setting otherwise spurious tripping could occur when synchronising or starting motors. However, it is not necessarily good practice always to employ the usual 5 s delay for the first stage of preference tripping. For example, in the event of a sudden loss of one of a pair of paralleled generators, the remaining machine may be subjected to an overload of perhaps 140% to 160% of its normal rating. This could cause a rapid fall in speed unless the excess load is shed rapidly. Ideally, when the system is designed the consequences of such an eventuality should be assessed and the time delay period and the magnitude of the load to be shed selected to avoid an undue fall in system frequency. The time delay and current settings chosen must, however, permit the starting of any large motors on the system.

If the overload condition is not removed by preference tripping and the current is of sufficient magnitude, the generator overcurrent relay will begin to time out. Typically the minimum operating current of the overcurrent relay will be between 110% and 130% of full load current and operation would only occur after a delay of some tens of seconds, perhaps allowing the engineer to take appropriate action. However, it should be noted that American regulations do not permit a setting in excess of 115% of full load current. Because of resetting difficulties with direct acting electromechanical trips it is usually advisable to use a separate relay if such a low setting is necessary.

For generators rated at and above 5000 kVA temperature detectors may be required in the machine windings to comply with certain statutory requirements. These will normally operate both temperature gauges and overtemperature alarms at the control panel.

Overcurrent protection

Each generator circuit breaker must be fitted with an overcurrent relay. On medium voltage systems this is usually an integral part of the circuit breaker in the form of direct acting trips (see Chapter 4) although at 3.3 kVa separate relay is used. An inverse time/current characteristic is normally employed. The actual operating curve of the relay should be selected on the basis of the following requirements:

(a) Proper system discrimination must be provided, the generator breaker only being tripped if a feeder breaker fails to do so or if a busbar fault occurs (see also Chapter 9).

(b) The minimum operating current should be in excess of the preference trip relay setting. The overcurrent relay must reset fully after non-essential loads have been shed. For simple direct acting trips the reset current is often as low as 80% of the setting current and consequently this can determine the minimum ratio of setting current to full load current. If the full load current is greater than 80% of the minimum operating current it is possible that, after a transient overload condition, the overcurrent device may remain in a partly operated state. From this position it may 'creep', even with normal load current flowing, and could eventually trip the breaker. This problem should not arise when a separate relay is employed as they tend to reset at currents much closer to their operating value. Static relays are particularly good in this respect and are now being made available as an integral part of the circuit breaker but a direct acting trip may have to be set to 125% full load current.

(c) Sufficient fault current must be available from the generator to ensure that the relay will operate in a reasonably short time if a busbar fault occurs. It must be remembered that although the generator will initially contribute as much as ten times full load current to the fault, the generator impedance will rapidly increase.

The fault current will decay until the a.v.r. begins to increase the excitation and the current rises again to a steady-state value. The overcurrent relay must be provided with a short time delay, even when responding to a short-circuit condition, in order to maintain discrimination with the feeder circuits. Because of this delay the relay will only usually respond to the steady state short-circuit current. If the relay operating current is too high, or if the fault current is too low, the circuit breaker may only be tripped after an excessively long time. Therefore, in order to ensure satisfactory operation of the protective equipment, the generator specification often calls for a minimum steady-state fault current capability of three or four times full load current when the machine is warm. (The American Bureau of Shipping requires three times full load current to be sustained without damage for two seconds.)

It should be noted that the steady-state current can be significantly higher when the generator is cold because the field resistance will then be low.

(d) The relay operating characteristic should reflect the thermal withstand capacity of the generator. Lloyd's regulations, clause 408, states that the generator should be capable of withstanding 50% excess current for a period of 15 seconds. Ideally the protection characteristic should pass through this point or even give a faster clearance, although this could increase the possibility of an undesired generator trip. In practice the setting used is often 20 s at 150% of full load current. Similarly, under short-circuit conditions, the circuit breaker must trip before the generator suffers thermal damage. The time delay under short-circuit conditions is usually between 0.1 and 3.0 seconds, the actual setting depending upon discrimination requirements.

When ordering a circuit breaker fitted with direct acting over-current trips it is important that the manufacturer be informed of the particular application. It can then be ensured that the oil dash-pot delay mechanism, if used, is calibrated for operation at the ambient temperature which is envisaged. (This will be higher than the room ambient because the dashpots are within the cubicle, but again the manufacturer will advise.) Also, for marine generator protection, an oil of higher viscosity will be required than that used for industrial circuit breakers. Similarly, if a clockwork escapement retarder is to be used, a long time delay type must be fitted.

A fully rated air circuit breaker will normally be required rather than an m.c.c.b. The thermal overloads fitted to the latter rarely have a characteristic suitable for generator protection. Also if, as is usual, the m.c.c.b. employs instantaneous magnetic trips, discrimination with feeder circuit protection will be extremely difficult. However, for small generators it may sometimes be more economical to use an m.c.c.b. without the thermal overloads fitted and with the magnetic trips set above the maximum generator fault contribution (say twelve to fifteen times full load current). Protection can then be applied using a separate relay.

Instantaneous overcurrent protection

In order to provide rapid tripping of a generator with an internal fault a high set instantaneous relay is sometimes employed. Naturally it must only operate for currents in excess of the maximum generator fault current otherwise system discrimination would be lost. Unfortunately this means that it can only be effective when three or more generators are being run in parallel. This form of protection is mandatory on American vessels if three or more generators are used.

Differential protection

If a fault occurs on a generator stator or its associated cables the tripping of the generator circuit breaker alone is not sufficient. While the machine will be isolated from the system the fault will continue to burn, probably causing extensive damage. This can only be stopped by removing the generator excitation. If only two machines are being operated in parallel at the time of the fault there will be the additional hazard of a complete loss of electrical supplies as almost certainly the circuit breakers of both generators will trip. If differential protection is employed this situation will be avoided.

This form of protection is also known as Merz Price or unit protection. Its advantage is that it will only respond to faults within a particular zone and in this case the generator windings and the cable to the circuit breaker are covered. Instantaneous operation can be permitted because the relay will be insensitive to faults outside the zone and therefore discrimination need not be considered. When a fault is detected the excitation is removed, the fuel or steam valve closed and the generator circuit breaker tripped. In order to provide both phase to phase and earthfault protection the scheme requires six current transformers, three at the generator neutral and three on the circuit breaker, together with three relays. The current transformers must be carefully selected to ensure that faults outside the protected zone do not cause spill currents on the secondaries of sufficient magnitude to operate the relay. A typical scheme is shown in Figure 8.8(a).

It would seem that convincing reasons exist for the use of differential protection, yet its application on marine systems is rare. There are a number of reasons for this but the most important probably concerns the earthing of the system neutral. Internal generator faults are rare but when they do occur it is usually between one phase and earth. On a typical marine system with an insulated neutral this fault can be tolerated until appropriate action can be taken. Cost and complexity also weigh against additional protection equipment.

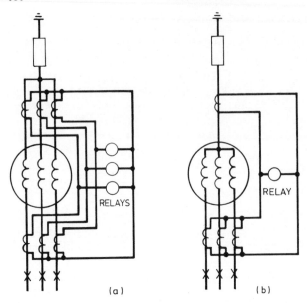

Figure 8.8 Two forms of generator stator differential protection
(a) Phase and earth fault protection
(b) Restricted earth fault protection

When the system voltage exceeds 1000 V it is usual to earth each generator neutral via a resistor and generator internal protection is mandatory. However, it should be noted that if the earth fault current is limited to a very low value the sensitivity of the differential scheme may not be sufficient to ensure operation.

Typically sensitivities of down to 10% of the circuit rating are possible. Occasionally, designers prefer to specify an unearthed neutral high voltage system and to increase the insulation to earth accordingly (see also Chapter 9).

Earth fault protection

Protection against internal phase to earth faults when the system is earthed can be provided by 'restricted' earth fault protection. A differential scheme similar to that described above is used but only four current transformers and one relay are required. The single current transformer is applied to the generator neutral as illustrated in Figure 8.8(b). Again this scheme will only respond to earth faults within the protected zone and therefore instantaneous operation is possible. While not covering phase-to-phase faults this arrangement does have the advantage that individual phases of the generator do not have to be brought out at the neutral end.

It is usual to 'back up' restricted earth fault protection with an unrestricted earth fault relay energised from a single current transformer in the generator neutral. This relay will respond to earth faults anywhere on the system and therefore it should be of the time delay type with current and time settings selected to give discrimination with feeder earth fault protection. When neutral earthing resistors are employed an additional relay providing standby earth fault protection may also be used.

Overvoltage protection

If an a.v.r. fault occurs, a generator may be driven to maximum excitation and cause a system overvoltage. The possibility of such a fault occurring is not great and therefore protection is rarely provided. However, many modern ships now carry a considerable quantity of expensive electronic equipment which can easily be damaged by overvoltages and in such circumstances suitable protection should be considered.

A simple relay which is arranged to trip the generator breaker and remove the excitation when an overvoltage occurs is unacceptable in a ship. If a number of generators are paralleled, each being provided with such a relay, any system overvoltage could result in all the machines being tripped. This can be prevented by only allowing a trip to occur if both over-excitation and an overvoltage are present simultaneously at a particular machine. In this way the machine causing the fault condition will be isolated. In fact, it may not be necessary to lose the generator. In the *Queen Elizabeth* 2 a scheme is employed in which the voltage control is automatically tripped from 'auto' to 'hand' on the offending machine[4]. When this scheme is used it will of course be necessary to ensure that the hand voltage regulator cannot be set excessively high.

Overvoltage protection at the generators can be supplemented by high speed tripping of feeder breakers supplying loads which are particularly susceptible to damage; e.g. navigation and communication equipment.

Loss of excitation

When excitation is lost on a generator the effect on the system will depend upon whether it is operating singly or in parallel with other machines. For single operation it will be obvious that the system voltage will collapse. However, when one or more healthy machines are connected in parallel the system voltage may only fall slightly, if at all. This is because the excitation on these other machines will increase and this will offset any tendancy for the voltage to fall.

The faulty machine will continue to supply kW by operating as an induction generator, provided that sufficient reactive current is available from the healthy generators. Unfortunately, this reactive current is seen as a large circulating current flowing between the faulty and the healthy machines. This current could eventually cause damage to the faulty machine but, of more immediate importance, the overcurrent condition could cause tripping of a healthy machine.

For other than brushless sets a simple undercurrent relay in the field circuit can be used to detect loss of excitation. However, brushless sets are now common and the field circuit is not then accessible. To detect excitation loss on such a machine it is necessary to monitor the power factor of the current, the latter being leading under these circumstances.

Relays are available which will respond to these conditions, a time delay also being provided to maintain stability under transient conditions. The operating current of the excitation loss relay should be set below the normal overcurrent setting, 75% to 100% of full load current being typical. Similarly the time delay of the excitation loss relay should be shorter than the overcurrent relay operating delay.

These settings will ensure that only the generator experiencing loss of excitation will be tripped, rather than healthy machines tripping on overcurrent. While not being mandatory the use of such protection is recommended by Lloyd's Register.

Reverse power protection

As reverse current protection cannot be applied in the case of a.c. it is necessary to utilise reverse power to prevent the generator acting as a motor in the event of loss of power by the prime mover. Loss of power may be accidental due to mechanical causes, fuel or steam deficiency, or may be an intentional stoppage by an engineer. If the generator were left connected in parallel with another generator rotation would continue with possible damage to certain types of prime mover.

On diesel driven sets it is unlikely that damage would occur but it is still important to trip the circuit breaker in order to reduce the load imposed on remaining sets; these will probably be overloaded anyway due to the loss of a generator and an additional motoring load of up to 20% of the rating of one machine should be removed as quickly as possible.

To prevent inadvertent operation of reverse power relays due to power surges, particularly when synchronising, a time delay should be incorporated. Where the prime mover is a diesel a fairly coarse setting of the order of 10% of full power is advisable, but steam turbines absorb very little power when motored and a very fine setting of 2½ to 3% reverse power is necessary.

Reverse power protection is normally a mandatory requirement of Lloyd's Rules, however it may be replaced by the provision of electrical interlocks or contacts which will respond to various conditions such as the closing of the fuel or steam admission valve, failure of lubricating oil pressure or, in the case of a turbine, excessive back pressure in the condenser.

Undervoltage protection

Undervoltage protection on low voltage systems is usually accomplished by an integral undervoltage release on the circuit breaker. Above 1000 V a separate relay would be required. It is commonly employed on marine systems:

(a) To prevent closing of the circuit breaker when the generator can be paralleled with other generators or the shore supply and its terminal voltage is less than 70%.

(b) To ensure that loads, particularly motors, are disconnected during a temporary loss of supplies. (Otherwise the generators could be tripped on overcurrent when supplies are restored due to the total starting current of all the connected motors.)

(c) To provide a 'back up' to short-circuit protection.

The undervoltage trip on the generator breaker must not operate if a feeder fault occurs. Consequently it must be time delayed to permit the prior operation of feeder protection. A time delay is also necessary to prevent operation when voltage transients occur during load switching or synchronising. A voltage setting in excess of 80% would not normally be employed because of the possibility of the generator being lost when starting large motors.

Whether undervoltage protection can provide effective 'back up' protection under short-circuit conditions is debatable. Often only the voltage across two phases is monitored and therefore the majority of phase-to-phase faults would only be detected when they developed into three-phase faults. It is notable that this form of protection is relatively uncommon in industrial systems except on motor feeders.

Combined protection

From the various forms of generator protection which have been described above, preference tripping, overcurrent and reverse power

Figure 8.9 Diesel generator protection relay comprising preference trip, inverse time over-current and reverse power elements (GEC Measurements)

are mandatory. Several manufacturers can now supply a unit which performs all of these functions within a housing of compact dimensions, a typical one being shown in Figure 8.9.

GENERATOR INSTRUMENTATION

The instrumentation required for three-phase a.c. generators is rather more extensive than is required for d.c. Where parallel operation is not involved it is sufficient to provide, for each generator, an ammeter in each line or alternatively an ammeter and a selector switch to enable the current in each line to be read, a voltmeter and a frequency meter. For generators above 50 kVA a wattmeter is required.

Where parallel operation is intended then in addition to the ammeters it will be necessary to have:

(a) A wattmeter for each generator.

(b) A voltmeter and a frequency meter connected to the busbars.

(c) A voltmeter and a frequency meter with switches to enable the voltage and frequency of any generator to be measured.

(d) A synchronising device comprising either a synchroscope and lamps or an equivalent arrangement.

Although ammeters for direct connection are available for quite large currents, it is customary to use current transformers. This not only avoids the necessity of carrying heavy current connections to the meter, but also facilitates the use of an ammeter switch to enable the current in each phase to be read. The same current transformer (c.t.) can also be used for the wattmeter and reverse power relay.

Similarly for voltage measurement it is customary to provide voltage transformers (v.t.) for use with voltmeters, wattmeters, synchroscopes reverse-power relays, etc.

The instruments must be capable of indicating abnormal operating conditions and therefore ammeter scales should read to 130% of the normal circuit rating and voltmeter scales to 120% of nominal voltage. In addition, wattmeters for use with generators which can be paralleled must have a scale extending below zero to 15% reverse power. This feature permits immediate identification of a motoring generator.

Current and voltage transformers

Except in certain special circumstances the current transformers will have a standard rated secondary current of 5 A which corresponds to rated primary current. It should be noted that the BS specification for current transformers, BS 3938 : 1973, does not allow an overload factor to be applied to the rated primary current. If an overload rating is required in a specific application this should be stated when ordering.

The secondary winding acts as a constant current generator. Thus, for rated current in the primary the secondary current, within the limits of saturation, will always be 5 A. If the impedance in the secondary circuit is increased the secondary voltage will also increase in order to maintain constant current. For this reason the current coils of ammeters, wattmeters etc, must be connected in series. Care must be taken not to overload the current transformer and manufacturers' catalogues of protective relays, meters etc, usually state the VA load or burden which they will impose. The standard rated outputs are 2.5, 7.5, 10, 15 and 30 VA. It must be remembered that the connecting leads also impose a burden on the c.t. and if this is high due to long leads it may be necessary to employ a rated secondary current of one amp. (The burden imposed upon the c.t. is proportional to the square of the secondary current.) A 1A secondary is also often used when the primary current is low. This increases the turns ratio and enables the required accuracy class to be achieved more easily.

Standard c.ts. are classed according to the degree of accuracy required (see BS 3938) and for general purpose metering either Class 1 or Class 3 is appropriate. These have current errors of 1% and 3% respectively at their rated primary current. When a c.t. is to be used for overcurrent protection a Class 10P transformer will usually provide sufficient accuracy. On a 3.3 kV system earth fault protection may be employed and greater accuracy could be required of the associated c.t., Class 5P then being used. For differential or restricted earth fault protection schemes Class X will probably be required.

For current transformers intended for use with protective relays it is usually important that the transformation accuracy be maintained up to currents equivalent to several times the rated primary current. In fact, the current at which reasonable accuracy is still maintained is defined by the 'accuracy limit factor' which is simply a multiplying factor applied to the rated primary current. The standard accuracy limit factors are given in BS 3938 as 5, 10, 15, 20 and 30. The actual limit which is specified will depend upon the system fault level at the point of application. It should be noted that a c.t. having both a high rated output and a high accuracy limit factor could be unduly large. Generally the product of the c.t. output in VA and the accuracy limit factor should not exceed 150.

A common error is to specify a VA rating which is far in excess of the expected load. Such a c.t. may operate outside its accuracy limits when only lightly loaded and could be unnecessarily large.

When current transformers are required for both protection relays and instruments it is good practice to isolate the two functions and to use separate c.ts. It is possible to use one unit for the dual purpose of both protection and measurement but the characteristics required are generally different for each of the functions. For example, when used for metering the c.t. must only maintain its accuracy for primary currents up to approximately 130% of rated primary current. If it begins to saturate at higher currents (i.e. the secondary current no longer increases at the same rate as the primary current) this is an advantage because under fault conditions the meter will be afforded some protection. Conversely, a c.t. required for overcurrent protection must maintain its accuracy up to several times its rated primary current. It is, however, perfectly acceptable to operate both a reverse power relay and instruments from the same c.t. because the former will only be required to operate at relatively low currents.

A typical unit for overcurrent protection with a rated output of 15 VA and an accuracy limit factor of 5 would be specified as 15 VA Class 10P5. Similarly, a c.t. for metering purposes may be specified as 5 VA Class 1, i.e. a rated output of 5 VA with a current error of one percent at rated current.

If a downstream fault occurs the c.t. must be capable of carrying the fault current without damage until the protection operates. It is therefore important that the manufacturer be informed of the maximum through-fault current possible and the time for which it could flow. For a bar-primary the usual short-time rating is 3 s but for a wound-primary type it may only be 0.5 s.

The secondary circuit must never on any account be opened or left open while under load. Not only would the secondary voltage rise to a dangerous level, but also the transformer may overheat. If necessary, a non-linear resistor wired in parallel with the c.t. will provide adequate protection against this possibility. Switches and plugs used to transfer ammeters from one phase to another, or to permit removal of the meter from the circuit, are invariably provided with contacts which bridge the c.t. before the meter is disconnected. The characteristics of c.t. are such that no harm will ensue if they are left short-circuited.

For voltage transformers the standard secondary ratings corresponding to line-to-line and line-to-neutral are 110 V and 63.5 V respectively. As for current transformers there are preferred values of rated output, these being 10, 25, 50, 100, 200 and 500 VA. The accuracy classes assigned to v.ts. are similar to those for c.ts. the class number referring to the percentage voltage error. The appropriate class for use with commercial grade meters or for synchronising would be Class 1.0 (BS 3941). Where ratio is relatively unimportant (e.g. polarity reversing transformers for synchronising) Class 3 would be adequate.

Current and voltage transformers to BS 3938 and BS 3941 are designed for use at a mean ambient temperature of only 35°C. Consequently, when employed in marine systems, it may be necessary to derate their VA output. Similarly the standard frequency is 50 Hz and, while such transformers can be used at 60 Hz, the specified accuracy may not be achieved. The manufacturer should be informed of both the frequency to be used and the mean ambient temperature so that a suitable transformer can be provided.

In order to safeguard personnel and the instruments from higher voltages in the event of a breakdown of insulation between primary and secondary, it is a requirement that one end of the secondary of v.ts. and c.ts. and the metal cases of the instruments shall be earthed.

Instruments such as wattmeters require two inputs, volts and amps, and it is important that the terminals of the c.ts and v.ts are wired correctly. This also applies to reverse power relays, particular types of excitation loss relays and a.v.rs. Although the quantities are alternating they have a vectorial relationship and therefore instantaneous polarity is inter-related. If some of the polarities are reversed unusual results can be obtained.

For c.ts the standard primary terminal markings are P1 and P2 and the secondary terminals are S1 and S2. These markings are directional and are so applied that at the instant when current in the primary winding is from P1 to P2 the direction of the secondary current through the external circuit forming the burden is from S1 to S2. Special markings for multiple winding transformers will be found in BS 3938.

For single phase voltage transformers the primary terminals A and B correspond to secondary terminals a and b. Thus, at the instant when A is positive with respect to B the secondary a is positive in relation to b. For three-phase star connected v.ts the primary terminals, A, B and C correspond to secondaries a, b and c. If the neutrals are brought out they are N and n for primary and secondary windings respectively.

Typical wattmeter connections are shown in Figures 8.10 and 8.11.

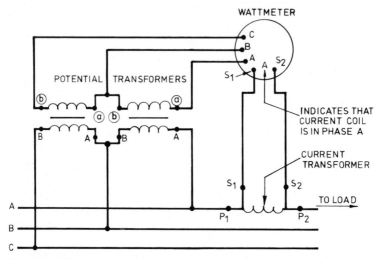

Figure 8.10 3-ph. 3-wire balanced load wattmeter used in conjunction with two single-phase voltage transformers and one current transformer

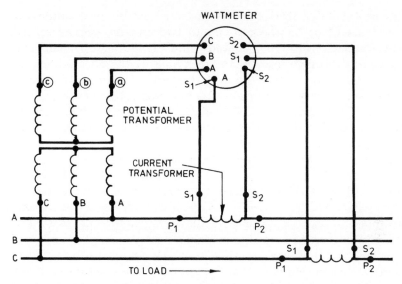

Figure 8.11 3-ph. 3-wire unbalanced-load wattmeter used in conjunction with one 3-ph. voltage transformer and two current transformers

NEUTRAL SWITCHING

In some circumstances a switch may be required in the neutral circuit of each alternator to prevent the circulation of third harmonic currents and also to provide isolation for maintenance.

While the majority of medium voltage marine systems operate with unearthed generator neutrals, at higher voltages it is usual to earth via a resistor. Occasionally a marine system may use solid earthing. When the neutrals are to be earthed, either solidly or via a common resistor, and if the generators are also to operate in parallel, the switching arrangements of the neutrals must be carefully considered.

Third harmonic circulating currents can flow between the neutrals of generators which are operating in parallel on a solidly earthed system. A path will still exist for these currents on a resistance earthed system if only one common earthing resistor is employed. (This subject is discussed in more detail in Chapter 9.) Switches may be required in the generator neutral circuits to prevent the circulation of such currents.

A further point to note concerning systems employing a single common earthing resistor is that, when maintenance work is to be carried out on a generator, it is essential to provide some means of isolating the machine from the earthing resistor. This is because if an earth fault develops on the system and two or more generators are earthed via one resistor, the generator end of the resistor could rise to the line-to-neutral voltage.

The neutral switches must be rated to permit safe closure against the maximum earth fault current possible and consequently circuit breakers are often used on industrial systems when solid earthing is employed. It will devolve upon the operators to see that one of the neutrals is always earthed. If the machine which has its neutral earthed is shutdown, whether intentionally or accidentally, the earthing of the system neutral will be interrupted. This should be prevented although circumstances may arise when it is inevitable. When a machine is intentionally taken out of service it will be the responsibility of the operator to ensure that before doing so the earthing is transferred to another machine.

On marine systems these complications are almost always avoided by using either insulated neutral systems or resistance earthing arrangements in which each machine is earthed via a separate resistor.

POWER FACTOR AND LOAD SHARING

When an a.c. generator is running alone the power factor is determined only by the load and altering the excitation merely changes the voltage (although this will also affect the load on the machine). Similarly, adjustment of the throttle or steam valve will directly affect the frequency.

On the other hand, with a.c. generators in parallel, the power and the reactive kVA contributed by each of the generators may be adjusted separately, i.e. it is possible to alter the p.f. of individual machines. In large grid systems as used on land the frequency is that of a system which is infinitely large with respect to any single generator and the amount of load carried by any one machine is determined by the throttle or governor setting. In small installations such as those in ships, where for example only two sets may be running, the frequency will depend not only on the governors (and to a certain extent on the total load relative to the total generator capacity) but also on the proportionate sharing of the load.

Assuming that the machines are approximately equal in rating, and are each carrying their share of load, then within limits the effect of changing the excitation of one of them is mainly to alter the individual power factor of each generator; alteration of active load sharing (i.e. kW) must be effected solely by throttle and governor settings. It is for this reason that matching of governor characteristics is so much more important in a.c. operation. It should therefore be noted that, for generators in parallel:

(a) kW loading is corrected by throttle or fuel valve adjustment.
(b) Power factor (and reactive volt-ampere or kVAr load) is controlled by excitation.

Speed and excitation controls must therefore be provided at the main switchboard for each generator.

In order to share both kW and kVAr in a stable manner it is necessary to have drooping machine characteristics. Thus, for kW sharing, the speed must decrease for increasing kW loading. If there is any tendency for the load on one machine to increase it will tend to drop its speed, thereby shedding part of it's load which in turn will be picked up by other machines. They will react similarly and a state of equilibrium becomes established.

In order to share kVAr between paralleled machines a drooping voltage characteristic is required. This is provided inherently with hand regulation but machines under the control of a.v.r.s maintain virtually constant voltage and instability will result unless this characteristic is modified. This can be accomplished by using a compounding or quadrature droop current transformer to develop a voltage across a resistor. This voltage is added vectorially to the system voltage and the resultant is applied to the input of the a.v.r. The effect of this is to reduce the excitation of any machine which is supplying excessive kVAr.

Sometimes, for operator convenience, compounding is applied to all machines. While this ensures kVAr sharing it does result in a degree of change in system voltage as loads are switched in and out. It is preferable to operate without compounding on one of the machines; this then becomes the 'master' and its a.v.r. will control the system voltage. kVAr sharing is effected by having the compounding switched in on all other machines (see also Chapters 6 and 7).

If an emergency should arise in service due to a failure of the kVAr stabilising feature of the equipment, a temporary expedient is to operate one machine under automatic voltage control and keep the second machine under hand control. The busbar voltage will be maintained by the a.v.r. controlled machine and the other, under constant excitation, will take approximately constant kVAr load leaving the controlled machine to take care of any change in total kVAr. From time to time sharing can be adjusted by hand control.

This will be fairly satisfactory provided the total load does not vary too frequently or too rapidly. If there is any choice in the matter, and one machine is larger than the other, the larger one should be chosen for a.v.r. control. If necessary more than one machine can be left under hand control under this system.

If it is necessary to operate a ship's generator in parallel with the shore supply then, unless automatic kVAr control equipment is fitted, it is usual to operate under hand control. If left under a.v.r. control large circulating currents can flow between the two sources if the shore supply voltage subsequently changes.

SYNCHRONISING

Although fundamentally the problem of paralleling two a.c. generators is the same as paralleling two d.c. generators, i.e. that the two voltages must be the same and remain the same after paralleling, the practical operation is vastly different. The voltage is alternating and the voltmeter registers the r.m.s. value of volts and not the instantaneous value, whereas for synchronising purposes the instantaneous voltages must match both in magnitude and polarity. Furthermore, they must remain matched, i.e. the frequencies must be identical. Prior to synchronisation slight variations within narrow limits are permissible.

The vectors must also rotate in the same direction, but this is a condition which must be established when the sets are first installed and connected. It is therefore essential in a new installation or when reconnecting a machine after repair to check phase rotation, i.e. that the phase voltages rise to their maximum in the same order for all machines which are to run in parallel.

When paralleling an a.c. generator with other sets already on load the following operations are necessary:

(a) The speed of the incoming machine must be adjusted until its frequency is approximately equal to that of the generators already connected to the busbars. Ordinary engine tachometers are not suitable for this purpose.

(b) The voltage must be adjusted to correspond with that of the busbars.

(c) The paralleling switch must be closed as nearly as possible at the moment when the two instantaneous voltages are in phase (i.e. phase angle zero) and equal in magnitude.

In practice these operations are just as simple as paralleling two d.c. supplies, but they require a little more patience to get the right conditions, as closing the switch when the two supplies are approaching 180° out-of-phase can have serious consequences.

To facilitate the operation a synchroscope is provided. This shows by the speed of rotation of the synchroscope pointer the difference between the two frequencies, and together with a set of lamps, indicates when the voltages are in phase. When the conditions are right the circuit breaker must be closed immediately.

There may be a current surge after closing the circuit breaker, the magnitude of which will depend on the difference of voltage and frequency and the angle of phase displacement. With equal frequencies and with phases coinciding, small differences in the voltages are not important. A difference of 5% in the voltages, with machines of average leakage reactance, would cause a transient surge of approximately 25% of full load current to circulate, and this would settle down to about 5%.

A difference of frequency results in a surge which after reaching a maximum gradually fades out. It is important however to remember that difference of frequency means that phase coincidence is continuously altering, and any delay in closing the circuit breaker may result in incorrect conditions. A frequency difference of 1.0% will correspond roughly with one revolution of the synchroscope in 1 s, and this would generally be found tolerable for synchronising. Movement of the synchroscope pointer clockwise indicates that the speed of the incoming machine is faster than that of the connected machine and vice versa.

It is the moment when the circuit breaker contacts touch which is important. If, for example, closing a circuit breaker takes one third of a second from commencement of the operation, in that time the phase angle will have changed roughly 90° with a frequency difference of 1.5%.

It is preferable that, before synchronising, the generator voltage and frequency should be not less than those already on the busbar so that the incoming machine immediately assumes a certain load (i.e. the synchroscope pointer should be moving clockwise). A typical synchronising panel is shown in Figure 8.12.

The synchroscope

This has two windings, one of which is connected to the busbars or running machine, and the other to the incoming machine i.e. on the machine side of the appropriate circuit breaker (Figure 8.13). Where there are several machines, the synchroscope winding intended to monitor the incoming machine is connected to each machine via a selector switch. A pointer rotates freely in either direction and indicates the phase angle between the two voltage supplies. When the voltages are in phase the pointer remains at 12 o'clock. The

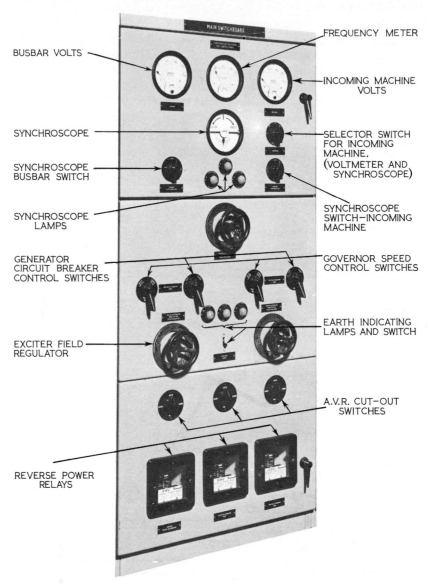

Figure 8.12 Synchronising panel for two 550 kW and one 200 kW a.c. generators

dial is marked 'Fast' and 'Slow' with appropriate arrows to indicate, according to the direction in which the pointer is rotating, whether the incoming machine is running too fast or too slow.

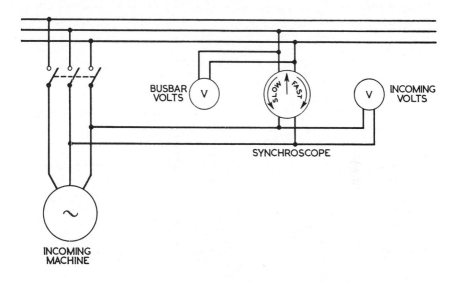

Figure 8.13 Connections of synchroscope and voltmeters

The synchroscope movement consists of a stator winding in which a rotating field is set up and a soft-iron rotor which is magnetised by a fixed coil. The rotor is supported in jewel bearings and its shaft carries the pointer. There are thus no moving coils, contacts, or control springs. When the frequencies are the same, the pointer takes up a position showing the angular phase difference between the two circuits, and when in synchronism the pointer is at 12 o'clock. To avoid false indications the pointer is made to fall away from the central position as soon as the windings are de-energised. The synchroscope should not be left in circuit for more than 20 min as it is not continuously rated.

To assist in synchronising, external lamps can be fitted to the instrument. The circuits for 'lamps bright' are shown in Figure 8.14 with an alternative arrangement for 'lamps dark' in Figure 8.15. In the 'lamps bright' method a one-to-one ratio transformer is arranged so that its secondary can be connected, with reversed polarity, in series with the secondary of the transformer connected to the running generator. Thus, when the two supplies are in synchronism double normal voltage is imposed on the lamps.

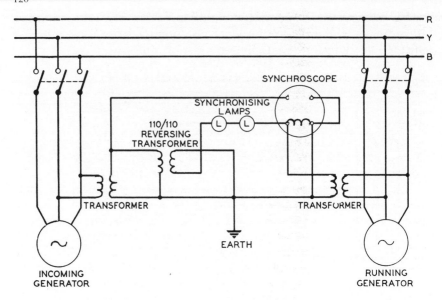

Figure 8.14 Schematic diagram of synchroscope and synchronising lamps for 'lamps bright' system

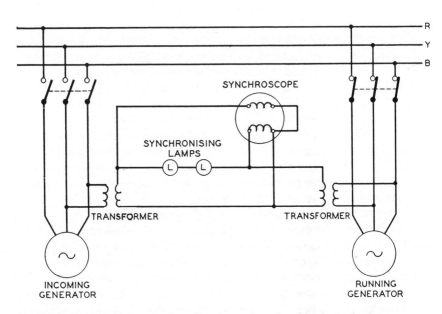

Figure 8.15 Schematic diagram of synchroscope and synchronising lamps for 'lamps dark' system

In practice it is almost impossible to adjust the speeds exactly so that the pointer remains stationary at 12 o'clock, and it is good practice to have the pointer rotating not faster than one revolution in 5 s in the 'fast' direction, and to initiate closing when the pointer is at about 11 o'clock (although the ideal point at which closing should be initiated will depend upon the closing time of the circuit breaker). In this way with the machine slightly fast it will immediately assume load, whereas if switched when running slow it would take a motoring load which might possibly operate the reverse power relay. It is in view of this possibility that the latter should be provided with a time lag.

Two voltmeters are necessary, one connected to the busbars and the other to the incoming machine. In practice up to 10% difference in voltage might be considered tolerable.

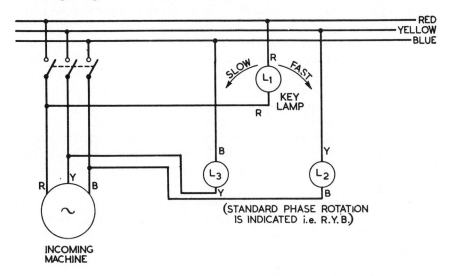

Figure 8.16 Connections of lamps for synchronising by the 'sequence' method

If, for any reason, a synchroscope is not available or is out of commission, lamps can be used to give the required indications and the 'sequence' method shown in Figure 8.16 is appropriate. One of the lamps, known as the key lamp, is connected in one phase but the other two lamps, are cross-connected. If the two frequencies differ the lamps will light up in rotation. If mounted in a triangular formation the lights will appear to rotate and the sequence in which they light up, i.e. whether clockwise or counter-clockwise, is an indication of whether the incoming machine is fast or slow. The moment to synchronise is when the key lamp (which should be at the top of the triangle) is dark and the other two lamps equally bright.

If the phase rotation is wrong all three lamps will brighten and darken together. To correct this, interchange any two phase connections of the faulty machine. As lamps suitable for voltage above 250 V are not generally available, it will be necessary to use lamps in series or to use voltage transformers.

The check synchroniser

Even a skilled operator may occasionally make an error when synchronising and the generators will then be subjected to undesirable stresses. This can be prevented by using a check synchroniser. This is a static unit which, in its more comprehensive form, monitors phase angle, voltage and frequency at both the busbars and the incoming generator. Each of the parameters are compared and, when the differences are within pre-set limits, the check relay output contacts will close. These contacts will usually be connected in series with the closing control-switch contacts in the closing circuit of the circuit breaker. Consequently the operator will only be allowed to close the circuit breaker when the conditions are correct.

With certain designs of check synchroniser an auxiliary 'seal-in' relay must be used because the check relay contacts will only remain closed for a brief period, perhaps insufficient to ensure closing of the circuit breaker.

It will be apparent that with such a scheme an operator could prematurely operate the circuit breaker closing control switch and hold it in that position until the check relay provided the closing signal. This could lead to the operator becoming lazy and unpractised in synchronising. In the event of failure of the check relay he would be handicapped. This can be prevented by specifying a check relay which does not permit premature closing. An extra input is provided on such a relay directly from the circuit breaker control switch closing contact. The exact instant at which the control switch contacts close can thereby be monitored and if the phase angle is outside pre-set limits at that time the check relay will not operate.

The great advantage of this check synchroniser is that the skill of the operator is still required to match frequency, volts and phase angle but errors are prevented. Other, more simple, variants of the check synchroniser are available which compare only phase angle, not voltage and frequency.

AUTOMATIC CONTROL OF DIESEL GENERATOR SETS

It is now becoming more common for diesel generator sets to be started, run-up, synchronised and shutdown automatically. Such arrangements would be specified when unmanned machinery spaces are required but a number of additional advantages are also obtained. For example, automatic schemes can start-up or shut down generators to accommodate changing load requirements and this results in fuel economies. Because machines are not operated at low load factors (less than 30% say) the corresponding detrimental effects on the diesel engine are avoided, (e.g. the rapid formation of carbon deposits). The probability of operator error is reduced and start-up and shutdown sequences can be accomplished both more rapidly and more smoothly.

Programmed automatic systems are available which can control several diesel generator sets. On a typical system the controller would first be 'programmed' to pre-select the order in which the sets are to start-up. The first set selected, the duty or base load set, will run continuously once started. The second set is the first standby and will only start when required. Further standby sets will start and stop as the load changes. The selection procedure is relatively simple and the sequence can be changed whenever required in order to build up the running hours of each set successively. This enables a maintenance routine to be operated which does not necessitate simultaneous servicing of all the sets.

A simplified block control diagram for a typical automatic controller is shown in Figure 8.17 and this should serve to clarify the following description. With the programming complete the system can be started via the 'start' push button. When this has been pressed all subsequent operations will take place automatically. The base load engine is started and as it comes up to speed a speed switch brings the alarm circuits into operation and permits closing of the circuit breaker when the frequency and voltage are correct. (Synchronising will not be required when the first set is started.)

The base load set will continue to run alone until the total load continuously exceeds a preset level, usually about 80% of rated kW, at which point the first standby set is started. (A momentary power demand in excess of this level, such as could be caused by a motor starting, will not cause this action to be taken because a time delay circuit is incorporated.)

The first standby set then runs up to speed and upon operation of its speed switch the auto-synchroniser is brought into service. This

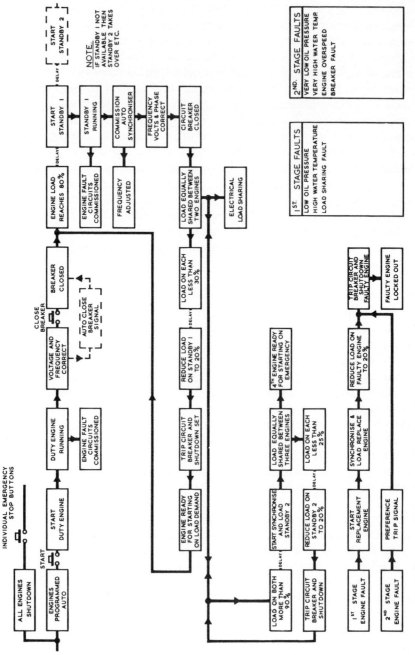

Figure 8.17 Block control diagram — automatic control of diesel alternators

unit compares voltage, frequency, and phase angle in the same way as the check synchroniser. If differences between the incoming set and the busbars are detected the synchroniser responds by pulsing the governor motor to raise or lower the speed as appropriate.

Normally it is not necessary to use the synchroniser to set the voltage because this is usually controlled adequately by the a.v.r. However, if the latter facility is required then motorised control of the a.v.r. voltage reference trimmer must be provided.

When the voltage and frequency are correct and the phase angle is approaching zero the synchroniser will initiate closing of the circuit breaker. At this point it is worth noting that the closing signal is given at a pre-set time before the ideal condition, zero phase angle, is reached. This allows for the closing time of the circuit breaker. However, if the breaker has a particularly long closing time, in excess of 0.3 s say, correct operation may not be possible.

If the first standby set fails to synchronise the second will start automatically. When two or more sets are operating in parallel it must be ensured that both kVAr and kW are shared between the machines. kVAr sharing is normally effected by the AVR with its associated quadrature droop circuitry and additional trimming by the automatic controller is not necessary. However, if it is envisaged that at some time the sets will be operated in parallel with the shore supply the AVR must be provided with a motorised potentiometer to enable the controller to adjust the kVAr sharing. This is because even a small change in the shore supply voltage will cause the AVRs to respond in an attempt to correct the change. Of course they will not be capable of effecting such a correction and the result is that large reactive circulating currents will flow. An alternative solution is to switch out the AVR and to operate at constant excitation when the sets are paralleled with the shore supply.

The sharing of the kW load is determined by the diesel governors. A load sharing module in the controller compares the kW load upon each of the standby sets with that of the base load set. Equal loading is then effected by pulsing the governor motor of the appropriate set. Alternatively, instead of running all sets with an equal load, some schemes permit all the sets except one to operate at thier most economic load factor. The last set takes up the remaining load.

If the busbar load is subsequently increased additional sets will be started and synchronised in the programmed sequence. Similarly, if the total load falls, sets will be shut down in the reverse order. However, before a set is tripped out the controller will first reduce its load to 10% or 20% in order to reduce the magnitude of transients on switching.

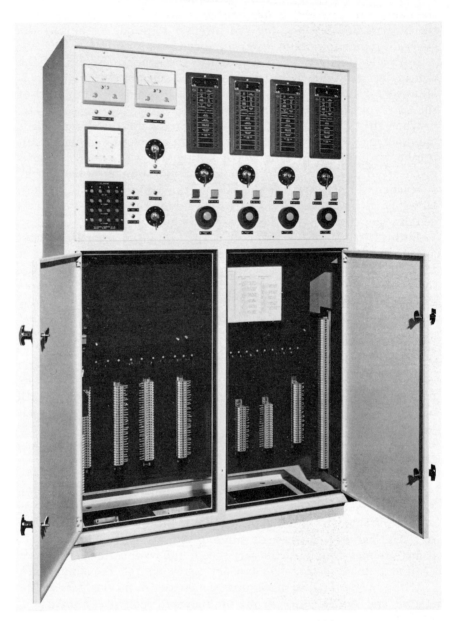

Figure 8.18 Diesel generator programmed automatic controller (Pyropress Engineering Co. Ltd.)

The power levels at which sets are started and stopped must be selected so that 'hunting' does not occur, i.e. when one set is shut down it must not result in the loading of the remaining sets exceeding the level at which a new standby set is required.

Frequency control is often achieved by circuitry which compares the busbar frequency with an internal reference. When a difference is detected the governor motor of the base load set is operated until the busbar frequency is correct. The standby sets need not be adjusted individually because they will of course be running in synchronism with the base load set. Such adjustments will obviously cause a slight change in load sharing which will then be corrected by operation of the load sharing module. While sets are running in parallel there will be continuous small adjustments of frequency and load sharing.

The automatic controller will usually provide fault surveillance and protection, covering such items as overspeed, lubricating oil temperature and pressure and cooling water temperature and pressure. Faults which can be tolerated for a short time are termed first stage faults. These cause an alarm to be given and the next standby set will be started and synchronised. The faulty set will be shutdown only when the new set has been connected. A second stage fault is one which requires immediate action, e.g. diesel overspeed or very low lub oil pressure, and the set will be shutdown at once. This could cause the remaining generators to become overloaded and to avoid this preferential tripping of non-essential loads will also be initiated. An illustration of a typical controller is shown in Figure 8.18.

References

1. Dwight, H.B. 'Skin Effect in Tubular and Flat Conductors' *Trans. A.I.E.E.*, 37, Part II pp 1379–1403 (1918).
2. *Copper for busbars*, Copper Development Association.
3. Wright, E.C. 'A.C. current ratings of rectangular conductors', *Electrical Review*, 199, 5 (20 July 1976).
4. Bolton, M.J. 'The electrical power system in the Queen Elizabeth 2 — design and operational experience', *I. Mar. E.*, (9th Feb. 1971).

BIBLIOGRAPHY

BS 88. Cartridge fuses for voltages up to and including 1000 V a.c. and 1500 V d.c.

Part 1: 1975. General requirements.

Part 2: 1975. Supplementary requirements for fuses of standardised dimensions and performance for industrial purposes.

Part 3: (In preparation)

Part 4: Supplementary requirements for fuse links for the protection of semiconductor devices.

BS 697 : 1977. Specification for rubber gloves for electrical purposes.

BS 387. Miniature and moulded case circuit breakers.

Part 1: 1965. Miniature air-break circuit breakers for a.c circuits.

Part 2: 1966. Moulded case circuit-breakers for a.c and d.c circuits.

BS 3938 : 1973. Current transformers.

BS 3941 : 1975. Voltage transformers.

BS 5752. Specification for switchgear and control gear for voltages up to and including 100 V a.c and 1200 V d.c.

Part 1: 1977 (IEC 157–1 and 157–1A circuit-breakers)

BS 5311. Specification for a.c circuit-breakers of rated voltage above 1 kV.

Part 1: 1976. General and definitions.

Part 2: 1976 Rating.

Part 3: 1976 Design and construction.

Part 4: 1976 Type tests and routine tests.

Part 5: 1976 Rules for the selection of circuit-breakers for service.

Part 6: 1976. Information to be given with enquiries tenders and orders: rules for transport erection and maintenance.

Part 7: 1976. The testing of circuit-breakers with respect to out-of-phase switching

BS 5405: 1976. Code of practice for the maintenance of electrical switchgear for voltages up to and including 1000 V a.c and 1200 V d.c.

Part 1: 1977 (IEC 439). General requirements.

IEC 157. Low voltage switchgear and control gear.

157–1 (1973) Part 1. Circuit-breakers.

157–1A (1976) First supplement.

IEC 363 (1972). Short-circuit current evaluation with special regard to the rated short-circuit capacity of circuit breakers in installations in ships.

9 Distribution

On new vessels d.c. distribution systems are now rarely used because the overall cost of a.c. systems is less. The a.c. system is also more compact and lighter and maintenance is reduced. However, where d.c. is found on existing vessels the two-wire insulated system is used almost universally,. except in American ships where the three-wire system is favoured.

Single-wire systems with hull return are now rarely used and under the 1960 Convention for Safety of Life at Sea special precautions must be taken to the satisfaction of the administration. Objections to the single-wire system, apart from the point of view of safety, are that the state of the insulation cannot be indicated while under load, and during surveys the conditon of circuits to consuming devices cannot be Megger tested without removing lamps or disconnecting apparatus. Hull return is not permitted in tankers.

A.C. SYSTEMS

With a.c. systems three-phase distribution with insulated neutral is still commonly employed. On medium voltage systems 440 V is usually selected in preference to 380 V because the former can result in significant economic savings due to the smaller copper sizes required. However, distribution at 415 V is sometimes used when ships have a large hotel load as this provides a line-to-neutral voltage of 240 V and enables standard domestic equipment and fittings to be employed. Such a system would use four wires with the neutral earthed but without hull return. 380 V is largely favoured for ships operated from the continent. At 3.3 kV a three-wire system with the neutral earthed via a resistor is normally employed but occasionally designers prefer insulated neutrals as at medium voltages. Neutral earthing is an important problem and is discussed later.

FREQUENCY

The two common power frequencies in use throughout the world are 50 Hz and 60 Hz. The frequency selected for a particular application may often be determined by the shore supplies available, thus vessels operating only in British waters will normally employ 50 Hz distribution. However, where a choice exists the advantages usually favour the higher frequency.

The power output of a motor is proportional to its speed and therefore a 60 Hz machine will generally be more compact and have a greater power to weight ratio than its 50 Hz equivalent. Less iron is required at 60 Hz and this results in a cheaper machine. Also, the motor speeds available from a 60 Hz supply are generally more suitable (see Chapter 12).

When a shore supply is taken it is permissible to supply a 60 Hz system at 50 Hz provided that the voltage is reduced. Thus, ideally 440 V 60 Hz motors should be supplied at 380 V when only a 50 Hz supply is available. At 415 V, 50 Hz the same motors will run with a slightly greater temperature rise but, provided that the ambient temperature is not too high, it is unlikely that any damage will result. It must be accepted that induction motor speeds will be reduced by about 20%. Heating and incandescent lighting are not frequency sensitive but of course, when they are operated at the lower voltage to accommodate the lower frequency, their output will be reduced.

The operation of a 50 Hz system from a 60 Hz supply is not to be recommended. The motors will run faster and therefore will produce more torque. In doing so they will demand more than their rated current and could be severely overloaded.

NEUTRAL EARTHING

With very few exceptions marine electrical design engineers favour the insulation of the neutral on medium voltage systems although this is contrary to almost universal practice ashore. In view of this it is worthwhile to examine the pros and cons of the insulated system.

Insulated systems were primarily adopted to avoid the risk of the loss of essential services, such as steering gear and vital engine room auxiliaries, following an earth fault on an earthed system. With solid neutral earthing a phase-to-earth fault constitutes a short-circuit on the phase concerned and causes operation of the protective fuse or circuit breaker. With motor circuit faults this may result in single phasing and the possibility of a burn-out unless adequate protective equipment is provided.

On an insulated system one earth fault does not interrupt the supply but raises a warning on the earth leakage detection system. This allows the operator to search for and clear the fault at a convenient time. This should be done as soon as possible because while an earth fault exists the voltage to earth of the two healthy phases will be at line volts, not phase volts. This 73% excess voltage on the healthy phases will further stress the insulation and could increase the possibility of a second earth fault occurring. Obviously this would now constitute a phase-to-phase fault and could result in the overcurrent protection on two circuits operating.

A particualr disadvantage of the unearthed system is the difficulty which can be experienced by an operator in locating an earth fault. Usually circuits have to be tripped out selectively until the earth fault indication is cleared. Even then the source of the fault on that particular circuit may be difficult to find. With an earthed system the faulty circuit is automatically isolated by operation of the protective device and at least the approximate location of the fault will be known.

A further advantage sometimes claimed for the insulated neutral is that the electric shock risk is reduced. In fact, while on a 440 V system the capacitive return current is usually only a few milliamps, a level unlikely to be directly fatal, on some larger vessels currents of approximately 60 mA have been reported and this can also be increased by surface leakage and the use of radio interference suppression units. Such levels would not be intrinsically safe. In addition, if there is already an earth fault on one phase the two remaining phases are potentially more dangerous. They will now be at 440 V to earth whereas, on a solidly earthed system, no phase can exceed 250 V to earth. It is therefore quite wrong to assume that live parts can be touched without risk of shock on an unearthed system. Both solidly earthed and insulated neutral systems should be regarded as equally hazardous.

One consequence of the low values of earth fault current on insulated systems is that the risk of fire due to such a fault is negligible. This is a definite advantage over earthed systems.

The main argument against the insulated neutral is that the system is subject to overvoltages caused by either resonant or intermittent faults. An earth fault on a winding, perhaps a contactor solenoid or a transformer, will result in a circuit in which inductance and capacitance are in series, the capacitance comprising that between the healthy phases and earth. If, unfortunately, this series circuit is resonant at or near the system frequency, or one of its harmonics, a voltage magnification of several times can occur. An investigation of a typical insulated 440 V 3-phase installation carried out on a network analyser showed that with an inductive fault between one line and earth overvoltages of 3.5 to 4.5 times the normal phase-to-earth voltage might occur.

An intermittent arcing fault on an insulated system can result in a rapid increase in the voltage between the system neutral and earth. Initially the system neutral will be floating at or about earth potential. When the earth fault first occurs the neutral will rise to phase volts to earth. If the fault now clears itself the neutral will remain floating above earth due the charge on the system capacitance. If no other disturbance arises the neutral will gradually return to earth potential as the system capacitance discharges at a rate determined by the leakage resistance between the system and earth. The time constant involved can be relatively long. Before the system has been discharged the fault may restrike and the neutral will experience a further rise in voltage above earth.

This sequence of events can be repeated rapidly and may result in the neutral, and hence the whole system, rising to a potential of several times the phase-to-neutral voltage above earth. The mechanism by which this occurs is examined more fully in reference 1 (see page 163). It may be noted that this rise in voltage can be prevented by employing an appropriate resistor between the system neutral and earth. This will reduce the discharge time constant of the system considerably.

Machines and equipment designed for medium voltage operation are insulation tested when new by the manufacturer at 2000 V, a level well in excess of the possible overvoltages. This is a 'once only' test on apparatus in new condition but there is no evidence that breakdowns due to over-voltages are a serious hazard.

Equipment rated for use at 3.3 kV does not normally have such a high margin of safety on the strength of its insulation. If an insulated system is used at these voltages, Lloyd's require all equipment to be tested at not less than 7.5 times the line to neutral voltage for one minute. This corresponds to a test voltage of 14.3 kV on a 3.3 kV system. Generally either it will be uneconomic to provide the degree of insulation required by this test duty or it will limit the choice of available machines. Most 3.3 kV systems are now designed to operate with an earthed neutral and in these circumstances the power frequency withstand test voltage specified by Lloyd's is only twice rated voltage plus 1 kV, i.e. 7.6 kV (see also Chapter 8 concerning the voltage rating of circuit breakers).

If a solidly earthed system were to be employed at these voltages the earth fault current would be excessively high. For example, with an earth loop impedance of 0.25 ohms the fault current would be 7.6 kA. In view of this it is common practice both ashore and afloat to earth the neutral via a resistor.

A further disadvantage associated with solidly earthed systems is that of circulating third harmonic currents. Although it is the aim to produce alternators having a perfectly sinusoidal voltage waveform this is seldom achieved in practice and the line-to-neutral voltage will usually contain harmonics of which the third will be predominant.

When two or more identical machines are being operated in parallel, each with its neutral insulated, there will be no return path for third harmonic currents (also known as triplen currents). Similarly, with only one generator neutral earthed, no path will exist. However, when more than one neutral is earthed a circulating current can flow if there is any inequality in the third harmonic voltages generated by each machine.

When two or more identical machines are being operated in parallel, each with its neutral solidly earthed, the third harmonic voltages generated by each will be identical and theoretically no third harmonic circulating currents will flow provided that the machines are equally loaded. However, when any one machine becomes unequally loaded its rotor angle will differ from that of the other machines. Immediately the third harmonic voltages will no longer be the same and the resulting voltage differential will cause a circulating current to flow, the magnitude of the current being proportional to the difference in the rotor angles, i.e. the difference in loading. Such a situation will occur when a generator is being synchronised with running machines. Since third harmonic currents do not produce armature reaction the current will be limited solely by the leakage reactance and not by the synchronous reactance.

The third harmonic current can therefore be very appreciable and, being additional to the load current, increases the stator losses with consequent extra heating. A further problem arises when earth fault protection is employed (as it could be on an earthed system) because third harmonic currents are of zero sequence and can be detected by earth fault relays. This can result in spurious tripping.

It is therefore recommended that the manufacturer of the generators be consulted as to whether it is advisable to operate with all the neutrals solidly earthed. In general such a system should only be considered for small machines of identical manufacture.

The circulation of third harmonic currents can be prevented by using neutral switches as explained in Chapter 8. The system will then be operated with only one generator neutral earthed. However, if the system includes any unablanced load such as lighting, heating, etc, the unbalanced current will be carried by the machine with the earthed neutral and it should accordingly be suitably rated to carry this load, (see also Chapter 6 on the effect of an unbalanced load on an alternator).

In conclusion therefore, insulated systems have been preferred at 440 V because the risk of failure due to overvoltage is not regarded as serious, whereas the risk of the loss of the vital services due to earth faults on earthed systems cannot be accepted. Faults to earth probably represent the most common form of insulation failure in ships. An additional disadvantage associated with the solidly earthed system is the possibility that measures may have to be taken to prevent the flow of circulating currents. At 3.3 kV and higher voltages economic considerations will often dictate that the system neutral should be earthed. This is usually accomplished via resistors.

Resistance earthed neutral

In selecting the ohmic value of the earthing resistor two factors must be considered. The current must be limited to a reasonable level yet must still be adequate to operate earth fault protection equipment. It is normal industrial practice to limit the maximum fault current to the rated full load current of the generator and this has proved to be satisfactory in service. In fact, Lloyd's Register stipulates that the resistor should be such that this current is not exceeded. In order to achieve positive operation of the protection devices the fault current should not be less than three times the minimum operating current.

At least one earthing resistor must be provided for each independent section of a switchboard. One possible method of earthing the generators on one section is to common all the generator neutral points on the generator side of a single earthing resistor as shown in Figure 9.1a. This has the advantage that, no matter how many generators are operation, the maximum possible earth fault current is substantially constant, being determined only by the ohmic value of the resistor. (This is because the zero sequence impedance of each alternator is negligible in comparison with the series resistance.) A further advantage is that only one resistor is required for each section. These merits can be heavily outweighed by one serious disadvantage. Third harmonic currents can circulate freely between the neutrals of each paralleled machine. In order to avoid this it may be necessary to switch the neutrals so that only one machine is earthed.

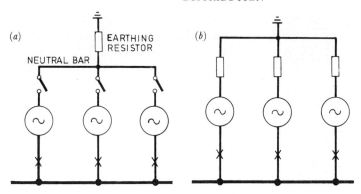

Figure 9.1 Two neutral earthing schemes used at 3.3 k V
(a) using one common earthing resistor
(b) using one earthing resistor per generator

A method of neutral earthing which is becoming more popular on marine systems employs one resistor for each generator with common bonding on the earthing side of each resistor (see Figure 9.1b). Neutral switching is not then required and the magnitude of third harmonic circulating currents will be negligible because there will effectively be two resistors in series between any two generators. (See also Chapter 8, neutral switching.)

It must be remembered that with this method of earthing the maximum possible earth fault current will be proportional to the number of generators operating. For example, a 3 MVA 3.3 kV alternator has a full load current of 525 A. In order to restrict the earth fault current to this value with a phase-to-neutral voltage of 1.9 kV a 3.63 ohm resistor will be required. However, if a second generator is operating in parallel and an earth fault occurs, the total current at the seat of the fault could be 1050 A. In this situation it is first necessary to determine how many machines would be expected to operate in parallel.

If, for example, this number is four the ohmic value of each resistor is increased accordingly, in this case to 14.5 ohms, so that the total fault current does not exceed 525 A. This will ensure compliance with Lloyd's Register Regulations. Naturally this may cause problems with earth fault relay sensitivity and discrimination if several machines could be operated in parallel. This is because under some conditions only one or two of these machines may be in operation and as a result the maximum fault current available to operate the relays would be quite low, e.g. 131 A from one machine in the example quoted. On such a system no earth fault protection setting should exceed 44 A.

In some circumstances it may be necessary to feed 3.3 kV busbars via a transformer, either from a shore supply or from an emergency 440 V generator. In this case the high voltage transformer winding should be star connected with the medium voltage winding in delta. This is contrary to normal practice but will allow the high voltage star point to be earthed via a resistor.

It must be remembered that neutral earthing resistors are usually only short-time rated and therefore the normal earth fault protection relays are sometimes supplemented by a standby earth fault relay energised from a c.t. at the resistor. This is set to prevent overheating of the resistor if the fault is not cleared by other means.

High resistance earthing

Some designers are now employing earthing resistors on 3.3 kV systems which limit the earth fault current to only a few amperes. This has the advantage that the fire risk is reduced considerably and, providing the ohmic value of the resistor is correctly chosen, overvoltages will not be a problem. In order to size the resistor it is first necessary to estimate the total capacitance, C, between the systems and earth. (This is three times the single phase to earth capacitance). The system capacitive reactance X_c is then given by

$$X_c = \frac{1}{2\pi f C} \text{ ohms}$$

where C is the total system capacitance in Farads and f is the system frequency in Hz. The ohmic value of the earthing resistor should not exceed the system capacative reactance X_c, the optimum value being when the two are equal[2] i.e.

$$R = \frac{1}{2\pi f C}$$

If this technique is adopted it must be ensured that detection of earth faults will still be possible in view of the low fault currents expected. It will often be necessary to use core balance current transformers to achieve the necessary sensitivity.

It may not be necessary to employ tripping in the event of an earth fault because of the low currents involved and sometimes only indication is provided. However, if the total earth fault current via the earthing resistor and the system capacitance exceeds about 8 A (equivalent to a resistor current of 5.5 A) then there will be a greater possibility of fault escalation if the fault is not removed automatically[3].

Multiple system

There is no reason why several different earthing systems should not be used on the same vessel so that the type most suitable for a particular application can be used. For example, if the main generation is at 3.3 kV this system would be earthed via resistors.

Two low or medium voltage networks could be fed from the 3.3 kV busbars, one supplying the machinery spaces and deck machinery and the second providing hotel services. The former could operate as an insulated system to preserve continuity of supply while the latter may be solidly earthed to simplify fault finding.

The lighting system is particularly subject to earth faults and, because of the nature of the equipment employed on such systems, these can take a considerable time to locate if an insulated neutral is used.

FUSES

It is good practice to use only high rupturing capacity (h.r.c.) fuses because of their consistent operating characteristics, durability and current limiting feature. The information in the following paragraphs relates only to h.r.c. fuses.

When selecting fuses for the protection of distribution circuits four factors must be considered:

(a) The fuse must have a fault rating which is equal to or greater than the system fault level at the point of application.
(b) The fuse normal current rating must not be so high that it fails to give adequate protection to the circuit.
(c) The fuse may have to be de-rated for particular service conditions.
(d) The fuse rating must be such that it will provide discrimination with both upstream and downstream protective devices.

Discrimination will be discussed later but the other factors governing fuse selection are described below.

Fault rating

The breaking capacity of the fuses must always exceed the r.m.s. symmetrical prospective fault current at each point where a fuse is to be applied. Often only a simple calculation will be necessary to check this (see Chapter 8). The standard breaking capacities listed in BS 88: Part 2 : 1975 are 80 kA a.c. and 40 kA d.c. Fuses with these ratings are adequate for most systems encountered in practice.

Fuse protection

The fuse can be considered as a device which is extremely efficient at providing protection under fault conditions. It is not so effective when called upon to disconnect overloaded equipment.

Probably the most valuable characteristic of the h.r.c. fuse is its ability to limit or 'cut-off' the peak current which can occur under fault conditions. It has already been explained in Chapter 8 that on an a.c. system a peak current of up to 2.55 times the r.m.s. symmetrical fault current can arise. However, the h.r.c. fuse can operate so rapidly that the fuse begins to arc internally before the prospective peak current is attained. At the onset of arcing the fault current begins to decrease and therefore the actual peak current occurs at this time.

Whether in fact current limiting does take place depends upon both the fuse rating and the prospective r.m.s. symmetrical fault current. For a given system fault level smaller fuses will provide a greater 'cut-off'.

Typical cut-off characteristics for h.r.c. fuses are shown in Figure 9.2. When using fuses to 'back-up' another protective device it should be ensured that the fuse cut-off current is lower than the peak making current of the protected device.

The high speed of operation of a fuse under fault conditions has the additional advantage of limiting the amount of energy which is released at the seat of the fault. Equipment damage is therefore restricted. The energy released can be expressed in terms of $I^2 t$, (amp squared seconds), and manufacturers data are available which indicate the $I^2 t$ 'let-through' of each fuse rating under given conditions. One set of such characteristics is shown in Figure 9.3. It will be seen that two values of $I^2 t$, are given for each fuse rating, 'pre-arcing' and 'total operating'. When a fuse is being selected to provide protection for an equipment it should be ascertained that the *withstand* $I^2 t$ of the equipment is greater than the total operating $I^2 t$ of the fuse.

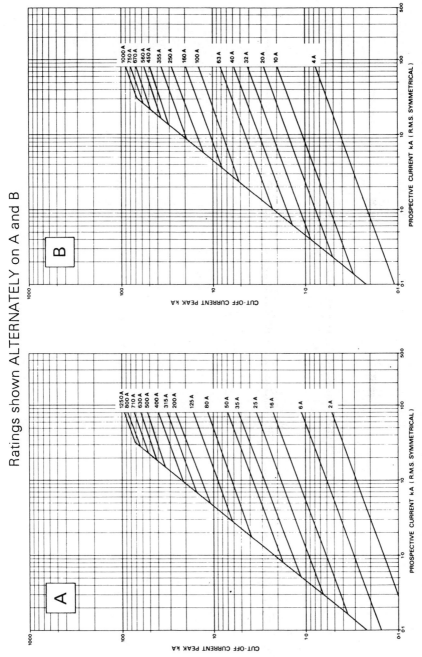

Figure 9.2 Typical cut-off characteristics for r.r.c. fuses

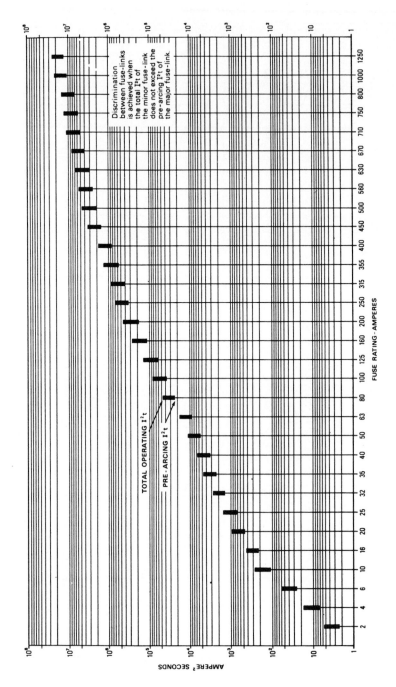

Discrimination
between fuse-links
is achieved when
the total I²t of
the minor fuse-link
does not exceed the
pre-arcing I²t of
the major fuse-link.

TOTAL OPERATING I²t

PRE-ARCING I²t

FUSE RATING-AMPERES

AMPERE² SECONDS

Figure 9.3 Fuse I²t characteristics

If a fuse with a high current rating is to be used it will be prudent to check that the fault current which is available from the generator is capable of operating the fuse within a reasonable time. The fault current can decay quite rapidly, perhaps falling below the fuse characteristic but not causing operation.

The degree of overload protection which is afforded by a fuse is given by its fusing factor where:

$$\text{Fusing factor} = \frac{\text{minimum fusing current}}{\text{current rating}}$$

The minimum fusing current is the minimum current at which a fuse element melts and this usually occurs after a period of about four hours. British cartridge fuses are divided into two standard classes:

Class	Fusing factor	
	Exceeding	*Not exceeding*
P	1.0	1.25
Q_1	1.25	1.5

The class quoted for most h.r.c. fuses is Q_1 which implies that over-loads of up to 150% of the fuse rating could be carried indefinitely. In terms of load rating the possible overload will obviously exceed 150%. (It should be noted that for re-wirable fuses the minimum fusing current can exceed 200% of the current rating).

While such figures compare unfavourably with the degree of over-load protection which can be provided by a circuit breaker it should be remembered that many distribution circuits will often have over-load protection provided somewhere downstream from the fuse. In such circumstances the fuse may be regarded as a protective device against short-circuit faults only.

Service conditions

Fuses complying with BS 88 : 1975 must be designed for use in a mean ambient air temperature of 35°C. It will be recognised that at the higher ambients possible on ships some derating may be required.

The degree of derating required at 45°C will be given by the manufacturer on request but in general it will be found that only fuses
with ratings in excess of about 250 A will be affected.

It will be appreciated that the local ambient temperature in the
vicinity of the fuse could be significantly greater than the general
ambient if the fuse is contained in a case with poor ventilation.
Again the manufacturer should be consulted.

MINIATURE CIRCUIT BREAKERS (M.C.B.)

The term 'miniature' applies to a compact small circuit breaker of
current rating not exceeding 100A, and with a short circuit capacity
of up to 9000A, (see Figure 9.4). The m.c.b. was originally
developed for use in factories and domestic installations in lieu of

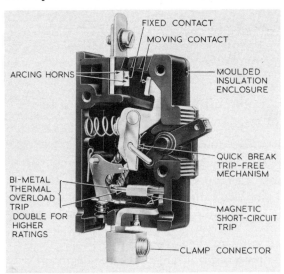

Figure 9.4 Miniature circuit breaker

fuses, and, as distinct from main switchboard types of circuit
breakers, it has a limited breaking capacity. This is not necessarily a
disadvantage because the m.c.b. will usually be used on sub-
distribution circuits and there will normally be cabling of appreciable
impedance between the point of application and the main switchboard.

Single and three-phase types are available but the nominal phase to
earth voltage should not exceed 250 V. They usually employ a
thermally operated bi-metal strip for overload protection, but have in

addition an instantaneously operating electro-magnetic trip to deal with short circuits. Without the latter there is a risk that the thermal trip, because of its inherently slow action, would burn out on a substantial overload or fault. There is no provision for maintenance on m.c.bs.

Thermal overload protection is provided by a bi-metal strip consisting of two materials, usually nickel alloys, which have different coefficients of expansion and which are firmly bonded together along the faces which are in contact. Change in temperature causes the composite strip to bend. Various methods of applying heat to the strip are adopted depending on the magnitude of the current and the operating characteristics required. The load current can either pass through the strip itself or through a separate wire coil; the latter may be either wound around the strip or placed alongside so that it heats the strip by radiation.

It will be apparent that bending of the strip will also occur due to changes in ambient air temperature independent of the load. There are several grades of thermostatic bi-metal, some of which are not recommended for use where severe corrosive conditions exist.

The degree of overload protection which is afforded is relatively close and is defined by the tripping factor (ratio of tripping current to rated current). This does not exceed 1.5 for current ratings of 10A or less or 1.35 for all other ratings. These factors correspond approximately with Class Q_1 and P fuses respectively (See 'Fuses'). The actual time/current characteristic cannot be adjusted.

The mechanism and contacts are lightly constructed and the arcing space restricted; consequently the breaking capacity is limited. They may be used in a circuit where the prospective short circuit current exceeds 900 A only if back-up protection is available. A conventional air circuit breaker or m.c.c.b. (moulded case circuit breaker) will not be effective in providing this protection and a fuse or current limiting circuit breaker must be used.

Standard industrial miniature circuit breakers are suitable for use in an ambient temperature with an average value of 30°C over any 24 hour period and peak values not exceeding 35°C. However, it is worthy of note that they can only carry their rated current at an ambient temperature of between 20°C and 25°C and 0.9 times their rated current at 35°C. For ships intended for unrestricted service, Classification rules stipulate cooling air temperature as 45°C so standard ratings must be adjusted accordingly.

If standard breakers which have been calibrated at the foregoing ambient temperatures are used it will be apparent that the standard tripping factors no longer apply at derated values. A 10 A breaker calibrated to operate at 15 A but derated to, say, 8 A will still operate at 15 A less a small amount due to the higher ambient. It is therefore important that breakers intended to operate in ambient temperatures of 45°C should be calibrated at that temperature. Amendment No. 2 to BS 3871 : Part 1 : 1965 recognises this and now lists two reference calibration temperatures, 20–25°C and 40–45°C.

Complete discrimination at all values of current between two m.c.bs in series is not possible, even if they are of different ratings, because at the higher currents both will open simultaneously due to the operation of the instantaneous magnetic trips. However, for currents lower than the instantaneous trip level of the major device, discrimination should be achieved.

MOULDED CASE CIRCUIT BREAKERS (M.C.C.B.)

In moulded case circuit breakers the insulated moulded housing forms an integral part of the unit upon which are mounted the various components (see Figure 9.5). The operating parts are inaccessible and the design is such that there is normally little provision for

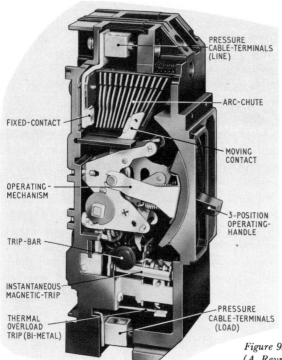

Figure 9.5 Moulded-case circuit breaker
(A. Reyrolle & Co. Ltd.)

maintenance but facilities for changing the contacts are provided on some recent designs. The current ratings available range from 100 A to about 2000 A. The manufacturer usually markets these circuit breakers in various frame sizes each covering a number of current ratings. The intermediate current ratings are obtained by changing the trip units.

The overcurrent trip releases are usually of the thermal magnetic type, however some manufacturers will provide breakers with only the magnetic trip. On modern m.c.c.bs a compensating thermal release is often employed such that operation depends solely on the current and is unaffected by ambient air temperature.

The circuit breaker thermal release is intended principally for cable protection. When a motor is to be supplied via an m.c.c.b. a separate thermal overload device will normally be required at the starter to give the closer protection which is required. Care should be taken in selecting the m.c.c.b. instantaneous setting (which is usually adjustable) on motor circuits. If this is too low the m.c.c.b. could occasionally trip when the motor is started due to asymmetry in the starting current. A setting equivalent to twice the rms starting current is usually sufficient. The manufacturer will sometimes give a choice between low and high instantaneous setting ranges, the latter being intended for motor circuit applications.

Until recently the instantaneous magnetic trip used on m.c.c.bs. had no intentional delay. This was to protect the circuit breaker itself which would be destroyed if the fault current were to be allowed to persist for any significant time. Because of this feature discrimination between m.c.c.bs. in series was impossible. In several designs now available the operation of the instantaneous trips can be delayed and discrimination achieved. Another new development is the solid state trip and m.c.c.bs. with these devices have more accurately defined tripping characteristics. The trip rating is relatively simple to adjust within a given frame size.

All m.c.c.bs. must now comply with the same specification as conventional air circuit breakers and short circuit ratings in excess of 50 kA are available. Many of the features of conventional circuit breakers are now to be found on m.c.c.bs. such as remote operation via solenoid or spring charging motor, shunt trip and undervoltage releases, withdrawable mechanisms with interlocks, etc.

Current limiting circuit breakers

It has been explained that h.r.c. fuses can operate so quickly under fault conditions that the prospective peak current is never attained, i.e. the fault current is 'cut off' or limited while it is still rising. Circuit breakers with similar current limiting features are now available with fault ratings well in excess of those found on marine systems. The high speed of interruption is achieved by employing the electromagnetic forces which are developed by the short circuit current to open the contacts.

The current limiting breaker can be used in the same way as an h.r.c. fuse to give back-up protection to other devices. Savings in the cost of cables and busbar installations can also be achieved. One disadvantage of the current limiting breaker is that because of its speed of operation full discrimination with downstream devices under fault conditions is not easy to obtain. Only h.r.c. fuses offer the speed of operation which is required under these conditions and the circuit breaker manufacturer will give guidance on this subject if requested.

PROTECTION

The distribution network is fed from the main switchboard through fuse-switches or circuit breakers according to the current rating of the circuit. For three-phase systems a triple-pole circuit breaker with overload protection in at least two phases is required for all outgoing circuits if the neutral is insulated, or on all three phases if the neutral is earthed or where four-wire distribution is used. Alternatively, a triple-pole linked switch with a fuse in each phase may be used when appropriate.

Two-wire circuits derived from a three-phase supply should be provided with a double-pole linked circuit breaker or alternatively a double-pole linked switch with a fuse on each pole. However, if the circuit is from one phase to an earthed neutral a single-pole switch and fuse connected to the line side will suffice.

Generally fuses with ratings in excess of 300 A are not used unless separate overload protection is also provided. However, when large fuse ratings are being considered it should be ensured that sufficient current is available from the generator under short circuit conditions to give fuse operation in a reasonably short time. For example, although the subtransient fault current available from a 625 kVA generator may be 5 kA or more, the rate of decay (decrement) may be such that a 315 A fuse will take over half a second to operate under short circuit conditions as shown in Figure 9.6. When two generators are running in parallel the same fuse will operate within one cycle. In practice the fuse operating times could be somewhat less than are indicated by this method[4].

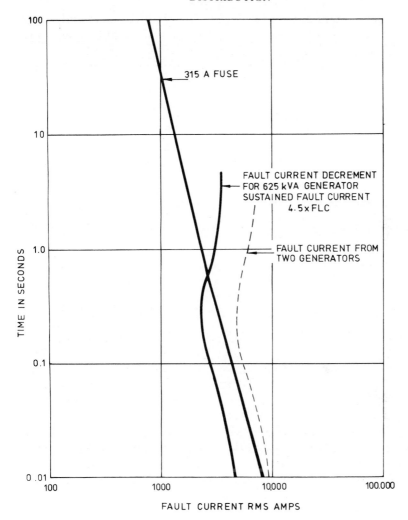

Figure 9.6 Effect of fault current decrement on operating time of fuse

For guidance as to the capacity of circuits and the correct replacement fuse to be used it is a requirement that labels be fitted providing the necessary information. Overcurrent releases on circuit breakers must be calibrated in amperes with the settings marked on the breaker. Whichever type of protective device is employed it should be ensured that it operates as quickly as possible, consistent with normal operation and discrimination, under fault conditions. This will limit the degree of damage caused by the fault current and will also serve to maintain system stability.

Steady load circuits

BS 88 defines these as 'circuits involving apparatus the load of which does not fluctuate much above its normal value'. A heating circuit would be a typical example. Such circuits are unlikely to have any protection additional to the main fuse or circuit breaker. Consequently a fuse or m.c.b. protecting such a circuit should be selected to have a rating equal either to the load rating or to the first standard rating which exceeds this.

A Class Q_1 fuse will normally be employed. Such a fuse could permit up to 150% of its rated current to flow without operating (see 'Fuses') and therefore in order to ensure adequate cable protec-, tion the cable should ideally have a rating equal to or greater than that of the fuse rather than the load. This is particularly important when p.v.c. cables are employed.

When a circuit breaker (other than an m.c.b.) is used to control such a circuit a typical value of minimum operating current would be 125% of the normal load current. In this case the cable can normally be selected on the basis of load current only. However, if the circuit breaker is of the non-current limiting type the short circuit withstand rating of the cable should be checked against the system fault level to ensure that cable fault protection is adequate (see 'Cable Protection').

Motor feeders

Overload and short circuit protection must be applied to all motors with ratings in excess of 0.5 kW with the exception of steering motors and possibly certain other auxiliaries such as main engine lubricating oil pumps. (For the latter overload protection should be replaced by an overload alarm.) It is normal practice to have the short circuit protection at the switchboard from which the motor is fed.

The overload protection is usually provided at the motor starter (see Chapter 13) and will typically be set to between 105% and 120% of the motor full load current. Such settings will obviously give excellent overload protection to the cable also and therefore the fuse feeding the motor circuit may be given a rating of up to twice the cable rating and will only be called upon to operate for short circuit conditions.

It must be remembered that the motor starter itself will only be capable of interrupting currents of up to six or eight times its rating and therefore the time/current characteristics of the fuse or circuit breaker and the motor starter thermal trip should cross below this critical current. It is this requirement, together with that of cable short circuit protection, which sets the upper limit on the fuse rating or circuit breaker setting which is permissible. The lower limit will be defined by the motor starting characteristic.

In general, when selecting a fuse for motor circuit protection, the lowest rating which will permit the motor to start without the danger of fuse operation should be used. Ideally the motor starting characteristic should be compared with that of the fuse in order to ensure this. However, if any doubt exists the manufacturers should be approached.

Manufacturers retail fuses specifically for motor protection applications and these offer the possibility of more compact equipment. This is accomplished by fitting into a smaller fuse body the elements from a fuse with a higher rating. Thus, the operating characteristic of the motor protection fuse is similar to that of a fuse with a higher rating (to permit motor starting) but its continuous current rating is determined by the body size selected. Such a fuse is given a dual rating, e.g. 100 A/160 A, where 100 A is the continuous rating but the time/current characteristic is that of a 160 A fuse. It will be obvious that switch-fuse units employing these fuses will, for a given rating of motor, be more compact than similar units using conventional fuses.

If the motor circuit is supplied via a circuit breaker it should be noted that the overload protection incorporated within the breaker is usually unsuitable for motors and separate protection at the starter will still be required. (This statement will not apply, of course, if a separate motor protection relay is used at the circuit breaker.)

Particular care will be required if the motor starter is to be supplied from a circuit breaker. This is because if a fault occurs below the starter, perhaps at the motor terminals, the contactor will have to carry the fault current until the circuit breaker opens. If the fault level is high and the circuit breaker total break time is relatively long, then the contactor may be called upon to withstand a higher I^2t rating than that for which it was designed. The damage which results could be such as to necessitate replacement of the starter.

This may occur even with moulded-case circuit breakers having opening times as short as 10 milliseconds. This is not to say that motor starters should not be supplied via circuit breakers, only that extra care will be necessary in the design stage. The I^2t 'let through' of the circuit breaker should be compared with the I^2t withstand rating of the motor starting contactor.

The manufacturer of the contactor should be able to provide information stating the maximum permissible I^2t and the peak currents relating to three degrees of damage to the starter. These are:

(a) Any degree of damage permitted (but enclosure should remain undamaged).
(b) No damage to starter (except contact welding) but characteristics of starter overload relay may be permanently altered.
(c) No damage to starter (except for contact welding), or overload relay.

These requirements are discussed in more detail in BS 4941 : Part 1 : 1973. If the motor starter is supplied via a current limiting circuit breaker or, particularly, fuses then this problem should not arise.

When a motor is started there will initially be a d.c. component which is superimposed upon the r.m.s. starting current. While this d.c. component will decay rapidly, perhaps within 20 ms, it is still possible that it could cause the instantaneous protection on a circuit breaker to operate. It is for this reason that the magnetic trips on moulded case circuit breakers should be set to about ten or twelve times the normal motor load current although the r.m.s. starting current may only be six to seven times the rated current.

On multiple voltage systems the larger motors will be operated at 3.3 kV. Such motors may be controlled by air circuit breakers, vacuum circuit breakers, motor switching devices or fused vacuum contactors. Generally the vacuum circuit breakers currently available are rather limited in fault rating although future designs will obviously improve in this respect. However the vacuum contactor, with suitable back-up fuses, has already been used successfully in several applications. This is discussed in Chapter 12.

The motor switching device is basically an air break contactor backed up by fuses. While an air circuit breaker could be used in this application a vacuum contactor or motor switching device will often be preferred for reasons of cost and low maintenance requirements.

With any of these devices the protection will be provided by separate relays. These will usually incorporate thermal overload and instantaneous overcurrent protection, although the latter will not, of course, be required when back-up fuses are employed.

Again the instantaneous protection should not respond to the initial asymmetry of the starting current and the relay may have to be set to ten or twelve times the rated motor current to prevent this. However, some designs of motor protection relay have an intentional initial operating delay of 30 ms and this enables them to be set just above the r.m.s. starting current. This can be a particular advantage when the relays have to be set as low as possible in order to discriminate with the generator protection.

3.3 kV systems will often be earthed via a resistor and therefore an instantaneous earth fault relay will be required. It is usually possible to supply this from the same CTs which are used for overload/overcurrent protection by employing a residual connection. However, if the earth fault current is limited by earthing resistors to a particularly low value it will become necessary to use a separate core balance CT.

Transformer feeders

Small transformers will generally be supplied via fuses and it is important to consider the magnetising inrush current when selecting the fuse rating. The inrush current is transient in nature and its magnitude depends upon both the point-on-wave at which the transformer is energised and the residual flux within the core. If a fuse rating equivalent to the normal load current rating of the transformer is employed there is a possibility that the fuse could operate during energisation. A useful 'rule-of-thumb' is to select a fuse rating which is about 50% higher than the full load current. The cable between the fuse and the transformer should be chosen on a basis of the fuse rating rather than the transformer rating.

When a 3.3 kV system is employed, transformers will be used to supply the 440 V busbars. Such transformers will usually be connected to the 3.3 kV busbars by either circuit breakers or fused contactors. If the latter are to be used it is prudent to obtain inrush data from the manufacturer to ensure that suitable fuses are employed. (For large transformers the inrush information will usually be required for other purposes anyway, for example, it will be necessary to determine the system volt drop when the transformer is first energised.)

If a circuit breaker is to be used overcurrent protection will normally be provided by separate inverse definite minimum time (IDMT) relays. Additional fault protection is sometimes provided by using 'high set' instantaneous overcurrent relays. The setting of the latter must be sufficiently high to prevent operation if a secondary terminal fault occurs (thereby maintaining discrimination with low voltage feeders) but will still provide 'instantaneous' clearance of high voltage terminal and winding faults. In practice a setting of fifteen to twenty times the full load current will be used.

Whichever form of overcurrent protection is provided it must be remembered that a low or medium voltage system short circuit must be removed within a certain maximum time if the transformer is not to suffer damage. The fault duration of commercial transformers is related to the transformer reactance and is 2, 3, 4 and 5 s for 4%, 5%, 6% and 7% reactance respectively. However the Lloyd's Register requirement is for a 2 s withstand only. The overcurrent protection will often be supplemented by an overtemperature device. This may be used to trip the circuit breaker or contactor or, more commonly, to raise an alarm.

The 3.3 kV system neutral will often be resistance earthed and therefore earth fault protection will be required for both circuit breakers and fused contactors. Where the latter are used the earth fault relay will be arranged to trip the contactor but it should be ensured that this is never called upon to interrupt a current greater than its rated breaking capacity. This is not usually a problem because the maximum earth fault current will be limited by the generator neutral earthing resistors.

It should be noted that earth faults on the low voltage side of a delta-star transformer will not be detected by high voltage earth fault protection and therefore no discrimination problems will arise if instantaneous earth fault relays are employed on the primary.

If during the operation of the system it will be possible to operate two transformers in parallel the effect which a fault on one may have on the other should be examined. It is possible that both transformers may be tripped out because, for a low (or medium) voltage terminal fault, both sets of high voltage protection will detect the same current. This may be prevented by using a low (or medium) voltage bus-section breaker with more sensitive overcurrent settings. Alternatively differential protection could be employed across each transformer. (See also Chapter 8 concerning differential protection for generators).

CABLE PROTECTION

This subject has inevitably been covered to some extent in the earlier discussion on the protection of particular items of equipment. However cable protection does merit a brief examination on its own account. As described in Chapter 10 the fault current to which a cable may be subjected must be limited in two ways.

First there is the thermal withstand of the insulation which is an $I^2 t$ function; any particular magnitude of fault current should only be allowed to flow for a defined time in order to prevent the cable limiting temperature from being exceeded. This sets the maximum interrupting time of the circuit protective device at that current.

The limiting characteristics of typical cables will be found in Chapter 10. These should be compared with the time/current characteristics of the proposed protection to ensure that the cable is always disconnected before damage occurs. It can normally be assumed that the cable will be adequately protected against both fault currents and overloads provided that the operating current of the protective device does not exceed 150% of the cable rating. Thus a fuse can be used to protect a cable of the same rating provided that the fusing factor does not exceed 1.5 (see Figure 9.7).

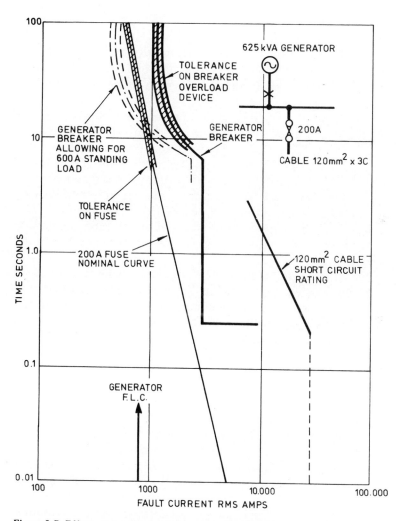

Figure 9.7 Effect of standing load current on discrimination

The second limit is concerned with the bursting of multicore cable due to electromagnetic forces and defines the minimum size of cable which may be used at a particular system fault level. If it is found that the maximum system fault current is greater than the bursting limit of the cable then either the cable size must be increased or it must be protected by fuses at the busbars. The latter solution is possible because the cut-off characteristic of an h.r.c. fuse will prevent the maximum peak prospective current from being attained.

DISCRIMINATION

Discrimination is said to be achieved when only the protective device immediately upstream of a fault operates, all other circuits remaining closed. This ensures that healthy circuits continue to operate normally.

In order to check that discrimination will be achieved on a particular system it will be necessary to conduct a discrimination or co-ordination study. This entails plotting and comparing the time/current characteristics of all the protective devices on graph paper. The wide range of currents and times involved make it convenient to use log/log paper. Naturally the characteristics of adjacent devices should not cross, but this alone will not ensure discrimination. The clearance between the curves should also allow for the possibility that some devices may continue to carry load current in addition to an overcurrent.

For example, consider a generator providing 800 A, 200 A of which is being carried by a particular feeder. This implies that 600 A is being supplied to all the remaining feeders. If an overcurrent condition now arises on the first feeder which is not of sufficient magnitude to cause a significant depression of the busbar voltage, the remaining feeders will continue to draw load current. Consequently the generator circuit breaker will always be carrying 600 A more than the feeder and it would not be correct to compare the time/current characteristics of the two devices directly.

However it is possible to allow for this condition by first drawing the actual feeder fuse or breaker characteristic and then constructing a second curve on which each point at a particular operating time is displaced by adding 600 A. Discrimination will have been achieved if the second curve does not cross the generator circuit breaker characteristic.

It would, of course, have been possible to make a similar comparison by constructing a second generator circuit breaker characteristic in which each point is displaced by subtracting 600 A. This has been done in Figure 9.7 where it will be seen that the apparent discrimination between the generator breaker and the 200 A fuse may in fact be lost for feeder currents up to 900 A when the generator standing load is taken into consideration.

The curves should also allow for operating tolerances, the opening time of circuit breakers, the arcing time of circuit breakers and fuses and any 'overshoot' inherent in the devices. Such a rigorous analysis will not normally be required because usually it will be obvious that there is sufficient clearance between the nominal curves. However, when several devices are to be placed in series it is prudent to examine the characteristics in more detail.

For two fuses to discriminate with each other it is not sufficient to ensure that the pre-arcing time/current characteristic of the major (or upstream) fuse is always above that of the minor (or downstream) fuse. Under short circuit conditions the principle factors which determine discrimination are the I^2t characteristics (see Figure 9.3). The total operating I^2t of the minor fuse, which is the sum of the pre-arcing and arcing I^2t, must be less than the pre-arcing I^2t of the major fuse. If this rule is not observed it will be obvious that if an arc is initiated in the upstream fuse, even if the circuit is interrupted elsewhere, this particular fuse will have blown.

When a fuse is supplied via a circuit breaker which is not fitted with instantaneous trips it is usually sufficient to ensure that the time/current characteristic of the breaker is always above that of the fuse (but allowance should be made for the standing load on the circuit breaker). However, if the fuse is supplied from a circuit breaker with instantaneous trips, or particularly from an m.c.c.b. or current limiting circuit breaker, the breaker manufacturer should be consulted concerning the maximum fuse rating to be used. Under these circumstances, even if the operating characteristics of the two devices do not cross, it is possible for the fuse to let through sufficient energy to operate the tripping mechanism.

Some devices are inherently faster in operation than others (although this relationship often changes according to the operating current). It is therefore possible to formulate a general rule concerning the use of protective devices in series. This is that the order of the devices, from the generators down, should be a.c.b., m.c.c.b., fuse. There will obviously be some occasions when this order may be reversed; e.g. when fuses are employed in a 'back-up' mode.

When both 3.3 kV and 440 V systems are involved it will be necessary to plot all the characteristics to a common base voltage. If, for example, the base voltage is 3.3 kV then the characteristics of all the devices used at the higher voltage may be plotted directly. However, for the 440 V devices it will be necessary to apply a correction factor to each curve which corresponds to the transformer ratio (because of transformer regulation this will differ slightly from the ratio of the voltage levels).

Particular care should be taken when allowing for discrimination between 440 V and 3.3 kV protective devices when a line-to-line fault occurs on the 440 V system. This is because for such a fault, with the normal delta-star transformer connection, one line supplying the primary windings will carry twice the current of the other two. There is therefore a greater tendancy for the protective device at 3.3 kV to operate rather than at 440 V. This must be allowed for by providing additional clearance between the two sets of time/current characteristics.

When several souces of power are provided the protection settings should be such that discrimination with a particular feeder is still achieved with the minimum number of generators which will normally operate in parallel. This is the most onerous condition.

When an overcurrent condition occurs on a feeder, the excess current will be shared between all the connected generators and therefore the feeder and generator time/current characteristics cannot be compared directly to assess discrimination. Current sharing between generators can be allowed for by displacing the generator breaker characteristic along the current axis by employing a multiplying factor equivalent to the number of generators in use. (This assumes that the generators are each of the same rating.)

Thus, if three generators are operating in parallel the curve for one generator circuit breaker is drawn first. Then, for each time/current point, the current is multiplied by three and re-plotted at the same time. This new curve is then used to assess discrimination with the feeder protection, and is shown in Figure 9.8. It will be seen that the 315 A fuse will not discriminate over the whole range of currents when only one generator is connected. With three generators connected there is no problem. For example, a fault causing 3000 A to be carried by the fuse will result in approximately 1000 A passing through each circuit breaker. Thus, while the fuse will operate in about 0.4 s, each breaker would take about 100 s to trip.

ARRANGEMENT OF CIRCUITS

On larger ships, if each service is fed from the main switchboard this results in an excessive amount of cabling and the more remote loads

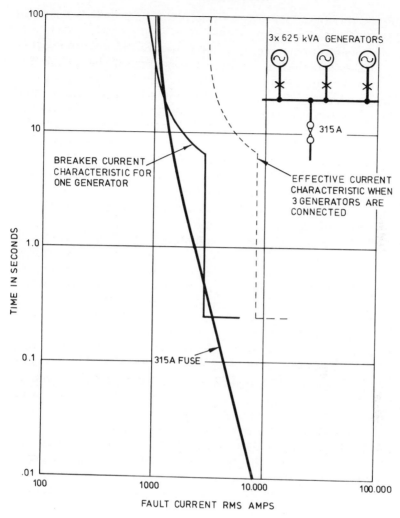

Figure 9.8 Effect of discrimination of generators in parallel

could be subject to large voltage drops unless the cross sectional area of the cable is increased. Consequently modern practice is to limit the number of feeder circuits from the main switchboard. These feeders supply section boards, sub-switchboards or load centres each of which is positioned as close as possible to the 'centre of gravity' of the various individual loads.

If this method of distribution is adopted most of the feeder cables will be of reasonably large cross section. However, when it is necessary to take small cables from the main busbars it will normally be advisable to do so via h.r.c. fuses unless the fault level is relatively low. (See 'cable protection'.)

It is permissible to connect the incoming cable directly to the busbars of the sub-switchboard, perhaps through an isolating switch, the necessary protection being provided by the fuse or circuit breaker at the main switchboard. The sub-switchboard will consist of a number of outgoing circuits, each protected by either fuses or a moulded case circuit breaker.

In some cases it may be convenient not to assemble all the distribution fuses for a group of circuits at the same point, while at the same time feeding them from the same cable. The practice then is to divide the fuses into two or more groups and to connect the individual busbars together by cable. This is known as 'looping-in'. When this is done the looping-in cables must always be of the same size as the feeder cable, even though the current to be carried is obviously less in the looping-in cables. This is a consequence of the fact that the fuse or circuit breaker at the main switchboard protects all the cables which it feeds and no reduction in cable size is permitted unless overcurrent protection with an appropriately lower setting is inserted downstream.

DIVERSITY FACTOR

In a comprehensive circuit which includes a number of consuming devices it is recognised that in many cases all of them will not be in service at the same time. It is then permissible to rate the feeder cable on an estimation of the probable maximum loading after allowing for any future increase in load when spare ways are available. The factor used is called the diversity factor and is always less than unity. A diversity factor is not permitted in a final subcircuit, i.e. the final circuit to a consuming device; it is only permissible for the feeder to a group of services.

There are no hard and fast rules as to either the factor or the nature of the circuits in which diversity can be taken into account, with the possible exception of winch circuits. Factors for these are given in Chapter 17. Each case is therefore treated on its merits based on practical experience. Incidentally, opinions differ as to whether 'diversity' is the most appropriate term, alternatives being 'demand' and 'utilisation' but 'diversity' is generally recognised.

It is common practice to connect capstans and windlasses to one of the winch distribution boards; as these are not in service at the same time as the winches they can be ignored if their rating is less than the winch load, which is generally the case.

NAVIGATION LIGHTS

These are perhaps the most vital circuits in a ship from the point of view of the laws of navigation, and require special attention. Navigation lights should be connected to a distribution board which does not supply any other service, so that they cannot be put out of action by the inadvertent opening of a wrong switch. Also they should have a changeover switch so that they can be transferred to another source of supply if the normal supply fails, for example by the blowing of a fuse. Warning devices are also required to indicate the failure of any individual navigation light.

The indicating panel may also comprise the distribution board previously mentioned, i.e. it may incorporate the fuse protection. The warning device may be visual, aural or both. The warning lamps are usually connected in series with the navigation lights and in such

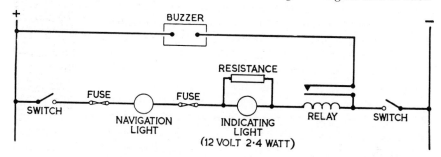

Figure 9.9 Schematic diagram of typical navigation light indicator

cases provision must be made to ensure a supply to the navigation lights should the indicating lamp open-circuit. The requirements for navigation lights are prescribed by International Convention, and lamps of special construction and appropriate wattages and performances are necessary.

A typical arrangement is shown in Figure 9.9, from which it will be seen that if an open-circuit occurs the relay will be de-energised and the contacts will close and operate the buzzer. If the indicating lamp fails the circuit is maintained through the parallel connected resistance.

STEERING GEAR CIRCUITS

In certain sizes of ships, two independent steering engines are required. If both are driven electrically, two independent circuits (each connected direct to the main switchboard) are necessary. These two circuits should be separated as widely as possible so as to reduce the risk that damage to one may also involve the other. One set of cables may be connected to an emergency switchboard having ships service and emergency feeds.

The 1974 Convention requires that short circuit protection only is to be provided for motors and power circuits of electrically or electro-hydraulically operated steering in all passenger and cargo ships irrespective of tonnage. In cargo ships of less than 5000 gross tonnage, this requirement may be waived for the auxiliary steering gear (but not the main steering gear) provided the administration is satisfied with the protection arrangements. Indicators for running indication of the motor must also be installed in a suitable location.

Short circuit protection only is generally interpreted as requiring a fuse or other protecting device having a minimum operating value of three times full load current. An overload alarm is also required.

Although the emergency supply is not required by International Convention to have sufficient capacity to supply steering gear in addition to the other compulsory services, it is useful to have a stand-by supply in certain emergencies, including steering when in tow when the normal supply has failed.

The 1960 and 1974 Conventions on Safety of Life at Sea (SOLAS) have detailed requirements for passenger and cargo ships, both mechanical and electrical. The exact position of the rudder, if power operated, must be indicated at the principal steering station. Where the main steering gear power units and their connections are provided in duplicate and the other requirements are met, no auxiliary steering gear is required.

SHORE CONNECTIONS

It is usual to provide terminals at a convenient position to receive shore supplies, enabling the ship's generators to be shut down when in port or in dry dock. These supplies will have overload protection at the shore end, but if the ship's cables for taking this supply are comparatively small the shore protection cannot be relied upon as it may be set too high. It is a requirement of Lloyd's Register that the connection box shall contain a circuit breaker or an isolating switch and fuses. A linked switch and/or a circuit breaker and an indicator to show when the cable is energised must also be provided at the main switchboard.

For three-phase shore supplies with an earthed neutral an earthing terminal must be provided for connecting the hull to the shore earth even if the ship's system is an insulated one. Alternative arrangements will receive consideration.

At this point it is worth noting that any earth fault on the ship will, under these conditions, result in a current of several hundred amps. (Even a total earth loop impedance of only 0.25 ohm will still limit the current to about 1000 A when the phase to neutral voltage is 250 V.) Occasionally this earth fault current will be insufficient to operate short circuit protective devices as the settings may be too high. If overload protection is provided in all three phases then the fault should be removed after a short delay.

However, it must be remembered that overload protection is only mandatory on two phases of an insulated three-phase system. If the earth fault is on the unprotected phase considerable damage may be caused. For this reason it is good practice to specify overload protection on all three phases, even if an insulated system is employed.

At the connection box a notice should be provided giving full information on the system of supply, the normal ship voltage (and frequency, if a.c.) and the procedure for carrying out the connection. If the ship's supply is a.c. and a three-phase shore supply to motors is required, a phase rotation or phase sequence indicator is necessary to ensure correct connections, as otherwise the motors could have the wrong rotation. For d.c. supplies means should be provided for checking the polarity and the terminals should be labelled.

TRANSFORMERS

A choice must be made when the system is designed between three-phase transformers and groups of three single-phase units. If a three-phase unit fails it is out of commission until either a repair can be effected or a replacement fitted. Greater continuity of service is possible if a group of three single-phase units is employed. If a fault occurs on one unit it is still possible to operate the other two. Also it is only necessary to purchase a single-phase unit as a spare.

The spare transformer itself can be a nuisance. It must be kept dry and, when required, must be moved into position. It can be advantageous to build the spare capacity into the three single phase units. If one unit fails the two remaining units can then be operated in an open delta arrangement.

With three single-phase transformers, the six primary connections being fed separately from the high voltage system, the current carried by each of the six cables will be reduced by a factor of 1.73 compared with a conventional three-phase unit. Consequently the

primary fuses can be reduced by the same factor and this can sometimes be of assistance when discrimination with the generator protection is difficult.

When the transformer primary is operated at 500 V or more it
is necessary to take precautions to prevent any lower voltage system
supplied by the secondary becoming charged from the primary. This
can be done either by earthing the secondary system or by using
screened windings in the transformer.

If transformers are to be operated in parallel they will share load
in proportion to rating provided that they have the same nominal
percentage impedance and the same primary and secondary voltage
ratings. Naturally the polarity on single-phase transformers and the
vector rotation on three-phase units must also be identical.

The certifying authority will give special consideration to transformers with either ratings exceeding 1000 kVA, or rated primary
voltages exceeding 3300 V. Similar consideration will also be given
when liquid cooled transformers are proposed.

Liquid cooled transformers have certain disadvantages and
normally should not be employed. Oil presents a fire risk and the
vapour from polychlorinated bipheryl (p.c.b.) liquids can be a health
hazard. However certain silicone fluids without these disadvantages
are now becoming available and could find widespread use in the
future. Dry type transformers with Class H or Class C insulation are
not usually suitable because of their higher operating temperatures.
To ensure adequate cooling all transformers must be well ventilated.

CONTROL OF VENTILATING FANS

In order to restrict the supply of air in the event of fire certain
facilities for the stopping of fans must be provided. Under the 1960
Convention control stations are required in passenger ships and the
stop buttons are located at these points.

Cargo ships come within the Convention and it requires an equivalent facility for stopping ventilating fans in machinery spaces from
an easily accessible position outside the machinery space. For accommodation spaces in passenger ships, master controls must be provided
at two positions as far apart as practicable.

PUMPS

Where oil fuel transfer pumps, fuel oil pressure pumps and cargo oil pumps are electrically driven, provision must be made for stopping the motor from a position which will always be accessible in the event of fire in the pump compartment. This provision is usually located near the engine room entrance.

Motor driven pumps which discharge above the light load line and in way of lifeboat launching should be provided with emergency stop controls installed in locked boxes having breakable covers, such as glass, conveniently located on deck.

References

1. Beeman, D., *Industrial power systems handbook*, McGraw-Hill Book Co., New York (1955).
2. Jones, D., 'Resistive earthing of electrical distribution systems in ships and similar installations', *Proc. IEE* 111, 10, (October 1964).
3. Dunki-Jacobs, J.R., 'The reality of high-resistance grounding', *Conference Record 76CH1109-8-1A*, I.E.E.E. Publication PC1-76-6.
4. Kelly, A.R., 'Allowing for decrement and fault voltage in industrial relaying', *First Annual Conference on industrial and commercial power systems* I.E.E.E. Pub. T-163 (1964).

10 Electric cables

The basic design of an electric cable consists of a metallic conductor surrounded by suitable insulation to form the core with one or more cores being covered overall with a common sheathing to provide protection from damage and external influences. Metallic coverings are sometimes applied to give additional mechanical protection or to provide electrical screening.

Cables should conform in detailed construction and test requirements to appropriate international or national standards, e.g. British Standard Specifications. The majority of cable specifications throughout the world, including those in the UK, adopt the metric system of measurement, based on SI Units. Some countries are still using Imperial and similar units but most of these are in the process of changing to the metric system.

CONDUCTORS

Cable conductors for marine fixed installations are invariably of copper except in the case of thermocouple cables for instrumentation purposes where special metals and alloys, e.g. cupro-nickel, are used for some cores. Welding cables, associated with ship repairs and work on off-shore drilling rigs, etc, may have aluminium conductors to deter pilfering.

Copper conductors are metal-coated in many cable designs although plain uncoated wires are used for some pvc-insulated types and all mineral-insulated cables. The metal coating, generally of tin base, serves as a barrier between the core insulation and the copper, reducing adhesion of the insulation to the conductor and also considerably reducing possible chemical interaction between certain constituents of some insulants and the copper conductor. A thin non-metallic tape of suitable material is sometimes interposed between the conductor and the insulation to further facilitate easy stripping of the insulation from the core.

Table 10.1. Circular non-flexible annealed copper conductors

Nominal cross-sectional area	Number and nominal diameter of wires in conductor	Nominal diameter of conductor	Maximum resistance per km of cable at 20° C			
			Plain		Tinned	
			Single core	Multi-core	Single core	Multi-core
mm²	mm	mm	ohm	ohm	ohm	ohm
1.0	7/0.40	1.20	20.8	21.2	21.2	21.6
1.5	7/0.50	1.50	13.3	13.6	13.6	13.8
2.5	7/0.67	2.01	7.27	7.41	7.41	7.56
4	7/0.85	2.55	4.52	4.61	4.60	4.70
6	7/1.04	3.12	3.02	3.08	3.05	3.11
10	7/1.35	4.05	1.79	1.83	1.81	1.84
16	7/1.70	5.10	1.13	1.15	1.14	1.16
25	19/1.35	6.75	0.66	0.673	0.666	0.679
35	19/1.53	7.65	0.514	0.524	0.519	0.529
50	19/1.78	8.90	0.379	0.387	0.383	0.391
70	19/2.14	10.70	0.262	0.268	0.265	0.270
95	37/1.78	12.46	0.195	0.199	0.197	0.201
120	37/2.03	14.21	0.150	0.153	0.151	0.154
150	37/2.25	15.75	0.122	0.124	0.123	0.126
185	37/2.52	17.64	0.0972	0.0991	0.0982	0.100
240	61/2.25	20.25	0.0740	0.0754	0.0747	0.0762
300	61/2.52	22.68	0.0590	0.0601	0.0595	0.0607
400	91/2.36	25.96	0.0451	0.0460	0.0459	0.0468
500	91/2.65	29.15	0.0357	—	0.0364	—
630	127/2.52	32.76	0.0283	—	0.0286	—

Table 10.2. Flexible annealed tinned copper conductors

Nominal cross-sectional area	Number and nominal diameter of wires, in conductor	Approximate diameter of conductor	Maximum resistance per km of cable at 20° C	
			Single core	Multi-core
mm²	mm	mm	ohm	ohm
6	84/0.3	3.3	3.23	3.39
10	80/0.4	4.2	1.85	1.95
16	126/0.4	5.3	1.18	1.24
16*	513/0.2	5.7	1.19	—
25	196/0.4	7.1	0.757	0.795
25*	783/0.2	7.1	0.780	—
35	276/0.4	8.5	0.538	0.565
35*	1107/0.2	8.5	0.552	—
50	396/0.4	10.3	0.375	0.393
50*	1566/0.2	10.3	0.379	—
70	360/0.5	12.4	0.264	0.277
70*	2214/0.2	12.4	0.268	—
95	475/0.5	14.5	0.200	0.210
95*	2997/0.2	14.5	0.198	—
120	608/0.5	16.0	0.156	0.164
150	756/0.5	18.0	0.126	0.132
185	925/0.5	20.0	0.103	0.108
240	1221/0.5	23.0	0.0778	0.0817
300	1525/0.5	26.0	0.0623	0.0654
400	2013/0.5	30.0	0.0472	0.0495
500	1769/0.6	33.5	0.0373	—
630	2257/0.6	37.0	0.0292	—

*These formations are for welding cable conductors

Except for mineral insulated cables, conductors for fixed wiring power and lighting circuits are composed of a number of wires stranded together (see Table 10.1). Unlike cables for shore installations, the smaller sizes do not consist of single wires but are stranded from seven wires in order to more adequately withstand the severe vibration often encountered in many parts of ships installations. Apart from the smaller sizes, circular stranded conductors are normally compressed to some degree during manufacture in order to produce smaller dimensions of the complete cable and also to assist with easier stripping of core insulation, especially with elastomeric insulants.

Mineral-insulated cables, because of their method of manufacture, have single-wire conductors in all sizes. Conductors of some communications cables are also composed of single wires.

Flexible cables of all sizes have conductors composed of a large number of small diameter wires (see Table 10.2). The use of individual small diameter wires results in a supple conductor and permits repeated flexing without fracture of the wires.

Copper conductors for British Standard cables are specified in BS 6360.

INSULATION

Modern cables used in marine and similar installations employ mainly the following insulation materials:

Polyvinyl chloride	(pvc)
Butyl rubber	
Ethylene propylene rubber	(epr)
Polythene	
Cross-linked polyethylene	(xlpe)
Silicone rubber	
Mineral insulation	(mi)

Natural rubber and also varnished-cambric were extensively used as cable insulants in ships in the past but these materials had rather severe limitations, particularly in high ambient temperatures, and have now been replaced by their modern synthetic successors. Present-day requirements call for more stringent fire resistance tests and these obsolete materials were not particularly satisfactory as they tended to support combustion and could cause spread of fire in a ship.

Polyvinyl chloride

Polyvinyl chloride (pvc) is used extensively as a cable insulant and also as a sheathing material for general wiring cables in buildings and for lower voltage power cables in land installations. However its use in marine applications has certain limitations because of its thermoplastic properties and operating temperature limitations.

PVC polymers and copolymers are white powders having the appearance of icing sugar and to produce compounds suitable for cable use polymers are blended with plasticisers, stabilisiers, lubricants, fillers and pigments to create the desired properties. British cable specifications call for pvc compounds in accordance with BS 6746 and a study of this specification will show that there is a range of compounds having different properties. The type of polymer, the type and proportion of plasticisers, together with the choice of the correct stabiliser, largely determines the properties of the finished compound. In general, two types of pvc insulating compound are used for ships cables — general purpose insulation and heat-resisting insulation.

Electrically, pvc compounds have adequate insulating properties for power and lighting circuits but because of the high dielectric loss angle and high permittivity such compounds are unsuitable for radio frequency circuits, although cables having pvc insulation can operate satisfactorily at audio frequencies in communications circuits provided the circuit lengths, and therefore the cable capacities, are not too great. With increasing temperature, the insulation resistance of pvc falls off rapidly, such that at about 70°C it is only approximately one thousandth of the value at 20°C.

As pvc is a thermoplastic material its softness and flexibility will vary with changes in temperature, but its behaviour at any temperature will depend to some extent upon the composition of the compound. As the temperature falls, pvc becomes harder and ultimately quite brittle and when installations are being carried out at temperatures below freezing-point (0°C) care has to be taken in handling the cables. If specially-formulated compounds are used, better performance can be obtained at low temperatures. Generally speaking, however, compounds which are flexible at low temperatures are softer at ordinary temperatures than general purpose compounds and are more easily deformable, particularly as the operating temperature increases. Such special low temperature pvc compounds would not normally be used for ship wiring cables unless specially ordered.

Operation of pvc compounds at high temperatures involves three factors; softening and deformation under load, volatalisation of plasticers and thermal degredation of the pvc compound. The maximum recommended operating temperatures for pvc compounds take these factors into account. These temperatures can be exceeded for short service periods under emergency or overload conditions, provided that the cables are installed in such a way that they are not subjected to sufficient mechanical pressure to cause an unacceptable amount of deformation as the pvc becomes progressively softer with increasing temperature.

The plasticisers in conventional general-purpose pvc compounds are somewhat volatile and operation above about 70°C will result in reduction of flexibility to an extent which will depend on service conditions. As plasticiser is lost, so the compound becomes more brittle. Heat-resisting grades, employing special plasticisers and stabilising systems, can operate at rather higher temperatures for longer periods without undue loss of flexibility, however, chemical degredation considerations must be taken into account. Prolonged exposure of any pvc compound to high temperatures can ultimately lead to chemical breakdown of the pvc polymer, accompanied by the formation of hydrocloric acid which may lead to severe corrosion of metal parts. This breakdown can take place after a number of days at temperatures as low as 115/120°C so care should be taken to ensure that pvc insulated conductors are not used as connections to equipment when the terminals and surrounding parts are at this order of temperature or hotter.

At lower temperatures pvc compounds are oil and solvent resistant and resistant to many acids but, as the temperature increases, so the resistance to the various substances falls off until at about 70°C many pvc compounds are not entirely suitable for use, for example, in hot engine oil.

PVC compounds are reasonably flame-retardant due to the fact that, when burnt, the formation of hydrochloric acid gas tends to blanket the area and prevents oxygen from the air from reaching the burning material. However, in certain circumstances, particularly when large groups of cables are involved, the self-extinguishing properties of individual cables may not be sufficient to extinguish the fire in the large group and in addition, the formation of large quantities of hydrochloric acid and other toxic fumes can probably lead to a dangerous situation. In recent years specially-formulated pvc compounds have been developed which overcome these problems to a certain extent and cables employing these compounds are used where spread of fire is to be minimised in large groups of pvc cables.

Butyl rubber

Butyl rubber was used extensively from the mid 1950's instead of natural rubber as insulation for ships' cables and this synthetic material has had a good record of service. Its great advantage over natural rubber is its superior ageing characteristics.

Natural rubber insulation, whilst being an excellent electrical insulant and having tough mechanical properties when new, suffers badly from the effects of oxidation at increasing temperatures. Oxidation eventually causes the insulation to become either hard and brittle, so that it can crumble from the cable conductor, or very soft so that deformation of the core insulation can occur. These effects with natural rubber insulation often developed after a relatively short service life if the cables were run at elevated temperatures and expensive rewiring of circuits was often necessary because of electrical failures.

The introduction of butyl rubber largely overcame these oxidation problems but butyl rubber has mechanical strength properties inferior to natural rubber and requires handling somewhat more carefully during installation. Butyl rubber has now been largely replaced by ethylene propylene rubber (epr) for insulating many ships cables. Both materials are often referred to as 'elastomeric' insulants.

As with natural rubber, the basic butyl rubber gum is not used on its own as cable insulation but has to be mixed with various inert filling materials to form the compound for applying to the cable conductor. As well as these filling materials it is necessary to include small amounts of special chemicals to achieve cross-linking of the molecules to bring about 'curing' of the rubber after the insulation has been applied to the conductor in order that it may be transferred from its soft, putty-like, nature into a tough elastic form. For cables made to British Standards, butyl rubber for the insulation must comply with BS 6899.

Although its tensile strength is not so good as natural rubber, butyl rubber has excellent electrical properties and its good ozone resistance makes it suitable for some high voltage cable applications.

Butyl rubber can operate satisfactorily at temperatures up to around 80–85°C for long periods without undue oxidation compared with natural rubber which is limited to about 60°C. At very low temperatures butyl rubber becomes somewhat harder than natural rubber but for all practical purposes it is entirely suitable for ships cables.

In moist conditions, even when totally immersed, butyl rubber is superior to natural rubber and is virtually unaffected by sea water. It is equally as conbustible as natural rubber. As with natural rubber, it is affected by mineral oils and many solvents, therefore cables having butyl rubber insulation require suitable overall protection from these substances.

Ethylene propylene rubber

Ethylene propylene rubber (epr) is a synthetic rubber material which is now tending to replace butyl because it is superior in respect of tensile strength, resistance to heat-ageing, resistance to ozone and corona effects and to deformation at elevated temperatures. Ethylene propylene rubber is included as an insulating material in BS 6899 and is recognised by Lloyd's Register of Shipping.

This elastomeric insulant, like butyl rubber, is compounded from the basic epr polymer by mixing it with various fillers and compounding ingredients, together with complex chemical substances for cross-linking, or curing, the compound after it has been applied to the cable conductor.

Similar to natural rubber and butyl rubber, epr is affected by many oils and solvents and is not a flame-retardant material. For ships' wiring, epr insulated cable cores are protected with oil and flame-retardant sheathing. The internationally accepted maximum operating temperature for epr insulation for ships' cables is 85°C.

More recent developments have resulted in the availability of epr compounds of a harder type than hitherto, known as hard ethylene propylene rubber, or HEPR. These compounds have a much higher tensile strength than conventional epr and their characteristics are specified in BS 5469. These compounds can operate at a continuous temperature not exceeding 90°C.

Polythene

Polythene, known also under its chemical term polyethylene, is a thermoplastic noted for its excellent insulating properties. Because of very low power factor (loss angle) and permittivity it is an excellent dielectric for use at high frequencies, e.g. for radar applications. However, it has a very sharp melting point around 110°C and in the semi-liquid form it can drop off the conductor. It must therefore not be allowed to exceed an operating temperature of about 90°C otherwise there is every possibility of failure and for this reason it is not used for power circuits where there is always a possibility of high conductor temperatures occuring due to heavy overloads or short circuits.

Polythene burns very readily and has the unfortunate property of dripping molten material when it burns with the result that it can easily cause spread of fire. Polythene insulated cables for use at radio frequencies are nearly always screened with a layer of metal for electrical reasons and this layer, usually in the form of wire braiding, is generally covered overall with a sheathing of pvc so that the completed cable is flame-retardant to a certain extent externally.

Cross-linked polyethylene (XLPE)

By causing the molecules of polythene to become cross-linked it is possible to change ordinary polythene from a thermoplastic material with a sharp melting point into a rubbery thermosetting material capable of reaching high temperatures without melting. This cross-linking has the same kind of effect as the vulcanisation or curing of natural and synthetic rubber and can be brought about by subjecting polythene to high-energy gamma-ray irradiation or by the addition of special chemicals to the polythene, followed by heat treatment. The chemical method of cross-linking is generally adopted so that XLPE insulated cables may be produced on standard manufacturing plant designed also for curing elastomeric insulation.

XLPE is used for insulating power cables for land use up to very high voltages and it has similar properties to epr. Although not yet used to any great extent in shipwiring, XLPE is finding increasing use as power cabling for off-shore applications where its maximum operating temperature is rated the same as epr.

It is not quite so flexible as epr and may be marginally inferior to epr in its moisture resistance, although in this property it is completely adequate for all marine applications at the normal voltages employed. XLPE, like epr, supports combustion and is affected by certain oils and solvents and must therefore be covered with a flame-retardant and oil resisting sheathing to produce a cable suitable for marine installations.

BS 5468 specifies requirements for XLPE insulation for electric cables.

Silicone rubber

Silicone rubber is a synthetic material having outstanding resistance to high temperatures. The material is rather expensive compared with the other cable insulants referred to in this chapter but for some special applications the extra expense can be well justified because of the superior properties imparted to the cable.

Silicone rubber can operate continuously at temperatures up to 150°C and even higher if there are no limits set by other component parts of the cable or by environmental conditions.

When silicone rubber is subjected to fire the material burns and is converted into an ash of silicon oxide, which is an electrical insulator. Therefore cables having silicone rubber insulation are able to continue operating during and after attack by fire (assuming that the conductor has not become melted and that the ash remains on the wire).

Silicone rubber is not so mechanically robust at normal temperatures as conventional insulants, such as epr and pvc, but modern grades are greatly improved over original types and have adequate mechanical strength to withstand reasonable handling during installation.

Silicone rubber remains flexible down to very low temperatures but its oil resistance is similar to that of natural rubber so normal precautions should be taken to protect it.

Silicone rubber insulated cores are often covered with a layer of glass fibre braiding which is itself saturated with a special oil-resisting and high temperature varnish. Multi-core cables are usually sheathed with heat, oil and fire-resisting sheathing which itself may be suitable only for continuous operation at about 85°C so it is at hot terminations where advantage can be taken of the superior heat resistance of the silicone rubber cores.

BS 6889 specifies the requirements for silicone rubber insulation for cables.

Mineral insulation

This insulation is magnesium oxide and because of its hygroscopic nature and due to the method of manufacture it requires a sheath of a hard metal, such as copper. The cable is also made with aluminium sheathing and other hard metals for special applications but the standard material is copper. The cable is for all practical purposes indestructible and will withstand very high temperatures without detriment to the insulation; the limiting temperature for the cable itself being the withstand temperature of the conductor and sheathing materials, which for copper is about 150°C.

Because of the hygroscopic nature of the insulation it is essential to seal the ends. The operating temperature of the complete cable system is therefore dependant upon the safe working temperature of the seals which, according to type may be from 105°C to 185°C. If the metal sheathing is protected with a further sheathing of pvc, the cable itself is limited in its operating temperature to that of the pvc which is generally 70°C.

Although the mineral insulation is applied around the conductors in a highly compacted form it has not the same good dielectric strength as elastomeric or plastic types of insulants which are extruded on to conductors and the impulse strength is comparatively poor. For this reason mineral insulation is not entirely satisfactory in circuits liable to voltage surges unless special precautions are taken by the fitting of surge diverters.

BS 6207 specifies the requirements for mineral insulated cables.

SHEATHING

Sheathing of electric cables is applied over the insulated cores for the purpose of providing protection to the cores. This protection can be simply for mechanical strength purposes or the sheathing may be to provide fire resistance or protection from moisture, chemicals, oils and similar substances, or to provide electrical screening, or a combination of any of these factors.

Materials used for sheathing cables for marine applications include:

Polyvinyl chloride (pvc).
Polychloroprene (Neoprene).
Chlorosulphonated polyethelene (cs.p., Hypalon).
Silicone rubber.
Lead.
Copper.

Some of the synthetic polymeric materials listed above may also serve partly as insulating materials.

Polyvinyl chloride sheathing

Sheathing compounds are basically similar to pvc insulants with the polymer/plasticiser composition being arranged to give the required physical properties, often insulation grades are used also for sheathing purposes. BS 6746 specifies the physical requirements and test methods for a number of pvc sheathing compounds having properties ranging from flexible supple grades to hard tough compounds for maximum operating temperatures of 70°C and 85°C with one special grade being suitable for use over cables working at a maximum conductor temperature of 90°C.

The ultimate use of a cable determines the type of pvc sheathing required, thus when tough mechanical strength is needed a hard grade might be selected whilst for flexible cords, which must be supple, a flexible grade of sheathing would be applied over the cores. Polythene-insulated cables for radio frequency operation could call for the special non-migratory grade of sheath which is specially formulated such that plasticisers do not migrate from the sheathing to the polythene core insulation and lower the electrical properties of the insulation.

Whilst BS 6746 offers a range of pvc sheathing compounds most complete cable specifications stipulate the actual type of pvc sheathing to be used.

Polychloroprene sheathing

This was the first synthetic rubber to be used extensively for cable sheathing and is generally known as pcp or Neoprene.

PCP sheathing compounds, when properly formulated, have very good resistance to oil and weather and are flame-retardant. When pcp is subjected to a flame from some other source of heat, the flame will cause the pcp to decompose and evolve a large quantity of chlorine gas which will then blanket the flame and tend to prevent oxygen from the atmosphere from allowing the fire to continue.

In its heat resistance, pcp is only slightly better than natural rubber and this type of sheathing in BS 6899 is rated for a maximum operating temperature of only 60°C. In this respect there is often the mistaken idea that because pcp is a flame-retardant material it must also be a good heat-resistant substance. Nevertheless, the compound can be allowed to run at high temperatures for very short periods in emergencies but, if very high temperatures are reached, there is a possibility of chemical decomposition which can lead to the formation of corrosive hydrochloric acid if moisture is present. At very low temperatures ordinary pcp compounds are not particularly good since the material becomes hard and is liable to crack when bent.

PCP sheathing can be made in the form of ordinary duty oil-resistant and flame-retardant grade or heavy duty oil-resistant and flame-retardant grade in accordance with BS 6899. To obtain tough mechanical properties it is necessary to incorporate carbon black in the compound and this results in the sheath being black in colour with the result that other colours are not obtainable in very tough form.

PCP is poor electrically, having a very low insulation resistance, but in the past it was used in conjunction with natural rubber to produce composite insulation having useful properties. Conductors of cables were first covered with a thin layer of natural rubber compound which was followed by a somewhat similar thickness of pcp compound.

This composite insulation had fairly good electrical properties but was also flame-retardant which made it very useful in many electrical installations where the spread of fire along cables had to be avoided. This type is now obsolete since the development of chlorosulphonated polyethelene synthetic rubber has replaced it.

Chorosulphonated polyethelene

This synthetic elastomer, generally known as csp or Hypalon, is a very useful cable sheathing material although quite an appreciable quantity is also used for electrical insulation. The mechanical toughness of csp as a sheathing is about the same as pcp but there are a number of properties which make it superior.

It is suitable for continuous operation at a temperature of at least 85°C so that it becomes an ideal sheathing for application over butyl or epr insulated cores which can also operate at this temperature. Whilst tough pcp compounds can only be produced in black form, csp can also be made in tough pastel shades with the result that cable sheaths can be supplied in various colours for purpose of identification, although in practice black is generally the standard colour for heavy duty csp sheathing and ordinary duty grade is grey.

CSP is a flame-retardant elastomer and in this respect it can be employed in the same way as pcp in order to provide a cable which will not spread fire. The oil and solvent resistance of csp is good and is similar to pcp. At low temperatures csp is better than pcp and compounds remain flexible down to about −30 to −35°C.

BS 6899 specifies the requirements for various forms of 85°C rubber sheathing which may be formulated from csp. This British Standard also includes requirements for 85°C flame-retardant composite insulations which consist of synthetic insulation applied first to the cable conductor followed by an outer layer of csp to provide the necessary flame-retardant properties.

CSP is sometimes used as combined insulation and sheathing in non-composite form, without the inner layer of insulating rubber, for covering conductors of welding and similar cables. For this use the csp compound is especially formulated to provide better electrical insulating properties than normal csp sheathing, whilst still retaining the excellent oil-resisting and flame-retarding properties of the csp. Such material is also included in BS 6899.

Silicone rubber sheathing

Sheathing based upon silicone rubber is the same type of compound as used for insulation and for British Standard cables the material should comply with BS 6899.

As with silicone rubber insulation compound, the sheathing is suitable for continuous operation at 150°C and may run for even higher temperatures for short periods. It supports combustion and can cause spread of fire, although, as with silicone insulation, the resultant ash is electrically non-conducting. Sheathing is not particularly robust and often requires protection from excessive mechanical damage. It is flexible down to very low temperatures.

Silicone rubber is expensive and is only used where cheaper alternatives are not feasible.

Lead sheathing

In the past lead sheathing was widely used for shipwiring cables as a protection over cores insulated with natural rubber, varnished cambric or impregnated-paper because it provided an excellent air and moisture barrier which enabled these insulants to perform satisfactorily. Since these cable insulants are now obsolete for shipwiring and their modern counterparts do not require the same degree of protection from air and moisture, there is considerably less lead sheathing used today.

However, lead is sometimes used where certain cables are required to have a protective metallic covering for providing either electrical screening against pick-up of undesirable interference or for ensuring electrical safety in hazardous atmospheres. Lead is also an excellent barrier to various solvents which might otherwise affect polymeric insulants of cables. Lead has a high specific gravity and therefore adds significantly to the weight of a cable and its poor electrical conductivity, only 8%, (approximately,) of copper results in rather more efficient screening materials often being used.

In its commercially pure state, lead is liable to crystallise and crack when subjected to mechanical vibration (such as is present in ships) so lead alloys which are better able to withstand these conditions are used. A number of standard alloys are available which contain small quantities of tin, antimony, cadmium or tellurium or combinations of several of these alloying metals and each alloy has particular mechanical properties suitable for particular applications. The cable manufacturer is best able to advise upon the most suitable alloy for a specific application.

Copper sheathing

As already stated, mineral-insulated cables have their insulation protected by an overall metal sheath. Copper used for this purpose requires special mention since it is not quite the same as copper used for cable conductors.

In order to withstand the cable manufacturing process, particularly the annealing operation required to produce a pliable sheath, it is necessary to use phosphorus deoxidised non-arsenical copper. This grade of copper is somewhat different from the tough pitch high conductivity copper used for cable conductors in that its nominal conductivity is about 80% of that of standard annealed copper.

BS 6207 covers the requirements for copper-sheathed mineral-insulated cables and includes various tests to verify the correct mechanical properties of the copper sheathing.

ARMOURING AND SCREENING

In the past it was common for ships' cables to be given added mechanical protection by applying a layer of galvanised steel wires helically around the sheathed cores and then protecting these wires from corrosion by means of an overall fibrous covering, thoroughly impregnated with paint or other suitable waterproof compound. This has now tended to give way to mechanical protection in the form of a braiding of a large number of smaller diameter galvanised steel wires applied as a basket weave. In addition to giving mechanical protection to the underlying cable this type of armouring also provides a reasonable degree of screening against radio interference.

Where a greater degree of electrical screening is required the wire braiding is composed of bronze or copper wires. Bronze wires afford greater mechanical strength but copper wires, because of their better electrical conductivity, provide better screening. The copper wire screening of elastomeric cables is generally composed of tinned copper wires.

Owing to its magnetic properties, steel wire is unsuitable for armouring single-core cables carrying heavy alternating currents and a non-magnetic wire, such as bronze, must be used.

Shipwiring cables generally have the wire armouring or screening protected by means of an overall sheath of pcp or csp if the core insulation is of a thermosetting polymeric material. Thermoplastic cables, e.g. pvc, polythene, have pvc sheathing overall since this does not require to be vulcanised and therefore the cores are not subjected to any heating process which would otherwise cause damage in the form of softening of the insulation.

FLEXIBLE CORDS AND CABLES

Although generally all flexibles are 'cables', if the cross-sectional area of each conductor does not exceed 4 mm² they are known as 'flexible cords'; larger sizes are 'flexible cables'. BS 6500 covers a range of flexible cords generally employed as connections for portable equipment and many of them are suitable for use within cabins of ships.

Twisted flexible cords consisting of two or more braided cores twisted together should not be used, as they are not sufficiently mechanically robust to withstand everyday service. Flexible cords made up in circular form and having extruded polymeric sheathing are preferable for most applications; where oil and grease is present sheathing of pcp or csp provides better protection than pvc in high ambient temperatures.

On no account should flexible cords be used for fixed wiring. Flexible cords are a frequent cause of fires mainly because, due to their vulnerability to physical damage combined with their light insulation and overall protection, they easily suffer injury. They should therefore be examined at regular intervals, particularly at their terminations, and faulty leads replaced or repaired.

Arc welding cables are quite different from flexible cords in that their design especially takes into account the very arduous conditions likely to be encountered in service. Single-core welding cables for connections between the transformer and electrode have very supple conductors composed of a large number of small wires and it is the modern practice for one single covering of elastomeric material, usually csp, to act as both insulation and mechanical protection. Previously a very thin layer of rubber insulation was applied between the conductor and the heavy outer sheathing.

For all constructions of electrode cables it is usual for a lapping of thin paper tape to be applied immediately over the conductor so as to prevent the elastomeric coverings from becoming embedded into the outer interestices of the flexible strand during the vulcanising process and in this way the resultant cable remains very supple. In use the paper tape tears and disintegrates but by this time it has served its useful purpose as a separator during the cable manufacturing process.

BS 6384, with amendments, specifies requirements for welding cables, including both copper and aluminium conductors.

For the very arduous conditions encountered on offshore drilling and production platforms heavy-duty flexible cables frequently embody galvanised pliable wire armour for providing the necessary mechanical protection. The flexible cores, generally insulated with epr, are twisted together then filled circular and sheathed with pcp over which is applied a helical layer of strands of small-diameter galvanised steel wires; each strand usually containing seven individual wires. The cable is sheathed overall with pcp to protect the pliable armouring from corrosion and damage. To provide the required conductance of armour for earthing purposes it is often necessary to include one copper wire in each of the seven strands of pliable armour, leaving six steel wires.

CURRENT RATINGS

The passage of current through a cable conductor results in a rise of temperature due to the power losses caused by the conductor resistance. The maximum current rating of a cable is based upon the maximum operating temperatures of the component parts of the cable, therefore current ratings of cables are related to the type of materials used for insulation and sheathing.

In practice the maximum continuous current ratings of cables are generally determined by the safe operating temperature of the core insulation since the majority of cables are sheathed with materials having safe operating temperatures compatible with the core insulation operating temperature. In the case of mineral-insulated cables, however, the insulation is able to withstand extremely high temperatures without deterioration and the limiting factors are the safe operating temperatures of the seals and any sheathing over the metal sheath. Where mineral-insulated cables have no covering over the metal sheath and where such cables are installed in positions exposed to touch, the current rating is limited to provide a sheath

Table 10.3. Maximum permissible service temperatures of cable conductors upon which
current ratings are based

Insulation	Conductor temperature
	°C
PVC, general purpose	60
PVC heat resisting	75
Butyl rubber	80
Ethylene propylene (epr)	85
Cross-linked polyethylene (xlpe)	85
Silicone rubber	95
Mineral — bare sheath	95
Mineral with pvc sheath	70
Mineral exposed to touch	70

temperature which is safe from the point of view of guarding against
burns to persons.

Table 10.3 shows the temperatures upon which continuous
current ratings for cables with various types of materials are based.
Table 10.4 shows typical continuous current ratings for different
types of cables.

Current ratings are based upon the temperature rise, due to the
passage of current, from ambient temperature to the maximum continuous operating temperatures, thus for high ambient temperatures
the permissible temperature rise will be less than for cables installed
in lower ambient temperatures and the current rating will be consequently less. For normal ships' installations an ambient temperature
of 45°C is assumed but in engine rooms and other areas where temperatures are high the cable ratings must take these higher temperatures into account and the ratings must be appropriately reduced
by applying the factors as given in Table 10.5.

For some applications, for example on offshore platforms, it may
be known that lower ambient temperatures will attain at all times in
which case current ratings can be increased by the factor appropriate
to the air temperature. The ambient, or cooling air temperature, as it
is sometimes called, is the temperature of the air in which the cable is
installed before the passage of current through the cable causes
heating.

When several cables are run close together or touching, the heat
from one cable affects the others and results in a lowering of the
current rating. The current ratings shown in Table 10.4 are based
upon six cables run bunched together in a ship installation but it is
assumed that not all six cables will be fully loaded at the same time

Table 10.4. Current ratings in continuous service for single-core cables
(Ambient temperature 45°C)

Nominal cross-sectional area	General purpose pvc (60°C)	Heat resisting pvc (75°C)	Butyl rubber (80°C)	EPR and XLPE (85°C)	Silicone rubber and bare sheath mineral insulation (95°C)	Mineral insulation exposed to touch or pvc sheathed (70°C)
mm²	A	A	A	A	A	A
1	8	13	15	16	20	16
1.5	12	17	19	20	24	19
2.5	17	24	24	28	32	26
4	22	32	35	38	42	34
6	29	41	45	48	55	44
10	40	57	63	67	75	60
16	54	76	84	90	100	80
25	71	100	110	120	135	110
35	87	125	140	145	165	130
50	105	150	165	180	200	160
70	135	190	215	225	255	205
95	165	230	260	275	310	250
120	190	270	300	320	360	290
150	220	310	340	365	410	330
185	250	350	390	415	470	375
240	290	415	460	490	—	—
300	335	475	530	560	—	—

Note: Ratkngs for 2, 3 and 4 conductor cables may be obtained by multiplying the above ratings by the following factors: 0.85 for 2-core cables; 0.70 for 3- and 4-core cables.

Table 10.5. Current ratings correction factors for various ambient air temperatures

Maximum conductor temperature (°C)	Correction factors for ambient air temperatures of										
	35°C	40°C	45°C	50°C	55°C	60°C	65°C	70°C	75°C	80°C	85°C
60	1.29	1.15	1.00	0.82	0.71	—	—	—	—	—	—
65	1.22	1.12	1.00	0.87	0.77	—	—	—	—	—	—
70	1.18	1.10	1.00	0.89	0.82	0.63	—	—	—	—	—
75	1.15	1.08	1.00	0.91	0.85	0.71	0.58	—	—	—	—
80	1.13	1.07	1.00	0.93	0.87	0.76	0.65	0.53	—	—	—
85	1.12	1.06	1.00	0.94	0.88	0.79	0.71	0.61	0.50	—	—
90	1.10	1.05	1.00	0.94	0.88	0.82	0.74	0.67	0.58	0.47	—
95	1.10	1.05	1.00	0.95	0.89	0.84	0.77	0.71	0.63	0.55	0.45

**Table 10.6. Current ratings for non-continuously loaded EPR-insulated cables without
metal sheath or armour
(Ambient temperature 45°C)**

Nominal cross-sectional area	Half-hour ratings		
	Single core	Two core	3 and 4 core
mm²	A	A	A
50	190	170	150
70	245	220	190
95	310	280	240
120	365	335	295
150	425	395	350
185	500	470	410
240	600	580	515
300	710	690	620

due to diversity of current loadings. Where more than six cables are run bunched together it is the usual practice in ships' installations to reduce the ratings to 85% of the value for six cables.

In particular cases where numbers of cables will be installed close together and will all be fully loaded for long periods it may be necessary to arrive at the safe level of current rating by mathematical calculation. The method of making these calculations is outside the scope of this chapter but valuable assistance is generally available from the cable maker.

If very heavy currents have to be carried it is often more economical to run two or more cables in parallel to share the load rather than run one very large cable. It is important, however, that each of

**Table 10.7. Current ratings for non-continuously loaded EPR-insulated cables without
metal sheath or armour
(Ambient temperature 45°C)**

Nominal cross-sectional area	One hour ratings		
	Single core	Two core	3 and 4 core
mm²	A	A	A
50	190	165	135
70	235	200	175
95	290	250	215
120	340	290	250
150	390	340	295
185	450	400	345
240	540	490	420
300	615	565	495

the cables in parallel should be the same conductor size, the same type and the same length. Otherwise the cable with the lowest impedance will carry an excessive share of the load and may become

Where it is known that cables will not be continuously loaded for long periods it may be possible to take advantage of the non-continuous loading values to Tables 10.6 and 10.7. These ratings are based on the assumption that the intermediate periods of rest are longer than the critical duration, i.e. longer than three times the thermal time constant of the cable. A shorter rating than one half-hour is not recognised, whatever the degree of intermittency. It is most important that the values of currents based on the one-hour or half-hour ratings should not be permitted to flow for longer than these respective periods otherwise overheating and permanent damage to the cables is liable.

Voltage drop

The tables of current ratings provide values of current based purely upon the temperature rise of the conductor due to the passage of

Table 10.8(a). Voltage drop in cables (copper conductors)
1.0 mm.^{2} to 35 mm.^{2}

Bunched and enclosed in conduit or trunking or clipped direct to a surface or on a cable tray, bunched and unenclosed

	Volt drop per ampere per metre							
Nominal area of conductor	Single-core cables				Twin and multicore cables			
	2 cables single-phase a.c. or d.c.		3 or 4 cables 3-phase		One twin, single-phase a.c. or d.c.		One 3 or 4 core cable 3-phase	
mm^2	*PVC	†Butyl	*PVC	Butyl†	*PVC	Butyl†	PVC*	Butyl†
	mV	mV	mV	mV	mV	mV	mV	mV
1.0	40	42	35	36	41‡	43‡	35‡	37
1.5	27	28	23	24	28‡	29‡	24‡	25
2.5	16	17	14	15	17‡	17‡	15‡	15
4	10	11	8.8	9.5	11‡	11‡	9.1‡	9.5
6	6.8	7.2	5.9	6.2	7‡	7.3‡	6‡	6.3
10	4.0	4.3	3.5	3.7	4.1‡	4.3‡	3.5‡	3.7
16	2.6	2.7	2.2	2.3	2.6	2.7‡	2.2‡	2.4
25	1.6	1.7	1.4	1.5	1.7	1.8	1.5	1.6
35	1.2	1.2	1.0	1.1	1.2	1.3	1.0	1.1

*PVC insulated cables, non-armoured, with or without sheath.
†Butyl or e.p. rubber or silicone rubber, non-metal sheathed. Also applies to EPR and XLPE
‡ Sizes 1.0 mm.^{2} to 16 mm.^{2}; flat cables only.

Table 10.8(b). Voltage drop in cables (copper conductors)
Single core cables 50 mm.² to 630 mm.²

Nominal area of Conductor mm.²	Volt drop per ampere per metre											
	Cables bunched and enclosed in conduit or trunking						Cables clipped to a surface or on a cable tray, bunched and un-enclosed					
	*PVC			Butyl†			*PVC			Butyl†		
	2 cables single phase		3 or 4 cables 3 phase	2 cables single phase		3 or 4 cables 3 phase	2 cables single phase		3 or 4 cables 3 phase	2 cables single phase		3 or 4 cables 3 phase
	a.c.	d.c.	a.c.	a.c.	d.c.	a.c.	a.c.	d.c.	a.c.	a.c.	d.c.	a.c.
	mV		mV	mV		mV	mV		mV	mV		mV
50	0.97	0.91	0.84	1.0	0.96	0.89	0.93	0.91	0.82	0.97	0.96	0.86
70	0.71	0.63	0.62	0.75	0.67	0.65	0.65	0.63	0.59	0.68	0.67	0.62
95	0.56	0.45	0.48	0.58	0.48	0.51	0.48	0.45	0.45	0.51	0.48	0.47
120	0.48	0.36	0.42	0.51	0.38	0.44	0.40	0.36	0.38	0.41	0.38	0.40
150	—	—	—	0.46	0.31	0.40	0.34	0.29	0.34	0.35	0.31	0.35
185	—	—	—	—	—	—	0.29	0.24	0.30	0.30	0.25	0.31
240	—	—	—	—	—	—	0.24	0.18	0.27	0.25	0.19	0.27
300	—	—	—	—	—	—	0.22	0.14	0.25	0.22	0.15	0.25
400	—	—	—	—	—	—	0.20	0.12	0.24	0.20	0.12	0.24
500	—	—	—	—	—	—	0.18	0.086	0.23	0.19	0.093	0.23
630	—	—	—	—	—	—	0.17	0.068	0.22	0.18	0.071	0.22

current. The current also results in a voltage drop along the cable and the value of the voltage drop may have as much influence in the choice of a cable size as the continuous current rating. Many cable runs in ships may be fairly short but there can be instances where voltage drop considerations are of great importance. Excessive voltage drop can seriously effect the proper operation of many types of electronic equipment and motors can give starting problems if the voltage drop at the starting current is excessive.

Tables 10.8(a), (b) and (c) provide voltage drop information for each conductor size for various types of cables. To arrive at the voltage drop for a particular run of cable at a known value of current it is necessary to multiply the appropriate value of circuit run in metres by the current in amperes and then multiply the product by the voltage drop factor in the table. This will give the voltage drop of the circuit in millivolts which should be divided by 1000 to provide an answer in volts. The factors suitably take into account the

Table 10.8(c). Voltage drop in cables (copper conductors)
Twin and multicore cables 50 mm.² to 300 mm.². Clipped direct to a surface or on a
cable tray and unenclosed

Nominal area of Conductor mm.²	Volt drop per ampere per metre					
	PVC			Butyl		
	One twin cable single phase		One 3 or 4 core cable 3 phase	One twin cable single phase		One 3 or 4 core cable 3 phase
	a.c. mV	d.c. mV	a.c. mV	a.c. mV	d.c. mV	a.c. mV
50	0.94	0.93	0.81	0.99	0.97	0.85
70	0.66	0.64	0.57	0.69	0.67	0.60
95	0.49	0.46	0.42	0.51	0.48	0.44
120	0.40	0.37	0.34	0.41	0.39	0.36
150	0.33	0.30	0.29	0.35	0.32	0.31
185	0.28	0.24	0.24	0.29	0.25	0.25
240	0.24	0.19	0.20	0.24	0.20	0.21
300	0.21	0.15	0.18	0.21	0.16	0.17

resistance of the cable conductor at the maximum operating temperature upon which current ratings are based but for all practical purposes the factors can be used at other lower ratings when in actual fact the conductor resistance will be somewhat lower.

Short-circuit ratings

In many instances it is necessary to match the cable size to the short-circuit capacity of switchgear and other circuit protection equipment which may take a fraction of a second to several seconds to clear a heavy fault or short-circuit from the system. For these conditions it is essential to be able to calculate short-circuit ratings of cables; the calculations being based upon the safe conductor temperature rise during the short duration of the fault current.

Chapter 8 gives details of the methods of calculation which are based upon the maximum permissible temperatures for various cable insulants as given in Table 10.9.

Under short-circuit conditions not only does the rapid rise in conductor temperature effecting the cable insulants have to be taken into account but the mechanical forces due to magnetic effects and longitudinal expansion of conductors have to be considered. It is possible that these could also cause destructive effects at the conductor terminations and at any joints.

Table 10.9. Short-circuit ratings. Permissable final
conductor temperatures after passage of short-circuit

Cable insulation material	Final conductor temperature
	°C
PVC (small cables)	150
PVC (large cables)	130
Butyl	160
EPR	160
XLPE	160

INSTALLATION OF CABLES

Because of the rigorous environmental conditions, cables in ships and in similar situations have to be installed with extreme care and proper thought must be given to the operating conditions.

Cable runs should be carefully chosen, particularly with a view to avoiding subjection to excessive heat and risk of mechanical damage. Cable runs should be so located that the cables are accessible for inspection and are not exposed to accumulation of water or oil. They should not be run under machines or floor plates as, although this is frequently done, it represents bad practice. In the majority of cases can be easily avoided by taking cables from the top of cable boxes instead of underneath and by attaching them to cable trays, racking or steel plating to carry them in an upward direction.

Cables which are exposed to exceptional risk of mechanical damage, e.g. in holds, storage spaces, cargo spaces, etc should be protected by suitable casing or conduits, if the ship's structure or attached parts do not afford sufficient mechanical protection. This should be the rule even if armoured cables are used.

As well as ensuring that cables are well protected after installation during service, consideration must be given to possible mechanical damage to cables during their installation or during construction of the vessel.

Except for those specially designed for use at high temperatures, cables should not be installed in any situation where temperatures greater than those in Table 10.10 are likely to be experienced. Because of the different temperatures permissible with various types of insulation, cables intended for different operating temperatures must not be bunched together in a common clip, gland or conduit.

Cables in cold-storage chambers should pass directly through the insulation or lagging of the chamber, suitably protected by a tube flanged at each end. They must not be concealed behind the insulation and must be either p.c.p.- or c.s.p.-sheathed or of the m.i.c.s. type. A space must be left behind the supporting galvanised trays, racking or plating, and the construction must be such that the cables cannot be used by stevedores, or anyone else, to place hooks on them for the suspension of cargo. All metal fixings, including

Table 10.10. Maximum ambient air temperatures in which cables should be permitted to operate

Insulation	Ambient temperature
	°C
PVC, general purpose	50
PVC, heat resisting	65
Butyl rubber	70
Ethylene propylene (epr)	75
Cross-linked polyethylene (xlpe)	75
Silicone rubber	140
Mineral with pvc sheath	60
Mineral, bare sheath 105°C terminations	95
Mineral, bare sheath 150°C terminations	140

screws, should be galvanised and the use of dissimilar metals such as brass screws or clips in contact with galvanised supports must be avoided, as this leads to electrolytic action and corrosion. Where supply and exhaust ducting is fitted in the chamber for air circulation purposes, cables should not be installed in the supply ducts as the heat losses in the cables affect the performance of the refrigerating plant.

Sharp bends in cables must be avoided as they involve risk of impairing the insulation and sheathing. Cables should not be bent to smaller radii than those recommended by the cable manufacturer. In the absence of such information cables should not be bent to a smaller radius (at the inside of the bend), of more than six times the outer diameter of the cable. An exception is allowed for small unarmoured cables not exceeding 25 mm diameter which may be bent to a radius of four times the outer diameter of the cable.

Cables having p.v.c. insulation or sheathing should not be bent unless both the cable and the ambient temperatures are above freezing point (0°C), and have been so for the previous twenty-four hours, unless special precautions are taken to maintain the cable well above this temperature. This is because of the thermoplastic nature of p.v.c.

and the fact that the material becomes increasingly stiff and brittle as the temperature decreases.

Cable supporting systems and clips

A commonly used method of fixing cables is on perforated trays, particularly for large feeder cables. Perforated trays should be galvanised or otherwise provided with rust-preventing coatings applied before erection.

Cables are held in position on trays by means of clips which, if metal, should be of either galvanised steel or naval brass. If of brass, only good quality soft metal should be used as the harder qualities are liable to fracture at sharp bends; if they do not do so immediately, they are prone to do so in service.

If non-metallic clips are used they should be of suitable flame-retardant material and if they are used to fix cables other than on top of trays there should be suitable metallic clips added at regular intervals of one or two metres in order to prevent the release of cables during a fire. All clips should be sufficiently wide and well radiused at their edges so that they do not bite into the cable.

Ladder racks are being more widely used and are constructed from flat section galvanised steel and are usually available in standard lengths which are attached to the main structure. Cables are either laid on top of the ladder rungs or attached to the rungs from below. Clips of suitable metal or flame-retardant material are used to fix the cables in a similar manner to cables as trays. Clips must be applied at sufficiently close intervals to prevent movement of cables in service due to vibration and thermal expansion.

Ladder racks should have sufficient mechanical strength, not only to adequately support the cable weight but also to withstand the possible weight of persons who might stand on the racking during construction and in service. This applies particularly in the case of off-shore platforms.

A well-established method for supporting larger cables is by cable hangers which are constructed of steel and attached or bolted to the main structure and must be protected from corrosion. Cables are either laid on top of the hangers or, alternatively, supported below the hanger by corrosion-resistant clips.

In order to economise in the use of steel and other expensive and heavy supporting materials, growing use is made of bunching cables together and strapping them by cable bands at short intervals to a longitudinal support, such as a steel conduit or steel pipe. The cable bands are made from suitable steel strip which is tensioned and terminated in a steel buckle. When this system is used in the open along weatherdecks the strap is often made from plastic coated steel.

In all the above methods the distance between cable fixings should be suitably chosen according to the type of cable and the possibility of vibration and should not generally exceed a value of 400 mm. For horizontal cable runs where cables are laid on supports in the form of cable trays, separate support brackets or cable ladders the spacing between fixing points for clips, saddles, straps, etc, may be up to 900 mm provided that the supports do not exceed a spacing of 400 mm. In case of cables run along weatherdecks where the cables may be subjected to forces from water washing over the deck, closer spacing between fixing devices is necessary.

In the case of large single-core cables consideration must always be given to the effects of electro-dynamic forces developing on the occurrence of a short-circuit in the system in which case the above mentioned distances may be insufficient for adequately restraining the cable and closer, substantial fixing methods may be required.

Cables enclosed in conduit, trunking, etc.

Whilst galvanised steel conduit is essential in locations subjected to corrosive conditions, the use of enamelled steel conduit is possible in many situations. All conduits should have their cut ends smoothed to remove burrs or bushes should be fitted to prevent damage to cables during the drawing-in operation.

In order to facilitate easy drawing-in and also easy withdrawal should it be necessary to remove a faulty cable, conduits and pipes should not contain too many cables, particularly if there are any bends in the run. As a general rule a space factor of 40% should not be exceeded, i.e. the aggregate cross-sectional area of cables should not exceed 40% of the internal cross-sectional area of the conduit. Since the cross-sectional area of the cables and of the interior of the conduit is proportional to the square of the diameter in each case it is unnecessary to work out the areas. Thus the requirement is complied with if the aggregate of the cable diameters squared is less than 0.4 multiplied by the square of the internal diameter of the conduit.

Ventilating outlets should be provided, preferably at the highest and lowest points, in order to allow a free circulation of air and to prevent the accumulation of water in any part of the run. On the other hand, as proved by experience, if it is possible to seal conduit runs effectively so that there can be no exchange of air with the outside atmosphere condensation can be eliminated. Ventilating openings should not be provided if they increase the risk of spread of fire, this applies also to trunking. Vertical trunking should be so constructed as not to afford passage of fire from one between-deck or compartment to another.

Metal conduits and trunkings must be earthed and must be mechanically and electrically continuous across all joints and fittings. Unless this is ensured there is grave risk of shock to personnel if the metalwork becomes live due to insulation failure, and there is also danger of fire. With long runs of conduit it may be necessary to fit expansion joints to prevent breakage.

Cables in d.c. circuits may have the lead and return in the same or in separate steel conduits or trunkings. For a.c. circuits all circuit conductors should run in the same steel conduit or trunking in order to reduce magnetic losses.

Cables penetrating bulkheads and decks

Where it is necessary to carry cables through watertight decks and bulkheads it is essential to preserve watertightness. Either individual stuffed glands or boxes containing several cables and filled with a flame-retardant packing should be use. Whatever type is used should be capable of complying with any specified gland-watertightness tests.

In choosing a particular method, care should be taken to ensure that the cable is not adversely affected by the heat from the compound being poured or from heat from any chemical reaction generated during the hardening of the compound e.g. from polyester resin compounds. Cables entering watertight apparatus must pass through suitable watertight glands.

Cables passing through decks must be protected from mechanical damage to a suitable height above the deck. Deck tubes are used for small numbers of cables passing through a deck; the tube may be circular or rectangular. On weather decks and main decks, the height of the tube must conform to freeboard requirements and must be the same as that specified for coamings.

Preparation of cable ends

When cable conductors are not connected at their ends by means of mechanical clamps, the ends of conductors should be fitted with soldering sockets or compression-type sockets of sufficient size to contain all the strands of the conductor. Where soldering is adopted, corrosive fluxes should not be used and care should be taken to ensure that the core insulation is not damaged by the soldering heat.

Apart from mineral-insulated cables, the core insulation should be cut back only sufficiently to enable the conductor to enter and completely fill the cable socket but any protective coverings should be removed for at least 13 mm from the ends of the insulation but not more than necessary. High-voltage cables having a semi-conductive layer over the surface of the core insulation should, however, be cleaned back for a sufficient distance to prevent tracking during service. This distance depends upon the operating voltage and cable design and manufacturers' instructions should be followed.

The ends of large cores may be lapped with suitable jointing tape or may be fitted with one of the many proprietary insulating sleeves. If heat-shrinkable sleeves are used care must be exercised in ensuring that excessive heat is not applied so as to permanently damage the cable insulation and sheathing.

Mineral-insulated cables require special terminations and the ends should be prepared in accordance with the instructions issued by the manufacturers of these cables. Owing to the hygroscopic nature of mineral-insulation it is essential that these cables are sealed very soon after the end is exposed to the atmosphere.

For all types of cable it is important to ensure that the terminations are suited to the currents to be carried and that they will withstand the temperatures likely to be encountered.

Earthing and bonding

The term 'earthing' or 'grounding', requires no explanation but the term 'bonding' is frequently misused, for example in the expression 'bonding to earth'. Bonding implies connecting the metal sheath or armour of one length of cable to that of another so that electrical continuity is maintained from one sheath or armour to the next. The cables may be lying together side by side, or a break may occur where a fitting is entered on two sides, as when two or more lighting fittings are fed from the same source. In this case steps must be taken to connect the two metal sheaths or armourings together electrically.

Earthing of metal sheathing and armouring is also essential. This should be accomplished by reliable clamps and not dependent on fortuitous contact with earthed metal which may be dirty or may eventually rust. The same requirement applies to steel conduit, both in regard to earthing and bonding. Where the cables enter metal cases the glands may act as a means for earthing. In this case it is important that provision be made in the gland to make effective metallic contact with the sheath and armour. Metal braiding must also be earthed. Sheaths and armour should be earthed at both ends of cables unless it is the final length for connecting to the consuming device, in which case it need be earthed at the supply end only.

Expansion joints

Where the structure of the ship embodies expansion joints, the fitting of cables across the joint should be avoided as far as practicable by running them on a lower deck. If this cannot be arranged a loop should be provided having a diameter at least twelve times that of the largest cable, to ensure flexability.

Cables for a.c. circuits

In a three-phase system with single-core cables laid parallel in flat formation, if each cable passes through a separate hole in a steel bulkhead, heating of the steel due to magnetic effects will occur. The temperature of the hottest point will amount to twice the conductor temperature rise under unfavourable conditions.

Unless a non-magnetic gland-plate is fitted, non-magnetic glands or bushes should be used, giving at least 10 mm clearance all round between the cable sheath and the steel. Axial spacing between the cables should where possible be not less than 150 mm. Similar precautions are also necessary where similar cables enter any steel enclosure, such as a cable box.

If a non-magnetic plate is used the opening in the steel bulkhead should be such that the distance between the edge of the opening and the centre of a cable is not less than 76 mm.

Metallic cable sheaths are conductors parallel to the copper conductor and when a.c. flows through single-core cables a voltage will be induced in the metallic sheath. For currents below about 100 A induced sheath current is negligible, but for higher currents careful consideration is necessary. On long cable runs this voltage may rise to an appreciable value and under fault conditions, i.e. short-circuit, it will rise rapidly and arcing to earthed metal may result.

For heavy currents of the order of 1000 A and above with single-core metal sheathed cables e.g. generator cables, careful planning and installation are necessary. The cable route should be as straight and short as possible and the cables run on trefoil formation, opening into single formation not more than a few cm from their terminations. The cable lengths should also be as nearly as practicable of equal length and securely held at intervals not exceeding 0.75 m with non-magnetic trefoil cleats. At the point nearest to the break from trefoil to single formation a substantial bond should be provided on each cable and efficiently connected by a copper strap to earth.

In circuits involving single-core cables in parallel per phase all cables should be of equal length and of the same cross-sectional area. Those cables pertaining to the same phase should be as far as practicable alternated with those of other phases to avoid unequal distribution of current. For example with two cables per phase the correct distribution should be:

$$\text{RYBBYR or } \frac{\text{RYB}}{\text{BYR}} \text{ and not RRYYBB or } \frac{\text{RYB}}{\text{RYB}}$$

Electromagnetic interference

Where cables are installed in the vicinity of electronic or radio-frequency circuits special precautions are necessary to avoid as much as possible the effects of unwanted electromagnetic interference.

This is a specialised subject and is dealt with more fully in Chapter 20 'Electro-magnetic compatibility'

Convention requirements

The Fire Protection requirements of the 1960 and 1974 SOLAS Conventions require that where main vertical zone bulkheads are pierced for the passage of electric cables the fire resistance of the bulkheads must not be impaired, i.e. arrangements for passing the cables through the bulkheads must be such that they do not constitute a means whereby fire on one side of the bulkhead might be transmitted to the opposite side. Cable trunks passing from one between deck or compartment to another must be so constructed as not to afford passage for fire.

The positioning of cables must be such that fire in any main fire zone will not interfere with essential services in any other main fire zone. This requirement will generally be met if main and emergency feeders passing through any zone are separated vertically and horizontally as widely as practicable.

11 Motors

The most common form of enclosure is 'drip-proof' which by definition ensures protection of the windings, commutator and terminals not only from falling liquids but also any other particles. Drip-proof protection as applied to motors in ships requires a slightly different interpretation from that applied to motors ashore, owing to the motion of the ship. For these motors, therefore, the requirement is extended to provide protection from falling water or dirt when the machine is tilted 22½° in any direction. Protection must also be provided against liquids striking a surface and running into the machine or being drawn in by the ventilating air.

Another type of enclosure commonly used is 'watertight', the standard requirement for which is that the enclosure will withstand complete immersion in water to a depth of not less than three feet for a period of one hour. 'Watertight' must not be confused with 'submersible'. The essential difference is that a watertight motor is only intended to be suitable for immersion under a comparatively low head of water and for a limited period, whereas a 'submersible' motor may be submerged under a considerable head for an indefinite period. Submersible motors are necessary for statutory bilge pumps. Other types of enclosure used aboard ships are 'hoseproof' and 'weatherproof' and 'deck-watertight' for which the test is the same as for watertight, except that immersion is for one minute only.

Totally-enclosed motors may also be used, but for d.c. they suffer from the disadvantage that carbon dust from the commutator brushes is deposited on the windings, core ducts, and brush gear insulation. Pipe-ventilation or duct-ventilation is sometimes used for large motors to enable clean cool air to be drawn from suitable places outside the engine-room. With pipe-ventilated motors the heated air from the machine may be discharged into the engine-room or may be piped so as to exhaust outside the engine-room.

Water cooling is seldom used for motors, except propulsion motors, though it is sometimes used for generators. The machine is then totally enclosed and the air is caused to circulate through a heat exchanger cooled by sea water. It is a good plan to keep commutators outside such enclosures for the reason already indicated.

Flameproof enclosures will be dealt with in Chapter 18 'Tankers'.

Axis of rotation

Horizontal-shaft motors should be placed with the axis of rotation in a fore-and-aft direction. If it is unavoidable for it to be athwartships, provision should be made to take end thrust and to reduce end-play which may arise due to rolling of the ship.

D.C. MOTORS

The characteristics of d.c. motors are fairly generally understood and a very brief reference is necessary.

Shunt or lightly compounded motors are suitable for fans, pumps, etc, and variable speed is obtained economically, i.e. without loss of overall efficiency, by shunt regulation. Up to four-to-one speed variation is obtainable but three-to-one is the more usual limit. Where a wider range is essential it can be obtained by a series resistance in the armature circuit. For very low creeping speeds a series resistance and a diverter resistance across the armature may be used. When a wide range of speed is obtained by shunt regulation it is necessary to ensure that the motor is not started with a weakened field. This would reduce the starting torque and cause sparking at the commutator. The regulator must be interlocked with the starter so that it must be returned to the full field position before starting.

Series wound motors are used where a high starting torque is required, such as for engine-turning gear, winches, windlasses and capstans, boat winches, etc. The speed varies with the load and such motors should never be run without load as the speed becomes excessive. Sometimes a light shunt field is incorporated in order to limit the light running speed. Winches and capstans incorporate special control equipment for dealing with the wide range of load and speed which is necessary for successful operation (see Chapter 17).

Ward Leonard systems are sometimes employed when a wide speed range is required such as for winches. In this system the motor is separately excited and the armature is connected to a generator, the voltage of which can be varied. The control is therefore on the shunt winding of the generator and as the field currents are comparatively small the control gear is correspondingly small. This system also has the advantage that very fine speed control is obtainable from zero to full speed.

A.C. motors

There are three main types of motor from which to choose:
(i) the asynchronous or induction motor,
(ii) the synchronous motor;
(iii) the Schrage or commutator motor.
There are also several variations of these types.

The synchronous motor, consisting of an a.c. winding and a d.c. field system, runs only at synchronous speed. It is used for a.c. electric propulsion schemes but is not generally used for auxiliary purposes. The commutator motor is essentially a variable speed machine, speed variation being obtained by altering the commutator brush positions. It also is not in general use for auxiliary purposes.

This leaves us with the induction motor which is the type generally used in ships. It may be of the cage type or of the wound rotor or slipring type.

The cage machine is virtually a constant speed machine, although its speed varies slightly according to the load. The commonest form has a simple cage winding, but it is also made with a double cage and the different characteristics obtainable by variations in design will be dealt with later.

The speeds obtainable with synchronous and induction motors are governed entirely by the frequency of the supply and the number of poles in the motor winding. Synchronous motors will run exactly at synchronous speed but induction motors will run two or three per cent slower due to the slip.

The synchronous speed is:

$$\text{r.p.m.} = \frac{\text{frequency of supply} \times 60}{\text{number of pairs of poles}}$$

Thus the following speeds (less the slip in the case of induction motors) are the only speeds obtainable:

Number of poles	50 Hz r.p.m.	60 Hz r.p.m.
2	3000	3600
4	1500	1800
6	1000	1200
8	750	900
10	600	720
12	500	600

Where two, three or even four speeds are necessary they can be provided by incorporating tapped windings or extra windings on the stator. The required speed is obtained by switching to a winding combination having the appropriate number of poles.

Cage motors

The single cage rotor suits the majority of applications ashore and also the majority of drives in ships, depending to a large extent on the size of the generating plant. As will be seen from Figure 11.1

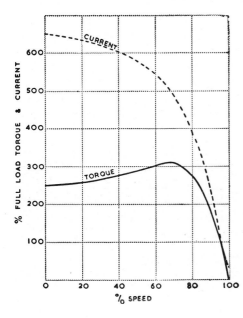

Figure 11.1 Typical torque and current characteristics of a 4-pole single cage motor

the initial starting current when switched direct-on-line (d.o.l. starting) is between six and seven times full load current, but it can be as high as eight times. It will be appreciated that if the motor is large in relation to the rating of the generators the starting of such a motor on an already loaded system might cause a momentary dip in voltage resulting in disturbances to other services. This factor must therefore be considered when deciding whether the single cage rotor is suitable. The starting current can be reduced by using a star-delta type of starter or by using the auto-transformer method.

It must be observed however that the starting characteristics vary considerably according to the number of poles. As the number of poles is increased the ratio of starting torque to full-load torque tends to decrease. Average ratios of starting torque/full-load torque

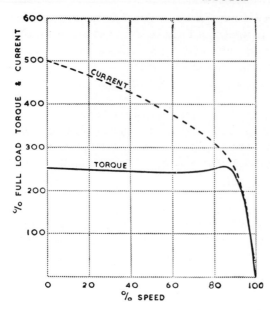

Figure 11.2 Typical torque and current characteristics of a 4-pole double cage motor

would be 2 to 2.5 for a 4-pole motor, 1.75 to 2 for 6 poles, 1.4 to 1.75 for 8 poles, and the corresponding ratio starting current/full-load current would be 5.5 to 8, 5.25 to 7.5 and 5 to 7 respectively with direct-on starting. Rotor resistance determines the slip at full load and therefore influences full-load efficiency. The higher the starting torque, the higher will be the full-load slip and therefore the lower will be the efficiency.

These values are independent of the load applied to the machine, i.e. they will be just the same whether starting light or starting against full-load torque. The only difference will be in the starting time which will be dependent on the amount of excess torque available for acceleration.

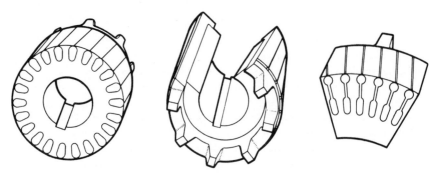

Figure 11.3 Single- and double-cage rotor sections

By adopting a double cage construction a high starting torque with a somewhat lower starting current, of the order of five times full-load current, is obtainable (Figure 11.2). The torque curve is much flatter than that of the single cage. The difference in rotor construction will be apparent from the sectional views shown in Figure 11.3).

The principle involved in this construction is that during the initial starting period the outer high-resistance cage carries practically all the rotor current and they are known as *current displacement* rotors. The inner winding, having a high reactance at the instant of start, does not take any appreciable current until the motor accelerates. As the rotor frequency (i.e. the slip frequency) diminishes the reactance of the inner cage becomes lower and this winding finally carries the major share of the running current. We thus have the advantage of a high-resistance rotor for starting purposes and a low-resistance rotor when up to speed. The relative proportions of the two windings can be varied according to the characteristics required.

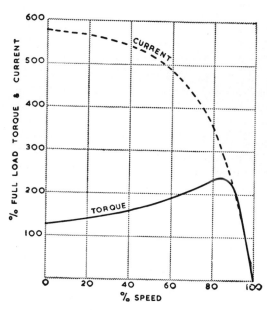

Figure 11.4 Typical torque and current characteristics of 12-pole motor with high-reactance rotor

Where starting currents must be restricted, but high starting and peak torques such as for centrifugal pumps, fans, etc., are not required, a high reactance rotor has a suitable characteristic. This construction is mainly confined to 2-pole and some of the larger 4-pole machines. To obtain the higher reactance the rotor bars are set back further from the periphery of the rotor. These characteristics may involve a slight reduction in overload capacity (Figure 11.4). Other constructions to obtain variations of the characteristic to suit special requirements are also obtainable.

A special design of motor in this category is the high-torque low-current motor developed by Laurence Scott and Electro-motors Ltd. and known as Trislot. Instead of the usual double cage rotor this machine has the slots arranged in three rows in the manner shown in Figure 11.5. In the outer row is a high resistance starting cage A

Figure 11.5 Partly-wound Trislot rotor of medium size. The end ring has been cut away to show method of jointing

similar to that of a normal single-cage rotor. The two inner rows of slots are occupied by low resistance running windings B and C. This winding consists of short-circuited turns in which each conductor in a slot of low reactance is connected in series with a conductor in a slot of high reactance, the closed loops spanning almost one pole pitch.

The material used for the outer cage A ranges from copper to a nickel alloy having up to sixty times the resistance of copper and is selected so as to obtain a bar section having the necessary mechanical strength and thermal capacity and requisite ohmic resistance. The series connection between the high and low reactance bars B and C ensures equality of currents under all conditions and an equal distribution of the m.m.f. around the periphery, an important consideration because of the secondary effects of unequal m.m.f. distribution. A very wide range of operating characteristics is permissible and a low starting current design suitable for applications where a high starting torque is not necessary, e.g. pumps, fans, etc., is shown in Figure 11.6. Higher values and lower values can be provided when needed.

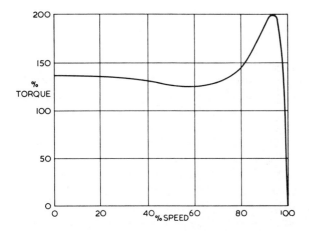

Figure 11.6 Typical speed/torque curve of Trislot motor. Starting current 4.25 × full load

Motors with wound rotor (Slipring motors)

Where finer speed variation than can be obtained with change-pole cage motors is required, or where lower starting currents are desirable, an induction motor with a wound rotor and sliprings may be found advantageous. For starting purposes resistance is connected across the sliprings. Speed regulation is obtained in the same way, except that the regulating resistance must be continuously rated. For constant-torque applications speed ranges of 3 or 4 to 1 can be obtained.

The disadvantages of this method of speed control are that it is inefficient because of the power wasted in the resistances, and also that the speed will vary with the torque. At full-load torque and half-speed, approximately half the energy taken from the line will be dissipated in the resistance.

Effect of changes in frequency and voltage

Since the frequency of supply is under the direct control of the engineer it is important to appreciate the effects produced by variations.

The effect of frequency on the speed of motors has already been dealt with and we have seen that synchronous speeds are proportional to the frequency.

At frequencies lower than those for which a motor is designed the stator flux increases and the magnetising current increases, so the heating of the windings and of the iron will also increase. Thus a motor on reduced frequency will tend to run hotter unless the reduction in speed also brings about sufficient reduction in load.

With an increase in frequency the stator flux will be reduced and this will affect the starting torque. The higher speed will also increase the h.p. output and, if the load is a centrifugal pump or fan, the h.p. will be proportional to the speed cubed. These effects are on the basis that normal voltage is maintained. The above considerations are important also when taking shore supplies. The frequency of shore supplies varies in different parts of the world and will generally be either 50 Hz or 60 Hz. If the ship's system is based on 50 Hz and it is connected to a shore supply of 60 Hz all motors will run at 20% overspeed and all centrifugal loads will increase 73%.

If, on the other hand, the ship supply is 60 Hz then on connecting to a 50 Hz shore supply all motors will run 17% slower. As already seen, overheating may take place but a slightly lower voltage may compensate for this; starters and contactors may however be adversely affected. These factors require special consideration when new ships are under construction.

Low voltage at the motor terminals may be caused either by a drop in the cables, or by failure to maintain correct voltage at the main busbars, or by dip in generated voltage due to appreciable loads suddenly applied.

Starting torques are practically proportional to the square of the voltage at the motor terminals. As a cage motor switched direct-on-line takes several times its full-load current the voltage drop in the line will be increased during starting.

In the feeder cables the extra line drop, in addition to the existing drop due to other loads, will be the starting current × cable reactance. In the motor cables to the final distribution board it will also be starting current × cable reactance. As this line drop also reduces the starting current below that which would obtain will full voltage, this must be allowed for in any calculations. If in addition there is a dip in the generated voltage this will still further reduce the available torque. Assuming that the combined effect is to reduce the terminal voltage to 85% of normal the starting torque of the motor, being proportional to the square of the voltage, will be reduced to 72.5%. With a single-cage motor having a normal starting torque of 2.5 × full-load torque this would be reduced to 1.8 times, or with a high-reactance rotor having a normal starting torque 1.25 × f.l.t. it would be reduced to 0.9 of full-load torque. In such a case, assuming the load torque required is equal to that at full load, the margin for acceleration is reduced from 1.5 to 0.8 and a longer starting time will be required. The motor with the high reactance rotor would remain stalled.

Motor heating with seven times full-load current is as the square of the current, i.e. forty-nine times full-load heating. So if the motor stalls due to the reduced starting torque it will soon burn out or receive permanent injury unless the protective devices operate very quickly.

If star-delta starting is used the voltage across each phase winding when star connected is reduced to 58% of line voltage. As the line voltage is depressed by the starting current this must also be taken into account. The current taken at any speed is directly proportional to the terminal voltage.

The effect of low voltage on the speed is negligible, so that the load will be unaffected, but the current will increase in order to maintain the same power input.

MAINTENANCE

Emphasis must be placed on the need for cleanliness, not only for motors but for all electrical apparatus. Accumulations of dirt in machines has two effects, firstly, on insulation, particularly on surfaces between exposed live parts of opposite polarity and between live parts and earthed metal where it forms a path of low resistance resulting in leakage currents. This may in time result in carbonisation of the deposit and of the surface of the insulation, and eventually a burn-out. Secondly, the ventilating ducts may become clogged with dirt, thereby obstructing or restricting the free flow of ventilating air. The machine temperatures will increase and if not remedied insulation failure will ultimately occur. Machines should therefore be kept as clean as possible in service.

As the inner parts are inaccessible they should be periodically dismantled and thoroughly cleaned. In oil-lubricated machines care should be taken to prevent any leakage of oil into the machine, for instance by way of the shaft.

For cleaning insulated windings the recognised practice is to use carbon-tetrachloride but certain precautions are necessary. This is toxic and care must be taken not to inhale the vapour; fatalities have resulted from failure to take precautions. If large quantities or a long process is involved a small portable ventilating fan may be found advantageous.

Carbon-tetrachloride is a powerful solvent and must therefore be used with discretion. Heavy deposits of dirt should first be removed by brushing or scraping, using a wooden (not metal) scraper, or by compressed air, reserving carbon-tetrachloride for finally cleaning the surface. Excess fluid should be wiped off and deposits of fluid in crevices should be avoided. If the customary high lustre on varnished surfaces has been destroyed there is a danger that the moisture-resisting properties of the varnish may have been impaired, and the surfaces should be re-varnished, using a good quality insulating varnish. Make sure that the carbon-tetrachloride has completely dried off before varnishing.

Commutator brushes, if of carbon or graphite, should be maintained at a pressure of between $9-13$ kN/m² in machines of normal design. In special cases $17-20$ kN/m² may be necessary particularly in machines subject to severe overloads or machines subjected to vibration. If metal graphite brushes are involved higher pressures are recommended, with minimum pressures of the order $17-20$ kN/m². The principle in either case is not to use a higher pressure than experience shows to be necessary. The pressure can be measured by a spring balance and it is good practice to measure the pressure and get familiar with the 'feel'.

The polarity of commutator poles follows the opposite rule to that of generators (see Figure 3.5); that is to say for a motor the commutating pole must have the same polarity as the main pole which *precedes* it according to the direction of rotation.

If for any reason it is difficult to find the netural position for the brushes of a d.c. machine the following method may be used, the machine being at rest.

(*a*) Connect a low-reading voltmeter between two adjacent brush arms, with the armature on open circuit.

(*b*) Connect the shunt winding to a suitable supply and adjust the current to about 25% of its normal value. A substantial switch capable of breaking an inductive arc must be connected in this circuit.

(c) Note the induced voltage on the voltmeter connected across the brush arms when the field circuit is quickly made or opened.

(d) Rock the brushes until the position is found which gives minimum voltage kick. This is the neutral position.

(e) Repeat the test with the armature rotated to two or three other positions and adopt the mean of the neutral positions thus found.

With grease-packed ball or roller bearings trouble is often caused by an excessive supply of grease. They should not be more than one-third to a half full of grease, but as it is impossible to determine this on an assembled machine the best course to follow is to leave them undisturbed if they are operating without undue noise or heating. If packed too tight they will run hot. The grade of grease recommended by the manufacturer should be used and a good grease should last six to twelve months. Fan motors in refrigerated compartments require special consideration. Not only must they operate at freezing temperatures but they must also run at tropical temperatures when cooling down cargo spaces in tropical waters. This represents a very wide range of operating temperature and accordingly requires special greases.

Commutation troubles may be due to a wide variety of causes such as high bars, low bars or flats, rough or grooved commutator, eccentric commutator, high micas, vibration, short-circuits or open circuits in the armature or commutator connections, inadequate clearance in brush-holders, imperfect bedding of brushes, incorrect brush position, incorrect spacing of the brushes circumferentially, incorrect brush pressure, unsuitable grade of brush, unequal air-gaps due to worn bearings, defective main field or commutating pole or incorrect pole strength, unequal current distribution due to unequal resistance of brush arms and interconnections, faulty or inadequate armature equaliser connections.

Single-phasing

Single phasing is the term used to denote the condition arising in a three-phase circuit when one phase becomes open-circuited. Much has been written on this topic and while some writers will assert that it is one of the commonest causes of burn-outs in motors, others, from their own experience, will deny this. The correct answer is probably that unless strict precautions are taken it can easily be the cause of failures.

The facts are simple and straightforward. When the supply to one phase of a three-phase motor with delta-connected stator fails we have the condition shown in Figure 11.7 where winding A receives full-line volts and windings B and C are in series.

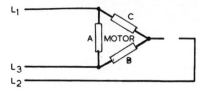

Figure 11.7 Three-phase motor with one phase open-circuited

Tests taken on a 10-h.p. motor under these conditions showed results as indicated in Figure 11.8 in which the percentage currents in the line and in the windings are plotted against the percentage currents with a normal three-phase supply.

If the motor is already running when the open circuit occurs it will continue to run on the single-phase supply but with the unbalanced distribution of current in the windings as shown. It will be seen that at 100% load the current in winding A is nearly three times its full-load current and in windings B and C it is about 30% above full load, while the line current is about 2.5 times full load. Under these conditions it would be expected that the overload protective devices would operate. But assume that the motor is only on 75% load at the time.

We then find that the line current is 50% above full load, so that if the overload protection is set to function above 50% overload it will not operate and the motor will continue running. Note however that the current in *A* is 80% above normal full load. Under these conditions the iron and rotor losses also increase, causing additional heating.

The torque developed by an induction motor is proportional to the flux and rotor current and as single-phasing causes a reduction in the flux, the rotor current and hence the stator current also increases if the same torque is to be maintained. Also as already shown the distribution of current in the windings is disturbed. The c.m.r. motor has a more limited overload capacity than c.r.p.o. motors and the setting of overload protective devices coupled with the need for single-phasing preventors assumes a new importance.

It is a vital principle that the cause of every breakdown should be sought in order to obviate subsequent failures. In the case of a.c. motors some guidance on the effects of single-phasing will enable this type of failure to be discriminated from burn-outs due to overloading.

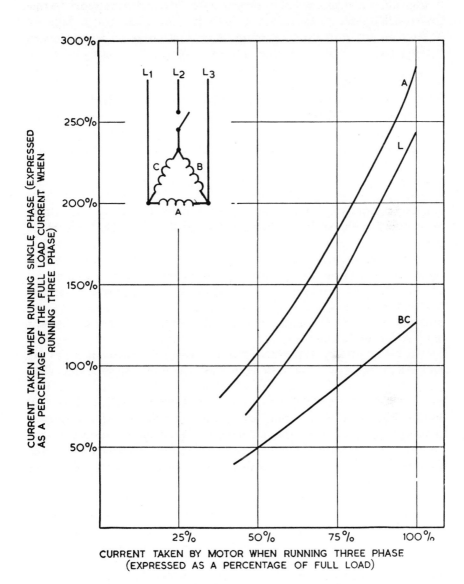

Figure 11.8 Curve showing division of current under single-phasing conditions
L. Line current in the unbroken lines L_1 and L_2
BC. Current in windings B and C
A. Current in winding A.

It is probable that single-phasing is more often the cause of failure than overloading.

Damage to the stator windings is characterised by uneven over-heating, the coils of either one or of two phases showing signs depending on whether the motor is star or delta connected. With two-layer windings the signs of concentrated overheating will be modified by the position of the coils and will be most marked with full pitch coils as each slot will then contain two coil-sides of the same phase. The number of poles comprising the winding can be determined from the speed and if single-phasing has occurred the damaged windings will be symmetrically spaced with angular spacing according to the number of poles. For example with a 4-pole motor there would be four symmetrically spaced zones.

Under single-phase conditions the motor will develop no starting torque and in the stalled condition the rotor will develop high rotor bar currents in positions corresponding to the number of poles. The healthy phase will produce a pulsating sinusoidal flux with con-centrated rotor heating. If this heating has melted the brazing metal or the rotor bars it will be evident from the appearance of the molten material whether failure occurred when stalled or when running, as under the latter condition centrifugal action will affect the distribution of metal.

It is by no means certain that a motor will continue running as the available torque will be less than half the three-phase value. The maximum torque demanded by BS 2949 is 1.75 × F.L.T. for motors above 50 h.p. up to 500 h.p. so a motor designed to this limit will deliver less than F.L. under single-phase conditions. If the pheno-mena existing under these conditions is analysed, resolving the vectorial components will reveal vectorial voltage components having positive, negative and zero sequences producing a forward rotating field and a reverse rotating field. The net result is an increased slip. With loads such as centrifugal fans, and pumps, for which torque is proportional to the square of the speed, equilibrium may be estab-lished at a reduced speed and the motor may continue running, assuming that the single-phasing occurs after the motor has been running. A complete and scientific analysis of the problem is com-plicated but sufficient has been said to indicate some of the prin-ciples involved.

To facilitate star-delta starting the majority of medium and small sized machines are supplied delta connected. The change from c.r.p.o. to c.m.r. ratings, increasing economic pressure to get the most out of machines, reduction in dimensions and weight all result in reduced design margins. Pump manufacturers know to a nicety what h.p. they require and they are encouraged not to overpower because this affects power-factor with the result that motors now operate much nearer their full-load rating than formerly.

Protection against single-phasing is dealt with in the following chapter.

12 Motor control gear

The 1960's saw radical changes in motor control gear for ship applications owing to the rapid change from d.c. distribution to a.c. Furthermore the advent of solid state devices thyristors, thermistors, etc. greatly influenced this trend, see Chapter 13. A trend away from magnetic protective relays in favour thermal types also occurred. An increase in the demand for automatic control will restrict the future of manually-operated starters. This chapter is mainly concerned with a.c. systems.

D.C. motors

In d.c. distribution systems, starters for d.c. motors can be of the traditional faceplate type or the drum type. In the former (see Figures 12.1 and 12.2) the contact arm is spring biassed to the off

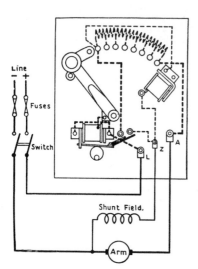

Figure 12.1 Starter for shunt- or compound-wound motor ('Off' position)

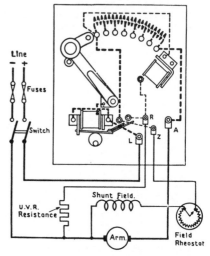

Figure 12.2 Starter for variable-speed shunt- or compound-wound motor with separately excited under-voltage coil and plain series-connected field rheostat

position and is retained in the running position by an electro-magnet which is either in series with the motor shunt field or is separately excited. An overload release coil in the motor circuit functions by shortcircuiting the low-volt release coil.

Where remote stopping is required a separately excited retaining coil is preferred (see Figure 12.2) in conjunction with a normally closed pushbutton. An alternative method is to use the arrangement shown in Figure 12.1 and a normally open pushbutton which is connected to short-circuit the retaining coil. This method is not to be recommended as the retaining coil has a low resistance and the shortcircuiting path must have a correspondingly low resistance. Any failure in the tripping circuit such as a broken connection will remain undetected until operation is required, thus offending the 'fail safe' rule.

For large motors and for heavy duties a drum type starter is appropriate, particularly where frequent starting or speed regulation is required such as for winches, i.e. cranes etc. For still heavier duties or where automatic operation by pushbutton, float switch, pressure switch, thermostat, etc is required contactor type starters will be necessary.

Alternative methods of controlling the rate of closing successive contactors in order to limit the accelerating current are available. Counter-e.m.f. systems depend on the rate at which the armature e.m.f. builds up. With current-limit control systems each contactor is locked out by the current peak resulting from the closing of the preceding contactor and is allowed to close only when the current falls to a predetermined value.

AC/DC motors

When a wide variation of speed is required from an a.c. supply a variable speed d.c. motor operated via a thyrister converter is appropriate, see Figure 12.3. It gives a fast response and is efficient. For

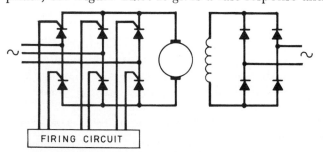

Figure 12.3 AC/DC motor circuits

small motors up to about 10 h.p. it can be adapted for single phase supplies.

For fixed shunt field applications the field is usually supplied from a single-phase supply through a diode bridge as shown. For variable field requirements the diode bridge would be replaced with a thyristor convertor.

A.C. motors

The great advantage of a.c. motors of the cage type is the facility of direct-on-line (d.o.l.) starting, i.e. without the use of external resistances. Nevertheless this introduces fresh problems for overload and shortcircuit protection because of the initial rush of starting current, usually of the order of 5 to 8 times full load current (f.l.c.). The protective device must be inoperative during the starting period but operative on normal moderate overloads and on short circuit and under stalled conditions.

Motors are now rated on a Continuous Maximum Rating (CMR) basis, i.e. they are not required to have any margin or capacity for continuous or prolonged overload operation. This entails overload protection at a low level, say 15% to 25% overloads for short periods. Overload protection should be set preferably at the working load current and not according to the motor current shown on the motor rating plate. Two speed change-pole motors require two overload relays to suit the f.l.c. of each speed.

Overload protection

Protective devices can be one or more of the following:
(i)   Magnetic overload relays;
(ii)   Thermal overload relays;
(iii) Protective devices built into the motor.

Thermal overload relays can be either bi-metal relays or fusible metal or solder-pot relays. The solder-pot type is rarely used in marine equipment.

Direct-on-line, at line voltage a.c. starters are dealt with in BS 4941 Pt 1. If the relay has a variable time-current feature the manufacturer is required to make available curves indicating how the tripping time, starting from cold, varies with current up to at least 8 times f.l.c. The ambient air temperature on which they are based must also be stated, preferably at +20°C or at +40°C. For marine applications +40°C would be preferred.

D.O.L. starters are not designed to interrupt short-circuit currents so suitable short-circuit protection must form part of the installation and not necessarily in the starter. It is usually accomplished by fuses in the supply circuit.

One of the difficulties encountered in designing an overload relay which can be set at, say, 15% to 25% overload after a short time interval is to prevent it from tripping on high starting currents before the starting operation has completed. The methods available will be dealt with later but there are two methods available which are external to the relay. The first is to leave the relays out of circuit until the starter is in the running position. This is sometimes done for centrifuge drives which have considerable inertia and long starting times of the order of 45 s to 60 s. The second method, more widely used is to feed the relays from current transformers having magnetic circuits designed to become saturated at about two to four times f.l.c. Although the line current may exceed these values the current in the relay coil will be restricted.

Protection provided in the starter is intended primarily for protection against the results of mechanical overloading of the motor except that for 3-phase motors the starter may also protect against the effects of single-phasing. Excess currents can also be the result of low voltage.

Direct-on-line starters rated for ordinary duty are required by BS 587 to be suitable for maximum motor starting times equal to 3 + h.p./10 s with a maximum of 15 s. Ratings are based on full line voltage starting current at standstill not exceeding 8 × f.l.c. for motors up to 100 h.p. and 6 × f.l.c. for motors over 100 h.p.

Bi-metal thermal overload relays

The elements of the bi-metal relays are susceptible to changes in ambient air temperature and some manufacturers incorporate temperature compensation in the design. Opinions differ as to the method by which correction should be made. One contention is that as it is the final temperature and not the temperature rise which is the determining factor in the life of the winding insulation, the relay should take into account the ambient temperature in such a way that it will trip at a lower value as the ambient temperature rises. By this means the motor will be disconnected at an approximately constant final temperature irrespective of the rise above ambient.

With the modern practice of grouping starters at a point remote from the motors, wide differences of temperature can exist between the environment of the relay and that of the motor and this renders such compensation ineffectual. Consequently, by making operation independent of ambient temperature it will always trip at the set value of current, which can be that which produces the maximum permissible winding temperature under the worst ambient condition.

The advantage of thermal relays compared with magnetic types is that they can be designed to follow approximately the motor heating curve and their ability to store heat. The latter property protects the motor from overheating when it is started too frequently or becomes subject to a succession of relatively small overloads of short duration whilst running. Should the relay operate the motor cannot be re-started until the thermal elements have cooled down. This however is not advantageous when circumstances demand an immediate restart regardless of temperature considerations.

Magnetic overload relays

These are of the solenoid type consisting of an iron plunger surroun-ded by a coil — one for each phase protected. The coil carries line current or a proportion of it if current transformers are used. At the predetermined value the plunger is attracted to the centre of the coil and a pushrod actuates a trip bar which opens an auxiliary contact in an operating coil circuit or actuates a mechanical latch. Adjustment of the trip current setting is by raising or lowering the plunger.

To prevent instantaneous tripping on momentary overloads, or on starting currents, a time lag device is attached to each plunger. This can be either a mechanical escapement or an oil dashpot, but is more usually the latter.

The time lag for all forms of oil dashpots is dependent also on the viscosity of the grade of oil used and this in turn is further affected by temperature. Silicone fluids are advantageous as their viscosity is less affected by temperature.

Magnetic overload relays are quicker acting than thermal types and therefore more suitable for a drive in which jamming is liable to occur. They are simpler in construction and less easily upset by unskilled or careless maintenance. Maintenance should not be so neglected that the dashpot becomes corroded or sludged. (See also Chapter 4, Figure 4.6, for typical time/temperature correction).

BS 587 requires magnetic trips to be capable of being set up to 15% above f.l.c. with a permissible tolerance of ±10%. This means that the actual tripping current can be 115% + 10% = 126.5 f.l.c. a condition not to be overlooked by users.

Thermal trips operate on a different basis. They are required to conform to a characteristic curve provided by the manufacturer, again with a tolerance of ± 10%. BS 4941, Part 1 stipulates no tripping in 2 h from cold at 105% f.l.c. and tripping in less than 2 h if the current is subsequently increased to 120% f.l.c.

Temperature sensing devices

Magnetic and thermal protective relays depend on sensing currents or current changes and cannot deal with overheating conditions which are not due to current alone. Circumstances which result in overheating without influencing current are too numerous to be catalogued here. To mention but a few would include lack of normal cooling such as blocked air vents, excessive local ambient temperatures and persistent periods of overloading.

Temperature sensing systems built into the motor windings, particularly thermistor probes provide for these conditions but for best all-round protection overload relays should also be incorporated. Thermal protection is not effective against all faults and abnormal conditions.

BS 4999, Part 72, deals with built-in thermal protection for motors rated at 660 V a.c. and below and in its introduction contains much useful advice. Current-operated relays related to the rated f.l.c. can be adjusted but the built-in systems are tailormade to suit the thermal properties of each machine and are not adjustable. A level of protection has to be chosen to accommodate the highest cooling air temperature condition and the maximum permissible temperature rise. The effective life of winding insulation is approximately halved for every 8–10% increase in continuous operating temperature. Control units are available which will give a warning signal when a chosen temperature below the tripping level is reached.

It will be appreciated that built in thermal protective devices are not usually a feature of standard machines and should be specially ordered when required. This form of protection is usually provided by thermistors attached to, or embodied in, the motor end-windings. The method generally acceptable is to use one thermistor in each phase section of the winding thus providing three thermistors in a normal machine. In change-pole machines, however, three devices for each speed would be required. Usually they are all connected in series.

Thermistors have an extremely large temperature coefficient, i.e. large changes in ohmic resistance with change of temperature. The usual tolerance for resistance at the reference point is ± 10% to ± 20% and because of variation in rate of change a substantial difference in operating temperature remote from the reference point may well develop. If a thermistor has to be renewed it will therefore be necessary to recalibrate. They are physically small and suitable for surface measurements of electric windings. Life expectancy is unlimited when operated within their temperature and power ratings.

Thermistors carry very small currents, a few mA only in the cold condition reducing to one-tenth or less when hot. They cannot be used directly in relay circuits so it is necessary to provide a separate system which will respond to the characteristics of the thermistor and yet provide a switching operation. This can be a solid state system with the thermistor giving the final switching component. It must be such that it is not sensitive to any pick up or capacitive effect in the connecting leads. The leads from the thermistors are very light, usually 7/.0076 flexibles and when motors are dismantled for maintenance purposes damage to a lead may occur.

It is a wise precaution therefore to connect each thermistor lead to a terminal so that in the event of damage to any of the thermistors or their leads it can be shorted out. Under these conditions, with only one or two thermistors remaining in service the degree afforded against single-phasing may be reduced but protection against other causes of overheating will remain.

Although thermistors capable of handling larger operating currents are available they are considered bulky and expensive.

An alternative system of operation is by means of a bridge network which is in balance under normal winding temperatures but unbalances and operates a control relay when an excessive temperature is reached.

Alternatives to thermistors are thermo-couples and thermostats. Thermostats would usually be attached to the external surface of windings, introducing an air space and also they sense only the temperature of the external surface which is not the hottest point. The alternative to attachment would be a cavity in the winding. An advantage is that they can operate directly on control gear without additional equipment.

Protection against single-phasing

The commonest cause of single-phasing is the blowing of one of the three fuses protecting the circuit. Filled cartridge fuses should invariably be used but reliable makes can be overloaded almost to fusing point without deterioration. They can also be regarded as calibrated fuses, i.e. variations between fuses of the same make are comparatively small.

However notwithstanding this it is prudent and sound practice when replacing fuses to replace all three. If any of the replaced fuses are still intact they can be transferred to another use such as a lighting circuit where matching is not vital. Fuse clips and connections should be examined when renewing fuses as an overheated contact may cause operation below the correct value.

Low-volt releases do not necessarily provide protection against single-phasing. Depending on which phase has failed a low-volt release may still be fed from the healthy phase. Also depending on where the failure has occurred the low-volt release may be fed by voltage induced in the motor.

Overheating will occur in star connected machines continuing to run single-phase but in these cases the line current is the same as that in the windings and there is a better chance that the overload relay will operate. It should be remembered that with either method of connection i.e. star or delta a motor can continue to run on single-phase but after stopping it will not restart. Also, depending on the loading and the setting of the overload relay a motor may stall and eventually burn out. Pilot lamps connected across one phase may continue to show for the same reason that a low-volt relay may continue and thus indicate 'live' if they happen to be across the healthy phase.

Some of these contingencies may be counteracted to a limited extent if the overload protection is set fairly low, say at 15% with a suitable time lag to prevent operation during starting but the most reliable is some form of single-phase protective device.

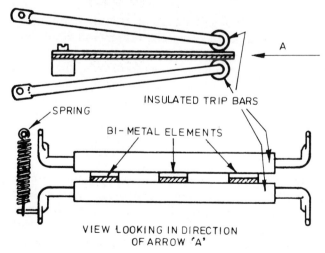

Figure 12.4 Diagrammatic arrangement of bi-metal elements of EAC thermal overload relay and single phasing preventer

One type of protection takes the form of three bi-metal thermal strips, one in each phase (see Figure 12.4), the ends of which project between two parallel guides, one fixed and the other movable and spring controlled. All three strips can respond in unison to a balanced three phase overload but one or two of the strips will act independently in the event of single-phasing. This action is accentuated by the open-circuited phase cooling off and thereby deflecting in the opposite direction. This unit is compensated for ambient temperature so will always trip at the same current irrespective of ambient temperature.

An alternative method, suitable for star-delta starting, is to connect overload relays in the delta connection in series with each winding. In systems with earthed neutral single-phasing will occur if a fuse blows due to an earth fault on one line.

Star-delta starter

After d.o.l. starting the next most common method is by the star-delta method. Both ends of each phase of the motor starter windings must be brought out and connected to the starter. In the start position the windings are connected in star; in the running position they are reconnected in delta. The voltage across each phase winding in the start position is 58% of line voltage with consequent reduction of starting current. The starting torque is also reduced to one-third of that which would obtain with d.o.l. starting (see Figure 12.5). With a single cage or a double cage rotor of average performance this represents about 80% of full load torque assuming normal line voltage but if there is appreciable line drop the torque will be proportionately lower. These factors must be taken into account when deciding whether star-delta starting is acceptable for the driven machine. It will be acceptable for centrifugal fans and pumps if, in the latter case, the stiction at starting is not excessive.

With centrifugal loads the motor can be accelerated to approximately 75% to 85% of full speed on the star connection which is the point at which curves of motor torque and load torque will cross. At or before this point the motor must be switched to the delta connection. This must be done as rapidly as possible because the motor is momentarily disconnected during transition and therefore delivers no torque. When the delta connection is established the motor will draw line current corresponding to its speed, which at about 80% speed will usually be about 3½ times f.l.c.

When this transition from star to delta is made transient effects are likely to occur. During this brief interval the rotor flux does not instantaneously collapse and e.m.f's are induced in the stator winding. When the stator is reconnected in delta the supply may be considerably out of phase in relation to the induced e.m.f's and violent current surges may set up depending on the amount of displacement. These disturbances reflect on the supply system and may

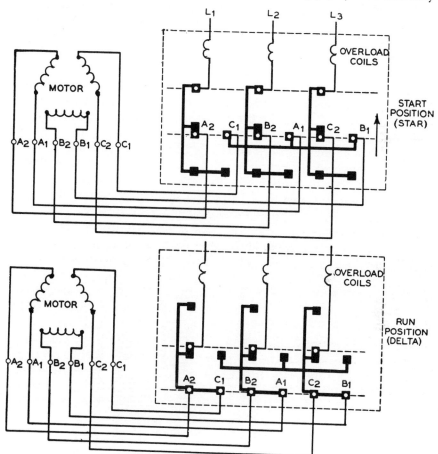

Figure 12.5 Star-delta starter

reach 2½ to 5 times the motor starting current and may persist for several cycles. This phenomenon does not occur at every start and is most likely to occur with manually operated starters if there is a delay in the transition stage. Automatic star-delta starters usually embody an electronic timer with adjustable timing on the star connection and with a short but definite time delay at the change-over. A similar phenomenon may occur with a two-speed or three-speed change-pole motor when switching from one connection to the other, particularly if a rapid deceleration of the drive occurs.

The maximum line current in the six connections to the motor can be taken as 58% of f.l.c. and the size of cables, subject to line drop, can be determined accordingly.

Vacuum contactors

Growth in the size of motors, particularly for such as cargo pumps, bow thrusters, etc is such that the size and capacity of medium voltage machines, cables and switchgear in marine installations tends to become uneconomical and 3.3 kV and 6.6 kV supplies become more attractive. A study of the problem for industrial applications indicated a changeover point from medium to high voltage to be advantageous in the region of 100 to 200 kW particularly where d.o.l starting is involved. Limitations of short-circuit ratings at medium voltage must also be considered. But the higher voltages also bring about other factors such as the physical size and space required for 3.3 kV and 6.6 kV air-break contactors and circuit breakers and their arc chutes. A comparison of the sizes is illustrated in Figure 12.6.

The vacuum contactor relies for its effect on the relative dielectric strength of vacuum; a small open gap is adequate and contact travel

Figure 12.6 Comparison of vacuum contactor and conventional contactor both suitable for 300A 3.3 kV operation (GEC Industrial Controls Ltd.)

is short. For 3.3 kV a travel of approximately 2 mm is sufficient. Current breaking takes place within the switch so there are no arc chutes and no ionized or other products of arcing to contend with.

The principles of vacuum switching have long been recognised but practical application has been delayed by difficulties of cleansing and assembling compatible insulation and metals having negligible included gases so that a vacuum below 10^{-4} torr can be maintained for periods of up to 20 years. This high degree of vacuum is essential for effective operation. For more than twelve years vacuum contactors have been thoroughly tried out in active service, coupled with research into the behaviour of different contact metals.

Separation of the contacts to break circuit causes an arc to be formed which vaporises metal on the contact surfaces but when the current falls to zero on the a.c. waveform this vapour condenses on the metal contact and current is interrupted. The arcing period does not exceed one half cycle. The fixed and moving contacts are sealed in a tubular envelope of glass or ceramic (see Figure 12.7). A sputter shield surrounds the contacts to prevent any stray arcing material depositing on the envelope and thus preventing a conducting path

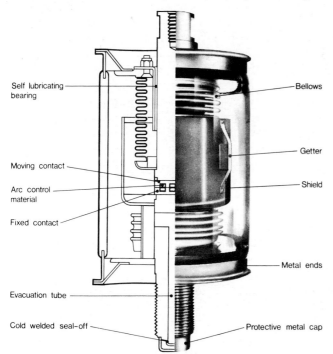

Figure 12.7 Sectional view of a typical vacuum switch (GEC Industrial Controls Ltd.)

from forming. Glass is favoured for the envelope due to the ease of forming a seal with the metal end caps.

Stainless steel bellows are provided to allow travel of the moving contact element while maintaining the vacuum intact. Atmospheric pressure outside the bellows is towards closure of the contacts. This pressure is overcome by springs opposing atmospheric pressure. They must be strong enough to hold the contactor in the open position and to maintain this until an operating coil has been energised at a voltage not less than 85% of normal. The design must also be such that any tendency of the contacts to bounce must be eradicated.

The provision of what are known as 'getters' originated with radio valves and their purpose in vacuum contactors is to provide means for absorbing gas molecules which may remain after evacuation or which are occluded in materials utilised in the construction and which are subsequently released. Barium is an active material comprising getters but not all designs are gettered.

Two forms of vacuum switching have been developed, viz. a contactor type suitable for frequent switching such as for motor starting, having a low 'chop' current and a circuit breaker type able to break fault currents for a limited number of times.

Current chopping is a phenomenon causing high induced transient voltage surges caused by abrupt interruption of current and can cause damage to cables, transformers and motors. A low current chop is attained if the current is always broken close to zero on the a.c. wave-form. The value of current at which the arc extinguishes must be kept as low as possible. In vacuum contactors this is determined to a large extent by the properties of the metal contacts. The aim is to maintain the arc as closely as practicable to the next zero in the waveform. Vacuum switches are available.

Under-voltage protection

Interruption of supply will cause the motors to stop and it is necessary to disconnect them so that on restoration of supply they are not immediately switched on, for the following reasons:

(a) Operating personnel may be injured due to a motor starting unexpectedly.

(b) With certain a.c. motors a definite sequence of starting operations must be gone through.

(c) If all the motors were to re-start simultaneously the generators might be seriously overloaded.

(d) Certain adjustments to the driven machinery may be necessary before re-starting.

For these reasons under-voltage release is necessary although it is not feasible in all cases. For instance automatic starters under the control of float switches or pressure switches, thermostats, etc., will re-start immediately, but as personnel will be aware of this they are not likely to be caught. However, if really necessary, even these can be locked out after a supply failure.

Except for the automatically controlled services mentioned and for a.c. motors, the continuous availability of which is essential to the safety of the ship, it is required that all starters be arranged for under-voltage release.

Although control gear, and contactors in particular, will function to close a circuit with the supply voltage reduced to 80% of normal for d.c. and 85% for a.c. as required by British Standards, nevertheless once they are closed they will hold on with very much lower voltages down to two-thirds of normal and in some cases much lower. With an induction motor, the available torque is proportional to the square of the voltage so that at two-thirds voltage the torque available will have fallen to about 40%. It will therefore most probably stall, causing considerable increase in stator current. Such drastic reductions in voltage although rare are not unknown and when they occur an immediate inspection of all running plant should be made. If it is thought necessary to provide against such a contingency under-voltage relays can be provided.

Three-phase A.C. starters

Direct-on-line starting is the method most commonly used, the most usual consideration being whether the generator and the distribution system can withstand the starting current. In the case of loads involving considerable inertia, such for instance as centrifugal oil separators, the starting time may also be a factor and in case of doubt the motor manufacturer should be consulted.

The starting current as we have already seen may be five to eight times the full-load current and the heating of the windings is proportional to the square of the current. At starting it will therefore be 25 to 64 times normal. Furthermore at the instant of start there is no windage and no radiation. There is a definite value of current at each speed, and therefore a very long starting period may result in overheating. Representative maximum safe starting periods may be taken as between 15 s for a 2-h.p. motor and 25 s for a 40-h.p. motor, with an initial starting current of not more than six times full-load current.

For these reasons also it is undesirable to make repeated successive starts without intervening periods for cooling.

Auto-transformer starter

The auto-transformer starter is more expensive than the two types so far described and is generally only used for the larger types of motor. It is suitable for motors in which each end of the three phases is not brought out, and which would therefore be unsuitable for star-delta starting. The starting conditions depend on the position of the tapping on the transformer winding, i.e. on the secondary voltage. Usually three or more tappings are provided so that there is a choice of starting conditions such as 40, 60 or 75% of line voltage.

From what has been said previously the starting torques on these different tappings can be estimated being proportional to the square of the voltage Figures 12.8(a) and (b). On the 60% tapping the torque will be approximately the same as with star-delta starting and on the 40% and 75% it will be proportionately lower and higher respectively.

The method of starting is similar to the star-delta method; the motor is first switched to the tapping and when it has accelerated sufficiently it is switched to the running or full voltage position (Figure 12.9).

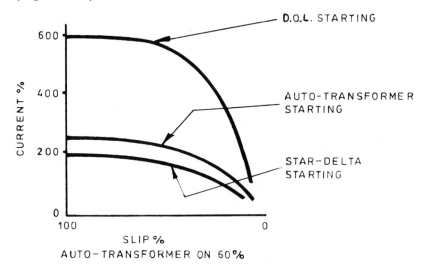

Figure 12.8(a) Comparison of motor starting currents

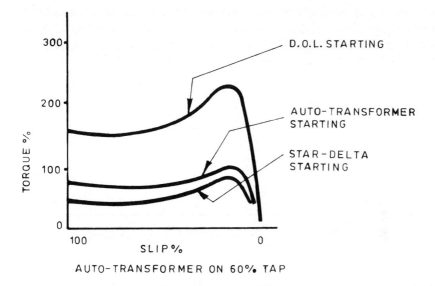

Figure 12.8(b) Comparison of motor starting currents

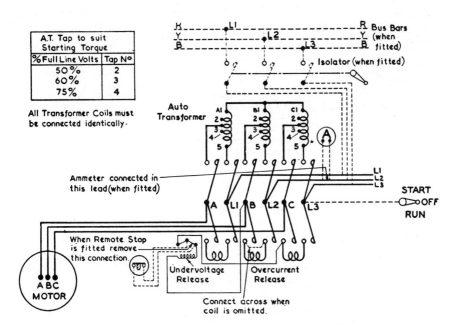

Figure 12.9 Typical diagram of connections of auto-transformer starter

Current surges similar to those experienced with star-delta starters are liable to occur if the connection to the stator is broken when switching from the tapping to full-line voltage. To overcome this disadvantage what is known as the Korndorfer method is now commonly used. The connections are shown diagrammatically in Figure 12.10.

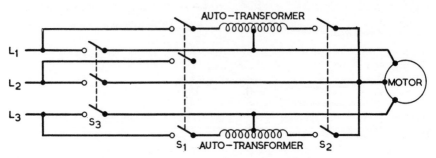

Figure 12.10 Auto-transformer starting by the Korndorfer method

S_1 closes first and part of the transformer winding is in circuit and acts as a choke; then S_2 closes and the motor is connected at reduced voltage. When the motor has accelerated S_2 is opened and S_3 closes. S_1 is now opened and the motor is connected to full-line voltage without interruption of supply.

The windings of the auto-transformer are short-time rated and the starting period must not be unduly prolonged. The rating for 'ordinary' duty is suitable for not more than two starts per hour, with starting periods not exceeding 6 + bhp/15 s on the 75% tap or higher, or 8 + bhp/8 s on the 60% tap or lower. After two consecutive starts a minimum subsequent cooling period of 60 min is necessary. If more frequent starting is required, starters rated for 'intermittent' duty (15 starts per hour) or 'frequent' duty (40 starts per hour) should be specified.

Rotor starters (rotors or slipring motors)

For high starting torques with low starting current a slipring motor is suitable, and it is started with resistance connected across the sliprings. The usual arrangement is to switch the stator on with the rotor starter in the 'off' or open-circuit position. The starter then closes the rotor circuit and cuts out resistance until the motor is up to speed. Speed regulation can be obtained with a suitable regulator or drum controller, with resistances rated according to the service conditions required.

Where speed regulation is not required it is usual to provide the motor with a short-circuiting device whereby the sliprings can be short-circuited when the motor is up to speed. As this switch must be in the open position before re-starting it is provided with interlocking contacts so that the stator switch cannot be re-closed with the sliprings short-circuited. In such cases it is also unnecessary for the rotor starter to be fitted with no-volt release and spring return, as it can be similarly interlocked with the stator switch or contactor.

Incorrect phase connections

It is very important, particularly after an overhaul or on new installations, to make sure that phase connections are correct. Otherwise the motor rotation will be wrong and damage may be done to the driven machine.

In the case of all-electric steering gear, lifts, hoists, planers, etc., in which the rotation in any case is reversible, it is equally important as, should the lift cage or steering gear be driven in the wrong direction the limit switches may not afford protection. For instance, if the lift cage travels up instead of down the top limit switch will open the control circuit which is not energised and the motor will not be stopped.

BS 822 for phase sequence i.e. the order in which the terminal voltages attain their maximum values of the same polarity, is for generators such that when the machine is driven with clockwise rotation when looking at (facing) its driven end the terminal phase sequence will be in the order A, B, C. (For colour marking the sequence is Red, Yellow, Blue.) When driven anticlockwise the sequence will be C, B, A. For single-speed 3-phase motors the terminals will be so marked A, B and C that when connected to a supply giving a terminal phase sequence in the order A, B, C, the rotation will be clockwise when viewed at (facing) its driving end. Anticlockwise rotation can be obtained and when connection to the supply is such that the phase sequence of the motor terminals is in the order C, B, A.

Incorrect motor connections

If a motor is designed for delta-connected windings it must not be connected so that the motor runs star-connected. By doing so the current in the windings would be three times the design value, but the line current will be normal, and the overload protection will therefore not protect the motor.

Synchros

'Synchro' is the lesser-known generic term for a system more generally
known as Selsyn and Magslip.

A synchro is a unit, similar in appearance to a slipring induction motor, which has a three-phase star-connected stator winding
and a two-pole rotor with a single winding brought out to sliprings
as shown diagrammatically in Figure 12.11. The effect of altering the

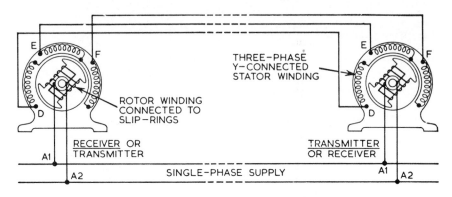

Figure 12.11 Connection diagram for transmitter and single receiver

angular position of one of the rotors (which then becomes the transmitter) is to cause currents to be induced in the other windings and
this results in a torque being generated in the other rotor or receiver.
The receiver then rotates until it assumes an angular position corresponding to that of the transmitter. We thus have a system in which a
transmitter can be placed in any desired position and a receiver some
distance away will automatically take up an exactly similar position.
The torque produced is comparatively small.

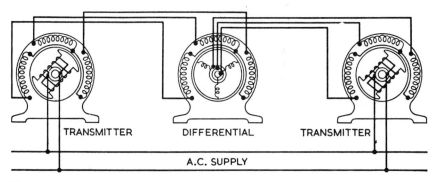

Figure 12.12 Connections for differential system

A further development of this principle is the differential synchro which is illustrated in Figure 12.12. In its simplest form it consists of three machines so designed that the motion of one is the algebraic sum of the motions of the other two. From Figure 12.12 it will be seen that two of the machines are the same as in Figure 12.11. The middle machine is the differential synchro and will function in the same manner with the exception that the relative angular positions of the two outer synchros when exerting no torque will depend upon the angular setting of the differential. Conversely if the differential synchro is free to rotate it will take up a position depending on the relative angular positions of the two outer synchros. The operation may be better appreciated from an example. If each of the transmitters is operated by a float forming part of a water-level indicator,

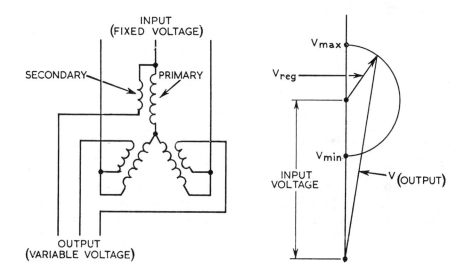

Figure 12.13 3-phase induction regulator (left) connections; (right) vector diagram

each in a separate tank, the differential synchro will indicate the difference in level between the two tanks. Similarly they can be used to indicate the difference in speed between two machines or shafts and if required the differential synchro can be coupled to a device controlling the speed of one of them in order to make both speeds identical.

Applications of synchros will be found in the descriptions of Sperry steering gear (Selsyns) in Chapter 16 and in Chapter 15 on Denny Brown Stabilisers (Magslips).

Induction regulators

An induction regulator gives voltage or phase variation and is based on the construction of the induction motor except that the constituent parts remain stationary. The angular position of the rotor can be adjusted but the rotor is not free to rotate.

In a 3-phase induction regulator the supply voltage is fed to both primary and secondary windings, the former being star connected and the secondary connected to the output terminals (Figure 12.13(a)) When connected to the supply a rotating magnetic field is set up which cuts the conductors of the secondary winding and induces an e.m.f. in them. The magnitude of the induced voltage remains constant but its phase angle in relation to the primary voltage can be varied by plus or minus the secondary voltage and at intermediate values as shown in Figure 12.13(b). The total movement of the rotor is 180° (elec.) and sliprings are unnecessary as the connections to the rotor winding can be made with flexibles. The primary winding may be on either the stator or the rotor, whichever is most convenient.

Maintenance of control gear

All moving contacts used in control gear have what is known as 'wipe' or follow through, that is to say if the fixed part were to be removed the moving part would follow on. In addition, particularly in the case of contactors, a rolling or sliding action takes place for which there are two motives, firstly to provide a cleaning action to remove any oxide which may have formed and thus ensure a good metal to metal contact, and secondly to provide that the point at which the contacts make and break and where roughening due to arcing occurs is away from the running position.

Contacts which make and break infrequently may never need more than an occasional cleaning but those which operate frequently, such as lifts, winches, windlasses, capstans, etc., may become so worn that not only is the contact bad but the 'wipe' is lost causing reduction of contact pressure, and overheating will occur. They must therefore be examined periodically and renewed in good time.

Provided the contact pressure is ample a rough contact surface may have a lower contact resistance than one in smooth new condition, so the file should be used sparingly and only on badly burnt and pitted contacts. A thin film of oil smeared on with an oily rag helps to reduce mechanical wear, but excess of oil or grease encourages burning and pitting. Mechanical wear on drum-type contacts can be considerably reduced by judicious greasing.

Silver-faced contacts and carbon contacts should not be lubricated. Copper contacts which have been closed for long periods tend to develop an oxide film which may cause overheating. When opportunity permits these contacts should be opened and operated several times to clean the contact surfaces.

Magnet faces should be kept clean and free from grease or oil and rust should be removed carefully with fine emery, making sure that metal particles are carefully removed and in no event deposited on contacts or insulation. See that the moving parts are free and without undue wear at pivots, and that magnets are bedding properly. The faces of a.c. magnets should on no account be filed.

13 Semi-conductor diodes

The developments which have taken place during the past few years leading to the availability of such types as the selenium, silicon and germanium diodes have proved a great asset in the trend towards a.c. They have replaced mercury arc rectifiers (never very suitable for use in ships) for many applications ashore and the consequent increase in manufacturing facilities also benefits shipping.

D.C. is still essential for some services such as battery charging, control of magnetic amplifiers and cathodic protection and is also advantageous for generator excitation, operating coils for contactors, etc.

Investigations have shown that in an a.c. installation instead of providing d.c. requirements from a central source, such as a motor-generator set, in certain cases a saving of up to 5.0% in cost and up to 40% in weight and volume can be effected by providing each auxiliary with its own local rectifier. In this estimation the elimination of the central d.c. switchboard was also taken into account.

The copper oxide rectifier which first became available commercially in 1925, gives way to the superior and more efficient types now available. Selenium followed ten years later, and germanium about 1952. Notwithstanding the outstanding progress and standards of efficiency and reliability which have now been reached semi-conductor techniques are still in their infancy and developments continue.

To explain satisfactorily the functioning of semi-conductors would be a lengthy and abstruse process involving atomic structures, so a simple version must suffice. Solids used for electical purposes can be divided roughly into conductors, semi-conductors and insulators. The gap between conductors and insulators is enormous; for example, copper has a specific resistance of 1.59×10^{-6} compared with ebonite at 1×10^{16}. Midway between these extremes lie germanium 47 ohms and silicon 67 000 ohms.

It is only the electrons in the outer orbits of an atomic structure which decide the chemical valence, and for electrical conductivity only these electrons are considered free, and only free valence electrons can conduct current. A germanium atom, for example, has 32 electrons but only four of these are 'free'. Conduction in metals occurs because these outermost electrons can migrate freely from one atom to the next and for this their energy must be increased. Insulators have no free electrons to move in this manner and therefore they cannot conduct.

Semi-conductors have a very limited number of free electrons. Pure germanium conducts to a very limited extent and to make it suitable for electrical purposes a minute quantity of impurity must be introduced. For example the addition of arsenic in the proportion of one part in 10 million will increase its conductivity 15 times. Arsenic has 5 free electrons so 4 of these will combine with the 4 valence electrons of germanium, leaving a fifth free for conduction. The resultant conductor is called n-type because the current carried by electrons is negative. Antimony having 5 outer electrons can also serve this purpose.

If on the other hand an impurity such as aluminium or gallium having only 3 free electrons were used there would be a shortage for pairing off with the 4 in in the germanium crystal, and so leave what is termed a 'hole'. This type of semi-conductor is called p-type because it has positive characteristics. Silicon can be rendered n-type or p-type in the same manner.

To obtain the properties required for rectifiers, transistors, thyristers etc., diodes are formed by placing n-and p-types together, but not merely in contact. A *junction* must be formed so that the atomic crystal lattice between them is continuous.

When an electron in the n region (i.e. the cathode) is energised it moves and finds a hole in the p region but leaves a similar hole behind. The holes in the p region are not in fact thereby neutralised. As soon as this happens the holes from the p region are transferred to the n region which becomes positively charged, and the p region becomes negatively charged. This instantly prevents a further flow of charge across the junction, thus building up a potential barrier so that few charge carriers can cross unless they have sufficient energy. The existence of this potential barrier is as though a battery existed at the junction. If now a voltage of appropriate polarity is applied across the pn junction its effective resistance is built up and only a few microamps reverse current will flow. If the applied polarity is reversed the effective resistance of the potential barrier decreases and a forward current will flow. In an electrical circuit the movement of electrons is opposite to that of the conventional interpretation of current flow, i.e., electrons flow from cathode (n-type) to anode (p-type), but the current is said to flow from anode to cathode.

Conventional methods of illustrating semi-conductor diodes are shown in Figure 13.1, but it must be appreciated that in practice diodes consist of extremely thin wafers. If voltage is applied as at (a) current will flow readily in the direction of the arrow, and resistance to current flow will be low. If the polarity is reversed as at (b) resistance to current flow will be high and only a negligible

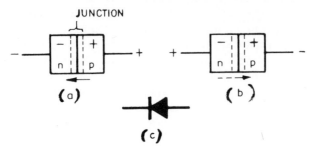

Figure 13.1 Semiconductor diodes

current will pass. It is evident from this that if an a.c. voltage is applied current will flow during one half-cycle but will be blocked during the other half-cycle. This is the basis of the semi-conductor rectifier. The conventional symbol is shown at (c).

Other combinations are also used such as for transistors which have 3 elements either *pnp* or *npn*. Thyristors have 4, i.e. *npnp*.

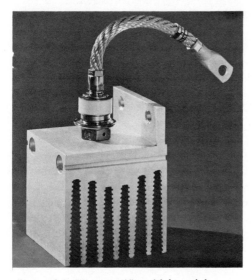

Figure 13.2 Silicon rectifier with heat sink

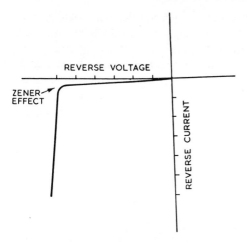

Figure 13.3 Typical characteristic of zener diode

When semi-conductors are required to be in circuit for any length of time the heat generated at the junction must be carried away, such as by a heat sink with radiating fins, by fan cooling, or by oil-immersion (see Figures 13.2 and 13.3). The necessity for controlling temperatures is not solely for physical reasons but also because important charges in operating properties such as 'thermal runaway' can be cumulative. If transformers or resistors are placed in the same enclosure they should be above and not below the diodes. Where forced air coolers or water coolers are provided they should be so arranged that the diodes cannot be loaded unless the cooling system is first started and subsequently maintained.

In all diodes there is a certain reverse voltage at which, if exceeded, breakdown will occur, and by providing a controlled impurity content the point at which this occurs can be controlled with great accuracy and can be as low as 1.5 V. Diodes so constructed are known as zener diodes. As shown in Figure 13.3 thre is a pronounced knee or break at what is known as the zener value. This phenomenon makes them invaluable as a voltage reference device for voltage regulators and for overvoltage protection.

A weakness of semi-conductor devices is their vulnerability to overvoltage and overcurrent, but provided that proper care and diligence are observed in designs, not only in the operational functions but in other factors, a very high degree of reliability over long periods can be ensured. The problem is accentuated by the fact that permanent damage can arise from transients of exceedingly short duration. Electronic gear connected in the diode circuitry and also in adjacent high power circuits in which rapid current changes or

switching transients may introduce surges or voltage peaks may
induce similar peaks in adjacent circuits. To minimise these effects it
is advisable to avoid running cables associated with diode circuits in
close proximity to those carrying power currents (see Chapter 20).

Malfunction of conventional machines and apparatus can as a rule
be observed or detected before ultimate failure but there is nothing
to indicate what has happened or is about to happen in solid-state
diodes. Only by judicious selection and knowledge of their characteristics can the very high reliability and simplicity of these devices
be fully guaranteed. They enter very largely into computer and data-
logging systems and the hieroglyphics and exclamation marks expres-
sive of computer bad language can be nothing compared with the
dire results of data-processing errors or the failure of electronic
control systems. In brushless a.c. generators it is common to incorporate two diodes in parallel in the revolving rectifier. If one of these
should open circuit the exciter will continue to function but there is
no indication of failure. If on the other hand a diode should short-
circuit a heavy current flows in this limb of the bridge, leading to
collapse of voltage or overloading of the exciter and the remaining
diodes. This is the most common type of diode failure. A fuse in
series with each diode will afford protection.

Environmental conditions

Although semi-conductors are mechanically rugged they can still be
damaged by shock, vibration or acceleration. They should accordingly
be so mounted that they will not be subjected to conditions beyond
their ratings and because of the large number of unknown quantities
involved a generous factor of ignorance should be allowed.

The effects of humidity can be accelerated by moisture traps i.e.
pockets of air not free to circulate. These can also become traps
for soldering flux and this in turn can lead to severe corrosion and
leakage. Moisture traps are particularly liable to occur in devices
mounted close to printed circuit boards and with certain types of
mounting pads.

Accelerated corrosion can occur in humid atmospheres due to
contact potentials between dissimilar metals. It is essential to ensure
that any metallic mounting or cooling fitting does not give rise to
undue potential differences.

Special precautions are necessary for devices connected in parallel,
e.g. for redundancy. If they are not adequately bonded thermally a
form of current hogging may occur leading to thermal instability and
possibly to catastrophic failure. If failure does not occur the effect

may pass unnoticed but reliability will be impaired. Devices in parallel should therefore be bonded thermally by being mounted close together on the same heat sink. Where this is impracticable the cooling requirements must take into account the maximum possible dissipation of each device under unbalanced conditions.

With extruded aluminium cooling structures difficulties can arise from formation of a surface oxide. The seating face should be cleaned abrasively under a coating of grease, the residue removed and the device mounted immediately. To improve heat transfer and inhibit corrosion it is usual to apply a light smear of a suitable paste e.g. a silicone heat sink compound.

Rectifiers

A typical construction for a silicon diode rectifier unit is shown in Figure 13.4. The diode is built upon a study of nickel plated copper and consists of a wafer of p-silicon on which the counter-electrode, a disc of antimony-doped gold is fused. It is in the junction between these that the blocking capacity of the diode occurs. To prevent mechanical stresses between the silicon wafer and the stud from damaging the former due to temperature changes, it is not brazed

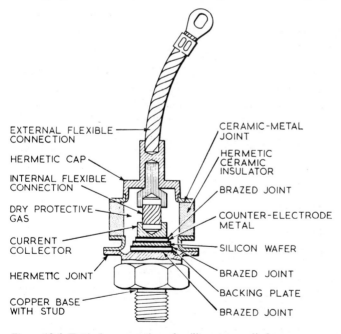

EXTERNAL FLEXIBLE CONNECTION

HERMETIC CAP

INTERNAL FLEXIBLE CONNECTION

DRY PROTECTIVE GAS

CURRENT COLLECTOR

HERMETIC JOINT

COPPER BASE WITH STUD

CERAMIC-METAL JOINT

HERMETIC CERAMIC INSULATOR

BRAZED JOINT

COUNTER-ELECTRODE METAL

SILICON WAFER

BRAZED JOINT

BACKING PLATE

BRAZED JOINT

Figure 13.4 Typical cross-section of a silicon power diode

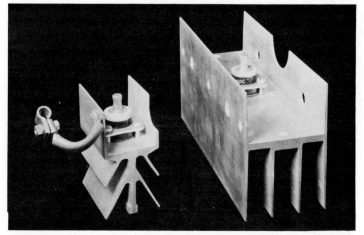

Figure 13.5 Rectifier cells on aluminium cooling fins (left) for fan cooling; (right) for natural cooling

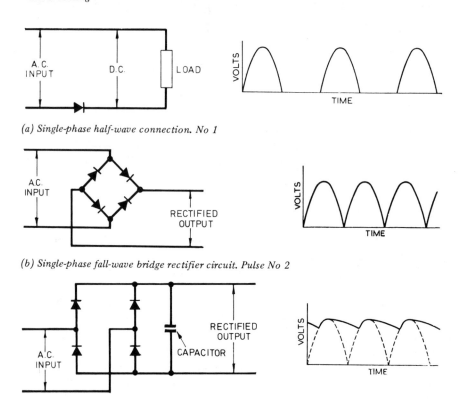

(a) Single-phase half-wave connection. No 1

(b) Single-phase fall-wave bridge rectifier circuit. Pulse No 2

(c) Single-phase full-wave bridge rectifier with capacitor acting across the output terminals. Pulse No 2

Figure 13.6 Typical rectifier circuits

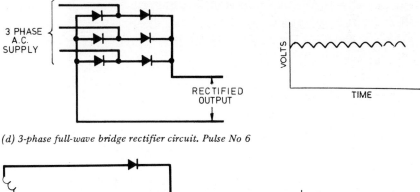

(d) 3-phase full-wave bridge rectifier circuit. Pulse No 6

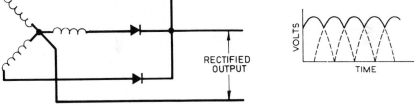

(e) 3-phase half-wave bridge connection with star-connected transformer secondary. Pulse No 3.

Figure 13.6 Typical rectifier circuits (continued)

directly to the stud but to a backing plate having the same coefficient of expansion. A flexible (internal) connection is brazed to the counter-electrode. The whole is hermetically sealed and enclosed with an atmosphere of dry nitrogen.

Some typical rectifier circuits are shown in Figure 13.6 from which it will be clear that the so-called d.c. is really an undirectional current containing ripples which are in effect a series of crests which pass through the rectifier from the a.c. side. Current in the other half-cycle would be of opposite polarity and is chopped off by the high resistance offered by the diode in this direction. This effect is shown more clearly in Figure 13.6 (a).

The pulse number is the number of these ripples or crests in the d.c. voltage during one cycle of the fundamental frequency of the supply. Thus in the 3-phase full-wave rectifier circuit shown in Figure 13.6 (d) there are 6 crests for every cycle of the primary supply and this circuit therefore has a pulse number of 6. By more complicated transformer secondary connections a pulse number of 12 can be obtained. In the diagrams the shape of the crests is shown as sinusoidal and corresponds to a theoretical rectifier having no losses, inductance or distortion; the actual shape, especially when loaded, will be slightly distorted.

Transformers for use with rectifiers require special characteristics and the standard specification for power transformers does not apply. If the rectifier is of a type subject to appreciable increase in forward resistance due to ageing, compensating taps or other means of adjustment should be provided.

Owing to the extremely low forward-voltage drop in germanium cells the transformer which supplies such rectifiers should have sufficient impedance to limit the prospective current under a d.c. short-circuit and as a general rule this is achieved with transformers of normal design with a correctly proportioned protective system. For use with selenium rectifiers, taps should be provided so that the reduction of d.c. voltage due to ageing can be corrected. The regulation of a rectifier is expressed in the same terms as for other electrical machinery and is the percentage increase in d.c. output voltage when the d.c. output current is reduced from full load to light load. It will vary for a given rectifier depending on whether it is rated at its maximum. Regulation will also depend on the circuitry adopted, i.e. whether full-wave, half-wave and so on. For example a 3-phase full-wave germanium rectifier may have an approximate regulation of 13.5% at its maximum current rating but this could be reduced to 5% if full load is one-third of its maximum rating.

D.C. loads which regenerate, i.e. return power to the system, can have serious effects on rectified supplies as the rectifier cannot absorb or pass this power back to the supply system and special precautions are necessary. If there are other non-regenerating loads connected in parallel with the regenerating loads and they are capable of absorbing all the returned power, this will be satisfactory but it is essential that the non-regenerating loads are switched on at the time. If necessary a fixed resistor can be used for this purpose and if the returned power is sufficient to warrant it this resistor can be arranged to be switched on only when re-generation occurs.

Germanium and silicon rectifiers as noted elsewhere can be operated at extremely high current densities in the rectifying element, and the closer to the maximum permissible value they are operated the more precise the protective system needs to be. When over-loads are imposed the junction temperatures will mount up very rapidly and under severe fault conditions can reach destructive values within fractions of a second. The fairly high forward resistance in selenium rectifiers does not present any problem.

Germanium and silicon require either a protective device which will clear a fault in less than about 5 s or a large amount of reactance in the supply circuit to limit the prospective short-circuit current or they must be derated. The degree to which these factors are important depends on how near to the maximum permissible rating the rectifier is operating.

All semi-conductor rectifiers are affected by excessively high surge voltages. Germanium and silicon rectifiers should be protected by a suitable surge-absorbing non-linear resistor or, more usually, by a capacitor circuit connected across the primary terminals of the transformer (Figure 13.7). Resistors are also usually connected in series with the capacitors to damp oscillations. The capacitors should be either metallised paper or paper and foil construction. The momentary voltages which these types of rectifier can withstand are about 1.5 to 2.5 times the peak working voltage.

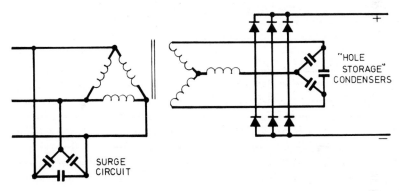

Figure 13.7 A 3-phase full-wave bridge circuit with surge protection

Another surge-producing phenomenon is what is known as the 'hole storage' effect which tends to produce voltage pulses on the inverse voltage applied to the diodes. During commutation, i.e. the transfer of load current from one rectifier to the next, at the point of changeover from forward conduction to the blocking state, there is a finite though brief time interval when 'current carriers' are swept from the junction region. If carriers are still present when the reverse voltage begins to rise substantial reverse currents can flow, and when the diode recovers its blocking characteristics this current, flowing in the reactive transformer secondary windings, will suddenly be interrupted, giving rise to a voltage surge. To disperse this oscillation, which has low energy content, capacitors are fitted as shown in Figure 13.7. When these are considered necessary they are supplied as part of the rectifier stack.

For short-circuit protection fuses are suitable if correctly chosen and must be fast enough in operation to prevent diode failure. They must operate under d.c. conditions at a voltage approaching the peak working voltage across the rectifier and the arcing voltage must be within the overvoltage limit which the cells can withstand. If the latter condition is not met the blowing of a fuse may start a chain reaction sufficient to destroy all the cells in the equipment. It is common practice to fit a fuse-failure alarm in conjunction with semi-conductor rectifiers. In order to reduce these risks to a minimum and allow an adequate margin of safety, operation at a smaller current density and therefore lower temperature is advisable. Special fuses with low arcing voltages are now designed for use in semi-conductor equipments. Operating a semi-conductor rectifier equipment at reduced current density, and therefore lower temperature, would not necessarily reduce the risk of cell failure due to fuse arcing voltages.

For the protection of the transformer normal circuit-breaker practice is satisfactory.

Germanium rectifiers

Germanium is polycrystalline after purification (zone refining) and must be converted into monocrystalline form by a crystal growing technique which demands a standard of purity infinitely higher than that commercially acceptable for other elements. Germanium crystals are refined until impurities are less than one ten-millionth of one per cent and special measures are necessary to prevent contamination or the introduction of impurities. This is a sensitive operation requiring close control and highly specialised equipment.

The first power rectifiers of appreciable size were produced about 1953 but since then remarkable progress has been made. If kept below 75° C. they are stable and exhibit no ageing effects. They can operate at high current density and for this reason are very small compared with selenium. On the other hand (not for the same reason) they may be destroyed by excessive overvoltage or overcurrent surges. Effective cooling is of extreme importance to ensure that the maximum safe barrier temperature is never exceeded. A silicon rectifier unit with cooling fins is shown in Figure 13.2.

As previously noted, one of the potential uses of semi-conductor rectifiers is in connection with magnetic amplifiers. A reverse leakage current in the d.c. control circuit of a magnetic amplifier has a de-saturating effect resulting in a lowering of the gain of the amplifier circuit. Germanium rectifiers are advantageous in this respect due to the extremely high reverse resistance. This feature is illustrated in Figure 13.8 from which it can be seen that current can pass in a

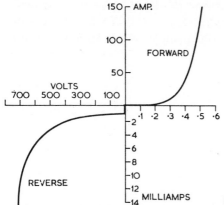

Figure 13.8 Voltage current characteristics (at 20° C) of typical rectifier

forward direction with a voltage drop of only 0.5 V whereas in the reverse direction 500 V will produce a current of only a few milliamps. Nevertheless improvements in production methods already indicate that with present production the reverse current trace at 75° C has its turnover point in excess of 600 V, whilst at room temperature this figure is considerably higher.

The overall efficiency of a transformer plus germanium rectifier depends to a certain extent on the output d.c. voltage but might be expected to be of the order of 95—97%.

Selenium rectifiers

Selenium diodes are polycrystalline and are unique in that the forming of the rectifier junction is accomplished in the final stages of manufacture by passing a current through the cell until the reverse resistance attains a maximum value. The high reverse resistance tends to diminish when standing idle for a long time but, however, is rapidly restored when again energised.

Actual puncture due to overvoltage is rare and when it occurs it will tend to burn out weak spots in the cell but these are self healing and performance is not permanently impaired. Over-current surges will also cause momentary heating but these can usually be absorbed without serious damage.

Selenium rectifiers are subject to ageing which results in an increase of forward resistance and consequently a reduction of d.c. voltage. Provision for adjustment should therefore be made such as by transformer taps. It is usually taken that the useful life is determined when the forward resistance has doubled. Ageing is very much affected by the working temperature and if kept below 75° C a life of about 80 000 hours might be expected.

The overall efficiency of a transformer and selenium rectifier might be of the order of 80–85%.

Silicon rectifiers

Silicon, like germanium, is polycrystalline after refining and must likewise be converted into mono-crystalline form for rectifier manufacture. The techniques involved are even more complex than those for germanium.

They have properties approaching those of germanium and are capable of high peak inverse voltages and a higher maximum operating temperature of about 200° C with current densities several times those permissible with germanium. Silicon rectifiers are suitable for use with magnetic amplifiers for the same reasons that have been noted for germanium. Except for very small sizes the current densities for power silicon and germanium rectifiers are for all practical purposes the same, i.e. approximately 100 amperes per sq. cm.

The effect of operating temperature on rectification is very pronounced. For example at room temperature the forward to reverse ratio would be of the order of 1 : 200 000 but at 150° C it would be in the region of 3000, and 2000 at 200° C. Compared with the germanium rectifier (see Figure 13.8) which has a forward voltage drop of 0.5 to 0.6 V, the silicon rectifier has a drop of 1.0 to 1.25 V.

The efficiency of the silicon rectifier is lower than that for germanium because the forward voltage drop is double and therefore it dissipates approximately twice the power loss for a given current.

Choice of type

The choice depends on several factors according to the operating conditions such as voltage, nature of overloads anticipated, initial cost, efficiency, available space, ageing and regulation.

At the lowest voltages germanium offers the best efficiency and at all voltages germanium and silicon are more efficient than selenium. Maximum efficiency of germanium and silicon is obtained when they are used at their full rated voltage and this also coincides with minimum initial cost. Efficiency assumes greater importance when the rectifier is in use continuously and is of less importance when only in service part of the time. Selenium comes into its own for low voltages, say below 50, where it is relatively unaffected by overloads and series connection of cells is unnecessary.

Thyristors

This device was previously known as s.c.r. or silicon control rectifier. The full term is reverse blocking triode thyristor but is abbreviated to thyristor derived from the Greek *thyra,* a door or gate. This comparatively recent development is equally as important and far-reaching as the original introduction of the semi-conductor rectifier. Many uses will undoubtedly be found, not least being the facility for obtaining a controlled d.c. voltage from a.c. to regulate the field current of d.c. and a.c. machines and to give a variable frequency and voltage a.c. supply from a constant a.c. source. A long life and the ability to withstand shock and vibration, high efficiency and fast time response are all important assets.

A typical construction is shown in Figure 13.9. The thyristor has the property that it can block the flow of current in either direction when no control current is applied to the gate electrode. A firing pulse applied between the gate and the cathode causes it to become conducting with a low resistance in the forward direction, i.e. from

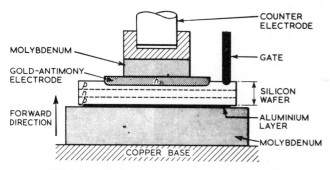

Figure 13.9 Schematic diagram of a crystal structure in a thyristor

anode to cathode. Current is blocked due to high resistance in the reverse direction as in a conventional semi-conductor rectifier. This state will continue until the current in the forward direction falls to zero when it again blocks in both directions unless a new firing pulse is applied. Re-blocking follows naturally in a.c. applications when the anode changes polarity, but with d.c. applications it is usual to return to the blocking state by applying a negative voltage to the anode, usually through a capacitor.

Heat sinks or cooling fins similar to those used on rectifiers are necessary.

A typical construction is shown in Figure 14.10. The active part is *n*-type with a layer of *p*-type on each side. In the example shown, see Figure 13.9, a gold-antimony contact is applied to one side of the wafer so that an *npnp* structure is formed. The gate electrode is fixed to the upper *p* layer.

Discs of molybdenum are used as backing plates at top and bottom and the complete structure is brazed to a copper base. The molybdenum has the same function as that described for Figure 13.4 and the encapsulation is similar. The base constitutes the anode.

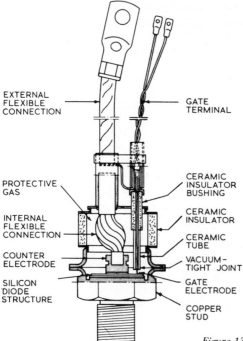

Figure 13.10 Typical cross-section of a thyristor

The twin flexible cord has one core connected to the cathode and the other to the gate. This arrangement eliminates the risk of mis-firing due to external stray magnetic fields. The triggering current for this construction is of the order of 50–100 mA and 1.5–2.0 V.

The gate electrode initiates an anode current but does not normally limit it. In the conductive condition it behaves like a conventional semi-conductor rectifier. It is in effect a 3-junction semi-conductor, i.e., a triode, normally blocking current flow in both directions until a signal is applied to the gate. Its function can be likened to that of a contactor which is in the open position until closed by exciting the operating coil.

Figure 13.11 shows a typical characteristic. The reverse characteristic is similar to that of a conventional diode and is unaffected by

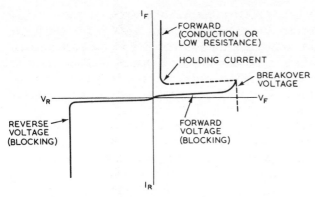

Figure 13.11 Typical thyristor characteristic

control signals at the gate. The forward characteristic also indicates low leakage current until the point of breakdown voltage is reached above which it will trigger automatically into a state of condition, i.e., without gate initiation. It is therefore clear that to function in a controlled manner the applied forward voltage must be less than the breakdown voltage. The effect of applying control current to the gate is to reduce the breakover voltage, depending on the value of

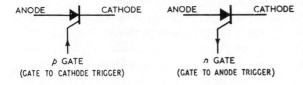

Figure 13.12 Graphical symbols for thyristors

gate current. If sufficient current is injected the breakover can be reduced virtually to zero. By this means a thyristor can be blocked or unblocked so that the current either flows or is blocked instantly by the application of a pulse. The forward resistance and therefore voltage drop is slightly higher than a normal rectifier and the maximum permissible junction temperature is lower so much more cooling is required to dissipate the losses.

Conventional graphical symbols are shown in Figure 13.12.

Transistors

This term is applied to a variety of devices but basically they all comprise an active semi-conductor with three or more electrodes. In typical forms they can be either *npn* consisting of a thin slice of *p*-type sandwiched between two pieces of *n*-type or they can be *pnp* type. In the former the middle slice forms the base, and the *n*-type slices form the collector and emitter and in the latter amplification is due to *hole* conduction instead of, as in the *npn* transistor, electron conduction. Variations consist of point contact, phototransistors etc; point contact types are now being replaced by junction transistors.

As indicated in the conventional symbol, Figure 13.13 there are usually three external connections, one to the emitter, one to the base and one to the collector, each being attached to one of the impurity regions, the base being in the centre.

Figure 13.13 Transistor graphical symbol

When positive potential is applied to the emitter of a *pnp* transistor, the *holes* in the *p* material are repelled from the region of the emitter and travel towards the *pn* junction. The barrier potential having been lowered by the biassing, the holes cross to the base, i.e. *n* region. They continue to drift by a diffusion process towards the collector and finally cross the *np* junction. In this process a few of the holes passing through the base (*n* region) will re-combine with electrons and to minimise this effect the width of the *n* region must be kept small. The holes which cross into the collector (*p* region) comprise current flow since each reaching the collector requires to collect one electron from the junction to neutralise it, and changes in emitter current produce proportionate changes in collector current.

An *npn* transistor behaves similarly except that polarities of applied voltages are reversed and electrons and not holes are injected at the emitter and collected at the collector. The characteristics are also similar except that as collector to base resistance is higher, the result is higher voltage and power gains. These functions are illustrated in Figure 13.14.

In operation a transistor is in effect a variable resistance employing a small input signal to change its resistance from a high value to an almost negligible value and it can be controlled much the same as with a rheostat. There are of course limits to the amount of current allowed to pass because of the internal heat generated in the process. Their application is also subject to the same considerations already dealt with in regard to temperature, overload and surge protection. Transistor characteristics change to a marked degree with temperature. In the present state of development, ratings are comparatively

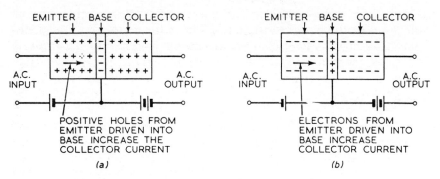

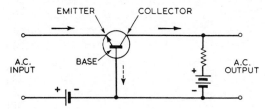

Figure 13.14 Diagrammatic representation of transistor
(a) pnp junction transistor;
(b) npn junction transistor

small and for power purposes are of the order of 50 A. depending on the cooling system.

The *pnp* junction transistor shown in Figure 13.14(a) can be represented diagrammatically as in Figure 13.15. It will be seen that the major electron flow passes through the emitter and collector in series while the base merely acts as a valve to control the flow. The arrows indicate the electron flow, the current of course being in the

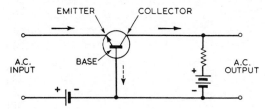

Figure 13.15 Typical pnp transistor circuit

opposite direction. For any given current flowing in the input circuit a small percentage is bypassed through the base and the balance goes in output. In the arrangement shown the base is common to input and output but alternative arrangements are also used in which either the emitter or the collector is common. Current flow is always through emitter and collector in series.

Amplification depends on the fact that the emitter has a low resistance and the collector a high resistance. The voltage level in the emitter circuit can be of the order of millivolts or a few volts whereas that of the collector circuit can be quite large, and the emitter to collector current can be regulated by a very small change in emitter voltage. The corresponding change in collector voltage will be enormously greater. The circuit must be devised to avoid excessive voltage at any stage as most failures are due to high voltages and transient voltages. All the characteristics will vary with temperature, e.g., the amplification will increase with increasing temperature at a rate of 0.5 to 1.0 per cent per °C.

Tunnel diodes

The tunnel diode is used in place of the transistor where very high frequency working is necessary. When suitably biased it has a negative resistance which results in the signal power in a circuit being increased. Therefore, if a tunnel diode is connected across a tuned circuit, any small electrical disturbance in the circuit will build up as an oscillation.

At present tunnel diodes have limited power handling capacity and are likely to be used as local oscillators in receivers rather than in transmitters.

The high frequency capability makes the tunnel diode suitable for various computer applications such as high-speed switching circuits for 'storing' information and extracting it from computer 'memories'.

14 Storage batteries and battery control gear

Storage batteries have played an important part in the electrical equipment of ships for very many years, not only for stand-by purposes in case of a failure of the ship's electric supply, but also for routine charge and discharge work. A battery is in the unique position of being able to supply electrical energy *immediately* upon demand and this gives it an advantage over any other stand-by device. The International Convention on Safety of Life at Sea, 1974, gives full recognition to this matter with a result that stand-by batteries are now an essential requirement on many classes of seagoing ships.

The successful use of batteries on board ship depends upon:

(*a*) The selection of the right type and size of battery and control gear.

(*b*) Correct installation.

(*c*) Regular inspection and maintenance.

Radio batteries in daily use are excluded from this chapter since they are normally under the direct control of the radio officers and are not the responsibility of the ship's electrical engineer. If, however, information is required about them, reference should be made to Dowsett and Walker's *Technical Instruction for Marine Radio Officers* or Harvey's *Battery Chargers and Charging.*

CLASSES OF BATTERIES

There are two distinct classes of batteries available: (*a*) primary batteries, and, (*b*) secondary or storage batteries. The primary battery will give only one discharge, after which it is discarded. The commonest example is the dry battery used in torches but special designs of primary battery are coming into use in conjunction with life-saving equipment. These remain inert until energised by water, after which they will give one discharge.

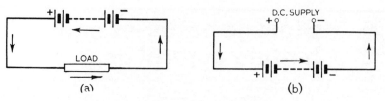

Figure 14.1 Elementary discharging and charging diagrams
    (a) Flow of current when a battery is on discharge
    (b) Flow of current when a battery is on charge

The secondary or storage battery can, however, be 'charged' as well as 'discharged'. This means that after the battery has been discharged it can be brought back to its original fully charged condition by passing an electric current through the battery in the 'charge' direction. This is illustrated in Figure 14.1. In the diagrams it should be noted that the long thin stroke represents the positive pole of the battery and the short thick stroke the negative pole. This convention should be followed in all circuit diagrams which include batteries.

TYPES OF STORAGE BATTERIES

Practically all storage batteries are of the alkaline or of the lead-acid type. Both are used extensively on board ship and it is essential, therefore, that designers and seagoing engineers should have a clear understanding of the constructional details and operating characteristics of each type.

The alkaline battery

A marine alkaline battery is normally of the flat-plate nickel-cadmium design. The active material of the positive plates consists essentially of nickel hydroxide with finely divided graphite added to improve the conductivity. The active material of the negative plates is a mixture of cadmium and iron.

These materials are enclosed in perforated steel pockets which are, in turn, assembled into steel retaining frames to form complete positive or negative plates. The required number of plates of the same polarity are bolted together and intermeshed with a group of plates of opposite polarity. A typical plate is shown in Figure 14.2. Thin ebonite rods are inserted between the plates to act as separators and the whole assembly is mounted in a welded steel container with cover. The electrolyte used is caustic potash solution.

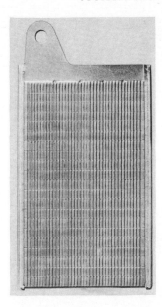

Figure 14.2 Nickel cadmium flat plate (Nife Batteries)

Figure 14.3 Sectional view of a nickel cadmium cell (Nife Batteries)

Figure 14.4 Crate containing five nickel cadmium alkaline cells (Nife Batteries)

Groups of cells are mounted into hardwood crates with air spaces between all the cells. They are suspended in these crates by means of bosses welded on the sides of the cells. This method of assembly ensures that each cell container is insulated from its neighbours and also from 'earth'. Figure 14.3 shows a typical cell with its sides cut away to illustrate the construction. Figure 14.4 is a picture of five cells assembled in a crate.

It should be noted that the steel containers or all alkaline cells are electrically 'alive' since they are in direct contact with the electrolyte or with one set of plates. Loose wires must consequently not

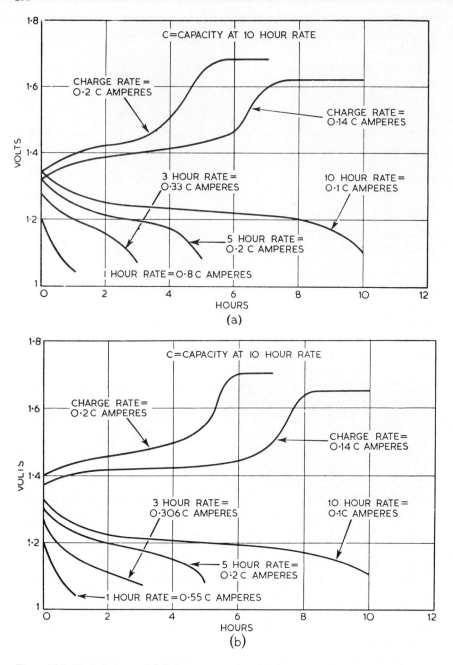

Figure 14.5 Typical charge and discharge curves for nickel cadmium flat-plate cells
   (a) Low resistance cells;
   (b) Normal resistance cells

touch any part of a cell container or its cover owing to the danger of severe sparking from short circuits. Similarly, tools must not be laid on top of the cells.

Nickel-cadmium flat-plate cells are made in two designs; a normal resistance design for applications involving cycles of discharge and charge, particularly for medium or slow discharge rates, and a low resistance design for applications where heavy discharge currents for short periods are required such as for engine starting, emergency steering and emergency lighting. The general description is the same for both but the low resistance design has closer separation and thinner plates to keep the internal resistance to a minimum.

Figure 14.5 shows typical charge and discharge curves for flat-plate nickel-cadmium cells.

The lead-acid battery

There are many different types of lead-acid battery available for specialised duties but for marine work the choice is normally limited to those in the 'armoured' category, i.e those in which the active material of the positive plates is almost completely enclosed within a protective barrier.

There are two principal types of armoured battery:

(a) The flat-plate battery with glass wool as an armouring, e.g. the D.P.-Kathanode.
(b) The tubular plate battery with slitted ebonite tubes for armouring, e.g. the Exide-Ironclad.

Figure 14.6 shows a grid from a Kathanode flat-plate marine battery. The grids are cast in a special lead alloy; they are filled with a suitable lead oxide paste and they are then electro-chemically 'formed'. The positive plates are chocolate brown in colour and consist mainly of lead peroxide. The negative plates are slate grey in colour with spongy lead as the active material. The electrolyte is dilute sulphuric acid.

The complete assembly of a typical Kathanode cell is shown in Figure 14.7. The armouring material consists of finely-spun glass felted into sheets. One sheet is mounted on each side of every positive plate. This 'glass wool' not only protects the plates from the worst effects of shock and vibration but also prevents the disintegration or loosening of the active material. Normal separators of grooved Porvic (a microporous plastic material) and wood veneers are fitted between the glass wool and the negative plates, and plastic

258

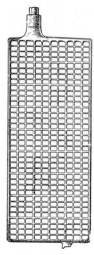

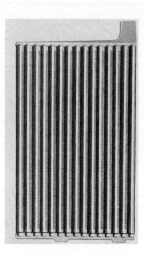

Figure 14.6 Typical kathanode (lead-acid) plate grid

Figure 14.7 Sectional view of typical kathanode cell assembly

Figure 14.8 Ironclad tubular positive plate

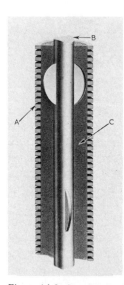

Figure 14.9 Cross-section of tube in tubular plate
A. Slitted ebonite tube
B. Antimonal lead spine
C. Active material of plate

Figure 14.10 Sectional view of ironclad tubular marine cell

insulating strips are fitted against the edges of the negative plates. These prevent internal shorts at the plate edges due to collection of spongy growth. The construction is clearly shown in the sectional view in Figure 14.7.

The tubular type of battery has positive plates generally as indicated in Figure 14.8. The active material is enclosed within

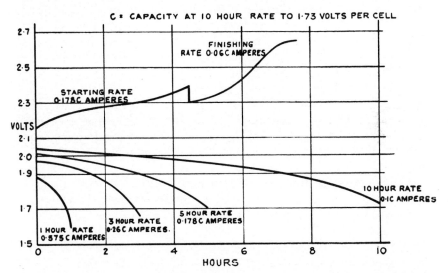

Figure 14.11 Typical charge and discharge curves for flat plate and tubular lead-acid marine cells

slitted ebonite tubes which hold it in close contact with the spines of lead alloy. A cross-section of one tube is shown in Figure 14.9. This indicates how fins are used to ensure that the spine is kept to the centre of the tube. The slitted ebonite tubes allow free access of the electrolyte to the active material but the slits are so fine that this material is effectively retained in position by the tubes. The tubular positive plates work in conjunction with pasted negative plates generally similar to the plate shown in Figure 14.6. Separators are inserted between the positive and negative plates. The final cell assembly is indicated in Figure 14.10.

Most lead-acid cells for marine use are assembled in 'wrapped' hard rubber containers. These are made up of several layers of rubber which are vulcanised together to form the complete box. Cells which incorporate wrapped boxes can withstand considerable mechanical shock without fracture. Two, three or more cells are assembled into waxed wood crates which have insulators at the bottom, sides and ends. The required number of crates is then fitted into the battery compartment in the ship.

Figure 14.11 shows the charge and discharge characteristics for flat plate and tubular lead-acid cells.

Selection of lead-acid or alkaline batteries

Lead-acid and alkaline batteries are both widely used at sea and in many cases the choice depends on personal preference. The alkaline type is generally higher in first cost but to offset this the manufacturers claim a longer life for them. The nickel-cadmium battery has very low open-circuit losses and this shows itself to particular advantage in the case of pleasure yachts and launches which may be laid up for long periods. A further point is that alkaline cells can be left in a discharged condition for long periods without deterioration.

For a given nominal circuit voltage an alkaline battery requires about 67% more cells than a corresponding lead-acid battery. This is due to the fact that alkaline cells have a lower nominal voltage than lead-acid cells.

The electrolyte in a lead-acid battery will normally last the life of the battery whereas in the case of an alkaline battery the electrolyte will require changing according to the particular duty. This falls into two categories as follows:

Batteries on regular charge/discharge cycles about every five years. Emergency duty and engine starting about every ten years.

MARINE BATTERY APPLICATIONS

Battery applications on board ship fall into three main categories:

1. *Emergency or stand-by* duties where the battery is brought into use automatically or manually immediately a failure of the ship's main supply takes place. Lead-acid batteries are normally on trickle charge while alkaline batteries stand on open circuit. Examples are:

General emergency lighting.
Engine-room emergency lighting.
Emergency steering.
Watertight door operation.
Starting emergency generators.
Life-boats.
Gyro-compass.

2. *Normal operation* where the batteries are subjected to regular cycles of discharge and charge. Examples are:

Port lighting in small cargo vessels.

Private yacht lighting.
Propulsion of river launches.
Engine starting and lighting of small craft.
Ferry-boats.

3. *Low pressure systems* for supplying low voltage current to bells, telephones, indicators and warning systems. Normally two batteries are used, one being on charge whilst the other is on discharge. Examples are:

Radio transmitters and receivers.
Distress call apparatus.
Direction-finders.
Depth-sounding equipment.
Telephone exchange.
Fire-detection apparatus.
Electric clocks.
Steward call indicators.
Engine-room signalling apparatus.

CALCULATIONS TO DETERMINE SIZE OF BATTERY REQUIRED

(a) Ampere-hour capacity

The capacity of a marine battery is normally given in ampere-hours at the 10-hour rate. For example a 250 Ah battery will give 25

LEAD-ACID TYPE

Discharge rate	Capacity factor	Final voltage (at the end of the discharge time)	
		Per cell	Per battery (55 cells)
10 hour	1	1.73	95
5 hour	0.89	1.70	93.5
3 hour	0.78	1.68	92.5
1 hour	0.58	1.59	87.5
½ hour (standard)	0.46	1.51	83
½ hour (high final volts)	0.29	1.80	99

ALKALINE (nickel-cadmium normal resistance type)

Discharge rate	Capacity factor	Final voltage (at the end of discharge time)	
		Per cell	Per battery (92 cells)
10 hour	1	1.14	105
5 hour	1	1.10	101
3 hour	1	1.06	97.5
1 hour	0.7	1.0	92
½ hour	Not applicable		

ALKALINE (nickel-cadmium low resistance type)

Discharge rate	Capacity factor	Final voltage (at the end of discharge time)	
		Per cell	Per battery (92 cells)
10 hour	1	1.14	105
5 hour	1	1.12	103
3 hour	1	1.06	97.5
1 hour	0.8	1.0	92
½ hour (standard)	0.7	0.9	83
½ hour (high final volts)	0.5	1.09	100

amperes for 10 hours. It does not follow that the same battery will give 250 Ah at the 1-hour rate; in fact, it will give less than 250 Ah and an appropriate Capacity Factor as detailed below must generally be applied for discharges other than the one at the 10-hour rate. The final voltages indicated are for a battery having a nominal 110-volt rating.

It will be seen from the above tables that two alternatives are available for the half-hour discharge rate in the case of lead-acid cells and nickel-cadmium low resistance cells. The second alternatives are used in those cases where it is essential that the battery should maintain a fairly high voltage during discharge. The final voltage of any battery can be adjusted (i) by altering the capacity factor, i.e.

a higher voltage is obtained with a lower factor or (ii) by altering the number of cells in the battery. Detailed information on these points can be obtained from the manufacturers concerned.

(b) Choice of voltage.

An emergency lighting circuit covering all important parts of a ship is generally designed to have the same nominal voltage as the main supply on the ship, e.g. 110 V or 220 V as the case may be. Where the circuit is of limited application, for example in the engine-room only, it is more convenient to use a lower voltage such as 25 or 50 V. This leads to simple control gear and fewer cells with comparatively simple maintenance.

The voltage required for low voltage devices such as the telephone exchange, stewards call indicators, etc, is usually fixed by the manufacturers but if there is any choice in the matter the voltage should be 24 or 50 V.

The number of cells is usually worked on a basis of 2 volts per cell for lead-acid cells and 1.2 V per cell for nickel-cadmium cells. Extra cells may be added if the discharge rate is high, if there are long cable runs or if accurate voltage control is required. In yacht lighting installations, for example, additional cells may be provided and tappings taken to an end-cell switch.

(c) Typical calculations

1. A lead-acid battery is required to supply a 5 kW. load for ½ hour at a nominal 110 V. The nominal current is 5000/110 = 45.5 amperes and the ampere-hours are 45.5 × ½ = 22.75 Ah at the ½-hour rate. The corresponding 10-hour capacity is obtained by dividing this calculated Ah capacity of 22.75 by the *Capacity Factor* 0.46 for the rate of discharge in question. This is 22.75/0.46 = 49.5 Ah. A standard size of 5 plate cell has a capacity of 52 Ah at the 10-hour rate and this would be chosen. The number of cells could be 55 but if a good voltage on discharge were important this could be increased to (say) 58 cells.

2. An alkaline battery is required to give 475 watts for 3 hours at a nominal 25 volts. The nominal current is 475/25 = 19 amperes which requires 57 Ah at the 3-hour rate. Since the 3-hour *Capacity Factor* for alkaline cells is unity, 57 Ah is also the required 10-hour capacity. The manufacturers have a cell rated at 60 Ah and this would be chosen for the job. The battery would consist of 25/1.2 = 21 cells.

(d) Emergency batteries

Where emergency batteries are installed in compliance with the 1960 Convention for Safety of Life at Sea they are required to have sufficient capacity to supply specified services as follows without recharging or excessive voltage drop.

1. In passenger ships the main source of emergency power may be a generator or a battery and must be adequate for a period of thirty-six hours.

2. In passenger ships if the main source of emergency power is a generator there must be a temporary source of power consisting of a battery which must be adequate for supplying specified services for thirty minutes. It must come into operation automatically on failure of the main electrical supply.

3. In cargo ships the requirements are similar to 1 but the period of supply is reduced to six hours for ships of 5000 tons gross tonnage and upwards and three hours for smaller ships.

'Excessive voltage drop' is interpreted by the Ministry of Transport to mean a voltage drop at the end of the specified time not exceeding 12½% of the nominal system voltage. The voltage variation should be within the limits of plus 10% and minus 12½% from fully charged to completion of full performance of the prescribed duty.

METHODS OF CONTROL

There are two methods which are used for controlling batteries on board ship each with its own range of applications.

(i) Charge-discharge.
(ii) Automatic switching.

Charge-discharge

In this method the battery is charged from the ship's mains or a generator and when fully charged is allowed to discharge to the load.

If the load is a continuous one this will mean the provision of duplicate batteries, one being on charge whilst the other is on discharge.

Automatic switching with or without trickle charge

With this scheme the battery is connected to the load in an emergency only, by means of an automatic switch. At other times the load is energised from the main supply. With lead-acid batteries it is usual to include a trickle charge circuit but this is omitted in the case of alkaline batteries. Marine type alkaline cells have very low open-circuit losses and any slight discharge which occurs due to leakage is replaced by periodical freshening charges.

The continuous trickle charging of lead-acid batteries ensures that they are always maintained in a fully charged condition until an emergency occurs. It compensates for open-circuit losses in the cells and also for any slight external electrical leakage. Normally a figure of about 1 mA per ampere-hour at the 10-hour rate is used. Thus a 52 Ah battery would require about 50 mA continuously, but this may have to be increased as the battery gets older. When a battery is on correct trickle charge its specific gravity does not fall and yet gassing is negligible. Falling specific gravity shows too low a rate; appreciable gassing shows too high a rate.

It must be emphasised that trickle charging is applied only to a fully-charged battery. If the battery has been discharged it must first be charged at the appropriate re-charge rate and then put on trickle charge.

TYPICAL WIRING DIAGRAMS

Figure 14.12 shows a typical wiring diagram for two batteries working on a charge-discharge cycle. One battery is on discharge to the load whilst the other is on charge from the d.c. supply mains through a series resistance. A blocking rectifier in the charge circuit ensures that the battery on charge does not feed back into the main supply network if the supply should fail. It is essential in this circuit to ensure that each change-over switch can be operated independently and that each one has an 'off' position.

This independent operation enables both batteries to be put in parallel to the load during the period of change-over thus ensuring continuity of supply to the load at all times. The 'off' positions are essential to avoid excessive overcharging. Each battery should be taken off charge immediately an adequate recharge has been given and then left on open circuit until it is required for another discharge. Excessive charging is not only wasteful of electric power but leads to shortened battery life, and more frequent topping-up of the cells.

A small emergency lighting set of the Keepalite or Katholite type would have a diagram as shown in simplifed form in Figure 14.13. The emergency lights are normally 'dead' but are illuminated from the battery in emergency. The battery is kept on continuous trickle

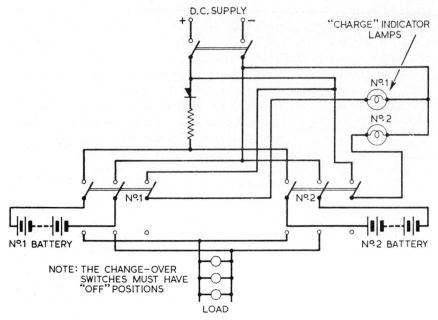

Figure 14.12 Simple circuit for control of two batteries on the charge/discharge principle
The indicator lamps show that No. 1 or No. 2 switch is in the 'charge' position

Figure 14.13 Simplified low voltage d.c.
'Keepalite' emergency lighting circuit (Note that
the trickle charge circuit is omitted in the
Nife-Neverfayle system)

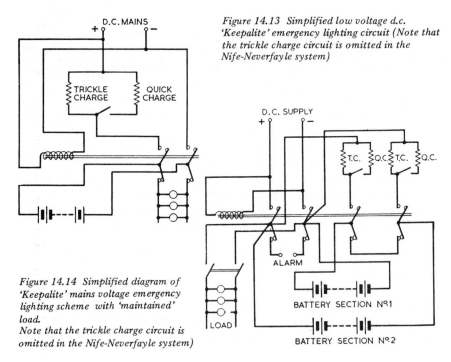

Figure 14.14 Simplified diagram of
'Keepalite' mains voltage emergency
lighting scheme with 'maintained'
load.
Note that the trickle charge circuit is
omitted in the Nife-Neverfayle system)

charge but facilities are provided for giving a quick charge after the battery has been discharged. The nominal battery voltage should not be more than half the main supply voltage if this circuit is used. In the case of the Nife-Neverfayle scheme (using alkaline cells) the diagram is similar but the trickle charge circuit would be omitted.

The larger batteries used for emergency lighting and power are normally of the same nominal voltage as the ship's main supply. They are divided into two halves which are charged in parallel and discharged in series. Figure 14.14 shows a simplified diagram of this nature. The emergency lights will be supplied from the mains under normal conditions. Independent trickle charge and quick charge facilities are provided for each half of the battery. The trickle charge is omitted with alkaline batteries.

WARNING DEVICES

All batteries can be damaged by serious overcharging or over-discharging and it is useful therefore to incorporate an alarm device in the control gear to remind the man responsible for the battery when attention is required. Typical devices which have been used include:

(a) An additional pole in the charging switch which connects a warning bell to the main supply via a process timer. At the instant of switching on the charge the warning bell rings and continues to do so until the process timer is set for the particular charging period. When the charging period has elapsed the contacts in the timer close again and operate the warning bell.

(b) The inclusion of an ampere-hour meter fitted with contacts whereby a warning bell comes into operation when say 75% capacity has been taken out of the battery and when the complete charge has been restored. This meter would have a differential between charge and discharge of 15% in the case of lead-acid cells and 40% in the case of alkaline cells.

A.C. MAINS

Ships mains have traditionally been d.c. at 110 or 220 V for very many years but recently there has been a tendency for some new ships, particularly tankers, to be provided with 60 Hz cycle a.c.

mains distribution. This supply must be converted to d.c. before it is used for battery charging and rectifiers are normally used for this duty. The general systems of control detailed above are used but with the addition of transformers and rectifiers. The complication of series parallel charging is, however, unnecessary because the required charge voltage for the whole of a mains voltage battery is readily obtained from a rectifier.

INSTALLATION OF BATTERIES AND CONTROL GEAR

The Institution of Electrical Engineers' *Regulations for the Electrical Equipment of Ships* include certain sections on the installation of batteries in ships. A brief summary is given below:

1. The cells must be suitable for use on board ship and must not emit acid or alkaline spray.

2. The cells must be accessible from the top and insulators must be used underneath and at each side of the battery. The cells must be fixed so as to prevent any movement arising from the motion of the ship.

3. Ventilating fans must be such that sparking is impossible in the event of the impeller tips touching the fan casing.

4. Acid from the cells must not damage the structure of the ship.

5. The battery compartment must be properly ventilated.

6. Rectifiers must not be located in positions where they would be subject to gases from the batteries.

7. Batteries must not be installed in living quarters.

8. Appropriate control gear together with an ammeter and voltmeter must be provided.

9. Switches and fuses must not be installed inside the battery compartment. The battery cables must be protected by a fuse or circuit breaker just outside the compartment.

10. Alkaline batteries and lead-acid batteries must not be placed in the same room.

Figures 14.15 and 14.16 show typical battery compartments on ships for lead-acid and alkaline batteries respectively. Points to note are the clear spacer permitted above the cells for maintenance purposes and the rigid fixing of the batteries to prevent any movement relative to the ship.

In the case of lead-acid batteries the battery compartment bulkheads should preferably be treated with anti-sulphuric paint and the deck should have a bitumen covering.

Figure 14.15 Typical lead-acid battery installation on board ship (The D.P. Battery Co. Ltd.)

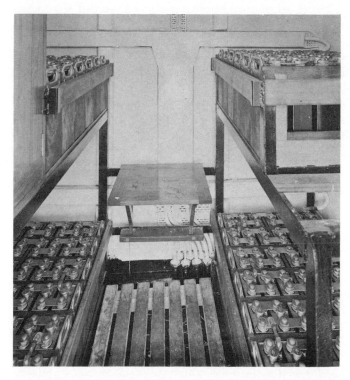

Figure 14.16 Typical alkaline battery installation on board ship (The D.P. Battery Co. Ltd.)

Location

Low voltage batteries for giving auxiliary supplies or for local emergency lighting protection should be mounted as near to their loads as possible in order to minimize voltage drop. Mains voltage emergency batteries and their control gear should however be mounted on the boat deck. Emergency circuits must take their supplies direct from the emergency switchboard and not via the main switchboard. An indicator on the main switchboard should show whether the emergency battery is in service or not.

If lead-acid and alkaline batteries are both installed in the same ship it is most important that they should be mounted in separate compartments. In such cases, too, each battery should have its own topping-up jugs, hydrometers, distilled water, etc. The slightest traces of acid can cause serious damage to alkaline cells.

Ventilation and safety precautions

The gases given off from any battery on charge whether of the lead-acid or alkaline type, consist of hydrogen and oxygen. If the hydrogen concentration becomes too great a spark or a naked flame can initiate an explosion. It is essential therefore that there must be proper ventilation of the battery compartment, particularly during quick charging. Furthermore every precaution must be taken to avoid sparking taking place.

All terminals should be examined from time to time to ensure that they are sound, metal jugs must not be used for topping-up purposes, and loose wires or tools must not be placed on top of the cells. Smoking must be prohibited in the battery compartment and a prominent notice displayed to this effect.

MAINTENANCE

Batteries must receive regular attention if they are to give satisfactory service. This is particularly the case with emergency batteries which are not in regular use. Unless the batteries and control gear are regularly examined and tested there is always the danger that they may not function properly under emergency conditions.

Cleanliness

If a battery is to be well maintained a first essential is that it must be in a clean condition. The tops of the cells must be kept in a dry clean state in order to reduce the risk of corrosion and electrical leakage. The cables, too, in close proximity to the cells require to be examined from time to time for signs of corrosion. All cable terminals must be well protected by a coating of Vaseline or any petroleum jelly (not grease).

The gas vents in the cell plugs should be kept free from blockage by dirt or in the case of alkaline batteries from crystallised electrolyte.

Topping-up

Pure distilled water only should normally be used for topping-up either lead-acid or alkaline cells but if supplies fail, drinking water may be used rather than allow the electrolyte level to fall below the tops of the plates.

It should be a general rule that acid is not added to lead-acid cells (except to replace accidental spillage) unless instructions are given by the battery manufacturer or a qualified Battery Service Agent. A similar restriction applies to the addition of alkaline solution to alkaline cells.

Specific gravity reading – lead-acid cells

The specific gravity of the electrolyte is a valuable indication of the state of charge of a lead-acid battery. A fully charged marine battery will have a specific gravity of 1.280 at 15°C (1.250 for sustained tropical use) and this will fall to something in the region of 1.110 when the battery is fully discharged at the 10-hour rate. The exact range of specific gravity varies with each design of cell and can be determined from actual tests or on application to the battery manufacturer.

Specific gravity readings in between the maximum and minimum values give an indication of the state of charge since the fall in specific gravity is directly proportional to the ampere-hours taken out on discharge. The figure 1.280 can be written as 1280 points; a reduction to 1.110 (or 1110 points) would therefore be referred to as a drop of 170 points.

Readings of specific gravity are taken with a syringe type hydrometer as illustrated in Figure 14.17. A sample of acid is withdrawn from a cell by means of the syringe, the level of the float is noted and the acid sample is returned to the same cell. The following details should be noted when readings are taken:

1. The low readings of the hydrometer are at the top of the float and the high readings at the bottom. This is in the reverse order as compared with an ordinary thermometer.

2. The bottom of the meniscus formed by the liquid gives the true specific gravity reading. This is illustrated in Figure 14.18.

3. Make certain that the hydrometer float is not sticking to the side of the float chamber.

4. A correction is required for the temperature of the electrolyte. The standard temperature for British marine batteries is 15°C. and the following table gives the corrections which should be applied if readings are taken at other temperatures:

Temperature °C.	ADD to observed hydrometer reading (points)
43	19
37	15
32	11
26	8
21	4

Temperature °C.	SUBTRACT from observed hydrometer reading (points)
10	4
4	8
−1	11

One cell in the battery should be selected as a pilot cell and labelled as such. Specific gravity readings should be taken every day on this cell in the case of batteries working on a charge/discharge basis (or once a week for emergency batteries). The specific gravity of every cell in the battery should be measured once a month. Record all these readings in a log book. (If the battery is divided into two sections for charging there should be a pilot cell in each section.)

Specific gravity reading – alkaline cells

In the case of alkaline cells the electrolyte undergoes no appreciable change during a charge and discharge cycle but it falls gradually during service. When the specific gravity has dropped to about 1.160 it is customary to renew the electrolyte.

Figure 14.17 (left) Syringe-type hydrometer

Figure 14.18 Method of reading hydrometer scale

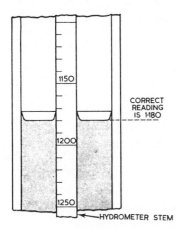

The period between renewals is dependent upon service conditions. This has been dealt with earlier in this chapter.

Temperature

A thermometer for measuring cell temperatures is essential for battery maintenance. It is used for hydrometer corrections as mentioned above, and it enables a check to be kept on high temperatures. The desirable upper limit for lead-acid marine cells is 37°C, but temperatures up to 51°C are permissible if 'low gravity' acid is used, e.g. 1.250.

The normal safe limit for alkaline cells is about 46°C.

Since charging causes a temperature rise in a battery it may be necessary to reduce the charge current or stop charging altogether during the hottest part of the day when the ship is in the tropics.

Voltage readings

Battery voltage readings are a valuable indication of the state of charge of discharge of a battery whilst current is actually flowing and reference should be made to the curves in Figures 14.5 and 14.11.

The voltage of a battery on open circuit is, however, rather misleading. If it is low the battery is definitely in a poor condition but if it is high it does not necessarily show that the battery is in good condition.

Individual cell voltages are useful for checking whether all the cells of a battery are in step. Here again, for readings to be of value, they must be taken when current is passing. Cell voltages are of particular importance in the case of alkaline batteries since they provide the principal means of determining that the cells are healthy. In the case of lead-acid cells there is, of course, the additional check by means of specific gravity readings.

Working conditions

The charge rates for batteries can normally be obtained from the instruction card but if this is not available the following information will act as a guide.

(a) *Lead-acid batteries on emergency duty only.* The 'Finishing' rate only is used. This is approximately 0.06 C amperes where C is the capacity in ampere-hours at the 10-hour rate.

(b) *Lead-acid batteries on charge-discharge routine.* The 'Starting' rate is 0.175 C amperes but this is reduced to the 'Finishing' rate (0.06 C amperes) when the cells begin to gas freely (at approximately 2.4 V per cell). Alternatively if there is ample time available the 'Finishing' rate can be used throughout charge.

(c) *Alkaline cells.* The recommended recharge rate is 0.1 C amperes.

Lead-acid batteries working on a charge-discharge cycle should preferably be taken off discharge when approximately two-thirds exhausted. (For example, if the battery is discharging at the 15-hour rate it is preferable but, of course, not essential for the discharge to stop after 10 hours.) Recharge at the rates recommended by the manufacturers as soon as possible after a discharge. If charging is once a week or less frequently, charge until half-hourly readings of the specific gravity of the pilot cell and of the voltage of the battery show no further increase over a period of one hour. This is called an 'extended' charge.

If the battery requires recharging more frequently than once a week it will be sufficient if the above requirements are met with every sixth charge. For intermediate charges, charge until the specific gravity of the pilot cell is within 10 to 15 points of that obtained during the last extended charge.

Thus is the specific gravity of the electrolyte in the pilot cell on the last extended charge was 1.280 continue the charge until the specific gravity reaches 1.265 to 1.270.

Alkaline 'working' batteries require a full recharge at the recommended rate after a discharge. Any reasonable overcharge will not cause damage but it causes a waste of current and leads to extra topping-up water being required.

A lead-acid battery used for emergency purposes and kept on continuous trickle charge does not require cycles of discharge and charge to maintain it in good condition. It is, however, a wise plan to carry out a test discharge to the load once every six months in order to ensure that the battery capacity is satisfactory and to make certain that all fuses, wiring, switches, lamps, etc., are in good working order. This should preferably be done when the ship is in port and should be followed by a thorough recharge.

Alkaline stand-by batteries should be given a freshening charge every month to ensure that any loss of capacity due to leakage or to testing the contactor, is replaced. This consists of a charge at the recommended rate until maximum voltage has been maintained for a period of three to four hours. A test discharge at six-monthly intervals is also recommended for the reasons mentioned in the previous paragraph.

Battery repairs

There are usually no facilities available on board ship for carrying out repairs to cells and consequently information on battery repairs has been omitted from this chapter. If individual cells fall out of step, e.g. are low in voltage during discharge (or, in the case of lead-acid cells have low specific gravity readings), they should be marked and examined at the next convenient port. Battery Service Agents are available at most of the important ports of the world for repairs to marine batteries and for advice on battery matters.

FIRST AID

Dilute sulphuric acid as used in lead-acid cells is not harmful to a healthy skin if it is washed off as soon as possible. A splash in the eye does, however, require immediate attention and as a first aid measure it should be swilled with water or a dilute saline solution immediately. (The saline solution recommended is one level teaspoonful of household salt to half a pint of water.) The chief essentials are rapid action and large quantities of water. A drastic method is to immerse the head in a bucket of water and open and shut the affected eye under the water.

The electrolyte of alkaline cells (caustic potash) should be handled with care as it is corrosive and should not be allowed to come into contact with skin or clothing. In case of burns to the skin or clothing, cover the affected part with boracic powder or a saturated solution of boracic powder. For the eyes, wash out throughly with plenty of clean water and then use immediately a solution of boracic powder — one teaspoonful to the pint. These should be available whenever electrolyte is being handled.

15 Denny-Brown ship stabilisers

Over the past twenty-five years, the stabiliser has become increasingly popular as a standard fitment for ships, especially on passenger/vehicle carrying ships and on certain classes of warship. Attempts to reduce the rolling motion of a ship date back more than a century but not until 1936 was a fully practical solution to the problem achieved when Brown Bros of Edinburgh and William Denny and Bros of Dumbarton successfully installed fin stabilisers on the steamer 'Isle of Sark'. Following this, the design rapidly gained favour over the clumsier, bulkier and less practical devices of earlier years. During the 1939–45 War, for instance, over one hundred ships in the Royal Navy were fitted with stabilisers to improve

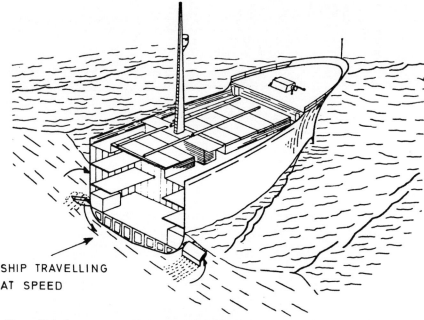

SHIP TRAVELLING
AT SPEED

Figure 15.1 Arrangement of Denny-Brown stabilisers

277

gunnery. After 1950, stabilisers were installed in increasing numbers on merchant ships.

The control system for the fin stabiliser can be classified as electro-hydraulic. On the electrical side, it includes heavy electrical gear (motors, starters, solenoid valves, etc), very sensitive electro-mechanical sensors and sophisticated electronic circuitry. To see what role these components play in the system, it will be worthwhile at first to consider some of the basic principles of roll stabilisation. For this purpose, it is convenient to consider how roll might be countered in the somewhat idealised condition of a ship rolling at its resonant period. (Although it is the easiest mode of roll to correct, it is, in fact, the most critical since at resonance large rolling motions are induced by relatively small wave forces).

Figure 15.3 shows curves depicting some of the factors involved in roll motion of the resonant mode type. Also shown for each curve (as a shaded region) is the action of one fin in countering the effect of that function of roll motion. Thus a downward position of the fin is shown correcting an upward roll. Comparison between the

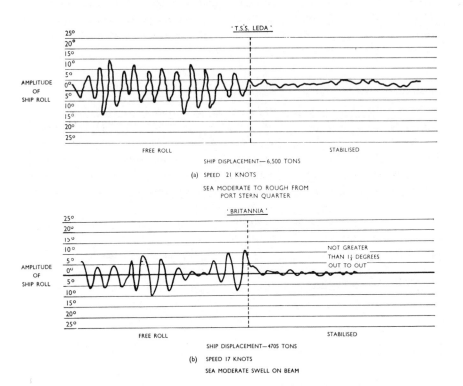

Figure 15.2 Roll and roll damping curves

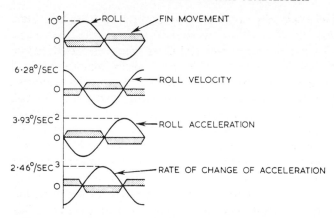

Figure 15.3 Derivatives of the rolling motion of a ship and the corresponding pin movements required for stabilising

diagrams shows, for example, that fin movement to oppose acceleration is exactly opposite to that required to oppose roll and that roll velocity requires the opposite fin movement to rate of roll acceleration. Clearly, if all four factors are used, total cancellation results. In practice, therefore, not all factors are used and when more than one is used they are not all used in the same amounts.

Beam Sea/Following Sea control

Early stabiliser control systems were designed on the assumption that rolling is the result of one of two distinct types of sea state, 'Beam Sea' or 'Following Sea'. Under 'Beam Sea', the tendency is for the ship to roll heavily at its own natural period especially if the natural period of the waves matches that of the ship. Stabilisation action in this case amounts to true damping of the periodic motion, i.e. fin

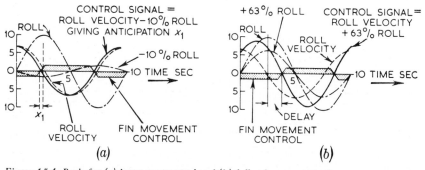

Figure 15.4 Basis for (a) beam sea control and (b) following sea control

position should be such as to oppose roll motion. In practice, some roll angle (actually about -10%) is added to roll velocity to effect a phase advance of the velocity signal and thus make up for the time lag between the initiation of a control movement of the fins and their actual movement. Figure 15.4(a) shows the curves used for 'Beam Sea' control, i.e. actual roll, a 10% inverted roll, and roll velocity (the latter to a slightly reduced scale).

In the 'Following Sea' conditions, the ship has a tendency, in addition to its own period of roll, to lie over on the contour of the waves in an irregular manner. Stabilisation here must include action to restore the ship to an upright position in addition to damping out of the periodic motion. Roll velocity is combined with a percentage of the non-inverted roll angle signal to produce a control signal which lags behind the pure damping (i.e. velocity) signal. The amount of lag is adjusted by varying the percentage of roll used. Figure 15.4(b) shows the curves when 63% roll angle is combined with roll velocity.

On occasions when sea conditions were neither entirely 'Beam' nor 'Following' the choice of which type of control mode to put into operation was left to the navigator.

The sensing elements of the Beam/Following Sea control system are two 150 mm diameter gyroscopes, one a vertical keeping gyro and the other a velocity sensitive gyro. The former is a pendulous wheel which is provided with automatic means for keeping it vertical when upset by ship acceleration, ship turning, etc. The velocity sensitive gyro has its spin axis horizontal and athwartships and as the ship rolls the gyro precesses about a vertical axis against centralising

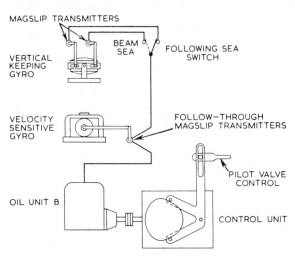

Figure 15.5 Original control

springs, the deflection of the springs being proportional to the angular velocity of roll. Magslip transmitters convert the motions of each gyro unit into electrical signals. These are then summed by a follow-through transmitter magslip and applied to an ARL Type B hydraulic unit. Two magslip transmitters are provided for the vertical keeping gyro so that the different roll angle signals required for Beam and Following Sea can be selected as appropriate.

The hydraulic unit acts as an amplifier, converting the low power electrical signals into hydraulic power sufficient to actuate the hydraulic pumps operating the fins.

MUIRHEAD COMPENSATED AND MULTRA CONTROLS

Working experience with stabiliser systems led to many improvements being made to the basic gyro system. It became evident, for instance, that ships rarely oblige by rolling in pure resonant mode but of necessity follow seas which may be highly confused. To deal with situations such as: suddenly applied roll, rolling at periods off resonance and rolling in conditions which are a combination of rolling at a number of frequencies at the same time, more sophisticated control systems were required. The Compensated System (and subsequently the K160A Multra Control System) by Muirhead were

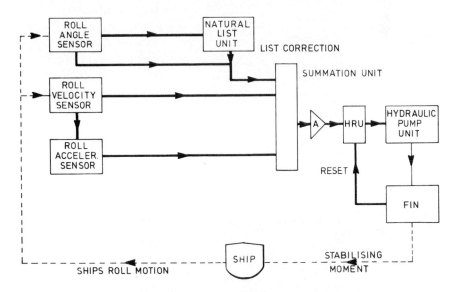

Figure 15.6 Principles of the 'Multra' control system

evolved to meet this requirement. In the Multra system, fin movement is a function of:

1. Roll angle.
2. Roll velocity.
3. Roll acceleration.
4. Natural list.
5. Ship speed, if a speed control unit is employed.

Roll acceleration

This control function opposes the commencement of any rolling motion. It is particularly effective in 'confused sea' conditions or when the ship is acted upon by large irregular waves. The control signal is derived from the velocity gyro by measuring the angular velocity at which the velocity gyro precesses about the vertical

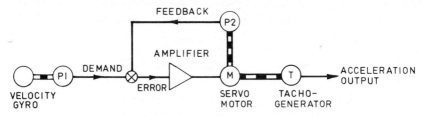

Figure 15.7 Roll acceleration

axis. Position sensor P1 (Figure 15.7) provides the input to a simple position servo, the position driver being servo motor M and feedback loop via sensor P2. The output of tacho generator T is proportional to the angular velocity of P1 which, of course, is roll acceleration.

Natural list

This control function allows the vessel to stabilise around a listed position (to avoid propulsive power being wasted using the stabilisers

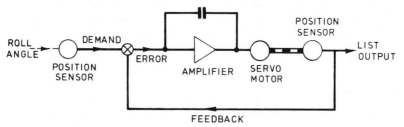

Figure 15.8 Natural list

to correct for list). This control signal is obtained by applying the roll angle signal to a position servo with a long time constant and using the steady list output to modify the roll angle signal (Figure 15.8).

Ship's speed control (fin angle reduction)

To a first approximation, the hydrodynamic forces on the fin are proportional to the square of the forward velocity of the ship, hence at higher speeds the generation of a given restoring couple requires a smaller fin tilt angle. In some ships, to avoid overcorrection and unacceptable cyclic stressing of the fin shaft as the fin oscillates, a fin

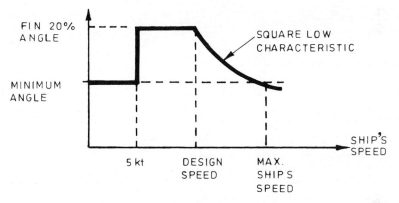

Figure 15.9 Fin angle reduction characteristic

angle/speed control system (Figure 15.9) is necessary. This automatically reduces the angle to which the fin is tilted as the ship's speed increases. The reduction is so arranged that the lift generated by the fins remains constant and the speed at which reduction starts is known therefore as the 'design' speed.

The ship's log signal is used as an input to control the necessary reduction in output from the gyro unit when operating above the 'design' speed. A fail safe facility brings maximum fin angle reduction into operation if the ship's log should fall below a certain level. This will come into operation if the ship's log fails (or if the ship is travelling too slowly for the fins to be of use anyway).

Hydraulic relay unit

Several stages of improvement have been made to the hydraulic relay unit since the Type B unit of the Beam/Following Sea control

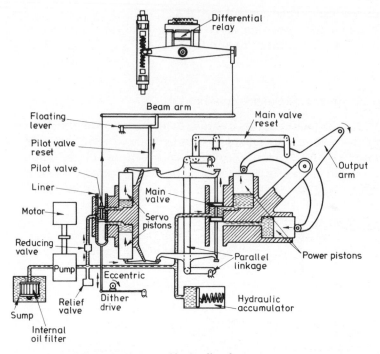

Figure 15.10 Schematic diagram of hydraulic relay

system (which had the disadvantage of providing rather harsh control of the main pumps). Figure 15.10 shows the hydraulic relay unit.

The unit is a sensitive, two-stage hydraulic amplifier which produces sufficient power to operate the tilt mechanism of the VSG pump. Two noteworthy refinements of the unit are a dither drive (to eliminate static friction), and a hydraulic accumulator (to reduce the size of the driving motor and pump yet still obtain a rapid step function response).

THE MUIRHEAD NEW MULTRA K-373 CONTROL SYSTEM

This system is the logical continuation in the line of self-contained stabiliser systems, that is to say, systems comprising their own attitude sensors.

In the Multra system, fin movement is a function of the same control parameters used in the system previously described, with the exception of helm correction, the desirability for which was considered marginal. Ship's speed control is included as part of the new system.

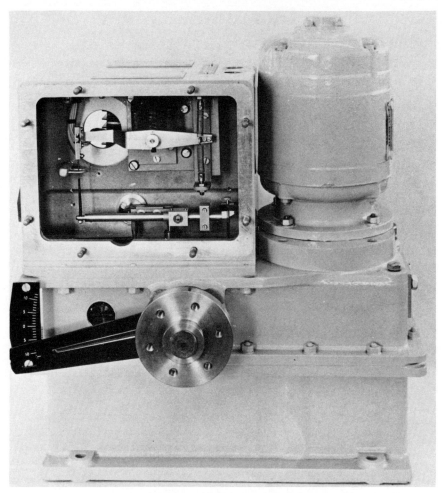

Figure 15.11 The D-696 hydraulic relay unit (Brown Brothers & Co. Ltd.)

The principal change in the system is the control unit (Figure 15.12). This has been redesigned and simplified for greater reliability by using electronic analogue computer techniques. The vertical gyro has been dispensed with, roll and roll acceleration being produced by electronically integrating and differentiating the roll velocity signal.

Only two synchros for picking up the roll velocity signal from the rate gyro. The output from the unit is a modulated 60 Hz carrier signal suitable for driving a hydraulic relay unit, or fin control unit for operating an electro-hydraulic servo valve. Where possible, it is preferable to use the electro-hydraulic servo valve because one time

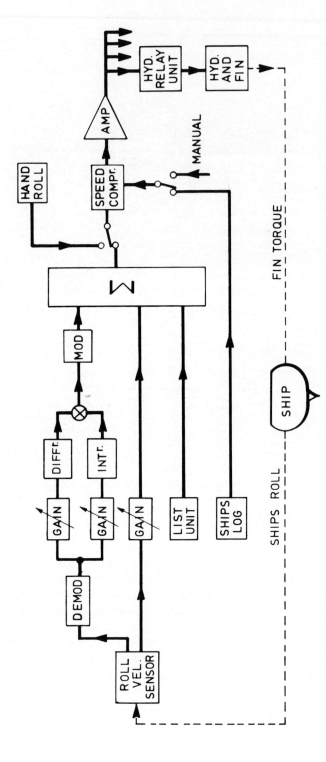

Figure 15.12 Block diagram of the 'New-Multra' system

delay in the system is eliminated. However, not every installation is adaptable to the direct use of an electro-hydraulic servo valve, particularly where a mechanical input is required, and there the hydraulic relay unit is used.

A feature of the system is that it operates from one power supply only, 150 V 60 Hz single phase. No supplies at other frequencies or d.c. are necessary.

Because the control unit no longer utilises a vertical gyro, stabilisation is about the mean or natural list position. List correction is available, if it is required to operate the ship stabilising with respect to the vertical. This is provided from a heavily damped pendulum system in the control unit with a synchro picking off the angle between the pendulum and the ship's structure. This signal can be switched to the summation unit within the controller to appropriately modify the roll angle. A switch is provided to enable the vessel to be force rolled.

The speed compensation circuit modifies the signal in the controller to give a fin angle/ship's speed characteristic similar to that of Figure 15.9. The method of doing this in the original system was by no means of a linear variometer in series with the fin control signal acting as an induction regulator and rotated mechanically by a cam lever system driven by a servo system controlled from the ship's log output signal. In the new system a linear variometer (i.e. a device giving an output voltage directly proportional to roll angle when coupled to a gyro) is used in the ship's log to provide the speed signal. The speed attentuation is obtained in an electronic potential divider. Speed parameters in the circuit are adjusted on test so that the attentuation commences at the design speed and provides the correct output voltage over the specified speed range. To make up the gain lost in the potential divider, an amplifying stage employing an operational amplifier is incorporated. A 'fail safe' feature is included in the circuit to prevent overloading of the fins in the event of failure of the log signal.

As an alternative to the hydraulic relay unit which provides a mechanical output for operating the pilot valve of the main fin hydraulic machinery, a fin control unit, may be used which will drive an electro-hydraulic servo valve directly. The unit takes the fin control signal from the control unit and the fin angle signal from the fin transmitter box to derive an error signal which is phase sensitively demodulated and amplified to give a voltage suitable for operating the electro-hydraulic servo valve.

The Muirhead Multra Minor

This is a simplified control system but suitable for small vessels.

Only roll velocity is used as a control signal which can still provide good stabilisation, especially at, or near, the ship's period so the control unit essentially contains a velocity gyro unit with synchro coupled to it giving a signal suitable for feeding on to either a hydraulic relay unit or a fin control unit. Speed compensation is again available if required.

DENNY BROWN STABILISER CONTROL UNIT LSR 2500 MARK 2

This control unit (Figures 15.13 and 15.14) is based on the use of an angular accelerometer rather than a gyro as the sensing device for roll motion. The accelerometer output, which is proportional to the roll acceleration of the ship, is integrated once to obtain roll velocity then a second time to obtain roll angle. The three signals, roll acceleration, roll velocity and roll angle, provide all the information about the ship's rolling motion necessary to obtain optimum roll reduction.

Figure 15.13 The LSR 2500 Mark 2 control unit is the main component of the Denny-Brown stabiliser system. It is suitable for use in ships with rolling periods in the range 5-30 secs. (Brown Brothers & Co. Ltd.)

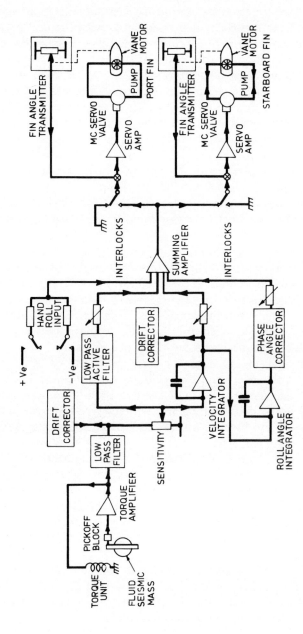

Figure 15.14 Block diagram of the LSR 2500 Mark 2 stabiliser control system

The control system comprises a control box (which houses acceler-ometer, electronic circuitry and sensitivity panel), an air supply unit and fin angle transmitters. Also associated with the control system is the control panel on the bridge which has essentially the same function as that used for the Multra system.

The low range angular accelerometer incorporates an annular tube or toroid filled with a sensing medium of silicone fluid for use as the seismic mass. A small 'paddle' blocks the tube and an inductive type of pick off senses the position of the 'paddle' as it is pushed by the inertial mass when the accelerometer rotates. This pick off signal is fed to a servo amplifier which, in turn, drives a torque coil forcing the paddle back to its central position and thus exactly countering the force applied to the 'paddle' by the fluid.

Since the torque is servo controlled, an electrical signal output is generated which is exactly proportional to the acting angular acceler-ation.

Conventional integrating circuits, employing high gain operational amplifiers, produce first velocity then roll angle signals. Each of the basic roll motion signals (i.e. acceleration, velocity and angle) is routed through a sensitivity switch before being combined with the other signals in a summing amplifier. Each sensitivity switch has 12 positions so that a precise 'mix' can be arranged between the three signals to suit the characteristics of a particular ship.

An interesting feature is the incorporation of drift corrector circuits on the acceleration and velocity output lines. Since both the average angular acceleration and average angular velocity of the ship must equal zero, drift correctors, which are constantly monitoring signal outputs, produce an output such that the average acceleration and average velocity is zero.

The use of a three term controller (acceleration, velocity and angle) ensures automatically that the amplitude and phasing of the fin angle demand signal is optimised over the whole frequency band. At low frequencies, the angle term predominates; at the resonant frequency, the angle and acceleration terms cancel and the velocity term predominates; and at high frequencies, the acceleration term predominates.

A separate servo amplifier is provided for each fin system. Current from the servo amplifier energises the actuating coils of the pump servo valves. Fin angle reduction circuitry is included in the system although the facility is not used on all ships.

The MC servo valve

Improvements to the control system resulted from the introduction of the MC servo valve. Amplification was eliminated and, as a result, the number of components in the pump servo system was greatly reduced. The system response was also improved. Current in the coils of the torque motor causes rotational movement of the rotor of the servo valve away from its neutral position. Balance is achieved when the torque of the feedback and centring springs match that produced by the torque motor. The new position taken up by the rotor allows hydraulic fluid to be admitted to one of the tilting cyclinders of the main pump and away from the other.

The direction and magnitude of tilt (and hence the stroking of, and sense of fluid flow of, the main pump) is determined by the direction and magnitude of current in the torque motor coils. As the pump tilt shaft rotates to the demanded position, torque is applied to the servo valve rotor via the feedback spring which equals the torque exerted by the torque motor and the centring spring returns the servo valve rotor to the neutral position. Pump output is thus directly related to the current input.

The electrical installation

Control of the stabiliser from the navigation bridge is carried out at the bridge control panel. This contains the switches for extending and retracting the fins, for ordering the starting and stopping the equipment, and a hand roll switch for testing the action of the fins in calm waters and permitting a roll to be induced in synchronism with the natural rolling period of the ship. The panel also includes lamps for indicating the states of various functions of the stabiliser system and indicators showing the position of each fin.

The largest panel in the electrical system is the compartment control panel (usually installed in the engine room). Within the unit are relays used in the interlock and power control circuits, system fuses, transformers, contactors and hours-of-use clocks for the stabilisers. On the front of the unit are the main isolator switch, state indicator lamps for the system and control switches for local control of the fins (but not including hand roll operations).

Other panels which have electrical components are the auxiliary power unit (which has a 3-phase electrical motor for driving a vane-type hydraulic pump) and the hydraulic valve panel (which carries a number of solenoid-operated hydraulic valves). Tappet switches mounted on top of each fin unit are used to work the fin locking gear and signal when the limits of travel are reached in the fin housing and extend operations.

The main power unit for hydraulic operation of the fin tilting gear (a Vickers VSG pump) is driven by a non-reversing continuous running, enclosed ventilated, 3-phase induction motor which also drives the constant delivery servo pump. The pump output is controlled by a moving coil (MC) servo valve mounted directly on the pump and described earlier in this chapter. Forced feed lubrication of the trunnion bearings supporting the crux member is provided by electrically-driven grease lubricators.

Fins

Torque to counter roll is generated by the combination of the ship's forward speed and the tilting of fins projecting laterally from each side of the ship's hull. The angle of tilt of the fins relative to their direction of motion through the water is determined by the control system (previously described) which produces appropriate control signals. Direction of tilt is such as to exert a moment on the hull opposing the incipient roll. For example, if a roll to starboard were to develop the port fin would be tilted nose down and the starboard fin would be tilted nose up.

In the early days of stabilisers, fins tended to be individually designed to suit each particular vessel, but with the introduction of the Denny-Brown-AEG stabiliser, a range of standard units became available from which a unit could be chosen to meet the ship designer's requirements. The development of the stabiliser came about through collaboration between the Scottish Denny-Brown firms and German firms AEG and Deutsche Werft of Hamburg, the stabiliser being known as the Denny-Brown-AEG stabiliser.

The basic difference compared with the older Denny-Brown design is in the method of housing and extending the fins. Previously, the fins were housed by retracting the fins athwartships into the hull but with the Denny-Brown-AEG fin, the fins are rotated forward into the hull so that they lie in a fore-and-aft position. This is shown in Figures 15.16 and 15.17. As the stabiliser is normally most effective when fitted at the ship's maximum beam the Denny-Brown-AEG stabiliser meeds less athwartship space in the main engine room than did the previous Denny-Brown design.

Another feature of the new fin is that few working parts are exposed to sea water, thus reducing maintenance in drydock. The fin assembly has been arranged so that the complete fin unit together with the fin shaft can be easily withdrawn from the crux for servicing and maintenance purposes.

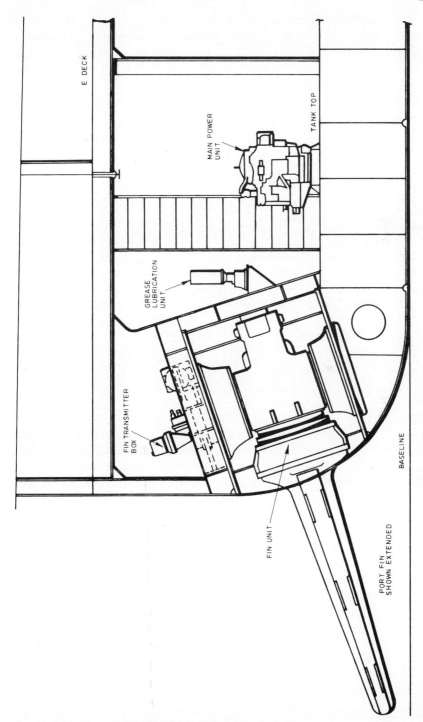

E DECK

MAIN POWER
UNIT

TANK TOP

GREASE
LUBRICATION
UNIT

FIN TRANSMITTER
BOX

FIN UNIT

BASELINE

PORT FIN
SHOWN EXTENDED

Figure 15.15 Denny-Brown AEG stabiliser. Elevation looking forward

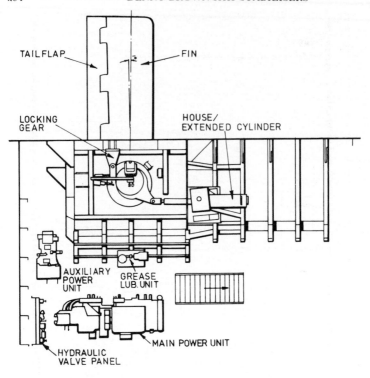

Figure 15.16 Sectional view of the Denny-Brown AEG stabiliser

The distinguishing feature of the Denny-Brown-AEG stabiliser is the use of a support member (called the crux) to carry the shaft on which the fin can pivot and serve as a swivel pin by means of which the fin can be swung in and out of its housing in the ship's hull. In addition to providing a rigid support for the fin, the arrangement also provides a convenient means of installing a vane-type hydraulic motor right at the root of the fin.

Rapid reversal of the attitude of the fins is essential and this is provided for in the mechanical equipment. The total period of double roll may vary from ten seconds for a ship of moderate size to twenty-five seconds for a ship such as the *Queen Elizabeth* and only a small part of this period can be allotted to the reversal of fins at the end of each roll in order that the righting moment may be retained effectively as long as possible. In practice the reversal time ranges from one second up to three and a half seconds. During this period each fin may have to be rotated through an angle of 40°. As a point of interest this may be contrasted with the thirty seconds usually required to move a rudder through 70°.

The fin tailflap is gear driven from a fixed rack so that, as the fin tilt angle increases from zero in either direction, so the tailflap angle changes in the same sense but at a higher rate (see Figure 15.16). For a given fin area and ship speed, the hydrodynamic loading on the fin (and the consequent anti-roll couple exerted on the hull) is increased by the use of such a tailflap.

TANK STABILISERS

Fin stabilisers provide the most effective means for controlling the roll of a ship when operating at its service speed. However, if stabilisation is required at low speed or when the ship is stopped (as is the requirement for a drill ship), some form of tank stabiliser has to be used.

Passive tank stabilisers derive their stabilising power through the transfer of fluid from one side of the ship to the other (Figure 15.17). The fluid (when in free motion) interacts with the ship in the same way as two, coupled, mass elastic systems interact. Normally, the

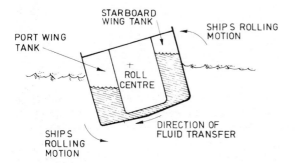

Figure 15.17 Passive tank

natural period of the fluid in the tanks is designed to be near or equal to the natural period of the ship; and, furthermore, the system is designed so that at or near resonance, fluid motion is 90° out of phase with the roll of the ship but in phase with roll velocity.

Unfortunately, if rolling is outside the natural period of the ship, the purely passive system just described can, in fact, increase the roll motion of the ship at certain roll periods. To overcome this disadvantage, a development of the Muirhead control system (called the Muirhead-Brown controlled passive tank system) was introduced. This prevents the fluid from moving naturally at non resonant periods by controlling the transfer of air from the top of one wing tank into the other by a simple air valve system.

The air valves are controlled after amplification by a signal from the control unit. This control system measures the acceleration of roll by means of a velocity gyro and a mechanical differentiating linkage. The output from this linkage passes to the master hydraulic relay unit which acts solely as an amplifier to drive the directional control valves via slave relay units.

16 Lighting

Developments in lamps and fittings over the past twenty years have contributed to the solving of many problems such as energy consumption, ambient temperatures, shock and vibration effects. Light sources are now available for mounting in the restricted spaces between ceiling and deckhead.

The technique of providing the correct kind of illumination and degree of brightness, particularly in passenger ships is a matter for lighting specialists and is outside the scope of this chapter. Suffice it to say that in a passenger ship each of the public spaces, e.g. lounges, dining-rooms, bars, cabins, etc. will require different treatment. Nevertheless crew accommodation in cargo ships, including tankers, tends to reach a higher standard of comfort than hitherto and also deserves specialist attention. Statutory regulations for the minimum intensity of illumination in crew's quarters have also to be observed.

A feature of cabin lighting recently developed is a control unit based on relays which enable all the lighting in a cabin to be controlled from a local point. A refinement permits one local light remote from the bed-head to provide soft general illumination to be switched from the door.

GLOSSARY OF TERMS

In this chapter terminology relating to illumination has been used, and it is hoped that the undermentioned glossary will assist in understanding these terms.

Angstrom: A unit expressing wavelength e.g. of light and is equal to one hundred-millionth of a cm. (Symbol Å).

Candela: The unit of luminous intensity, of such a magnitude

The illustrations and documentation in this chapter are the copyright of Philips Industries Ltd., to whom acknowledgement is due for their kind permission to reproduce the material.

that the luminance of a full radiator (*q.v.*) at the temperature of solidification of platinum is 60 units of luminous intensity per sq. cm. (abbreviation cd).

Colour temperature: The colour temperature of a light source is that of a full radiator (*q.v.*) which would emit radiation of substantially the same spectral distribution in the visible region as the radiation from the light source and which would have the same colour.

Direct lighting: A system of lighting in which the greater part of the luminous flux after leaving the sources passes directly towards the area illuminated.

Indirect lighting: A system in which the greater part of the luminous flux reaches the area to be illuminated after reflection from a ceiling or other object external to the sources.

Efficiency of a light source is the ratio of luminous flux emitted to the power consumed by the source and for electric lamps is expressed in lumens per watt.

Foot-lambert: A unit of luminance, the luminance of a uniform diffuser emitting one lumen per sq. ft. (abbreviation ft.-l.) (The use of 'lambert' by itself is officially deprecated.)

Full radiator: A light source emitting radiation, the spectral distribution of which is dependent on the temperature only and not on the material and nature of the source.

Luminance. The quotient of the luminous intensity of a surface in a given direction of an infinitesimal element of the surface containing the point under consideration on a plane perpendicular to the given direction (symbol L).

Lumen: The unit of luminous flux (symbol lm.) emitted in unit solid angle of one steradian by a point source having a uniform intensity of one candela (abbreviation 1m.).

Lumen per sq. ft. (abbreviation lm/ft^2) 1 lm/ft^2 = 10.764 lux.

Lux: A unit of illumination of one lumen per sq. metre (abbreviation lx).

Luminosity: The attribute of visual perception in accordance with which an area appears to emit more or less light.

Luminous flux: That quantity characteristic of radiant flux which expresses its capacity to produce visual sensation, evaluated according to the values of relative luminous efficiency for the light adopted by the CIE (Commission Internationale de l'Eclairage). (Symbol F or O.)

Luminous efficiency: The quotient of luminous flux by the corresponding radiant flux (symbol K).

Maintenance factor: The ratio of average illumination maintained on the working plane at a given time to the average illumination obtained when the installation was first fitted. This factor includes deterioration from all causes.

Radiant flux: Power emitted or received in the form of radiation.

Working Plane: The plane on which illumination measurements are made. Unless otherwise stated the plane is assumed to be horizontal and 0.85 m. (2 ft. 9 in.) above the floor.

MOUNTING OF LIGHT SOURCES

Alleyways, stairways, lobbies and lifts

Almost invariably these localities will be entirely without daylight or with very little. They will be entered from spaces already either daylit or artificially lit and the transition must be smooth. In the spaces themselves contrasting brightness and shadows must be avoided.

In general, spacing between fittings should not be less than the height nor greater than 1½ times the height in an alleyway except where a continuous row of recessed ceiling fittings with diffused panels is installed. Because of low ceiling height in lights the lighting should not be too glaring and fluorescent lamps are very suitable.

Galleys

The galley is one of the most important working areas, particularly in passenger liners. Good illumination brings improved productivity, faster working, fewer mistakes, a reduction in accidents and better hygiene. Tubular fluorescent lamps are suitable for general lighting and a colour close to tungsten lighting is recommended because food will be seen in this quality of lighting when it is served and chefs can take pride in the appearance of the food they are producing. In special circumstances watertight fittings may be necessary when it comes to washing or hosing down.

Recessed dustlight diffusing fluorescent fittings also have their uses. Avoidance of shadows in working areas may need the provision of local lighting. Locations where grease and fat easily collects require special emphasis. Perspex covers must be avoided where temperatures are liable to exceed 60°C as they will distort.

Machinery spaces

The importance of adequate and effective lighting in these spaces needs no emphasis. Machinery rooms are usually of great height and obstructed by gangways, piping and other interferences. Narrow beam light sources are desirable e.g. 250 W fluorescent-reflector lamps in fittings with integral control gear.

A suitably constructed fitting requires practically no maintenance being independent of atmospheric pollution. Local lighting of gauges, switchboards etc. require higher illumination levels. Fittings with fibreglass bodies reduce maintenance i.e. no painting or rust problems.

In boiler rooms heat problems must be taken into account in order to maintain the correct lumen output. For the shaft tunnel fluorescent diffusing fittings are most suitable.

Cold rooms and refrigerated spaces

Fluorescent lamps are unsuitable for these conditions unless the temperature is higher than −5°C. At lower temperatures starting can be slow and light output poor. A suitable light source is the 50 W or 80 W mercury fluorescent lamp which will operate down to −50°C.

Deck lighting

The vicinity of cargo hatches requires effective lighting, usually in the form of 1000 W halogen floodlights fixed to the ship's structure — a minimum of two to each hatch.

Open decks are lit by watertight (hoseproof) deck and bulkhead fittings which have a protective guard except in covered passenger areas and promenades. In the vicinity of stairways and narrow spaces safety lighting is necessary. Sports decks can be lit with floodlights mounted on the windscreens. For swimming pools, either indoor or outdoor underwater lighting can consist of mercury fluorescent reflector lamps (125 W or 250 W) flush-mounted in the walls. Reflector lamps can be recessed in the perimeter ledges.

For special occasions strings of coloured lamps are sometimes used. Subject to navigation safety regulations floodlighting of the superstructure, mast and funnel can be bathed in light of different colours. Floodlights with 1000 W halogen lamps or 400 W high-pressure mercury lamps or watertight lampholders with pressed-glass reflector lamps are suitable light sources. Many passenger liners have luminous name signs.

For lifeboat launching positions, two lamps of the pressed-glass reflector type (300 W PAR56 or 150 W PAR38) with special watertight lampholders can be used. Their location should be such that they can be directed on to the boat or on to the launching gear. Assembly areas can be lit by fittings at regular distances.

Wheelhouse and navigation spaces

For night sailing conditions special considerations apply. Essential instruments should be illuminated by red lamps radiating light of wavelengths not less than 60 nm and a luminance not greater than 0.1 footlambert. Otherwise, during night sailing the wheelhouse must be in complete darkness.

The sole purpose of lighting will be to provide adequate light for operation and maintenance tasks on steering, navigational and radar equipment. In the chart room and operation control rooms ceiling mounted or recessed fittings are suitable, including lighting supplied from the emergency system.

Emergency lighting

Statutory regulations (when applicable) require emergency lighting to be embodied in the general system. All public and crew areas, alleyways, cabins, service spaces, stairways and exits must be provided with emergency lighting to facilitate escape. Also all boat stations and lifeboat launching gear.

Requirements for emergency lighting are prescribed in the 1974 Convention for Safety of Life at Sea and by Lloyd's Register of Shipping and the Department of Trade (Marine Division). Fluorescent lamps are unsuitable unless it can be shown that they will operate satisfactorily (including restriking) at the reduced supply voltages and lower limits of ambient temperature that may be expected to obtain in an emergency. All emergency lights must bear a distinguishing mark for identification. Radio telephone stations must have an emergency light independent of the normal lighting system.

Container ships

In areas in which dangerous gases could be present there is a requirement for Division II type of lighting unit. Fluorescent fittings for these areas must normally be of the starterless type unless, special dispensation by the Board of Trade has been obtained, permitting starters which are sealed within the fitting. Details concerning Division II areas are obtainable from the British Standards Institution.

A minimum illumination level of 50 lux is required for the loading of containers. Fittings equipped with 400 W/40 000 lm medium pressure sodium lamps have been found suitable for general lighting purposes.

Tankers

The vast deck areas of super-tankers present a special problem and illumination levels of the order of 60/70 lux must be contemplated. The choice at present is limited virtually to high-pressure sodium lamps, preferably in twin-lamp fittings to minimise mounting space and thereby obtaining approximately 80 000 lumens per unit.

A 250 000 ton tanker would require 30 to 32 units to obtain the average lighting required.

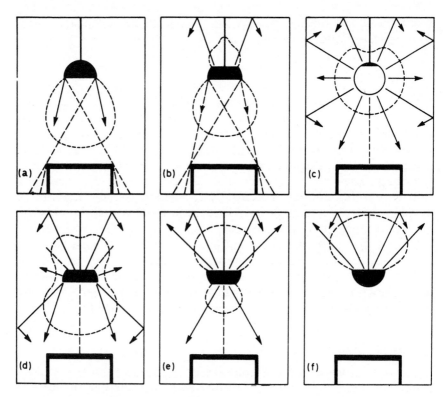

Figure 16.1 Types of lighting distribution

Systems	Downwards	Upwards
(a) Direct	90–100%	0– 10%
(b) Semi-direct	90– 90%	10– 40%
(c) General diffuse	approx. 50%	approx. 50%
(d) Mixed diffuse	40– 60%	40– 60%
(e) Semi-indirect	10– 40%	60– 90%
(f) Indirect	0– 10%	90–100%

The light distribution of fittings

Light radiated mainly downwards from the fitting is termed direct and if it is upwards it is indirect. Naturally there are intermediate forms, partly direct and partly indirect.

Figure 16.1 gives a rough indication of these systems, light distribution being expressed in percentages.

LIGHTING DATA

Brightness of light sources

In service areas, a level of 1000 lux or more could be provided by fluorescent lamps fitted to unscreened mounting channels against a white ceiling but, in practice, this would give rise to complaints of 'too much light'. The real cause is usually glare.

There are two main forms of glare; disability glare and discomfort glare. The former is usually from too bright or inadequately screened bare lamps or from maladjusted reflector lamps. Discomfort can arise from unscreened fluorescent lamps in the field of vision. For the avoidance of glare the system used in the UK is that of the Illuminating Engineering Society Code of Practice. The following measures are advised:
1. Screen the light source by means of a reflector, louvre or cover.
2. The contrast between fitting and background should not be too great (light-coloured ceilings).
3. Place light sources as far as possible outside the field of view, mounted to the ceiling or recessed.
4. The working surfaces of control desks and worktables should be given a matt or eggshell finish and strongly reflecting objects avoided.

Luminance measurement

The working terms of illumination are lux (lm/ft^2) rather than luminance (cd/m^2 or cd/ft^2). A well-known instrument for measuring lux is a light meter but calculation of luminance is more complicated and the ratio between luminances more difficult to forecast.

Hitherto there has been a lack of handy luminance meters but various types are now becoming available. Also more practical methods of calculation are being investigated on a basis of luminance ratio.

Uniformity of illumination

Too great a distance between fittings causes excessive variation from average illumination. The schedule which follows gives a guide to the maximum permissible distances between light sources. This is mainly a matter of the spacing/mounting-height ratio of the light sources, mounting-height being the height above working plane. The narrower the beam of reflector lamps the smaller will be the spacing distances.

1. *Direct and predominantly direct lighting:*
   150 W Pressed-glass 'Spot' $S \leqslant 0.4$ h.
   150 W Pressed-glass 'Flood' $S \leqslant 0.7$ h.
   Closed fittings with louvres $S \leqslant 1.35$ h.
2. *Diffusers, semi-direct and semi-indirect:* $S \leqslant 1.7$ h.
3. *Semi-indirect fittings mounted against the ceiling:* Fluorescent lamps, without diffuser, flush to the ceiling; $S \leqslant 1.5$ h.
4. *Predominantly indirect lighting:* $S \leqslant 3 \times d$.
5. *Indirect lighting:* Ordinary incandescent lamps or fluorescent lamps in coves on two sides $S \leqslant 3 \times d$.
where:

S = Max. spacing between light sources, in order to ensure sufficient uniformity.
h = height of light source above the working plane.
d = distance from a fitting to the ceiling.
$\leqslant$ = less than or equal to.

Colour of the light

'White' light is composed of a number of the colours of the spectrum, i.e. red, orange, yellow, green, blue and violet. The proportions of these colours determine the appearance of colours in a room, i.e. colour rendering.

When red is lacking the red colours become invisible or are suppressed according to the amount of red in the light and this will apply to food, furnishings and human complexion.

Light sources – chief characteristics and methods of operation

A great many types of lamp are now available to the lighting engineer. Seven major considerations will influence his choice:

1. Required output.
2. Efficiency.

3. Lamp dimensions and relevant fitting.
4. Operating conditions and life performance.
5. Source brightness.
6. Colour.
7. Ease of maintenance.

The minimum level of illumination in crew spaces is stipulated in *The Merchant Shipping (Crew Accommodation) Regulations; Amendment Regulations 1954; Statutory Instrument 1954 No. 1660.* From these the total light output required from the fittings can be calculated, bearing in mind the utilisation and maintenance factors. Thus the light output per lamp and number of lamps required can be determined.

In areas where a continuously high level of lighting is required, a high efficiency is important but for indicator lamps and those used only occasionally efficiency is secondary compared with size and simplicity. Lamp life is an important consideration and in many cases is affected by shock and severe vibration. Cleaning and lamp replacement must be capable of being carried out quickly and efficiently.

Incandescent lamps are still the simplest and most convenient for many purposes. Their efficiency is limited and if used to provide adequate lighting over large areas they increase the problem of heat removal, particularly in the tropics.

The high efficiency of discharge lamps of the sodium and mercury types is offset by poor colour rendering and long starting times. The development from these types of the tubular fluorescent lamps of similar efficiency but of good colour rendering and quick starting which can be switched as incandescent lamps makes them eminently desirable for high level general lighting.

Incandescent lamps

In 1879 Swan and Edison first demonstrated practical lamps in which light was produced by electrically heating a carbon filament. The efficiency and life was low, limited by evaporation of the carbon filament. In 1907 the first lamps using a tungsten filament were introduced.

The use of gas fillings permitted higher filament temperatures and coiled and coiled coil filaments increased the efficiency until it is now ten times that of the original Swan lamp. Lamp bulbs are available in different shapes and with different finishes for influencing the quality or colour of the light. A selection of types is shown in Figure 16.2.

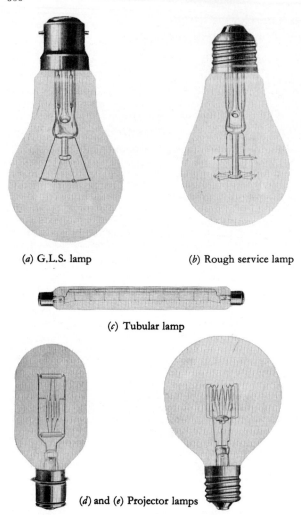

(a) G.L.S. lamp   (b) Rough service lamp

(c) Tubular lamp

(d) and (e) Projector lamps

Figure 16.2 Types of incandescent lamp

The front of the pressed glass bulb has special patterns depending on whether spot or floodlighting purposes are required.

Life and luminous flux are influenced by the filament temperature. The higher the temperature the greater the efficiency (lumens emitted per watt) but the shorter the life. An economic balance is arrived at depending on the purpose of the lamp. For general service (GLS) lamps where low replacement cost and relatively long life is desirable a life of 1000 hours is the accepted standard.

Effect of voltage variation

An increase of voltage means a higher operating temperature resulting in increased light output and a proportionately greater emission of the shorter wavelengths so the colour becomes whiter. The filament is nearer the melting point so the life is shortened. An overvoltage of 5% will increase the lumen output 20% but will halve the life. On the other hand a reduction of 5% reduces the lumen output 20% giving a perceptible reddening of the light but with double the life. Variations in consumption, lumens, efficiency and life are illustrated in Figure 16.3.

In spite of the increased life obtained by running below rated voltage it is uneconomical. The lamp will not be operating under the conditions for which it was designed, which are intended to be those most economical to the user. Lighting installations are sometimes spoiled by inadequate wiring giving a voltage drop so large that lamp performance is affected.

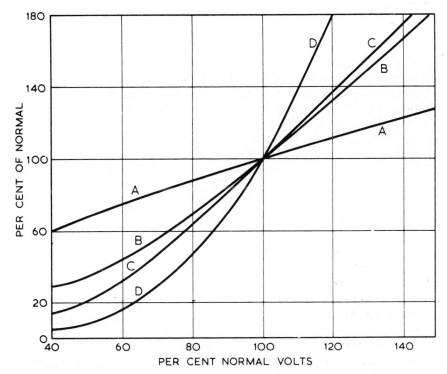

Figure 16.3 Variation of characteristic of incandescent (tungsten) lamps with applied voltage
A. Amperes. B. Watts. C. Lumens/Watt. D. lumens

The relationship between lamp characteristic and applied voltage can be expressed as follows:

(V = rated voltage V_1 = applied voltage)

$$\frac{\text{luminous flux}}{\text{nominal luminous flux}} = \frac{V_1}{V}^{3.55}$$

$$\frac{\text{wattage}}{\text{nominal wattage}} = \frac{V_1}{V}^{1.55}$$

$$\frac{\text{luminous efficiency}}{\text{nominal luminous efficiency}} = \frac{V_1}{V}^{2}$$

$$\frac{\text{life}}{\text{life at rated voltage}} = \frac{V_1}{V}^{-14}$$

INCANDESCENT LAMPS

For general lighting (GLS): These are the jack-of-all-trades lamps, but are also used for many special purposes (see Figure 16.2).

Vacuum lamps: Single coil lamps for small ratings up to 25 W.

Gas-filled lamps with coiled coil for ratings 25 W to 150 W.

Single coil gas-filled lamps for ratings up to 200 W clear of pearl, frosted or opalised or 300 W to 1000 W practically always clear.

Originally all lamps were clear but in course of time they have been almost entirely replaced by the inside-frosted (pearl) type which owing to its limited glare has a wide application. Nevertheless the clear bulb is still used in well shielded fittings and in those cases where brilliance and sparkle are more important than avoidance of glare.

Lamps are available having two separate filaments, each of a different wattage, which can be lit individually or together making it possible to obtain three different illumination levels. The medium wattage should be regarded as normal, the lower for decoration or subdued lighting and the combined wattage where visual requirements are important.

Bowl-reflector lamps are normal inside-frosted lamps (60 W–200 W), the bulb having a silvered bowl. The glaring filament is completely shielded from view and used with suitable fittings these lamps give diffused lighting with an indirect component. For spot-lighting of small areas 24 V reflector lamp with clear bulb is available.

Reinforced-construction lamps (often loosely called 'Rough Service' lamps) have a particularly strong filament which makes them suitable for places subject to shocks, bumps and vibration. They are available in inside-frosted finish in sizes 25 W to 200 W. (see Figure 16.2).

Among the special types are tubular incandescent lamps with a cap at each end (Figure 16.2). Because of the small diameter tube, lamps of this kind can be concealed behind small coves, showcases, aquaria, pictures and mirrors.

There is an increasing demand for coloured lamps for outdoor use e.g. for lido decks. The colour coating being flushed inside the bulb it cannot chip, scratch or fade or be affected by weathering. Two shapes can be supplied — *normal* or *drop* shape.As decorative lamps are in prominent positions their luminance must be low to exclude glare and they are invariably of low wattage.

PRESSED-GLASS REFLECTOR LAMPS

One of the latest technical advances is the pressed-glass reflector lamp. Heat- and weather-resistant hard pressed-glass of compact construction ensures an accurately controlled beam-pattern making them an excellent and rapid means of providing a highly efficient and economical lighting media. They can be used either inside or outdoors and have a higher light output and longer life than blown-bulb reflector lamps (2000 hours versus 1000 hours) and blend successfully with fluorescent lamps. By suitable shaping, flood-lighting or spot lighting can be obtained suitable for directional lighting on dance floors, the exterior of upper decks, swimming pools etc.

Blown-bulb reflector lamps

This is a well-established group used exclusively for indoor lighting which can be used in conditions where a large number of light sources of lower luminous intensity than that of pressed-glass reflector lamps is preferable to a small number of the latter of higher luminous intensity.

Par 38 lamps

Lamps of 100 W and 150 W with beam width $2 \times 7.5°$ with a stippled front refractor producing narrow homogeneous light beams of very high luminous intensity. They are used mainly for illumination of small surfaces and for objects placed at greater distances and for dramatic effects.

Par 26 lamps

These are narrow beam spot lamps 300 W beam width 2 × 7.5° horizontal by 2 × 4.5° vertical for strong local lighting or, when used in batteries, for high levels of floodlighting.

They are usually focused on distant objects e.g. mast, funnel and superstructure when in port.

Pressed-glass spot and wide floodlight Par 38 lamps

Lamps (100 W and 150 W) with a front glass made of prismatic elements produce homogeneous floodlight beams of 2 × 17.5° (flood) or 2 × 25° (wide flood). Suitable for modelling effects and for obtaining high illumination levels in large areas e.g. lounges and dining-rooms.

Pressed-glass colour floodlamps

This is a range of lamps with a weatherproof coloured silicone coating in red, blue, yellow or green on the refractor face providing opportunities for decorative lighting, creating colour effects in indoor and outdoor situations.

Figure 16.4 Pressed-glass floodlamp (Philips Industries)

Halogen lamps

The addition of a halogen vapour to the filling gas is one of the latest developments in incandescent lamp manufacture. Halogens are in a group consisting of the elements fluorine, chlorine, bromine and iodine. The vapour combines with the evaporated particles driven off the filament forming tungsten halogenide which then spreads over the filament where, owing to the high temperature, the tungsten settles and the halogen is released to start a new cycle, known as the regenerative cycle. It makes possible an increase in the temperature of the filament to about $3000°K$.

Figure 16.5 2000 W tubular quartz halogen lamps (Philips Industries)

The luminous efficiency of present day high wattage halogen lamps (Figure 16.5) is 20—25 lm/W with a lifetime of about 2000 hours. When suitably housed they are suitable for outdoor flood-lighting and are also often used for stage lighting (Figure 16.6).

Figure 16.6 Floodlight tungsten-halogen fitting for outdoor floodlighting (Philips Industries)

Projector lamps

These are specifically designed for high brightness and the filament is arranged for maximum utilisation in optical systems (Figure 16.2). The high temperature results in higher efficiency but a shorter life. They are usually fitted with special prefocus caps to ensure correct location in the optical system.

Bulb size is reduced to a minimum and, to avoid overheating the glass, many types can be operated only in one position, usually cap down or at a limited angle of tilt. Early lamp failure can occur if the ventilating system is not efficiently maintained.

Lamp caps

For general lighting purposes, screw and bayonet caps in several sizes have been standardised. They are designated by the letters E (Edison) and B (Bayonet) followed by figures indicating cap diameter and length in mm.

General service lamps have E27 screw caps up to 300 W or B23 bayonet caps up to 150 W. Higher wattages use E40 screw caps (called Goliath). Some of the lower wattage lamps such as candle, lustre, tubular, pilot and decorative types are made with E14 screw (also called Mignon) or B15 bayonet caps. Special dispensation must be obtained if these are to be used at mains voltage.

GAS DISCHARGE LAMPS

Generation of light in these lamps is the result of an electric current passing through a gas and/or metal vapour such as sodium or mercury (mercury lamps, fluorescent lamps). Passage of current is initiated when a sufficiently high voltage is applied. Once this has taken place there is no limit to the discharge and in a very short time the current would increase and the lamp soon burn out unless suitable devices were embodied. Every gas discharge lamp, therefore, has a ballast to limit the current to an appropriate value, usually a choke or sometimes a leak transformer.

Properties of the ballast are very important as they determine the correct lamp current and voltage on which depend the light radiated, luminous efficiency and life of the lamp.

Mercury fluorescent lamps

These are available in wattages from 50 W to 2,000 W and have an outer bulb with an inner coating of fluorescent powder. Ultraviolet radiation from a quartz tube is converted into visible radiation by the fluorescent material. This is mainly in the red region of the spectrum. The resultant colour rendering is considerably better than that of a mercury lamp without the fluorescent coating.

If a stroboscopic effect is to be avoided in interior lighting, lamps should be distributed across other phases of the supply. With a 15% light depreciation a life of about 9000 hours can be expected. They can burn in any position.

Blended-light mercury lamps

These may be considered as a variant of ordinary mercury lamps the lack of red radiation being compensated for by radiation from a filament. This is in series with the mercury discharge tube and also serves as a ballast. As this is incorporated in the lamp, the blended lamp can often replace incandescent lamps without further change especially in cargo holds etc. In this way the luminous efficiency (25 lm/W.) of an installation can be increased considerably without extra installation costs and under normal conditions the life is several times that of incandescent lamps.

FLUORESCENT LAMPS

In the early 1930's research was directed towards better efficiencies than those obtainable from filaments and free from the poor colour radiation of sodium and mercury vapour lamps. The tubular low-pressure fluorescent lamp emerged in 1939, producing a white light obtained from fluorescent material excited by ultraviolet radiation from a low pressure discharge. The efficiency was several times that of filament lamps.

Fluorescent lamps are grouped according to methods of starting and operation. Each method requires a different combination of lamp and auxiliary equipment.

The range comprises the following types:

1. The standard range operating with starter switches and ballasts. (Figure 16.7).
2. Rapid start lamps without starters but with special ballasts which incorporate pre-heat transformers for the electrodes.
3. A reflector type with an internal reflecting powder layer, normally starter operated but can also be supplied as rapid start.
4. For d.c. operation some versions need auxiliary equipment such as a stabilising lamp and magnetic relays, others operate on stabilising tubes.
5. Lamps with an inside ignition strip can operate with stabilising lamps as well as with a ballast. No starter is required.

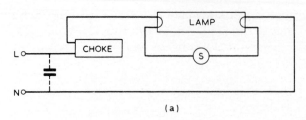

(a)

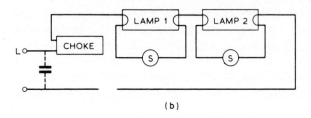

(b)

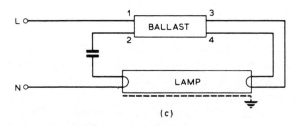

(c)

Figure 16.7 Fluorescent circuit diagrams
(a) Single tube switch start circuit
(b) Up to 2 ft. twin lamp switch start circuit
(c) 20/65 W switchless start circuit

6. When housed in flameproof fittings a type is available which operates on the same ballast mentioned above, without starter.

Colour rendering index

In strict lighting technology colours are given numbers for identification and coding purposes. Fluorescent lamps are popularly described as follows:

Warm white	(Colour 29)
Warm white de luxe	(Colour 32)
Daylight	(Colour 33)
White	(Colour 35)

There are many others but these are the common types applicable to ship installations.

For classifying the light colours of fluorescent lamps an internationally agreed index (Ra) has recently been adopted. The colour rendering properties of a particular fluorescent can be read off immediately from a certain index figure. A *full radiator* is given index 100 so that a lamp showing complete agreement would score 100. Deviations in characteristics in relation to *full radiator* are expressed by an index less than 100. On this scale a 40 W. Warm White de Luxe (Colour 32) lamp has an index as high as 86 while a clear mercury vapour lamp may be as low as 17 and that of colour 27 for example is index 94. It is important to keep in mind that a direct comparison of colour rendering properties is only possible between lamps of the same colour temperature category.

Fluorescent lamp colours are divided broadly into two classes, high efficiency (standard colours) and de luxe. In the former, most of the luminous flux is emitted towards the middle of the range of visible wavelength while in the de luxe type a better rendering is achieved by a mixture of powders which produce a better spread — but inevitably at the cost of efficiency.

The colour rendering index Ra does not show that one colour of light source is inherently better than another. It simply rates each specific colour in terms of its own colour rendering purpose i.e. it determines how closely it approaches the *full radiator* of the same colour temperature.

For lighting of rooms in ships, various recommendations state that for visual comfort and pleasant colour rendering the colour rendering should be approximately 3000° K with an Ra index of at least 80. During the past decade the emphasis has changed from the quantity of lumens emitted to their quality but as so often is the case compromise has to be accepted and a balance between lumen output and colour rendering.

Ballasts

Ballasts in fluorescent lighting installations are an essential and decisive factor in correct operation. Their three most important functions are:

1. Pre-heating the lamp electrodes to start electron emission.
2. Providing the high voltage necessary to start the arc between electrodes.
3. Stabilising the current and power to the correct value.

Their design must be such as to keep their power loss low, resulting in long operating life, and size and weight should be minimal. High quality ballasts are filled with a thermosetting specially compounded polyester which remains hard and does not flow; temperature rises are stipulated in IEC and CEE specifications. Being hermetically sealed they are unaffected by ambient conditions and ballast hum is virtually absent.

To convert d.c. supplies to the a.c. required for fluorescent lamps special transistor ballasts without moving parts and without need for servicing are necessary.

Some types of fluorescent lamps may give rise to radio interference in certain locations and will then require to be fitted with suppressors usually in the form of a capacitor.

Glow starters

The function of the starter is automatic starting and its closing voltage must lie between two limits. The upper one is the lowest voltage at which it should operate and the lower one is governed by the highest value which the arc voltage can reach. Should the switch reclose under the latter condition, i.e. under the influence of arc voltage the lamp would be short circuited and begin flickering off and on. Since the no-load voltage of the ballast is, in most cases, roughly twice the arc voltage of the lamp it is evident that, for lamps of different arc voltages, different starter switches are necessary.

The stated initial luminous flux of a fluorescent lamp is only guaranteed when the tube wall is at a temperature of approximately

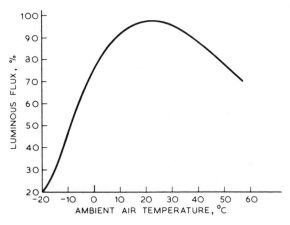

Figure 16.8 Luminous flux of a fluorescent lamp as a function of ambient air temperature (Philips Industries)

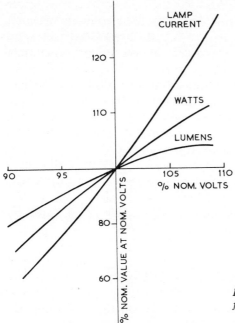

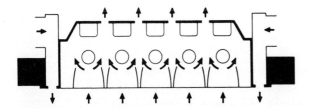

Figure 16.9 Effect of voltage variation on fluorescent lamps

45°C. (Figure 16.8). Especially in the case of inexpensively built narrow reflectors carrying three or even four lamps the temperature at the lamp wall and at the ballasts may rise to 75°C. or even to 85°C. This can cause a decrease of 10–25% in luminous flux. The effect of voltage variation is shown in Figure 16.9. Where the ceiling is provided with air outlets for the ventilating system it is possible to utilise the lighting fittings in conjunction with the air ventilation. A typical arrangement is shown in Figure 16.10.

Figure 16.10 Cross-section of a recessed mirror reflector fitting with slots in the top plate for return air.
Fresh air is supplied through slots parallel to the sides of the fitting. (Philips Industries)

NEON LAMPS

Although popularly known as neon tubes they are more correctly described as cold cathode tubes and various gas fillings, other than neon, are necessary if other colours are required. The cold electrodes, consist of pure iron and very long tubes call for the use of very high voltages of the order of 6000 V. Lengths can be up to about 750 cm with diameters from 12—25 mm and can be bent into any required shape. Current is very low and varies from 50 mA to 200 mA.

The colours available and the appropriate gases used are red (neon), pink (helium), golden yellow (nitrogen), yellow (sodium), pale blue (krypton, carbonic acid and mercury vapour), violet (argon). Variations can be produced by using either coloured glass walls with a filter or by colour powder. The luminous flux can be regulated by means of a thyristor light regulator.

LIGHT REGULATING EQUIPMENT (DIMMING)

With incandescent lamps the light can be regulated by varying the applied voltage but this simple method cannot be used with gas-discharge lamps as the lamp must be reignited every half-cycle and a certain ignition voltage is necessary. Ignition will no longer take place if this voltage is reduced, neither will the lamp remain burning.

Several systems of dimming, as it is called, of starterless rapid start fluorescent lamps are known, such for instance as the use of thyristors. With these systems the voltage is maintained fairly constant but the moment of ignition and thus the current in the lamp is controlled. Two thyristors are connected anti-parallel and this combination is included in series with the lamps in one circuit.

To avoid radio interference a filter is connected in series with the thyristors. In order to give good pre-heating of the electrodes of the fluorescent lamps specially developed ballasts are applied. The ballast contains a preheat transformer for which two secondary windings and one series impedance are provided. The lamp is connected in series with the impedance to the dimming apparatus. During each half-cycle the thyristors will, in turn, allow current to pass provided a suitable signal ensures that they become conductive.

A phase-changing network postpones the moment at which the signal operates so that the average current is regulated. A circuit which ensures that the luminous flux is constant in each set position, independent of mains voltage fluctuations is included in the apparatus.

INSTALLATION AND MAINTENANCE

Wiring

The wiring of fluorescent lamp circuits requires special consideration and this applies also to switches. Because the circuit, unless fitted with power factor correction devices, operates at less than unity power factor the current is greater than that calculated from the rated lamp watts.

Whenever possible, the lamp fitting supplier should be consulted as the power factor and control gear losses vary with different types. In the absence of maker's ratings, the demand in volt-amperes should be taken for the purpose of switch and cable ratings as 1.8 times the rated lamp watts. This is based on the assumption that the power factor is not less than 0.85 lagging and takes into account control gear losses and haromonic currents.

High voltage connections in the vicinity of cold cathode (neon) tubes must be ozone resistant or suitably protected. Appropriate requirements will be found in BS 559.

Lamp replacement

The basis of good maintenance for the majority of lighting installations, particularly in passenger ships, should be group replacement of lamps. This is becoming widely accepted as the most economical form of relamping.

The most economic point in lamp life can be assessed in two ways:

1. By taking account of the lumen depreciation of the lamp during life.
2. By considering the failure pattern of lamps.

The lamp lumen values used in designing the lighting system should be that point in the life of the lamp at which it is intended to change the lamps. This will ensure that at least the required minimum illumination level will always be maintained. The illumination level should therefore be measured and after the installation has been in operation for some time the level compared with that initially obtained will in most cases show a noticeable depreciation (known as the maintenance factor). This can be due to four causes:

1. Soiling of the lamps.
2. Soiling of the installation.
3. Reduced radiation by ceilings and walls.
4. Mechanical ageing of the lamps.

It is a mistake to assume that a lamp maintains its value as long as it still functions. The luminous flux decreases considerably due to age but the power consumption remains the same and the wasted power may exceed the value of a new lamp.

Fluorescent lamps are assigned average lives but manufacturing tolerances are inevitable and it is impossible for every lamp to attain exactly the average life. Gradually the number of lamp failures increases until the average life approaches; then failures increase relatively rapidly. The best time for replacement of lamp is, in general, before the point is reached at which the failures begin to increase rapidly. This point lies at 60—70% of the average life. It is only possible to determine the average life statistically i.e. on the basis of tests embracing a very large number of lamps which are tested under precisely defined conditions and special statistical methods have been developed for this purpose.

Factors which influence the life of gas-discharge lamps are:

> The switching frequency i.e. number of burning hours per switching.
> The ambient temperature.
> The quality of the ballast.
> The method of ignition.
> The circuit: inductive or capacitive.
> The humidity of the surroundings.

It will be obvious with so many factors involved that, with fluorescent lamps, the spread in life is much greater than in the case of incandescent lamps. Summarising, the conclusion can be reached that there is a difference between the electrical life of a fluorescent lamp and its life based on luminous efficiency. Since the electrical life is much longer than the luminous efficiency it is essential for rational maintenance to replace all fluorescent lamps at the end of the luminous efficiency life. Group replacement is preferable to haphazard replacement and this provides an opportunity for regular cleaning of the fitting. It can be arranged at a convenient point in time e.g. annual overhaul or when the ship is in dock.

End of life is usually accompanied by flickering caused by regular opening and closing of the starter. At each closure a short-circuit current flows through the ballast and this produces excessive temperature in the ballast. An increase of $10°C$ means halving its life. If excessive flickering has occurred the starter should always be replaced.

17 Electrical deck auxiliaries

These auxiliaries, in the main, comprise cargo winches (which may include warping as a subsidiary duty), cranes, capstans, warping winches, mooring winches, windlasses and hatch-cover winches. Except for cranes, each of these may sometimes be used for duties other than those for which they are primarily intended. The systems of control as between these various applications bear a similarity but with variations to suit the operating conditions. It will be convenient to deal with them under their different headings, but there are divergencies between the methods favoured by different makers and descriptions will therefore be confined to representative schemes.

Electro-hydraulic winches do not call for special mention as they use a continuous running motor, which can be either a.c. or d.c. They can be operated either singly or in groups from one pump.

Many electrical deck auxiliary schemes make use of contactors for control purposes and where these are of such size and numbers as to warrant it they can be accommodated in a separate contactor deckhouse instead of in the winch assembly. This increases the amount of cabling but on the other hand it economises deck space in the vicinity of the winch, making for cleaner lines and unobstructed viewing by the operator. It also facilitates maintenance work which in any case is not always opportune to carry out when the ship is in port and when the winches are in use. While at sea maintenance can be carried out under protection from the elements.

In every winch, etc., in which the load is lowered while the motor is mechanically coupled such as in systems employing power lowering it is essential to prevent the load taking charge and lowering at a speed which will damage the motor armature. To safeguard against this contingency earlier drives utilised a form of mechanical braking system such as centrifugal or foot-operated brakes. Present day devices rely on inherent electrical braking systems.

321

Brakes

All brakes should be of the 'fail safe' type, i.e. in the event of failure the brake should be automatically applied, thus preventing the load running back. A type of brake which meets these requirements is as shown in Figure 17.1.

A number of brake pads are located in a carrier keyed to the motor shaft. The armature plate, by means of a number of springs located in the periphery of the magnet applies pressure to the pads which are free to move axially and these are forced against the friction surface of the brake backplate thus preventing the motor

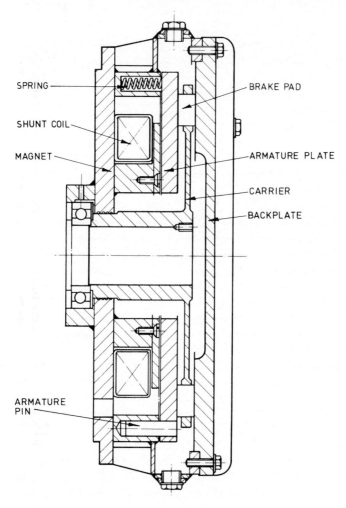

Figure 17.1. Section of a typical 'fail-safe' brake

shaft from turning. When energised the armature plate is attracted to the magnet, thus releasing the pad pressure and allowing the shaft to rotate.

Quick release is achieved by initially applying 3 × rated d.c. voltage to the shunt coil, this being reduced to rated voltage after a short interval by means of a timer circuit which inserts an economy resistance. No adjustment of the brake is necessary during the working life of the pads and to renew these requires only the removal of the backplate.

Warping

Warping is carried out on a drum of different shape from those used for handling cargo. These drums are of such a shape that the hawser will always slip towards the waist of the drum. They also have a flange which will prevent the hawser running over the rim. Exceeding a pre-determined torque can be prevented by automatically inserting a resistance in the motor circuit or by other means according to the control system.

Capstan barrels are normally mounted on a vertical driving shaft, the barrel having whelps cast on. The driving motor is frequently mounted below deck in order to leave as much free space as possible for handling lines. The commonest method of operation is for one end of the line to be attached to a fixed bollard on the wharf or on another adjacent vessel and the line is then given three or four turns round the capstan barrel with the free end held by the operator. When the free end is pulled so as to tighten the grip of the line on the barrel the line between the capstan and the fixed end is wound in by the friction on the barrel. If the operator slackens or surges his line it loses its grip on the barrel and the line is freed. There are, of course, other more complex uses for capstans.

Anchor windlasses are vital to the safety of the ship, its crew and cargo and there is no standby; they are subject to Classification Rules and individual government requirements.

The cable lifter is specially shaped to fit the links of the cables and will normally fit four or five links around its circumference which is then known as four or five snug although actually only two links are engaged at any one time. The lifter runs freely on a shaft or can be disengaged from the drive and has on one flange a rim to take a hand-brake. The lifter is disengaged for lowering, the paying-out speed being controlled by the brake or if paid out under electrical power the speed is controlled electrically.

Undue stress must not be applied to the cable and a slipping clutch is incorporated between the motor and magnetic brake and the driving shaft and set to slip at approximately 150% of full load torque. Otherwise excessive stress could be applied to the cable by the momentum of the motor armature, by the magnetic brake, or by a sudden obstruction when heaving or when bringing the anchors into the hawsepipe. The electrical equipment should give a crawl speed to enable the anchor to be housed safely and to allow the motor to stall when it is fully home.

The hauling speed is usually regulated to about 0.15 m/s at rated load but as the chain is recovered and the load is thereby reduced the characteristic of d.c. windlasses is such that the hauling speed will increase. In some waters where there is a fast-running current or stream the speed at which the cable can be recovered is important.

When dropping anchor it is lowered as speedily as possible, usually in bursts of 5 fathoms at a time while the anchor is free to drop. The friction brake is applied to the lifter by means of tightening screws and is used to control the lowering. A bow-stopper is normally fitted at the head of the hawsepipe and relieves the windlass from strain when riding at anchor. This bow-stopper is in the form of a jaw holding a link by a wedge action. When it is necessary to take in cable the jaw holding the link is self-releasing. To break out anchor the vessel is moved into a position directly above the anchor thereby reducing the strain of breaking out.

It is usual practice for windlasses to also perform warping duties which involve a pull of approximately 40% of that of the cable lifters but at a faster speed and a still faster speed when recovering warping lines after they have been cast off from the quayside bollards.

Windlasses are in the main divided into two classes: one which will stall for short periods for use, in particular while navigating the locks of the St. Lawrence Seaway, and the other for constant tensioning against rising and falling tides or lock waters and during rapid loading or unloading. For the former requirement a torque limiting feature is provided.

Cargo winches are also adapted for dual purposes, by providing a two-position switch, one for cargo and the other for mooring. When Ward Leonard systems are used, the generator field is weakened on the mooring side providing a reduced torque on all control steps ensuring reduced heating under stalled conditions. Further details of these winches are given later in this chapter.

Cargo cranes are being used to an increasing extent and many leading cargoship owners are now using cranes to replace derricks and winches. The hoist requirements and control systems are to a certain degree similar to those of winches, and in addition there will usually be two extra motors. The luffing drive is straightforward and does not require an elaborate control system.

A controlled lowering system is generally employed and the equipment can be similar to that used for the topping unit on derricks, i.e. for raising or lowering the derrick to the position required except that as luffing is an essential feature of crane operation a speedier movement becomes necessary. For the slewing motion special consideration is necessary. The mass in motion involves not only the load on the hook but that of the crane itself. It must be accelerated and decelerated gently and without jolting. Dynamic braking is appropriate and where the drive is taken from a squirrel-cage motor this can be arranged by injecting d.c. into the stator winding via a transformer and semi-conductor rectifier just prior to switching off. This has the effect of producing a static (as opposed to rotating) field in the machine. Rotation of the rotor induces an e.m.f. in the rotor windings and the interaction of the stator field and the rotor current produces a torque which opposes the rotation, braking power being dissipated in the form of heat in the rotor winding and in rotor iron losses. The effectiveness of this method can be adjusted to the requirements of the crane by transformer tappings or by an adjustable series resistance. When the crane comes to rest the magnetic brake is applied and the d.c. fed to the motor is switched off.

Luffing and slewing controls of cranes are frequently combined in one controller with a single operating lever having motion in two planes. The operator thus has only two levers to handle for the three motions on the crane.

APPLICATION OF DIVERSITY FACTORS

The Rules of Lloyd's Register of Shipping permit the application of a diversity factor to circuits supplying two or more final subcircuits in accordance with the total connected load where this can be justified. The diversity factor, where justified, may be applied to the calculation for size of cable and the rating of the relevant switchgear and fusegear. For winches, the diversity factor proposed has to be submitted for approval.

Where justifiable the diversity factor applied to the calculation of cables, switchgear and generators supplying groups of cargo winch motors or crane motors should be based on the estimated duty cycle of motors in the group. The frequency and duration of motor starting loads must be taken into account in these calculations.

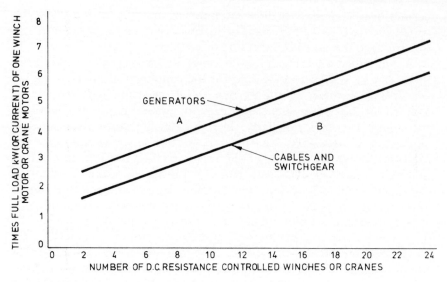

Figure 17.2 Typical curves for series resistance-control of d.c. motors. In the case of cranes with hoist, luff and screw motions the sum of the kW inputs of the three driving motors should be allowed for

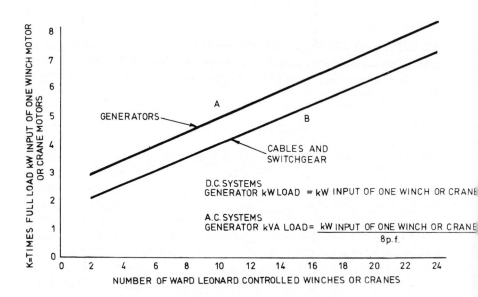

Figure 17.3 Typical curves for Ward Leonard controlled d.c. and a.c. systems
Note that in the case of cranes employing Ward Leonard control with hoist, luff and screw motions the sum of the kW inputs of the three driving motors should be allowed for

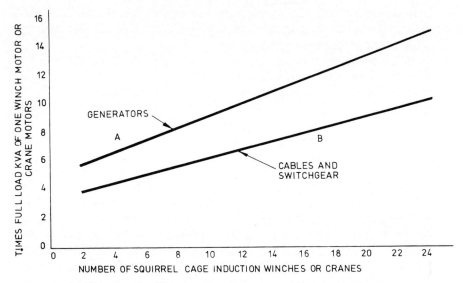

Figure 17.4 Typical curves for a.c. systems
In the case of pole changing 3-speed motors the kVA of the middle-speed should be
allowed for. In the case of cranes with hoist, luff and slew motions the sum of the kVA
inputs of the driving motors should be allowed

For series resistance controlled d.c. motors the curves in Figure 17.2 have been found satisfactory. For Ward Leonard controlled equipments operating on d.c. or a.c. systems, the curves in Figure 17.3 apply. For a.c. cage motors, the curves in Figure 17.4 are satisfactory if the voltage regulation of the generators meets classification requirements.

All these assessment curves are based on motors of equal rating; if they are of differing values suitable adjustments would be necessary. All the diversity factors should be taken as minimum and subject to voltage drop. Where the cables feeding winch motors and/ or crane motors supply in addition other equipment the current upon which the conductors of the cables is based should allow for the coincidence of such loads.

A mathematical justification for these factors cannot be formulated and they are based on experience and observation. They are extracted from the fifth edition of the IEE Regulations for Electrical and Electronic Equipment of Ships, 1972.

Whereas cables and switchgear are concerned solely with the heating effect of the current, generator loading must also take into account peak loads which must also be within the overload capabilities of the generator and its prime mover. It should be emphasised that whereas these peaks are at low power factor and affect the kVA rating of the alternator the kW loading is unaffected and it is this which determines the rating of the prime mover.

If the frequent starting periods are troublesome from the point of view of their effect on lighting, the practice of using a separate set for lighting services when in port can be recommended.

DERRICK SYSTEMS

For many generations when loading and unloading of mixed cargos use was made of dockside cranes, when available, or by the ship's winches in conjunction with derricks rigged in what became known as 'union purchase'. Because of rising labour costs and the need for quick turn-around times various alternative systems have now become generally adopted. Union purchase systems also have a useful limit of the order of about one and a half to two tons. For the heavier loads, which are now common, other systems are in demand.

The union purchase system

The union purchase system is based on the use of two derricks each with its own winch. When in operation one derrick is arranged so that its head is vertically over the ship's hold from which, when unloading, the cargo is to be lifted. The second derrick is positioned over the ship's side over which the cargo is to be landed. The first winch takes in slack wire until the load is lifted sufficiently to clear the hatch coaming and the ship's rails. At this point the first winch is reversed and the second winch hauls on the load while the first winch pays out and by skilful control of the relative winch speeds the load is traversed across the deck and over the quay.

During this operation the weight of the load is gradually transferred from one derrick to the other and finally lowered to the quay while the first winch pays out slack wire. By reversing the process the empty hook is returned to the hold for the next load.

The winch controls are so arranged that they result in high speeds when returning the empty hook but a low speed obtains when breaking out cargo. This is usually accomplished by load discriminating relays.

An advantage of the system is the good acceleration and fast speeds obtainable by skilled operators at all loads and from the point of initial installation cost it is regarded as the cheapest solution for handling general cargo. Also, due to the hook being under the control of two wires at a wide angle to one another, swinging of the load is practically eliminated. A disadvantage is the difficulty, and hence the time and labour involved, in rigging the derricks in the first place and in manoeuvring the derricks when it is necessary to reposition them to suit the stowage requirements in the hold or on the quay.

Deck cranes

For heavier loads than those mentioned above it is necessary to employ deck cranes.

These are normally jib-type cranes permanently mounted on the deck and powered for all motions required. They provide a clear working deck and are always available for immediate use on either side of the ship. On the other hand there is higher initial cost and a greater deck space taken up by the crane base.

Swinging-derrick systems

Considerable attention has been given in recent years to powered swinging-derrick systems and many are being installed, particularly for heavy lift purposes.

The principle involved is to use a single-derrick boom and to have two topping wires from the derrick head, one taken to the port side and the other to the starboard side extremities of cross-trees or to the head of a mast mounted on each side of the ship. Hauling on one wire and paying out on the other provides the slewing motion and, by varying the relative speeds, any combination of topping and slewing can be obtained.

These swinging-derrick systems combine to a large extent the advantages and also eliminate the disadvantages of the union-purchase system and the deck crane. On the other hand a single-boom swinging-derrick system tends to set up a swinging pendulum motion of the load, particularly when slewing the derrick.

First cost of swinging-derrick systems is more than that for union purchase due to the increased number of winches required and to the larger mast structure. However, they are cheaper than deck cranes and can be designed for very heavy lifts.

At the present time there are several well-tried systems available under trade names such as, the Hallen system; the Vell system, the Thomson Ship Crane and the Stulcken derrick. Space will not permit a detailed description of these systems which in any case are principally concerned with the physical arrangements of the derricks.

The Hallen system comprises a single derrick stepped in the centre-line of the ship and two topping/slewing guys each led from the derrick head to guy pennants secured to each yardarm of the cross-trees. The two topping/slewing winches are controlled from a single 'joystick' control lever. The controller consists of two cam-type controllers mechanically coupled, each providing three steps of speed control in both heave and payout directions. The topping/slewing winches are virtually standard cargo winches electrically.

In the Velle system, also based on a single derrick, the slewing and topping duties are handled by separate winches although the slewing/topping wires are common. Power for the winch motors is provided from two motor-generator sets. One generator supplies the hoist winch motor while a dual output generator supplies the topping and slewing winch motors. A single motor-generator comprising an a.c. motor driving a single and a dual generator to supply the three motions is also commonly used. The control systems described else-where for cargo winches have much in common but differ in the application of load discriminator relays. A delayed brake application reduces the tendency towards swinging pendulum action.

Thomson Ship Cranes (marketed by Thomson Ship Cranes Ltd) are electrically similar to the Hallen. The manufacturers have given consideration to the problem of pendulum motion and have devised an outrigger arrangement of the derrick head whereby the hoist or purchase wire forms a tripod of wires at the derrick head. The three angles formed by the wires at the hook are equal.

The Stulcken Derrick is designed principally for handling very heavy loads and derricks have been supplied capable of handling lifting capacities of from 30 tons to 180 tons. A lift of 260 tons has been accomplished by using two 130 ton Stulcken masts. The derrick is normally mounted amidships between two separate derrick posts which may either be upright and parallel to each other or inclined in an outward direction. The normal arrangement of winches consists of four units, two for the hoist wires and two topping/slewing winches for the span tackles. Standard type winches with speed control in both directions are suitable but special consideration needs to be given to the design of the barrel.

Ward-Leonard control is commonly used on all the foregoing.

D.C. AUXILIARIES

The deck winch is required to lift and lower a load either by a fixed rope on a barrel or by whipping on the warp ends; it may also be required to top or luff the derricks and to warp the ship. A favourite method of handling cargo is that known as 'burtoning' in which two derricks are used. One winch raises the load which is then slewed in the direction of the second winch which takes up the load and lowers it in the required direction. For heavy loads the derrick may be slewed to carry the load across towards the lowering position.

After depositing the load it is necessary to transfer the light hook back to the loading position and much ingenuity has been exercised in devising methods for gaining time by speeding up this operation in the ratio of from three to four and a half times the full load speed. However the necessity for this facility depends to some extent on the nature of the cargo, the method of handling and the distances over which the load must be raised and lowered. If it is considered that a high light hook speed is advantageous it must be obtainable in both directions, i.e. raising and lowering. When lowering it is undesirable to exceed a speed of about 400 ft min in order to ensure that the rope unwinds evenly from the drum.

The final choice of the characteristic most suited to the intended operating conditions rests with the shipowner and some selected examples will be given to illustrate the systems currently in use.

Over the last decade the majority of vessels built have been based on a.c. power systems so it is proposed to limit details of the three basic systems to one example of each, i.e.

(a) Series resistance control
(b) Electrically controlled lowering
(c) Variable voltage control.

Series resistance control

This is probably the most straightforward and most commonly used system of control and comprises a master controller, contactors and resistance. The scheme is the same whether the master controller is integral with the winch or separately mounted and the contactors can likewise be self-contained in the winch or placed in a deckhouse.

An example of this type is represented in Figure 17.5. There are three steps of speed control in both directions with a light-load discriminating relay on the fourth step to give double speed at half load and a higher speed with light hook. The correct rate of acceleration, keeping control of the current taken from the line, is provided by the contactor gear even when the controller handwheel is swung to full speed without pausing on intermediate steps. Too rapid operation due to rapid reversal of the controller is also taken care of by a reverse delay relay.

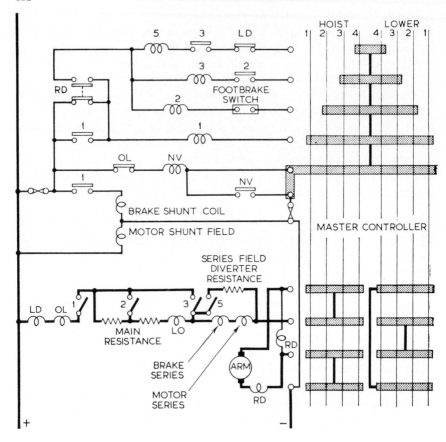

Figure 17.5 Schematic diagram of series resistance control for cargo winch

When the footbrake is applied a switch is operated which causes the main resistance to be inserted thus limiting the current and protecting the motor if it should stall. On releasing the brake the motor will accelerate to a speed corresponding to the setting of the controller.

Note. In Figures 17.5 to 17.12 the coil numbers and letter symbols correspond with the contactor or relay contacts of the same number shown elsewhere in the diagrams. For the sake of simplicity, economy resistances in coil circuits and discharge resistances, etc. have been omitted. All contacts are shown in the de-energised position. The following symbols will also be used:

OL = overload relay   H = hoist
LD = load discriminator   L = lower

RD	=	reverse delay relay	TDR	=	time delay relay
NV	=	no-volt relay	HS	=	high speed
LO	=	contactor lock-out	LS	=	low speed.
TL	=	torque limit relay			

In the control system shown in Figure 17.5 resistance contactor 3 has a lockout coil to regulate its closing so that it is locked out while the accelerating current is high and released at a predetermined current. If extra resistance points are added the additional contactors will also have lockout coils.

The series diverter resistance is under the control of contactor 5 which is in turn controlled by load discriminator relay LD and contactor 3. Contactor 5 can close only when the current in LD is low, and when contactor 3 is also closed, and the controller is on the final step. The effect therefore is that the current in the series winding of the motor is reduced and the motor is speeded up on light loads.

Relay RD has shunt and series coils and it delays the reclosing of contactor 1 on a rapid reversal.

In the arrangement shown the reversal of the armature connections is done in the controller and this method is suitable up to about 35 h.p. As with all winches were the speed on the lowering side is not under electrical control a foot-operated brake is essential.

Where the equipment is watertight and no provision is made for ventilation the problem of accumulation of moisture due to condensation must be considered. Silica-gel dessicators are fitted in some cases where there is no ventilation and it is then necessary to seal off cable entries, etc, to ensure that the equipment is airtight. The silica-gel must be reconditioned periodically.

As an alternative to silica-gel dessicators, electric heaters are used in many cases to inhibit condensation. It is important they be switched on when there is a risk of condensation. If drain plugs are fitted they should also be attended to if there is evidence of an accumulation of water. In some cases non-return valves are fitted instead of plugs.

Electrically controlled lowering

In this category, potentiometer control circuits are used or proprietary systems are available such as 'Selector' (Laurence Scott and Electromotors Ltd.) and 'Autocon' (Clarke, Chapman & Co., Ltd.). Lowering of all loads without the use of footbrakes is possible by manipulating the controller lever alone.

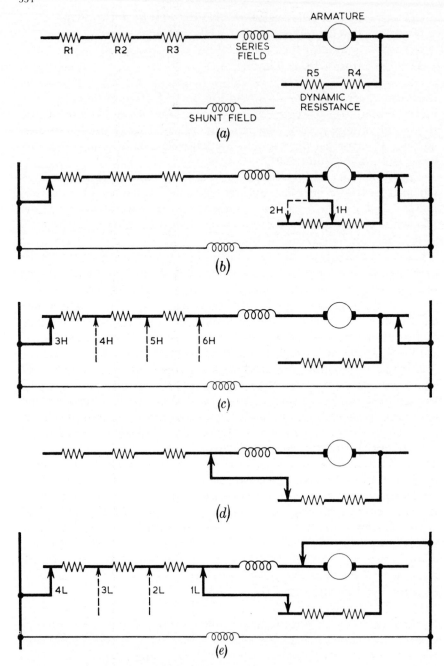

Figure 17.6 Elementary diagram of simple potentiometer control
  (a) Circuit arrangement.
  (b) Slow speed hoisting steps.
  (c) Medium and fast speed hoisting steps.
  (d) Off position
  (e) Slow, medium and fast speed lowering steps

The systems employed differ fundamentally so typical examples are not feasible but basically a potentiometer connection is usually employed, using a compound-wound motor in which the series field predominates but with a shunt winding for limiting the maximum speed, usually referred to as a 'shunt limiting winding'. The basic elements are shown in Figure 17.6.

The shunt field is not varied and is connected across the supply in all control positions except the 'off', in which it is disconnected. On the first two hoist notches R_1 is connected to the line and R_4 across the armature on the first notch, and $R_4 + R_5$ on the second notch, these connections constituting a potentiometer arrangement and giving a slower stable speed than is possible by plain series control. On subsequent hoisting steps the resistances R_4 and R_5 are disconnected and speed regulation is carried out by short-circuiting the series resistance in the usual manner.

For lowering purposes the connections are as in Figure 17.6 (e), speed being regulated by notching from 1 to 4 as indicated. The connection shown in the off position provides dynamic braking. This type of control has a limited speed range of about 3:1 for light hook speed in the hoisting direction and 2:1 in the lowering direction and as the operation is by drum controller, and not by contactor, an unskilled operator might possibly harm the motor.

To counter these limitations the Clarke Chapman Autocon system shown in Figure 17.7 has been devised. On the first hoist step, armature diverter connection is provided which gives a slow speed for tightening up the sling, an essential feature for a winch not provided with footbrake for crawl speeds. On the fourth step a series field diverter enables the winch to lift light hook or light loads at high speed. The series diverter is controlled by a load discriminating relay which operates on armature current.

Lowering employs a potentiometer circuit, i.e. part series and part armature diverter resistance. The starting resistance $R_1 - R_3$ is supplemented by an economy section $R_0 - R_1$. By this method graduated voltage can be applied to the armature, combined with a strong shunt field. A current controlled pilot relay limits the weakening of the shunt field. A current controlled pilot relay limits the weakening of the shunt field on step 4 to light loads only.

Dynamic braking is used in the 'off' position and on the first lowering step enabling heavy loads to be handled safely at low speed. As this step is not powered the winch stops as soon as the load is landed and does not pay out slack rope unnecessarily.

The operator selects the speed at which he wishes to lift or lower and the automatic features ensure that very high speeds can be

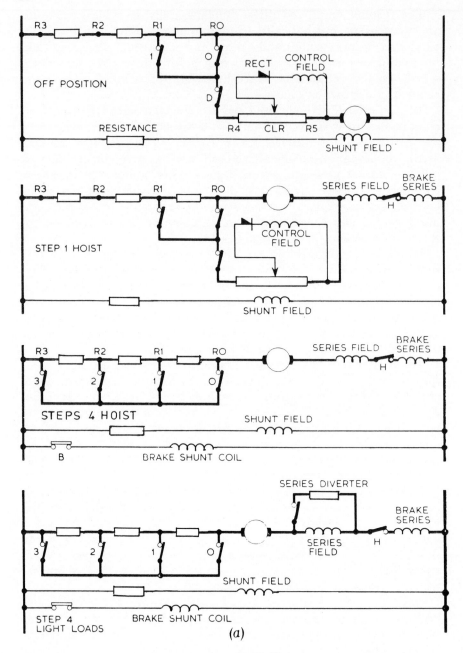

Figure 17.7(a) Elementary diagram of Clarke Chapman Autocon control showing 'off' and hoisting

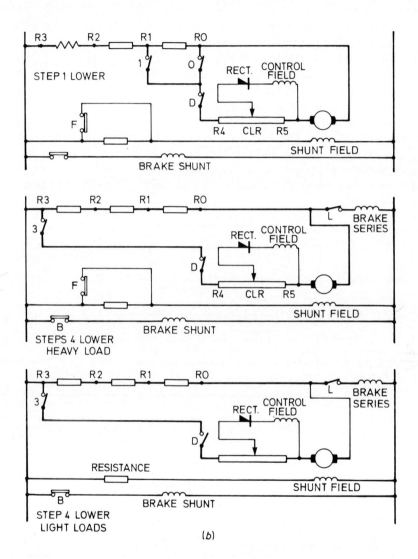

Figure 17.7(b) Step four lower light loads — lowering

obtained with only light loads. All speeds are attained step by step
and without undue current surges irrespective of the way the controller is handled. Stall limiting protection is also incorporated to
prevent overheating.

A patented feature is the use of a control winding in the winch
motor. This is a shunt field connected across a portion of the current
limiting resistance (CLR) and hence the current it carries is proportional to the armature current. The rectifier in series with this
winding permits the flow of currents whilst the motor is driving and
hence it acts as a stabilising field, shunt connected during lowering.
When the motor is regenerating the polarity across CLR reverses and
the rectifier blocks the path of the current which would tend otherwise to make the machine unstable.

A further and even more important function is to ensure good
commutation when the speed of a fast falling load is checked. As

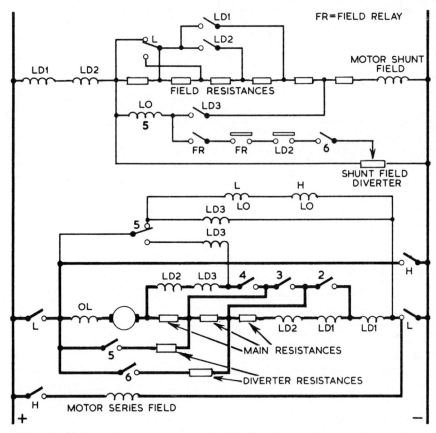

*Figure 17.8(a) Clarke Chapman Autocon control for lowering and incorporating
potentiometer circuit*

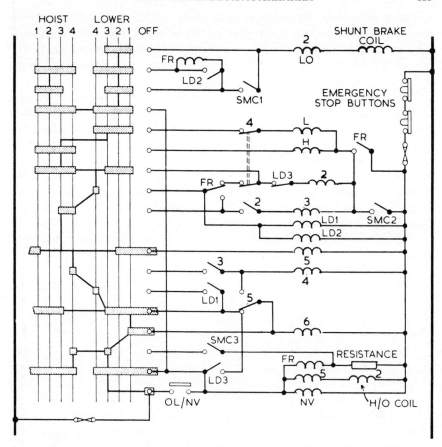

Figure 17.8(b) Schematic diagram of selector winch — master controller and operating coils

this is accomplished by strengthening the shunt field in one step, the rapid build-up of the shunt field would cause a surge detrimental to good commutation. The rectifier therefore is momentarily shorted by a contactor and during this condition a reverse current is allowed to flow in the control winding which slows down the rate at which the shunt field builds up and experience has shown that commutation is then completely satisfactory.

A time delay relay in conjunction with field contactor (F) controls the momentary closing of a contactor (not shown in the diagram) which shorts the rectifier in the control field and the circuit is arranged that no notching to earlier steps occurs until the time delay provided for the surge condition expires.

The Laurence Scott Selector deck winch system is also designed to overcome the disadvantages previously referred to. This is shown schematically in Figure 17.8(a) and the speed is electrically controlled with the aid of load discriminator relays to a safe value dependent on the load and not on the operator.

Each reversing contactor (H^1 and L) when closed operates contacts SMC, Figure 17.8(b). SMC1 completes the shunt brake circuit on all steps except 1, 2 and 3 lower. SMC2 is a retaining interlock to maintain the feed to L and H and also to 2 and 3 when FR is open. SMC3 completes the short on one of the two coils of FR on steps 4H and 4L of the controller. Contactor (L) also has an interlock of the changeover type which, when L is open, shorts one section of the shunt field ballast resistance and, when closed, it shorts another section.

Voltage lock-out coils fitted to H and L ensure that neither can close if the armature volts are in excess of predetermined values except when 5 closes to break these lock-out coil circuits.

Accelerating contactor 2 has a double wound lock-out coil, one excited by main voltage and the other, in opposition, by shunt brake current to prevent the contactor closing until the latter reaches a predetermined value.

Diverter contactor 5 also has a double wound lock-out coil, both shunt wound, one being line excited and the other, in opposition, energised by motor shunt field current. This locks out the contactor until the field current reaches a predetermined value.

Hoisting includes one slow speed step with armature diverter control and high speed at light loads are obtained by shunt field weakening under the control of two load discriminators. In the 'off' position contactors 5 and 6 are closed thus providing dynamic braking in this position. Contactor 5 has two auxiliary contacts of the changeover type. One of these makes one or other of the shunt coils of load discriminator LD3, either the line excited coil or the coil connected across the motor armature. When 5 is open this contact also makes the circuit of lock-out coils on reverser contactors L and H. The second auxiliary contact on 5 breaks the feed to the coil of 6 when 5 is closed, except in the 'off' position and on the first 'lower' step.

Load discriminators 1 and 2 control the speed according to loading conditions and the position of the controller and whether hoisting or lowering. Load discriminator LD3 controls contactor 2 on steps 1H and 2L, to close it if the armature volts are low in order to provide sufficient torque to enable full load to be lifted at slow speeds. Conversely at high armature volts it opens 2 to reduce the value of current at light loads. On step 4H protection is required if the winch is operated with the rope fed to the centre barrel incorrectly, i.e. it becomes necessary to use 'hoist' control for lowering. Under these conditions and with medium or heavy loads excess speeds would arise on step 4H. LD3 under the control of the line excited coil and the current coil will close for a small value of regenerated current and it then shorts resistance in the motor shunt circuit to maintain maximum field strength. LD3 also gives protection if the power supply fails when the motor is regenerating. Under this condition the armature voltage will rise and at a suitable value above normal voltage the line excited coil causes the discriminator to close and this gives full motor field, opens contactor 2 and closes 6.

The field relay FR has two coils, an upper, line excited coil, and a lower coil energised by shunt brake current, one coil on each side of a central pivot and controlled in such a manner that the relay armature is closed in either direction after a short delay.

Variable voltage control

Where fine control of both hoisting and lowering speed is required either booster control or a modified form of Ward-Leonard control is suitable and footbrakes are not essential. A magnetic brake provides against power failure or when returning the controller to off. Generally speaking for straightforward Ward-Leonard schemes the motor for the generator set can be either a.c. or d.c. and as the set runs continuously and in one direction only it is started in the conventional manner. Typical Ward-Leonard connections are shown in Figure 17.9. If the supply is a.c. the exciter would be replaced by a static rectifier.

An example of Ward-Leonard control for a combined cargo/mooring winch which enables the winch to comply with the St Lawrence Seaway Regulations and so can be used when navigating the Seaway is shown in Figure 17.10. Under these Regulations vessels of 200 gross tons or less must have two lines of hawsers, one at the bow and the other at the stern quarter, each leading through a closed chock. Larger vessels must have at least four lines so arranged that they can be used on either side of the vessel. Two must lead from the bow and two from the stern quarters and not from the extreme bow or stern. For vessels between 200 and 300 gross tons the windlass forward and the capstan aft may be used for the two lines ahead but those leading aft must run from the main drum of power-driven winches and not from capstans or nigger heads. For all larger vessels

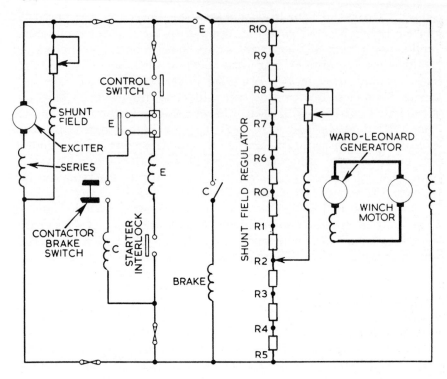

Figure 17.9 Schematic diagram of typical Ward-Leonard winch

all four lines must be power-operated and run from the main drum of power-driven winches and not from capstans or nigger heads.

Booster control systems are variations of the Ward-Leonard system except that the generator armature or booster as it is termed is connected in series with the winch motor. Performance can be said to equal that attained by conventional Ward-Leonard systems with the advantage of greater compactness which, for ship work, is a great asset. With Ward-Leonard the whole power for the winch motor is supplied by the generator of the motor-generator set so both machines of the latter are equal in output to the winch motor but with the booster system smaller motor-generator sets can be used as the booster is not called upon to handle full power. The fundamental circuits are shown in Figure 17.11 and the complete system in Figure 17.12. The booster voltage is reversible and can therefore add to the supply voltage or oppose it. When adding to the line voltage the booster will be generating but when opposing it will be motoring the motor generator set and returning energy to the supply system.

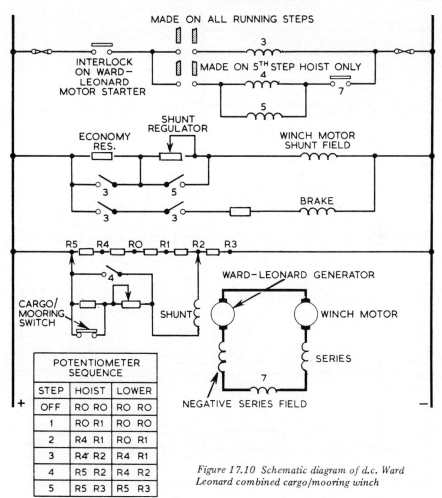

POTENTIOMETER SEQUENCE		
STEP	HOIST	LOWER
OFF	RO RO	RO RO
1	RO R1	RO RO
2	R4 R1	RO R1
3	R4 R2	R4 R1
4	R5 R2	R4 R2
5	R5 R3	R5 R3

Figure 17.10 Schematic diagram of d.c. Ward Leonard combined cargo/mooring winch

Since control is via the field system of the booster the change from step to step takes place smoothly and without jerk and there are no current peaks on the supply system. Main circuits are not broken while carrying current and the currents handled by the controller are small field currents with consequent elimination of excessive wear and burning of contacts. The power taken from the mains is proportional to the work done and not, as with conventional resistance control schemes, a constant demand while the winch is in operation, irrespective of the winch speed. Although this description is included under winches this system finds its most appropriate application for windlasses and capstans.

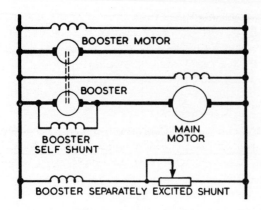

Figure 17.11 Elementary diagram of booster arrangement

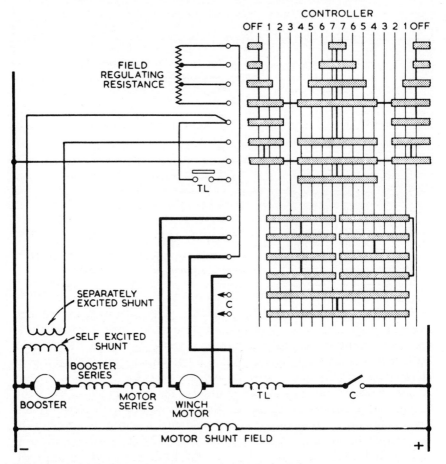

Figure 17.12 Schematic diagram of booster control scheme (Clarke, Chapman/John Thompson Ltd.)

An alternative to the booster system is the reducer which is connected as shown diagrammatically in Figure 17.13. Armatures A and B constitute a tandem set, both being on the same shaft, in which B supplies the motive power for A. It differs from the booster scheme in having the armature B in parallel to the capstan armature. When A is fully excited it generates full voltage in opposition to the line voltage and there is therefore no voltage on the winch motor.

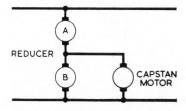

Figure 17.13 Elementary diagram of reducer shceme

By gradually reducing the voltage of A the main motor voltage is correspondingly increased and it speeds up until eventually armature A idles round at zero voltage and the motor is at full running speed. In this system the reducer set has to be big enough to carry the full current required at slow speed but at top speed it is doing no work. The overall performance is such as to give the necessary falling characteristic.

WARPING WINCHES AND CAPSTANS

Winches and capstans of the contactor series resistance type are similar to the cargo winches previously described except that they are fitted with a torque limit relay to permit stalling with power maintained. Also if the normal speed is on the high side, such as with a dual-purpose winch, an armature diverter is provided to give creep speeds with light loads as already described.

The equipment should give the same duty in either direction and load discrimination to give double speed at half load is undesirable. On the other hand some steps of the controller giving suitable light load speeds are considered essential for handling slack ropes; if slack ropes are not brought in quickly they are liable to become wrapped round the propellers.

The equipment includes a torque limit relay which opens contactors to insert the main resistance so that the circuit is automatically switched back to the equivalent of the first step. If the load falls off the winch automatically returns to the position on which the controller was left.

There is also an armature diverter which is inserted by a contactor on the first step only, in order to give slow speeds for handling light loads. This contactor is provided with a voltage-controlled lockout to prevent closing when the armature voltage is high.

When the booster control system shown in Figure 17.12 is used for these applications the stalling pull is usually arranged at a higher value than is required in ordinary use, such as 100 per cent excess torque. To prevent overloads of this magnitude occurring when warping ship a torque limiting relay is fitted. When an overload occurs the separately excited shunt field circuit is broken, giving the same effect as returning the controller to the third step, and in this condition a stalled pull equivalent to full load is obtained. When the overload is removed the torque relay will re-set and normal operation will resume. If this system is used for windlass duty the torque relay can be put out of action in an emergency if a particularly heavy pull is desired.

WINDLASSES

Systems of control are in general similar to those of winches with additional features to take care of the following requirements.

A falling speed/load characteristic enables the motor to stall ultimately when overloaded whilst still maintaining a live pull; conversely it will allow the motor to accelerate as the length and thereby the weight of the cable diminishes. It is usual to fit an excess-torque device set slightly below that of the slipping clutch to reduce the torque to a safe limit as it is important to avoid disconnecting the motor on overload when it is heaving.

If, as is commonly the case, the windlass is also used for warping duties the control system will embody an additional provision for giving high speed with light load for hauling slack lines. Subject to the inclusion of these additional features any of the systems previously described for winches are suitable.

The overall efficiency of a windlass is about 60% and as much as 30% can be lost in friction at the hawsepipe although this can be improved by the modern practice of including rollers.

A.C. AUXILIARIES

Recent years have witnessed an ever increasing demand for electrical power in ships. This has resulted in the majority of new vessels utilising a.c. systems which greatly simplify the generation and distribution of electrical power.

The development of suitable deck auxiliaries became universally acknowledged as the key to the problem of the use of a.c. for general purposes as the alternative to d.c. Much ingenuity has been exercised in devising means for simulating the well-proven characteristics and performance of d.c. systems and although it is not practicable in this chapter to describe the many schemes evolved, a selected few examples are described.

One of the many difficulties which have had to be faced is that of providing high light hook speed hitherto thought to be essential and this has led to a closer study of operating conditions. Time studies have tended to show that for some, though not all, operating conditions, little is gained in the long run by this facility. For instance the period taken for acceleration and deceleration are largely determined by the inertia inherent in the winch and that the load on the hook is a small proportion of the total. Thus depending on the height of lift and the operating time cycle, the time taken for accelerating the light hook plus the braking time may leave very little running-time at full speed and the time gained by higher speeds may be but a few seconds. It therefore became evident that an alternative solution was to reduce the inertia inherent in the winch and to improve the rate of acceleration.

The cage motor appears to go some way towards meeting these requirements and its rate of acceleration is much higher than that of a comparable d.c. machine. Given the right conditions a high light hook speed is undoubtedly a decided advantage and it is for the shipowner to weigh up his conditions and decide whether they merit dispensing with this requirement and installing the simpler and cheaper type of winch.

These considerations have led to the development of winches based on the use of single-speed squirrel-cage motors, to meet the cases where a high light hook speed and a fine speed control are not essential. Where these refinements are necessary the answer lies in the adoption of multi-speed (change pole) motors or Ward-Leonard control and other more ingenious methods.

A broad grouping of winch systems for use on a.c. is as follows:

1. Single-speed cage motor winches
2. Dual-motor three-speed cage motor winches
3. Ward-Leonard controlled winches
4. Specialised systems of control.

It will perhaps be better to deal first with the simplest form of winch driven by the cage induction motor before describing Ward-Leonard and other alternatives. As this type usually involves direct-on-line switching each time the motor is started, a word should be said as to the effect on the generators. The motor is usually designed with this disadvantage in view and the starting current is therefore generally limited to about four times full load current but the power factor is very low and the combined effect of several winches operated simultaneously may have repercussions on the generator heating. The makers of this type of winch have experience of this problem and their advice should be sought if such is contemplated.

Whilst the operating characteristics of any of the types enumerated do not compare with those of the series resistance controlled d.c. winch they all have the advantage of electrically controlled lowering of loads.

Three speed a.c. cage motor driven cargo winch

Present day cargo winches must be able to meet high cargo handling rates involving frequent starting and stopping. To overcome the inherent disadvantages associated with direct switching cage motors a specially designed dual stator/rotor low inertia, high torque motor is necessary. This minimises the starting and accelerating losses which are responsible for a large proportion of the overall losses and subsequent heat generated.

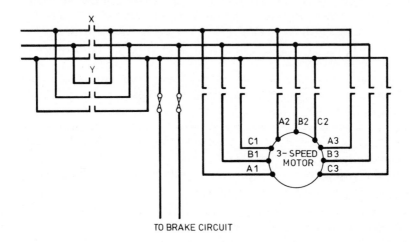

Figure 17.14 Typical 3-speed a.c. cage motor-driven cargo winch (Clarke Chapman/John Thompson Ltd.)

The three-speed motor has two stators (see Figure 17.17) and three contactors; a low speed stator with a 24-pole winding controlled by contactor 1 and a medium/high speed stator with two independent windings, one wound for 8 poles and the other for 4 poles controlled by medium speed contactor 2 and high speed contactor 3. All windings are star connected. These are in turn fed by reversing contactors x and y.

To run the motor through its speed range, first the low speed contactor 1 is closed and then the forward or reverse contactor is energised and the motor will run at low speed, the electro-magnetic brake being simultaneously released by an additional contactor. As the controller is moved to steps 2 and 3 the motor accelerates first to medium speed and then to high speed. To make the system foolproof, much interlocking is provided and, in addition electrical deceleration is provided to reduce wear on the brake shoes.

Auxiliary contacts on each succeeding contactor open to trip out the preceding contactor but each succeeding contactor comes under the control of a timing device to ensure the current peak which occurs while accelerating has died down before the next acceleration takes place.

Windlass with three speed a.c. cage motor drive

This type of drive (see Figure 17.15) is one of the alternatives for windlasses and enables three discrete speeds to be selected by means of a controller. This type has been found to be adequate to meet the requirements of anchor handling and warping duties.

The motor has two stator windings, one wound for 16 poles connected in delta for use for housing anchor. The other is a tapped pole-changing winding, 8 pole star connected for breaking out and raising anchor and 4 pole delta-connected for handling slack lines. The motor has an integral fitted fall-safe disc brake, spring applied and electro-magnetically released.

Power is supplied via reversing contactors. Speed selection is obtained using five contactors numbers 3, 11, 12, 21 and 22 (3 high speed, 11 low speed star, 12 low speed delta, 21 and 22 medium speed). Timing relays prevent over rapid acceleration or deceleration. Torque limit relays TL1, TL2 and TL3 in each circuit are provided for low, medium and high speeds. In the event of overload a control relay is tripped out, connecting the low speed winding in star connection, enabling a reduced torque 'live' pull to be maintained for a limited period. If the overload is removed within this period the motor will re-accelerate to the particular step of control previously

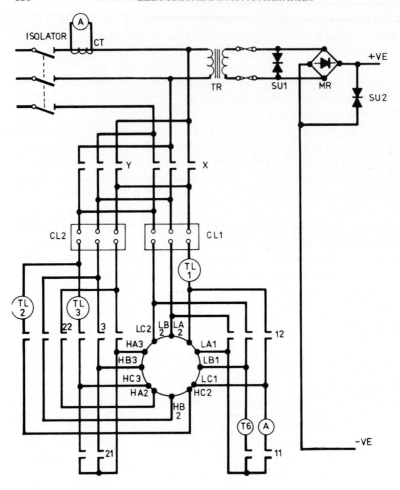

Figure 17.15 Power circuits for 3-speed cage motor for windlass

set. If the overload is maintained beyond this period the motor will shut down and the brake applied. Thermal overload relays protect the windings.

Capstan with two-speed a.c. cage motor drive

This is a typical alternative type of drive for capstans and operates in a similar manner to the 3-speed windlass drive except that two independent stator windings, 8 and 4 pole are used for two speeds only. They are connected delta and star respectively.

The two separate stator windings are connected to reversing contactors as appropriate. A timing relay is energised to prevent undue acceleration.

A fail-safe integral disc type magnetic brake is located at the top end of the motor for easy maintenance.

Warping winch with a.c. slipring motor drive

In this typical example of a slipring motor all manually controlled switching of power circuits as demonstrated in Figure 17.16 is done at the controller. This has a heavy-duty control drum and finger contacts able to handle the current of the motor up to approximately 40 kW.

Motor reversing is carried out directly from the controller without reversing contactors. The controller also switches the controller

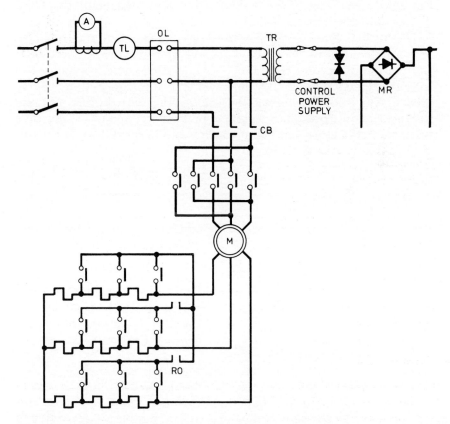

Figure 17.16 Typical a.c. slip-ring motor drive for warping winch drive

resistors from maximum resistance resistance on step one to zero resistance on the last step.

As the controller contacts are handling live currents it is desirable that the control handwheel should move deliberately from step to step, pausing on each step sufficiently to allow the motor to accelerate in order to minimise arcing and burning of contacts.

Two contactors are in the power circuit of this winch. Contactor CB interrupts the three supply lines to permit either the overload relay OL or the brake thermal trip switch to shut down the winch. A contactor RO is provided to permit the torque limit relay to step back the control system to step one conditions if the load becomes excessive. As the controller passes through step one, contactor RO is energised and maintains its own control circuit on subsequent steps of the controller. Contactor RO, when closed, gives common connection to the three sets of resistors in the rotor circuit. In other words RO gives a star centre point connection independent of the fixed star point connection DI.

The torque limit relay also uses this independent star point to obtain its control of the rotor resistance, if the winch is overloaded and the motor current rises above its operating value, contactor RO will be tripped out and the independent star connection will be broken. The fixed star connection will then become the effective one and all the rotor resistance will be re-inserted in circuit. The motor is fitted with a fail-safe disc brake which is spring applied when electromagentically released.

Ward-Leonard cargo winch

This uses a dual output generator to supply two winches (see Figure 17.17). The a.c. cage motor of the Ward-Leonard set is switched directly on line by means of contactor RU. The dual d.c. generator has two completely independent output circuits permanently connected to the two d.c. motors driving two winches. The winch motor shunt field windings are energised at approximately half current when the controller is in the 'off' position. Since the operation of each of the winches is identical the control system of only one need be described.

With the controller on any running step, the excitation contactor is energised and the brake is released. In addition the line of resistors is energised so that the generator shunt field becomes excited and the generator will supply the winch motor according to the controller position. A contactor becomes energised simultaneously

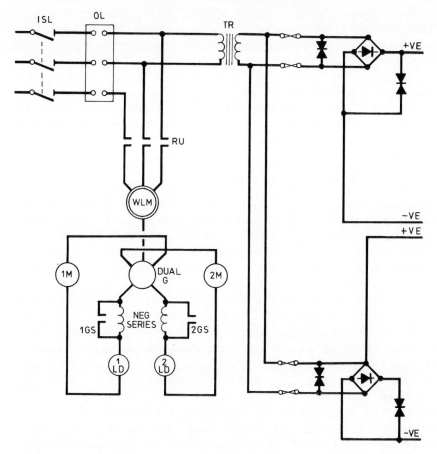

Figure 17.17 Typical Ward Leonard cargo winch using dual output generator to supply two winches (Clarke Chapman/John Thompson Ltd.)

with the excitation contactor so that the motor shunt field steps up to full strength.

When the controller is returned to the 'off' position a timing relay maintains control for approximately one second to allow regeneration from the motor to reduce speed before the brake is applied.

A load discriminator (1LD and 2LD) relay is provided which performs two separate functions. When the winch is hoisting a light load on step 5 hoist, normally-closed contacts of a relay will remain closed and energise a contactor which short-circuits a resistor to increase the generator output and so increase the hoisting speed. When the winch is hoisting a heavy load with the controller on step 1, the load discriminator relay will operate due to the heavy current in the relay assisted by a shunt winding of the relay on this step. The relay will close contacts to energise a contactor whose contacts will short circuit a resistor to increase generator excitation to prevent the winch stalling.

Contactors 1GS and 2GS are provided to short-circuit the generator negative series windings after the controller has been moved to 'off', during the brief period while a timing relay delays the dropout of the excitation contactor. This increases regenerative braking to further reduce wear on the brake.

Deep sea automatic mooring winch

This has Ward-Leonard control with a dual output generator to supply two winches. The type of winch shown in Figure 17.18 is suitable for mooring a vessel permanently alongside a berth with the winch motor energised and unattended. It is primarily intended for vessels trading deep sea but is also suitable for navigating the St. Lawrence Seaway.

The control system, although similar to that used on the Ward-Leonard cargo winch is less complex. There is no load discriminating relay provided, no timing relay to delay brake application and no contactor to short-circuit the generator negative series winding since the duty imposed on the brake is very light for this application.

Loading and unloading rates of modern types of vessel are becoming extremely rapid, particularly in the case of bulk carriers. As a result the elevation of the vessel in relation to the dock is constantly changing even in non-tidal harbours. By using automatic mooring winches line adjustments are automatically taken care of without attendance by the crew.

Tidal waters also create problems for the mooring of vessels. Again adjustments for rise and fall can be taken care of automatically; the winch heaving, stalling, or rendering to suit the conditions.

The automatic mooring winch is arranged with both 'hand' and 'automatic' mooring control. The value at which the winch will operate will be dependent on the size of the winch and on the particular step of automatic control to which the controller is set. Normally there are three steps for automatic mooring control and five steps for automatic mooring control and five steps for hand control.

Mooring lines are protected against breakage as the render value can be predetermined at a tension below the yield strength of the wire rope. Line speed is automatically adjusted to line tension with a high recovery rate for light line.

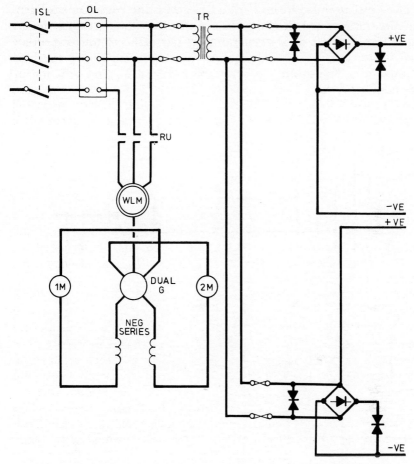

Figure 17.18 Ward Leonard control using dual output generator to supply two winches (Clarke Chapman/John Thompson Ltd.)

DECK CRANES

Since the introduction of deck cranes in ships for general cargo handling, their use has been extended to cater for all forms of modern cargo handling requirements.

Cargos can be divided broadly into the following categories:
1. General cargo
2. Bulk cargo
3. Containerised cargo

The most popular form of electric drive is the Ward-Leonard drive and the basic system has already been described. In general there is one Ward-Leonard motor-generator set per crane comprising an a.c. cage motor driving a single output generator supplying the hoist motor and a dual output generator for the luffing and slew motors (see Figure 17.19).

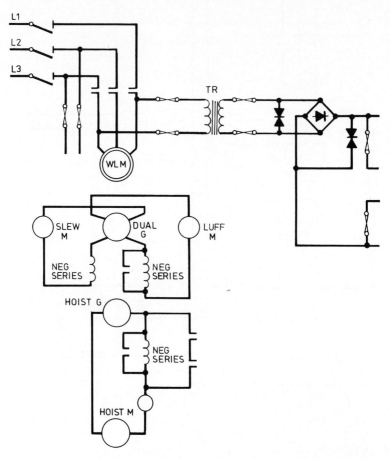

Figure 17.19 Typical Ward Leonard system for single deck crane

Bulk cargo

For this application a grab is used instead of the conventional hook. There are basically two types of grab commonly used:

(a) Electro-hydraulic, in which the grab operating mechanism is contained within the grab and only requires an electric power cable from crane to the grab, using a cable reel.

(b) A four-rope type which requires an additional hoist motion to close the grab and hold it closed during lifting.

For grab cranes the electrical equipment has a higher duty rating as there is no 'hook on' and 'hook off' time involved, thus the duty cycle rates can be much higher.

Containerised cargo

For this system the cargo hook is replaced by a container spreader which fastens on to the container by latches. This is normally actuated mechanically or electro-hydraulically.

Figure 17.20 Twin crane installation (Clarke Chapman John Thompson Ltd.)

To increase flexibility, twin cranes have been developed which can operate individually for general cargo handling or in tandem for handling containers or similar lifts. When operating in tandem the hoist motions of each crane are synchronised with each other as also are the luff motions.

The two cranes, in addition to having their individual turntables, are also mounted on a common turntable which is used when working in tandem, both cranes being controlled from the 'master' crane (see Figure 17.20).

The control circuits of the 'master' and 'slave' cranes are basically similar. When the two cranes are being used individually, the control systems of both cranes work in very much the same way as the Velle

Figure 17.21 Double crane installation (Clarke Chapman John Thomspon Ltd.)

system cranes but, in order to permit the master crane controls to operate both cranes in synchronism, the master crane has certain differences in its control systems.

The double crane illustrated in Figure 17.21 has 23 ton and 5 ton cranes mounted on a common turntable. This is not a true twin installation but is intended to allow either a 23 ton or 5 ton lifting facility in any one of two adjacent hatches.

18 Tankers

The special requirements for tankers which are specified by the various Classification Societies and the Statutory Authorities are, in the main, based on the recommendations set out in Publication 92 of the International Electrotechnical Commission *'Electrical instalations in ships'*. In this publication the chapter dealing with tankers defines such a vessel as a 'sea-going cargo ship constructed or adapted for the carriage in bulk of liquid cargoes of a flammable nature'. As such cargoes are very varied the Recommendations distinguish between four different types of tanker, i.e:

1. For carrying all cargoes having a flashpoint (closed test) not exceeding 60°C — e.g. crude oil carriers, gasoline carriers, etc.
2. Cargoes having a flashpoint (closed test) in excess of 60°C — e.g. vessels designed for the carriage of bituminous or asphaltic products or for the carriage of fuel or diesel oils.
3. For the carriage of liquefied natural gas (LNG) or liquefied petroleum gas (LPG) — such vessels are commonly referred to as gas carriers.
4. For the carriage of other flammable cargoes. This category deals with vessels carrying products which are potentially more hazardous than those conveyed by vessels under (1) and (3) above, or products which may be prone to chemical instability or reaction or which produce gases or vapours which could cause the deterioration of electrical equipment. The vessel designed to carry certain specific chemicals is an example of a tanker falling into this category.

GENERAL RECOMMENDATIONS

Irrespective of the intended cargo there are certain recommendations which are common to each of the four types of tanker referred to above and which differ from those applicable to dry cargo ships. Examples of these are given in the following paragraphs:

Ships service system of supply

Hull return systems or systems with an earthed neutral are not permitted excepting for:

Sacrificial anode protective systems or impressed current cathodic protection systems for outer hull protection only;

Limited systems or locally earthed systems such as starting and ignition systems of an internal combustion engine;

Insulation level monitoring devices, subject to any circulating current not exceeding 30 mA under the worst conditions;

The earthing of the neutral of a high voltage power network providing any possible resulting current does not flow directly through any dangerous area defined in the Recommendations.

Power supply and distribution

Generating plant, switchboards and batteries must be separated from the cargo tanks by a cofferdam or an equivalent space and from a cargo pump room or a cargo compressor room by an oil and gas tight bulkhead.

Cable or cables which may be exposed to cargo oil, oil vapour or gas must be sheathed with a lead sheath plus a further mechanical protection such as armourbraiding or a non-metallic impervious sheath, or, alternatively, a non metallic impervious sheath with an armourbraiding for mechanical protection and earth detection. A copper sheath is to be used in the case of mineral-insulated cable. Where there is risk of corrosion, cables having an armoured or metallic sheath are required to be covered additionally by a non-metallic impervious sheath.

A number of recommendations are made in respect of cable installations. Cables installed along the foredeck of a tanker may be subjected to movement due to the working of the ship's structure and consequently the cables and their supports must be installed in a manner which avoids any strain or chafing which could be caused by this working of the structure; allowances must also be made for consequent expansion and contraction. Cables which are associated with intrinsically safe circuits must be used only for such circuits and they should be separated from cables containing non-intrinsically safe circuits.

DANGEROUS SPACES (OR HAZARDOUS AREAS)

Dangerous spaces in a tanker are defined as areas where flammable or explosive gas/air mixtures would normally be expected to accumulate. A 'hazardous area' is sometimes referred to in preference to a 'dangerous space' as the former term is now in general usage when referring to land installations. Unlike land practice the requirements for tankers do not recognise degrees of danger or hazard; in a tanker spaces are either 'dangerous' or 'normally safe', whereas in land practice such hazards are graded into Zones 0, 1 and 2. Definitions covering these three zone categories are given later in the chapter.

When considering the type of vessel described in (1) above, the following are considered to be dangerous spaces:

Cargo tanks;
Cofferdams adjoining cargo tanks;
Cargo pumprooms.

Enclosed or semi-enclosed spaces immediately above cargo tanks (e.g. between decks) or having bulkheads above and in line with the cargo tank bulkheads.

Enclosed or semi-enclosed spaces immediately above cargo pumprooms, or above vertical cofferdams adjoining cargo tanks, unless spearated by a gastight deck and suitably mechanically ventilated.

Spaces, other than cofferdams, adjoining and below the top of the cargo tanks (e.g. trunks, passageways and holds).

Areas on open deck, or semi-enclosed spaces on open deck, within at least 3 m of any cargo oil tank outlet or gas or vapour outlet.

Areas on open deck over all cargo tanks, including all ballast tanks within the cargo tank block and to the full width of the vessel plus 3 m forward and aft on open deck, up to a height of 2.4 m above the deck.

Compartments for cargo hoses.

Enclosed or semi-enclosed spaces having a direct opening into any of the spaces or areas mentioned above.

The designated spaces and the areas listed above have been formulated as a result of experience gained over a number of years. It is, however, readily recognised that liquids, gases and vapours do not always obediently remain within the boundaries which have been laid down. Attention is, therefore, drawn to the following hazards:

(a) Large quantities of gas can be present during loading, ballasting and during gas freeing by mechanical means. Therefore, consideration must be given to possible dangers arising from gases or vapours outside the areas which have been mentioned.

(b) Spaces which are forward of the cargo tank block and are below the level of the main deck are prone to the accumulation of heavier than air gases. They must, therefore, be considered dangerous if they are not provided with suitable self closing air lock doors and, in addition, adequate mechanical ventilation;

(c) In cases where the cargo tank deck continues along the sides of an accommodation block a spillage barrier should be provided to limit the spread of any product spilt on the deck in order to limit the extent of any resultant gas or vapour.

Electrical equipment and wiring is only permitted in dangerous spaces or areas where it is essential for operational purposes. Echo-sounding devices, providing they are hemetically enclosed and their associated cables are installed in heavy gauge steel pipes with gas-tight joints, may be fitted in cofferdams adjoining cargo tanks, cargo pumprooms and in spaces other than cofferdams which are adjoining and are below the top of the cargo tanks. Cables for external hull impressed current cathodic protection systems may also be run through these areas providing they are installed in a manner similar to those for echo sounders.

Should the compartment or cofferdam be subjected to sea water filling, as in the case of permanent ballast tanks, the cable pipes must be corrosion resistant to offset the effects of sea water. Flame-proof or pressurised enclosure type lighting fixtures may be fitted in a cargo pumproom, in enclosed or semi-enclosed spaces immediately above a cargo tank or above a cargo pumproom and in compartments used for storing cargo hoses. Switches and protective devices associated with the lighting circuits must be located in normally safe spaces and additionally must interrupt all poles or phases of the circuit.

In the case of cargo pumproom lighting systems at least two independent final branch circuits must be provided. This arrangement allows the disconnecting of one circuit for the maintenance of fittings whilst the other circuit provides the lighting necessary for this purpose. With the exception of the cargo tanks, through runs of cables are permitted in most of the dangerous areas. In some instances, however, they are discouraged if a suitable alternative routing can be found. Cable expansion bends should not be located within 3 m of any gas outlet such as a cargo tank hatch, sight port, etc. Within cargo tanks the only electrical equipment permitted is that of the intrinsically safe type.

Electric motors are not permitted in cargo pumprooms. Where they are used for driving cargo pumps or any other equipment, which may be located in the cargo pumproom spaces, they must be separated from those spaces by means of a gastight bulkhead or deck. Shafting between the motors and the driven units must be suitably glanded where the shafts pass through the gastight bulkhead or deck. It is normal practice for the ventilation pressure of the pumproom to be less than that of the compartment which contains the motors; should the bulkhead glanding become defective air passes from the normally safe space (in this case the motor room) to the designated dangerous space (the pumproom) thereby preventing any ingress of gas into the former.

For the vessels which are described under (2) dangerous spaces are not defined. The Recommendations nevertheless emphasise prudence in reducing potential sources of ignition and suggest certain practices which may be followed. These are:

Using intrinsically safe apparatus for any monitoring equipment which is in direct connection with the cargo tanks or with the oil circuits.

Employing increased safety type motors for driving pumping equipment when such motors are located in the cargo pumproom, and

Ensuring that any portable electrical equipment which may be used in the cargo tanks is of a certified safe type.

For this type of vessel the Recommendations also stress that they should not be used for the carriage of flammable cargoes other than those for which they are designed.

In the case of gas carriers, the vessels described under (3), the dangerous areas defined in IEC Publication 92 have been superseded by those given in the IMCO *Code for the construction and equipment of ships carrying liquefied gases in bulk.* The following definitions are, therefore, extracts from this Code:

A space in the cargo area which is not equipped with approved arrangements to ensure that its atmosphere is at all times maintained in a safe condition.

An enclosed space outside the cargo area through which any piping, which may contain liquid or gaseous products, passes, or within which such piping terminates, unless approed arrangements are installed to prevent any escape of product vapour into the atmosphere of that space.

A cargo containment system with cargo piping.

(i)   A hold space where cargo is carried in a cargo containment system requiring a secondary barrier;

(ii) A hold space where cargo is carried in a cargo containment system not requiring a secondary barrier;

A space separated from a hold space described in (i) by a single gastight steel boundary.

A cargo pumproom and cargo compressor room.

A zone on open deck, or semi-enclosed space on open deck, within 3 m of any cargo tank outlet, gas or vapour outlet, cargo piped flange, cargo valve or of entrances and ventilation openings to a cargo pumproom and cargo compressor rooms.

The open deck over the cargo area and 3 m forward and aft of the cargo area on open deck up to a height of 2.4 m above the weather deck.

A zone within 2.4 m of the outer surface of a cargo containment system where such surface is exposed to the weather.

An enclosed or semi-enclosed space in which pipes containing products are located.

A compartment for cargo hoses, and

An enclosed or semi-enclosed space having a direct opening into any dangerous space or area.

As with the vessels described in (1), electrical equipment and wiring is only permitted in dangerous spaces or areas when it is essential for operational purposes. That which is permitted is in most instances similar to that for the vessels in (1). There are, however, two significant additions, these being:

(a) Submerged cargo pump motors and their cables are permitted in cargo tanks subject to the atmosphere of the tank being controlled to prevent presence of a gas/air mixture when the motors are energised.

(b) Motors driving gas compressors, may, in certain circumstances, be sited in the same space as the compressors. In these instances the motors are required to be of a 'pressurised' type, the pressurising medium being air, inert gas or water, or of the type which combines 'Increased safety' construction within a flameproof enclosure.

The present section in IEC Publication 92 which deals with gas carriers is currently (1980) being revised to remove any ambiguities which could arise between it and the IMCO Code.

The for the type of vessel described under (4), such as chemical carriers, the possible hazards in relation to electrical equipment by the products intended to be conveyed are identified with the aid of an Appendix. In this Appendix the designer is given guidance on whether the product is:

(a) Similar to those normally conveyed by vessels of the types listed under (1), (2) or (3); in this case the recommendations given for those types of vessel would apply.

(b) Potentially more hazardous than in the case above; in these instances the distances determining the extent of the already defined dangerous areas would have to be increased from 3 m (or 2.4 m) to 4.5 m.

(c) Prone to chemical instability or reaction resulting in the generation of flammable gases or vapours; such cases must then be dealt with in accordance with whichever of the foregoing is most appropriate.

(d) Liable to damage electrical equipment either by liquid gaseous or vapour contact; here the need to carefully select the materials or to encapsulate equipment must be considered in order to avoid or prevent corrosion.

For some products it is necessary to consider more than one of the points mentioned. Ammonia displays what might be regarded as 'normal hazard' from the gas evolution aspect as well as 'corrosive' effects.

Brief mention has already been made of the electrical equipment and cables which may be used in dangerous spaces or areas on board a tanker. It is not proposed to give here a comprehensive list, sufficient to say that these are adequately covered in IEC Publication 92 where the equipment suitable for use in dangerous areas are referred to as being of a Certified Safe type.

This term means that the equipment has been constructed in accordance with a recognised specification, mainly based on IEC Publication 79 *Electrical apparatus for explosive gas atmospheres* and examined and certified by a recognised testing authority. In the UK the organisation responsible for such a certification is the British Approvals Service for Electrical Equipment in Flammable Atmospheres (BASEEFA). There are similar organisations in other countries — Physikalish-Technische Bundesanstalt (PTB) in the Federal Republic of Germany; Underwriter's Laboratories, Inc. (UL) in the USA; Laboratoire Central de Industries Electriques (LCIE) in France, Nippon Hakuyohin Kentei Kyokai (NHKK) in Japan, etc.

Equipment certified by any of these testing authorities as well as those in other countries, are normally accepted by the major Classification Societies but is not always the case with governmental bodies. It is advisable to check the acceptability of any proposed equipment and its certification with the government authorities appropriate to a vessel's registry.

It is of course, essential that the certification of the equipment is applicable to all types of flammable atmospheres which will be encountered due to the types of cargo carried by the vessel.

Recommendations and/or standards based on IEC Publication 79 are primarily intended for equipment used in land installations. Consequently, equipment constructed in accordance with such standards are not always suitable for use in the marine environment and special features may require to be incorporated. Such features are covered in another Appendix in the tanker chapter of IEC Publication 92; examples of which are: resistance to corrosion; suitability for operation in higher ambient temperatures; increased creepage distances on terminal blocks.

Accepting that the most appropriate equipment has been selected for its intended location and duty and that it has been correctly installed and commissioned by the shipbuilder, and/or an appointed sub-contractor, the continued safe and reliable operation of the equipment is dependent upon certain inspection and maintenance procedures being carried out. Many manufacturers issue recommended procedures with respect to their equipment or systems and these should be followed when available. In the absence of such instructions the following guidelines should prove to be of some assistance.

FLAMEPROOF (TYPE EXD) EQUIPMENT

Flameproof equipment relies upon the integrity of its enclosure and its ability to withstand the internal pressures generated by an ignited gas. The flanges between the cover(s) and the main body of the enclosure should be able to cool any transmitted flame sufficiently to prevent it igniting any gas which may surround the enclosure. The equipment should, therefore, be examined for cracks in the metal enclosure and in any glass ports and for the failure of the cement fixing of glass ports. Corrosion or wear of flanges or components must be remedied. All securing nuts and bolts must be in position and should be checked for tightness.

When enclosures are dismantled for maintenance, or joints are broken for any reason, it is essential that the flanges are clean when reassembled. No packing should be applied to the flanges except when this has been provided by the manufacturer.

In the event of replacement being necessary the correct O-ring or gasket must be used.

When replacing lamps in lighting fittings the correct rating and type must be used otherwise an excessive surface temperature may result which could thereby invalidate the temperature classification of the fitting. This applies equally to the replacement of other components such as a transformer, relays, etc.

The accumulation of dust and dirt on an enclosure can interfere with the heat dissipation and result in an excessive surface temperature. The equipment must, therefore, be kept free of such deposits.

The cable installation associated with the equipment should be inspected periodically to ensure that entry glands are secure; conduit runs are free of slack joints and corrosion and that equipment and cable arm on ring is effectively earthed.

INCREASED SAFETY (TYPE EXE) EQUIPMENT

Increased safety can be described as a type of protection by which additional measures are applied to give electrical apparatus increased security against the possibility of excessive temperatures and of the occurrence of arcs or sparks in the interior and on the external parts during the service life of the apparatus. Safety can only be applied to electrical apparatus consisting of components which do not produce arcs or sparks nor exceed the limiting temperature during normal service, for example, a lighting fixture or a cage-type induction motor.

The information given above on flameproof equipment in respect of component replacement, removal of surface deposits and the associated cable installation apply equally to increased safety apparatus. Enclosures should be checked for damage and the condition of any gasket should be such as to render the enclosure effectively dust proof, weatherproof or deck watertight, according to the location.

The protection devices associated with increased safety motors are of considerable importance and should be checked periodically to ensure that they function correctly at their prescribed settings.

INTRINSICALLY SAFE (TYPE EXI) EQUIPMENT

Intrinsic safety is a protection technique based upon the restriction of electrical energy within apparatus and of interconnecting wiring to a level below that which can cause ignition of an explosive atmosphere by either sparking or heat effects.

Intrinsic safety can be applied to either a complete system — e.g. a sound powered telephone system — or part of the system (a cargo tank temperature monitoring system using shunt diode safety barriers) or a single circuit (a 'stop' push using an interposing intrinsically safe relay).

There are so many variations that it would be imprudent to give any specific guidelines here other than to state that the manufacturers' instruction manuals should be referred to. One general point can, however, be made in reference to insulation and earth continuity testing. Excepting where it can be established without any doubt that no flammable atmospheres are present only certified testing instruments should be used. The maximum output parameters of these instruments do not exceed 1.2 V, 0.1 A and 25 mW nor the energy storage capability exceed 200 μJ.

It should be added that for other circuits, e.g. power and lighting, insulation tests should only be carried out when no flammable atmospheres are present in the areas concerned. Even though certified intrinsically safe test apparatus may be used, the total circuit being tested may not be intrinsically safe.

PRESSURISED (TYPE EXP) EQUIPMENT

Pressurisation is a type of protection which prevents entry into the equipment enclosure of a surrounding flammable gas by maintaining within the enclosure a protective gas (which may be air or inert gas) at a pressure which is higher than that of the surrounding atmosphere. This over-pressure can be maintained with or without a continuous flow of the protective gas. Pressurisation is frequently applied to lighting systems and on occasions to motors; usually the non-continuous flow method is applied in both cases.

With pressurised equipment it is necessary to purge the enclosure(s) before the circuits are energised. This is to ensure that any flammable gas which may have entered during shut-down periods are expelled. The functioning of associated control equipment should, therefore, be periodically examined to ensure that the require purging cycle (equal to ten times the free volume of the enclosure) is fulfilled. The settings of the 'flow meters', if fitted, should be checked also that of the system pressure switch which, when the purging cycle is completed, detects a fall below the minimum acceptable pressure and automatically disconnects the electrical supply.

The information given for increased safety equipment also applies to pressurised equipment.

GENERAL

Before attempting to carry out maintenance on any electrical equipment, all associated supplies must be disconnected. None of the equipment must be modified in any way as alteration could impair the effectiveness of the protection as well as invalidating the Testing Authorities Certification. In conclusion two further points should be made:

1. All portable apparatus such as hand torches and UHF/VHF transceivers of the 'Walkie-Talkie' type on a tanker should be approved for use in hazardous areas irrespective of wherever it is intended to operate.

2. When alongside a loading or discharging terminal a tanker can be partially embraced by the hazardous areas ascribed to a terminal. According to the operational procedures applicable to the terminal it may be necessary to isolate certain electrical equipment which is not of a certified safe type. Radar and main radio transmitters should not be used except when authorised by the terminal authorities. For further information on operational procedures, see the *International Safety Guide for oil tankers and terminals.*

As mentioned earlier, for land installations hazardous areas are classified into zones 0, 1 and 2. IEC Publication 79—10 defines these different zones as follows:-

Zone 0 : In which an explosive gas-air mixture is continuously present or present for long periods.

Zone 1 : In which an explosive gas-air mixture is likely to occur in normal operation.

Zone 2 : In which a gas-air mixture is not likely to occur and if it occurs it will only exist for a short time.

Marine engineering circles are currently discussing the possibility of applying this 'zoning' concept to the hazardous areas on tankers. Whilst the experienced designer is well able to liken many of the defined tanker hazardous areas with the three zones mentioned the advantages of applying the zoning concept could arise when dealing with vessels having hazardous areas which fit none of the definitions presently applied. This situation is arising quite frequently in connection with vessels associated with the offshore oil industry. When dealing with these special vessels a designer will, once the zones have been identified, be given a lead on the type of electrical equipment which may or may not be used as each of the types referred to earlier are recognised as being suitable for operation in one or more of the three zones mentioned.

International agreement will be necessary before the zoning concept can be implemented. The 'dangerous' and 'normally safe' approach will, therefore, continue to be applied to tankers for a number of years to come.

19 Control engineering

Control engineering embraces instrumentation, alarm systems, control of machinery and plant previously known under the misnomer of automation. Its application to ships was initiated in the early 1960s to ease manpower problems and routine tasks of engine room watchkeepers and these functions have been revolutionised. The concept of unattended machinery spaces has given rise to special notations by all the leading classification societies to the extent that about 25% of all ships classed with Lloyd's Register in the 1970s have the special UMS notation for unattended machinery spaces.

In the early years, lack of appreciation of marine conditions and environment led to the supply of unsuitable equipment and bad planning although reliable equipment was in fact available. An analysis of malfunctioning and a study of shortcomings of these early equipments has resulted in new specifications and the drafting of rules now resulting in extremely reliable installations. One of the contributory factors in this state of affairs has been the establishment by the leading classification societies of test requirements and type approval of control equipment. These tests take into account environmental and working conditions such as temperature and humidity, vibration, inclination, saline atmospheres, drip-proof and waterproofing properties and intrinsically safe requirements.

Type approval however does not ensure complete success of every unit. Occasionally conditions not envisioned in the type test will arise, such as excessive vibration or a sensor subject to exceptionally high ambient temperature e.g. if mounted in an excessively hot situation. These exceptions will usually be dealt with by the surveyors during construction. Test requirements are drafted for two categories (a) A minimum test and (b) additional tests. All equipment has to meet the minimum test.

Minimum test requirements include:

Visual inspection.
Performance tests.

Fluctuations in power supply.
Vibration test.
Humidity test.
Dry heat test.
Inclination test.
Insulation resistance. ⎱ Electrical
High voltage test. ⎰ only.

Additional tests comprise:

Low temperature tests.
Alternative vibration test.
Salt mist test.
Watertightness.
Extended dry heat test.

Generally speaking life tests and corrosion tests are not included except where already covered in national or international standards.

The alternative vibration test is intended for equipment normally attached to reciprocating machinery where greater severity is involved. The standard vibration test is based on an acceleration of $\pm$ 0.7 g, the alternative requires $\pm$ 4.0 g.

Equipment which has proved to function well and reliably in land-based industrial environments proved quite the reverse when applied to ship conditions. Much of this was due to entry into this field of firms with little or no experience of marine hazards. Another factor was lack of coordination and planning caused by several firms supplying units independently without coordination. The employment of a single manufacturer assuming complete responsibility for the design and supply of comprehensive systems is therefore to be recommended. It not only reduces unnecessary duplication and complication but for the shipowner facilitates service, maintenance, and repair problems when the ship is in service.

Control engineering can be applied not only to propelling and auxiliary machinery but also to electrical installations, refrigeration, cargo handling (especially in tankers) and deck machinery, e.g. Windlass Control. Opinions still vary on such matters as the relative merits of pneumatic versus electronic systems and whether the control centre should be in the engine room or adjacent to the navigating bridge. Arguments against the exclusion of the engineer officer from close contact with the machinery are countered by the fact that electronic systems are based on changes other than those of human response. Automated ships operate closer to prescribed standards and therefore operate with greater efficiency.

Nomenclature

To avoid misunderstandings it is important to learn the jargon and new terms inevitably introduced by control engineers. The design and specifications for systems are prepared by *control engineers* who devise not only marine systems but also shore installations. Following are just a few of the more commonly used expressions but for those interested in a more comprehensive coverage BS 1523 *Glossary of terms used in automatic controlling and regulating systems, Section 2 'Process control' and Section 2 'Kinetic control'*, can be recommended. For interpreting diagrams BS 3939 *Graphical Symbols, Section 20 'Semi-conductor devices'* and *Section 21 'Pure logic and functional symbols'* are useful.

Closed loop: A control system, sometimes called *feedback,* possessing a monitoring feedback, the deviation signal from this being used to control the action of a final controlling element in such a manner as to tend to reduce the amount of deviation to zero (see Figure 19.1).

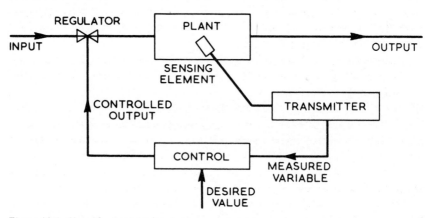

Figure 19.1 Closed loop control system

If the deviation control is too small the plant will be caused to oscillate about the desired value (hunting). Alternatively a residual error will remain.

A *manual closed-loop* system is one which includes a human operator as an element of the closed loop. An *automatic closed loop* is one in which there is no human operator in the loop. Inherently faster and more accurate than manual or open loop.

Open loop: A system, sometimes called *feed forward,* without a monitoring feed back. It may operate an alarm device or register an effect on an instrument or data-logger (see Figure 19.2).

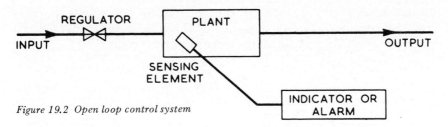

Figure 19.2 Open loop control system

Computer: Any equipment capable of carrying out calculations or of storing and handling data. A *digital computer* deals with discrete digits and performs ordinary arithmetic. An *analogue computer* deals with variable functions and where variables are changing with time e.g. transient conditions in an engine room. Analogue computers are quite common in ships.

Data-logger: Any equipment producing by means of a typewriter or strip printer a regular print-out log of events, all time identified in tabulated form to provide an accurate record at predetermined intervals of selected conditions or of movements (e.g. of bridge/engine room telegraph) or an indication of changes in operational conditions liable to lead to failure.

Desired value: A value which has to be preserved or memorised by the controller whether human (open loop) or automatically (closed loop).

Measured values: The variable which has to be controlled.

Feedback: A signal from some part of the system to be controlled e.g. a variable at an earlier stage or a signal to a display, instrument or alarm.

Gain: The amplification of an element or system in which the input and output signals are of the same physical kind.

Attentuation: The reciprocal of gain.

Hardware: The component parts of a system, computer, etc.

Software: The information fed to a computer, data-logger or system as distinct from hardware (*q.v.*).

Module. A standard interchangeable unit.

Mean time between failure (MTBF): The average life or operational time between failures.

Redundancy. Safeguards incorporated into a system to ensure continuity of operation. For example, in an electrical circuit two diodes connected in parallel so that the system will continue to function if one should fail -- known as *parallel redundancy*. In *automatic redundancy* a failing unit is automatically replaced by a reserve unit.

Availability: The probability that a device or system can function satisfactorily for a given period. It is the ratio between *MTBF* and the sum of *MTBF* and the replacement or repair time *T*:

$$A = \frac{MTBF}{T + MTBF}$$

Transducer: A device for converting a signal or physical quantity of one kind (the input) into a corresponding physical quantity of another kind (the output). For example, the input may be pressure, temperature, torque, speed, etc. and the output an electrical or pneumatic signal which can feed a control system, instrument, data-logger' alarm, etc

Planning

Experience has shown that where there has been some failure to achieve all that was expected it is largely due to lack of planning. Successful planning involves integrating and coordinating the system as a whole and this cannot be achieved if sections are in different hands. Haphazard methods by independent concerns have resulted in conflicting and unworkable systems. For example, sensors have been used at the instigation of one interested party and without consultation with, for example, the supplier of the computer or the data-logger only to find later that the output is incompatible.

It is also essential the control engineer should have practical knowledge and experience of the plant to be controlled and that the plant supplier should concur regarding facilities for accommodating and positioning the sensors.

A procedure which has been advocated for ensuring success is that the shipowner should, at the outset, state in broad terms what he requires. The shipbuilder should then prepare an outline specification to meet the owner's requirements and from this the control engineer can prepare a detailed specification. All three parties should then get together and agree the control specification. Hitherto there has been too little feed-back of information and experience from the ship but control engineers and shipowners are now appreciating that this is important. If owners or builders have preferences for any particular make of component, it is at the planning stage that agreement should be reached.

The owner will need to consider operational and economic issues to decide how far to go and what financial benefits he can expect from each section. For example, in a refrigerating plant, push-button starting from the control console may not be justified as it is an infrequent operation which can be performed manually and so centralisation can be confined to instrumentation and alarms. The essential factors for a successful system are:

1. Reliability.
2. Simplicity.
3. Ease of operation and maintenance.
4. Suitability for marine conditions.
5. Facilities for servicing (especially in foreign ports).

Marine conditions involve not only ambient temperatures, humidity, vibration and saline atmospheres but also the physical conditions inevitable during construction, installation and trials. These apply to all parts of the system — sensors, instruments, consoles, computers, etc. Paint spraying, asbestos lagging, welding, staging and dirty surroundings can play havoc. Fitters and erectors have no respect for such equipment and many a sensor has served as a footstep.

Systems must embody 'fail safe' features and this aspect must be studied analytically in the planning stage. All possible sources of failure and their consequences must be covered. For example, if a fuel injection system is such that a spring is balanced by fluid pressure acting on a piston then loss of fluid may result in full fuel admission to the engine and a dangerous condition exists. The arrangements must ensure that failure of the controlling medium will result in either the speed remaining constant or that it is reduced.

Fail safe principles can be interpreted in different ways, such as complete stoppage of an operation or reverting to some other (safe) state. In suitable cases it can mean 'fail-as-set', i.e. continue as at the time of failure, sometimes referred to as 'fail-as-is'. It is essential that an alarm be operated to direct attention to the failure.

A vital part of planning procedure is planning the precommissioning trials and calibration. This must be considered and agreed by the builder at an early stage so that he can include it in his overall programme and delivery date and, when the time comes, provide the essential facilities.

It is not unusual for a comprehensive system to include 300—400 control points widely distributed and each requiring individual checking for operation and possibly calibration. This is time-consuming and can only be done when installation is complete and ship's services are available. It cannot be postponed until after the sea trials. A detailed test programme and timetable, agreed by the shipbuilder is therefore essential. With all systems there is an initial period of teething troubles and these must be tracked down as far as possible before the sea trials. This applies particularly to closed-loop systems.

Simulators can be provided in some cases which make it possible to test the entire electronic equipment by providing similar responses to those anticipated under service conditions. They can form part of the permanent installation so that, for example, prior to arrival in port, the navigating officer can himself simulate operation of the engine telegraph.

Methods of measurement

The methods to be taken into account are those which can be recorded from a distance and can be used for instrumentation, alarms and data-logging.

Temperatures may range from sub-zero to 54° C and several methods are suitable, their choice depending on the range involved. Thermocouples, resistance thermometers and thermistors have wide ranges.

Thermocouples consist of two dissimilar metal wires such as NiCr-Ni in intimate contact at each end. One end is maintained at a known temperature and the other subjected to the temperature to be recorded. The difference in temperature results in an electrical potential and generation of a current which can be measured by a micro-ammeter or potentiometer calibrated as temperature. They are suitable for high temperatures such as diesel exhaust gases. The *thermistor* is a recently developed form of semiconductor having an extremely large change in resistance with temperature and can have either a positive or a negative temperature coefficient but are now mostly made negative. Thermistors are made from specific mixtures of very pure oxides of nickel, manganese, iron, cobalt, copper, magnesium, titanium and other metals. A mixture of these oxides formed to the desired shape, usually with a binding mixture is sintered under controlled conditions of temperature and atmosphere.

The usual tolerance for resistance at the reference point is ± 10 to 20% and, because of variation of rate of change, may well develop a substantial resistance difference at temperatures removed from the reference point. If a thermistor has to be replaced it will therefore be necessary to recalibrate. They have unlimited life expectancy when operated within their temperature and power ratings. They can be used in the same way as a resistance thermometer. They are physically small and very suitable for surface measurements such as those of bearings and electric windings. Resistance thermometers depend on the change of resistance with temperature of a wire-wound element, usually platinum, the change being recorded by Wheatstone bridge. They are generally used for temperatures up to 100°C.

Liquid expansion thermometers consist of sealed tubes filled with liquid which expands when heated and usually acts on bellows. This type has a limited range and is commonly used for refrigeration controls.

Pressures: These may vary from high vacuum to 10 000 N/m² and can be measured by means of bellows, diaphragms, Bourdon tubes changing an electrical output by moving a slider on a resistance. Pressure dampers may have to be inserted to protect pressure sensors from surges such, for example, as from compressors. Static head balanced against mercury or air pressure may also be used; so also may strain gauges consisting of a grid of fine resistance wire mounted on a suitable supporting medium. When cemented to surfaces subject to strain the variation of length of the wire grid changes the electrical resistance. Static pressure e.g. steam pressure can make use of differential pressure measurement.

Levels (liquid): Hydrostatic pressure can be utilised or if the actual level of liquid is not vital a simple indication of high, normal, or low level can be recorded by float switches or, if the fluid is electrically conducting, electrodes may be used.

Speed is measurable by means of three-phase tachogenerators, pulse generators, by frequency meter or by magnetic pole-pieces on a shaft in close proximity to a stationary electro-magnetic pick-up.

Electric power: The sum total of power from two or more a.c. generators can be obtained from the secondary windings of current transformers connected in series ahead of the input to a phase-sensitive rectifier.

Miscellaneous: Other quantities suitable for use are indicated in Table 19.1.

Table 19.1

Function	Method of measurement
Torque	Strain gauge, magnetic reluctance
Viscosity	Differential pressure
Salinity	Electrical conductance
Flow	Impeller rotation, venturi tube
Smoke	Photo-cell, transistor
Acidity	pH meter
Humidity	Hygrometer, dry and wet bulb thermometer
Electricity	Wattmeter, ammeter, voltmeter

Alarms

Alarms are usually audible and visual with provision whereby the operator dealing with the signal can silence the audible signal but retain the visual. It is important that the alarms be restored when the emergency has been satisfactorily dealt with and the visual signal cancelled. Alarms can be of two types, those which are vital requiring immediate action and those not so urgent and usually the different audible alarms are distinguishable.

Vital alarms are those which could require a reduction of engine speed or even a stoppage e.g. failure of lubrication. Less urgent might be tank level alarms. It is advisable to exercise restraint on the number and nature of alarms in order to prevent confusion. Fire alarms originating in the engine room should also operate simultaneously on the navigating bridge and in the engineer's quarters.

A typical example of good practice is to be found in a bulk carrier intended for service with unmanned engine room for up to 12 hours. If for any reason an alarm is not accepted by the duty engineer it will be repeated in all engineer's cabins thus avoiding the risk of an emergency condition not being dealt with. The engine room is also provided with a test panel and facilities for feeding artificial signals into the system so that checks can be made prior to sailing. In another example the alarm system extends to the bridge, smoke room, dining-room and, by selector switch, to the duty officer's cabin.

The International Standards Organisation (ISO) is studying standards for signal lights and present proposals, subject to ratification are:

Red for danger; flashing for conditions requiring immediate action, changing to steady when the condition is receiving attention.
Yellow for less urgent conditions.
Green for safety; flashing to indicate that a standby machine has automatically come into service and steady for normal operation.

Sensors

Sensors play an essential role in all systems for transmitting information to control and other remote positions. The quantities necessary to sense include counting, fluid flow, humidity, liquid levels, noise, position, pressure, salinity, smoke density, speed, strain, temperature, viscosity, torque, power, etc.

The type of sensor must take into account the relative importance of the effect of its presence on the quantity to be measured, together with the extraneous effects by or on the sensor. For example:

1. It should not affect the quantity to be measured, e.g. flow metering.
2. The effect of ambient and adjacent temperatures should be either known or be capable of elimination.
3. Speed of response in respect to rapid changes.
4. Independence from magnetic fields, humidity, barometric pressure, local heat.
5. Independence from variations of electrical supplies (e.g. frequency and voltage) or be provided with means for compensating for variations.
6. Linearity, hysteresis, repeatability and zero-point drift are also important.

Sensors may be required to initiate mechanical operation, for example, such as the high forces required to operate cargo valves in tankers and for hatch closing and opening and as most sensors cannot provide the mechanical effort required this can be provided via transducers. The electrical or pneumatic signals obtained from them can in turn operate alarms, relays or instruments. Bourdon tubes, diaphragms and floats can provide sufficient power to operate instruments directly or can act as transducers.

Pneumatic systems

Pneumatic control is naturally favoured by most engineers as it is effective and relatively easy to maintain. Nevertheless electronic systems can be equally reliable and in fact become indispensable for sophisticated systems especially those incorporating computers and data loggers. Many systems employ both pneumatic and electronic controls.

Pneumatic systems can give a speed of response sufficient for marine applications and have been used for example for fuel and lubricating-oil temperature recording, boiler control and in numerous other directions.

A very high standard of clean uncontaminated air supply free from the slightest trace of lubricating oil, fuel oil, salt or moisture is essential. The apertures in nozzles and pilot valves may be of the order of a few thousandths of an inch and any contamination can become dangerous. Duplex filters of the ceramic, sintered or activated carbon duplex type combined with fine gauze filters at strategic positions will normally give the required protection provided strict routine attention and draining of traps is observed. Filters should not be provided with by-passes. Air pressures are normally of the order of 551–827 kN/m² for operational purposes but lower pressures of 20–103 kN/m² and 20–206 kN/m² are usual for recording and signal purposes, the former being an international standard.

Electronic systems

For some functions electronics beoome indispensable and in a properly designed system can be equally as reliable as pneumatic systems. Advantages are low power consumption, reduced size and cost of components, high speed of response. For accuracy and stability there is not much difference.

Precautions are essential in the layout and installation of circuits incorporating semi-conductor diodes to avoid electrical disturbances. These devices are vulnerable to momentary over-voltages (known as spikes) which may arise from a variety of causes, including switching. Spikes in main distribution circuits can be of the order of four to five times normal voltage and can affect diodes connected to those circuits or other diode circuits if these are laid too close to main cables from which spikes can be induced. For redundancy it is common practice to connect diodes in parallel and the necessity for ensuring adequate thermal bonding is fully explained in Chapter 13.

Transmission

A slight time lag may occur with pneumatic transmission in long air lines and this is not usually a problem in operations confined to the engine room but in some controls operated from the navigating bridge it may have significance. In some instances a limiting distance of 120 m has been stated. The use of larger diameter piping may be necessary for long lines.

Because of the incidence of voltage spikes previously mentioned the location of electric wiring associated with electronic circuits in relation to power circuits is of importance. In the *QE2* for example a separation of 18 in. was stipulated. Relationship between different electronic circuits and radio-frequency systems is also important if electro-magnetic compatibility is to be ensured.

Data loggers

Data loggers owe their origin to shore installations such as chemical plants and have been specially adapted and modified to perform the special functions needed. As the name suggests their primary purpose is to log data but they also serve other useful purposes. The owner must decide whether he requires both or only one of these functions. Primarily they will log the quantities and movements tranditionally required of engineers but in addition they can, if so required, record data useful to designers and shore staff for future use or for statistical purposes. Also to record for the attention of the engineers malfunctioning of the plant.

To sum up, the purposes of data-logging can be:

1. To relieve operators of irksome logging.
2. To monitor and log important quantities at predetermined intervals.
3. To record quantities or conditions which are approaching or exceeding specified limits.
4. To provide a printed log of variables at set intervals e.g. propeller speed, ship speed, etc.
5. To record engine telegraph orders and the responses and the times. Normally two engineers are on duty when manoeuvring, one to carry out the movements, the other to write the log; similarly on the navigating bridge. This is unnecessary with data loggers. Results noted by hand are open to challenge and are completely eliminated by automatic systems.

Data loggers need not be confined to engine rooms but can be applied to navigation e.g. ship's log of speed, ship's headwind, sea temperature, cargo refrigeration temperatures and can also aid research (hull stresses, etc.).

The functions to be recorded, the quantities, time intervals etc. must be planned in advance. For the engineers it can show trends which require actiona and vital conditions requiring urgent attention. By automatically recording conditions at predetermined intervals, transient states are revealed which would not otherwise be observed. For timing purposes a digital clock provides timing pulses. As ship's time may change from day-to-day, the data logger must also be corrected and adjusted by means of a selector switch. The number of points to be monitored is a matter of choice and 300 to 400 is common practice. One standard equipment monitors and logs 250 points every 4 minutes and 100 of them will be scanned every 22 seconds.

The scanning circuits contain sealed-reed relays, usually with gold-plated contacts in order to inhibit oxidation. Each transducer is associated with a relay connected directly to the transducer output. The relay output is in turn connected to the input of an amplifier system to bring the signal up to the required strength. The amplifier also converts the signals to the required form before transmitting them to the digital converter. In alarm circuits the measured value is compared with the desired value. When two or more alarms occur simultaneously the data logger write-out unit records them in chronological order. This is one of the most important functions and must indicate to the engineer the location and if possible the nature of the trouble. Failures are apt to cascade and the sequence of events may reveal important information. Print-out is of course additional to audible and visual alarms.

The printing device consists of a fixed carriage typewriter and can operate on either a fixed programme or in conjunction with a computer. The trend is towards the latter. The type of computer used operates on a fixed programme basis and a knowledge of computer programming by the operator is unnecessary. The computer includes a memory system and the 'programme' fed to it is supplied with the equipment and written according to the owner's specified requirements.

In some installations the print-out machine is duplicated. Any channel in an alarm condition will be printed in red and the operator can select any particular point to be printed out at any time. Continuity of supply is of vital importance, particularly for alarms and the scheme should incorporate an automatic transfer to an alternative source in the event of failure e.g. to a battery or to a feeder from the emergency switchboard.

A data logger is not an essential requirement for unmanned engine rooms and in suitable cases a cheaper alternative known as an event recorder is available. This consists of a fast monitoring system, scanning at the rate of one microsecond per point and recording any change of status. As a 250-point recorder scans all points four times per millisecond and the print-out cannot operate at this speed a 20-point memory storage provides a print-out of events a a minimum spacing of one millisecond. A record of events in the sequence in which they occur sometimes helps when dealing with an emergency.

The event recorder does not accept or record actual values but accepts binary signals (i.e. on/off) and identifies the point against a statement of condition. The exact time and order of events is recorded and a description of the actual point can be printed out in full thus dispensing with the need to refer to a key list of numbers for point identity.

Centralised control

In early applications the control station was of the open type placed in a strategic position in the engine room and consisted of a console for the operating controls flanked by essential instruments. The modern concept is an enclosed space, soundproofed, vibration proofed and air conditioned. It may be situated in the engine room or adjacent to the bridge.

A variation of either is to embody the essential manoeuvring controls in a navigation console on the bridge flanked by radar and other navigational aids and a minimum of instruments indicating propeller speed and direction etc. The more sophisticated systems embodying data-logging or electronic equipment should undoubtedly be in an enclosed space with resilient mountings and facilities for maintaining a minimum temperature at all times.

Such control stations will include one ore more of the following:

1. A manoeuvring console for control of main and auxiliary machinery with start/stop of essential motors.
2. Instruments.
3. Alarm and warning indicators.
4. Communication facilities for the bridge, chief engineer, etc.
5. Data logger or event recorder.
6. Mimic diagram.

In some cases certain engine speeds are barred because of torsional vibration problems and control systems must automatically bar continuous running at these speeds. If bridge control is used it will be duplicated at the engineer's console and in all such cases provision must be made for manually-operated controls to be readily available in the event of remote or automatic control failing. All Classification Societies insist on this. Sufficient instrumentation must be provided in the vicinity of the manual controls to ensure efficient operation for lengthy periods.

Control stations should be reasonably free from noise and kept at a uniform temperature. Acoustic and thermal insulation including the use of double glazing and in combination with air conditioning will assist in achieving this. Some components are vulnerable to moisture and to prevent condensation when idle permanently installed heaters are advisable (see Figure 19.3).

Where engine control is from the bridge and, as is sometimes the case, from two or more positions the station in control at any one time should effectively block out all other positions. Transfer should be possible only when authorised and accepted and when both controls match.

Figure 19.3 Main control console of the QE2
This gives push-button control of electrical distribution, boilers, air conditioning, bow thrusters, stabilisers and other machinery

The temptation to include too many instruments and pilot lamps should be strongly resisted. The watchkeeper's attention should be focused on really important items and diversion and confusion by less important matters avoided. Those of prime importance and requiring most frequent attention should be segregated and placed adjacent to the console, others being grouped on separate panels. When sequential operations for starting or controlling systems are provided, indication to show successful completion of the sequence should be shown at the console. This is particularly necessary with bridge control of main engines. If the sequence is interrupted the indicator should identify the point so that remedial action can be taken.

Bridge control

Damage in collision is often accentuated or increased by the unavoidable delay which occurs between the time an order is telegraphed and the carrying out of the order and any reduction of this interval is a substantial advantage. Bridge control is ideally suited to controllable pitch propellers and for diesel-electric propulsion, but can be complicated and costly for other systems. It may not offer any economic gain for ships on long ocean voyages compared with those on short voyages.

It is essential the officer on watch should not be burdened with operational details with which he is not concerned. His instrumentation and operational requirements should be simple and just sufficient to assure him that the required response has been made or immediate warning, if this is not the case. For docking purposes portable remote controls which can be taken to the wings and used for controlling speed can in some cases be provided. Transfer of control to the engine room has already been dealt with. It must be accepted and acknowledged by a suitable and reliable signal.

The bridge layout must be carefully analysed and studied to ensure an arc of vision for the navigating officer in relation to the instruments and controls which he must observe and operate. Lighting is of special importance at night and red or orange lighting on black dials, as in aircraft, with provision for variable dimming is to be recommended. Where access is needed only for adjusting or setting purposes a light-sealing flap can be fitted.

It is now generally agreed that it is undesirable for a man to remain alone in an engine-room for a full 4-hour watch and the location of the centralised control at or adjacent to the bridge may be a solution.

On the other hand it is a disadvantage for an engineer to be out of sight, sound and smell of the engine room—all good senses with which to detect trouble. To ease this problem some progress has already been made by the use of closed-circuit television directed to selected areas.

Control of generators

Installations invariably include two generators but more often three or four. For reasons of economy it is undesirable to run more sets than necessary for the load for the time being. On the other hand an increase in power demand which would overload the sets may occur and call for another set. Under present regulations, preferential tripping switches off non-essential loads when overloading occurs. This is only a temporary expedient and systems are now available for the automatic starting, stopping and synchronising of sets according to demand.

Load variations will occur frequently and rapidly with deck machinery or gradually as with refrigerating plant when passing from temperate zones to the tropics. In confined waters it is necessary for safety reasons to retain a margin in reserve and to have not less than two sets on the board so an overriding provision must be included in automatic schemes.

The automatic system should include the following features:

1. Pre-start preparations. For diesel sets these will include lubricating oil priming and, in some cases, cooling water pump and fuel oil preparation.

2. Starting and stopping governed by load demands.
3. Synchronising.
4. kW and kVAr sharing.
5. Maintaining frequency.
6. Protection against engine mal-operation.
7. Protection against electrical faults and overloads.
8. Preferential tripping of non-essential loads and restoration when sufficient power becomes available.

Standby sets can be pre-warmed by continuous circulation of hot water from the main engine cooling system. Engines using heavy oil may require straight diesel fuel for starting, changing over automatically to heavy oil when warmed up. It is usual to bring in another set before the load reaches full load on the running —say 80 to 90%. It is also good practice to incorporate a short time delay, say 20 s, to prevent starting on a spurious load demand. To prevent an incoming set being switched repeatedly on to a short-circuit it is usual to arrange that it be locked out after being connected once.

In one system the starters of all large motors are connected to the generator control system by means of relays. If the available margin of power when the start button of a motor is pressed is insufficient, a new generator is brought in and as soon as the extra power is available the motor starts automatically.

A selector switch is used to determine the starting order when there are three or more sets and it will also establish which is to be the base load set. A set under maintenance can also be locked out.

The arrangements for steam sets are more complex and although the synchronising and load-sharing techniques, etc. are the same as for diesel sets it is more common to have manual control for starting and stopping. The sequence is basically the same whether on remote manual control or fully automatic, the latter being by a programmed control system. A typical sequence would be:

1. Emergency stop valve closed.
2. Auxiliary lubricating oil pump started.
3. Sea water circulating valves opened.
4. Gland steam admitted.
5. Extraction pump started.
6. Steam admitted to air ejector.
7. Steam valve opened.
8. Synchronising and load sharing as for diesels.

As each stage is established a pilot lamp is illuminated; if a failure occurs the sequence is stopped until it is cleared.

Automation on tankers

Automation and computers can play an indispensable part in tanker operation, particularly in the super-tankers now in service. It is of vital importance, for instance, to take account of stresses raised in the hull due to bending moments resulting from unequal buoyancy. These may arise from ballasting or from different grades of oil or may occur during loading or discharging.

There are three main systems of pipelines used in tankers and each requires a different method of handling:

(a) *The ring system:* A pipeline ring has suction pipes connected separately to each tank and each controlled by a gate valve. By opening the appropriate valve each tank can be emptied separately. When loading, the main pumps are bypassed and the ring becomes a gravity flow line and individual tanks are loaded by opening the appropriate valve.

(b) *The direct system:* The tanker is divided into three or more 'compartments' each of which is in turn subdivided into tanks. Each compartment is served by a pump and a pipeline which in turn is connected to tanks by tail pieces and gate valves. The main pipelines are interconnected by cross-over sluice valves.

(c) *The free-flow system:* This dispenses with pipelines and has the disadvantage that tanks can only be emptied simultaneously or in a fixed sequence. Oil from the after tank is drawn through a suction pipe and then from the forward tanks through valves in the transverse bulkheads. A variation consists of combining free flow and direct systems so that the latter is used for port and starboard wing tanks and free flow from the centre tanks.

It will be apparent that with modern tankers a large number of valves is involved which must all be operated in a logical sequence. Not only is this important from considerations of hull stress, but also when a mixed cargo of different grades is involved. For protection against incorrect operation some valves require sequence interlocking. Trim and list must also be controlled. There is obviously a fertile field for centralised control and for computer operation (see Figure 19.4).

Risk of explosion rules out electrical operation of valves and because of the power requirements for operating mammoth valves (up to 30 in.) hydraulic power is favoured. On the other hand for instrumentation and control purposes pneumatic and *intrinsically safe* electronic circuits (subject to classification approval) are admissible. The latter circuits are such that in no circumstances, including short-circuit and open-circuit, can an explosion be caused.

Figure 19.4 Cargo oil control panel for Shell vessel (Mangelia) built by Kawasaki Dockyard Co

1. *Stripping pump control valve, position indicator No. 1.*
2. *Cargo pump tachometers.*
3. *Ballast pump tachometer.*
4. *Stripping pump control valve, position indicator No. 2.*
5. *Discharge pressure gauges for the pumps*
6. *Suction pressure gauges for the pumps.*
7. *Clock.*
8. *Tank washing water heater temperature control and recorder*
9. *Sound powered telephone.*
10. *Pressure gauges for cargo line valve control system.*
11. *Mimic diagram and associated valve position indicators.*
12. *Discharge valve position control for cargo and ballast pumps (hydraulically-operated).*
13. *Speed controllers for the seven pumps.*
14. *Trips for the cargo and ballast pump turbines.*
15. *Cargo valve position controls.*

(Shell Oil Tankers)

When tanks have been emptied, sediment and dirt deposited at the bottom must be removed by *stripping pumps* through a separate pipeline and valve system. To facilitate the quick turn round now required, the stripping must be brought into action immediately the tank has been emptied.

For centralised control systems accurate measurement of tank contents when loading and discharging must be transmitted. Two main types of measurement are currently in use:

(*a*) a pneumatic sensing system, and,
(*b*) tape and float systems.

In the pneumatic system, compressed air is fed into a sensing pipe in the tank and when the air pressure balances the hydrostatic pressure air bubbles from the pipe. The actual air pressure in the pipe is transmitted by small bore tubing to the control room where it is applied to a U-tube manometer, one limb of which is connected to the space above the cargo. Various readings can be obtained from such a system e.g. direct reading of cargo tonnage, rate of loading or discharge, cargo temperature, pressure or vacuum above the cargo, etc.

In the tape and float system, a float is suspended on a stainless steel tape, the float is guided by a stainless steel wire. The tape

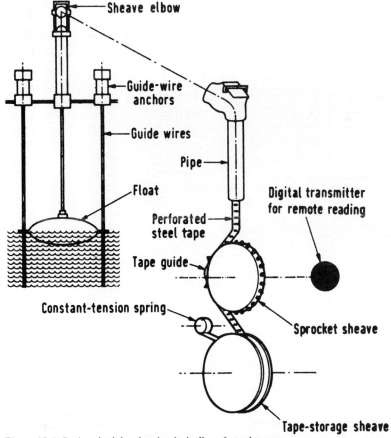

Figure 19.5 Basic principle of an intrinsically safe tank gauge

passes over a sprocket operating a counter for transmitting the data to the control room. Automatic devices for preventing overfill can also be incorporated. An approved intrinsically safe system (see Figure 19.5) is now available in which the movement of the float rotates a counter mechanism in the gauge head geared to an encoder/ transmitter. Coded data is fed via cables to a play-in high gain transmitter amplifier whose output feeds a data translator and digital display. Additional remote indicators can be mounted in different parts of the ship if required. High and low-level alarms and indicator lights are available on each indicator.

Container ships

It is essential if containers are to locate accurately in guides in ships' holds that the ship stays on an even keel during loading. Careful control is also necessary during unloading. Detection of the heel can be utilised to automatically control pumps and valves for the transfer of ballast between tanks. Systems have been developed for operating for lists greater than one degree (see Figure 19.6).

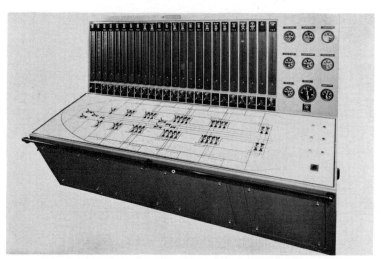

Figure 19.6 Ballast and fuel tank contents and valve control console for maintaining an even keel, while loading, on a container ship (Dobbie McInnes Ltd.)

Diesel engines

Small diesel engines in tugs, ferries, coasters, etc have been controlled from the bridge for many years but large cargo ships and tankers are being so controlled in increasing numbers. This requires not only the

usual starting and reversing operations but additionally the conditions imposed with way on the ships and barred running speeds.
   The sequence of starting is as follows:

1. Check that turning gear is disengaged.
2. Check that starting air pressure is correct and cooling water,
   lubrication and fuel supplies are in order.
3. Check camshaft correctly positioned.
4. Admit starting air.
5. Shut off starting air.
6. Adjust speed to value required.

If the sequence is not completed it is usual to repeat it, still under
automatic control. After a set number of false starts, usually three,
an alarm operates. If acceleration to the firing speed is not reached
within about 3 s a further period of about 4 s is allowed and then
the complete cycle is repeated.
   These times are subject to variation in consultation with the
engine builder and depend on the size of engine and its thermal time
constant. Control of starting air can be entirely pneumatic or, more
usually, electrically by solenoid-operated valves controlling an air
supply to pneumatic actuators.
   Various methods of controlling the fuel supply are used, for
example a pneumatic cylinder and hydraulic dashpot controlling the
rate of fuel supply by flow regulators. When the fuel lever matches
the telegraph position, further movement of the lever is arrested.
   There remains the separate problem of monitoring, controlling,
instrumentation and alarms concerning the following:

1. Lubricating oil temperature.
2. Fuel oil viscosity.
3. Cylinder jacket cooling water.
4. Piston cooling.
5. Exhaust gas temperatures.

Maintenance and efficiency will be improved by automatic control
of these items as compared with manual control but they need to be
co-ordinated and integrated at the design stage.
   Temperature sensors at the cylinder jacket cooling water outlet
have not been entirely satisfactory with wide load variations and
thermal inertia, so special systems have been evolved. It is normal to
control the temperature at the outlet by either by-passing on the
freshwater side or by controlling the flow of sea-water.

Temperature of lubricating oil is usually maintained constant at the inlet, preferably by bypassing or by throttling the sea-water to the cooler. Fuel oil viscosity can be controlled by regulating the steam supply to the heater and, with heavy oils, adjustments to suit different oils can be eliminated by maintaining constant viscosity. Viscosity is an important factor in reducing wear and tear.

A low temperature for the scavenge air is preferable and accordingly it is passed through a cooler but control is necessary as a low sea-water temperature can induce condensation. This can be achieved either by combining with the jacket water and lubricating oil coolers or by recirculating the water from the discharge side back to the pump suction.

A reduction of engine speed would be called for in the event of excessive temperatures of exhaust gases, main bearings or reduced lubricating oil pressures and the presence of heavy oil mist in the crankcase. Exceedingly low lubricating oil pressure would call for an immediate stop.

Steam raising

Automatic control of steam raising has been practised over a considerable period and although it offers the greatest scope for efficiency and economy both in manpower and in fuel consumption it is by far the most complex problem.

The correct relationship between fuel supply, feed water supply and temperatures, forced draught, engine load and sea-water temperatures depends on a large number of independent controls. Optimum efficiency is rarely, if ever, achieved without some form of automatic control so this may well pay dividends.

Two basic factors are:

1. Maintenance of steam pressure under varying loads by control of fuel.
2. Optimum combustion control of combustion air flow and maintenance of correct ratio of fuel and air at all combustion rates.

Human control cannot equal the automated instantaneous computation of corrections to be applied under varying conditions e.g. the correct relationship necessary between the performances of fuel pumps and F.D. fans to mention only two items. Combustion is influenced by flue-gas temperature and oxygen supply, fan load, superheat, boiler pressure and temperature of condensate and feed water. Complete elimination of firemen can only come about when there is available an oil-fuel burner with a sufficient turn-down ratio with high stability and a tolerance of impurities. Steam assisted or spill-return type burners with high turn-down ratios and consequently seldom withdrawal are a step in the right direction. A fast and large turn-down ratio in excess of 10 to 1 is necessary. Apart from this, combustion control and feed water regulation and desuperheater temperature control have been successfully automated.

A closed loop will comprise the steam cycle through main turbines, condensers, feed-water heaters and pumps and back to the boiler, controlled at the turbine throttle by either steam header or flow. Sub-loops will regulate water levels in the hot well, de-aerating feed water tank, the boiler and the main circulating pumps.

Rules and regulations

There are at present no Governmental Regulations for automatic control systems and IMCO has deferred action on the grounds that it is still in the development stages and it would be preferable to gain further experience. Nevertheless several countries have expressed concern about the need for additional protection against fire and flooding in unmanned engine rooms and this is receiving attention. Liberia has adopted a code of safety measures in co-operation with a classification society for vessels designated UMS and they are being applied to a number of vessels on an experimental basis.

Some classification societies have adopted special notations for ships suitable for operating with unattended engine rooms and which comply with their special requirements. The notations are:

UMS (unattended machinery spaces). Lloyd's Register of Shipping.
AUT. Bureau Veritas.
EO. Norske Veritas.
✠ ACCU. American Bureau of Shipping.
AUT-16/24 or AUT-h/24 Germischer Lloyd.

Lloyd's Register in its Annual Report for 1976 records that 60% of all types of ship classed by them during that year were automated and that 33% of all ships qualified for the notation UMS. For cargo ships and tankers alone the corresponding figures were 70% and 48% respectively. Chapter L of Lloyd's Register Rules specifies the requirements necessary to qualify for UMS. All control systems applied to essential machinery must be inspected and tested to the satisfaction of the Society even if UMS is not contemplated. The chapter is in general terms thus allowing scope for flexibility but details have to be submitted for approval.

The requirements of Bureau Veritas for the notation AUT are in Chapter 19 of their Rules and this is also brief and in general terms, but a separate Guidance Note publication outlines technical conditions.

Det Norske Veritas describes their requirements for the notation EO in their Chapter VII. They also make provision for Type Approval and for this a separate publication contains a component test programme.

Automatic and remote control systems which comply with the requirements of the American Bureau of Shipping are distinguished in their Record by the symbol ✠ACC and requires constant machinery surveillance by at least one attendant but if approved for an unattended engine-room the symbol is ✠ACCU. Section 46 of the A.B.S. Rules details their requirements for Automatic and remote control systems.

A committee appointed by the Danish Ship Research Institute sponsored by several Danish shipyards has made a Report in general terms applicable to mechanically coupled propulsion plant and steering gear and intended to enable a ship to operate safely with a periodically unattended engine room. A separate report deals with additional features not essential for safety but which will improve operational efficiency.

The requirements of Germischer Lloyd for the notation AUT-16/24 or AUT-h/24 for vessels equipped for operating with unattended machinery spaces are in Chapter 3 Section 18 of their rules. An alternative notation AUT-Z is for vessels with *attended* main propulsion machinery and centralised monitoring and control installations.

The U.S. Coast Guard, the Governmental authority for U.S. shipping has published (January 1969) Navigation and Vessel Inspection Circular 1–69 on automated main and auxiliary machinery containing a comprehensive code applicable to all spheres amenable to automatic control. It is not mandatory and is intended at this stage for guidance purposes only. For unattended machinery spaces, flooding of major proportions but within the maximum capacity of the bilge pumping system a simple timing device which will sound an alarm if the pump operates excessively e.g. more than ten minutes in any fifteen minute interval is envisaged. In all cases an oil detection alarm is also required in the bilge overboard discharge line and in the event of oil being detected an automatic shut down is required but with manual overriding facilities.

20 Electro-magnetic compatability

Electro-magnetic compatibility is a general term covering the more familiar subjects of interference generation and the susceptibility of equipments to interference. The term now includes radio interference, radar interference, sonar interference, telephone interference, computer interference, general electronic interference, etc. It takes account of the susceptibility of all equipments. Electro-magnetic compatibility is thus defined as the ability of all equipments — electrical, electronic, radio and mechanical — to work together without fortuitous electrical coupling between them causing any malfunction.

Failure to achieve a high degree of electro-magnetic compatibility can result in degradation or failure of radio communication circuits, erratic behaviour of automated electronic equipments, spurious echoes on radar or sonar displays, etc. Indeed, if equipment functions in the laboratory but does not give identical results when correctly installed in a ship, then it is probable that a compatibility problem exists.

Theory

Compatibility problems are simply due to electrical energy in the wrong place! How does this energy get there? Firstly, every movement of current along a conductor sets up a magnetic field which surrounds that conductor; secondly, wherever there is a potential difference an electric field extends into the space in the vicinity. These two effects give rise to 'transformer action' and 'charging action' respectively.

Such actions follow time variations in the original currents and voltages which in turn give rise to secondary voltages and currents in adjacent conductors. As the rate of change of such variations increases a third effect becomes more prominent; this is the ability of part of the electrical energy to detach itself from the original source and become a self-supporting electro-magnetic wave — familiar as a radio wave and capable of transferring energy through enormous distances. The amounts of energy transferred can be either quite large, as illustrated by transformer couplings at power frequencies, or very small, micro-volts or micro-microwatts in the case of radio waves.

Another way of transferring energy from circuit to circuit is by the use of common return paths to complete electrical circuits. Such paths may be either common wire conductors, common earth paths through a metallic chassis or case or, very frequently, a common path via the ship's hull. In general it has to be realised that the lead and return wires of any circuit, in the absence of special precautions, are not balanced in relation to the earth plane. That is the distributed capacitances and inductances in each leg of a circuit are not identical and compensating out-of-balance currents will flow in the earth plane. As frequencies rise, this effect becomes more significant and the complex phenomonen of common impedance coupling arises.

Earthing and bonding

In the context of electro-magnetic compatibility the terms 'earthing' and 'bonding' need precise definition. 'Earthing' is the connection of any conducting material to the general mass of the sea, either via the ship's hull or via a specially installed earth plate in contact with the sea. 'Bonding' is the connection of any number of conductors, frames, chassis, etc each to each and *not* to earth.

Earthing and bonding of equipments provide many complex problems in the field of electro-magnetic compatibility due to the formation of loops and common return paths, and it is difficult to give simple guidance. However, since the earth/bonding connections can provide these parallel paths to couple or distribute fortuitous energy, care must be taken to avoid completing circuits in this fashion. Thus, in order of preference:

1. If possible, choose equipment which does not require earthing.
2. If earthing is essential, then bond all the earthing points together and connect to earth at one point only. These bonding connections should follow the signal cables.
3. As an alternative, bond to earth at as many points as possible and avoid 'two point earthing'.

The requirements for safety earthing to avoid shock hazard take precedence over the foregoing requirements and indeed it requires specialised knowledge to deal with some of the more complex installations. In these cases the equipment designers' instructions should be followed implicitly.

Susceptible equipments

Equipments that suffer from interference are classed as 'susceptible', and various arrangements can be employed to reduce this susceptibility. The reduction process is termed 'electromagnetic hardening' and is complementary to the measures to control interference and the use of suppressors.

The susceptibility of an equipment to interference depends upon the number and nature of sensitive circuits employed and the amount of energy involved in those circuits. Circuits which use only small amounts of energy are the most sensitive, e.g. aerial input circuits to radio receivers.

Where it is possible to make a choice from among several types of equipment which may be susceptible, the following points should be considered:

(a) Avoid equipment using very sensitive input circuits.
(b) Prefer low impedance input circuitry to high impedance.
(c) Prefer the use of input circuitry which is balanced to earth and has a high 'common mode rejection ratio'
(d) Use input circuits of the minimum possible bandwidth consistent with the required signal acquisition.

A very simple test to check the immunity of equipment to interference consists in passing a current of approximately 1 amp d.c. through the framework or chassis of sensitive equipment including in the circuit the screens of any connecting cables. The 1 amp current should be interrupted several times by making 'splash' connections; the object being to cause pulses of current to traverse the earth paths of the equipment. The equipment (which must be operating during this test) should not malfunction.

Causes of interference

Almost every type of electrical apparatus is potentially capable of giving rise to interference under the right conditions and even certain non-electrical equipments may also cause trouble due to the generation of static electrical charges. Typical examples of the latter are seawater-lubricated rubber or plastic bearings, especially if they are fluted. In these cases minute electrical charges produced by the rotation of the shaft on the rubbing face of the bearing will give rise to a crackling noise in any adjacent radio set of the portable type.

Interference results from any sudden interruption or change of electrical current such as surges from switches, control gear, motor starters, etc, or it can arise from steady-state conditions which in themselves are a series of current interruptions or reversals. Examples of this type of disturbance vary from the familiar fluorescent tube (even if operating on d.c.) to thyristor control gear, and motors and generators of all kinds.

Erratic or fortuitous connections can also cause an enormous amount of trouble because by their very nature the trouble is intermittent and consequently difficult to trace.

Planning the installation

Fortunately, if electro-magnetic compatibility is considered at the design stage of a ship, a great deal can be done to control and minimise problems and in many cases to eliminate them completely. It is only when this aspect of design is ignored and problems are allowed to develop in a completed ship that investigations and remedies are likely to prove expensive.

Precautions against interference start with the purchase of equipment. All equipment should meet the requirements of BS 1597 : 1975 *Radio interference suppression on marine installations* and associated standard BS 5260 : 1975 *Code of Practice for interference suppression.*

Most of the apparatus used in modern ships is the composite product of a number of manufacturers, e.g. a main supply system will have the generator produced by one manufacturer, the control gear by a second, the surveillance gear a third, the prime mover by a fourth, and so on. This entails a detailed scrutiny over even quite small items and it may happen that equipment, which in itself is inoffensive, will require suppression due to associated small electronic components. A typical example of this is a large motor starter switch where the switch, although physically large is quite innocuous from an interference viewpoint, needs the addition of interference suppressors due to the inclusion of thyristors in the monitoring circuits. Circumstances can arise therefore, where it is necessary to suppress to one manufacturer's equipment in order to control interference from other components from a different manufacturer.

The control of interference starts with a voltage measurement using a very sensitive radio frequency voltmeter. These meters in themselves are highly specialised instruments, but are available from various firms who undertake this type of investigation. The recorded voltage at various frequencies is a measure of the amount of interference that may be expected from the particular piece of equipment under test. Acceptable limits have been set by BS 1597 : 1975.

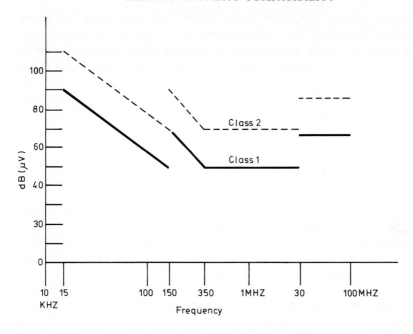

Figure 20.1 Radio frequency terminal voltage limits (From BS 1597 : 1975 and reproduced by permission of the British Standards Institution, 2 Park Street, Lodnon W1)

The graph shown in Figure 20.1 is reproduced from this standard.

It will be seen that the co-ordinates of the graph are frequency ranges and voltages. The voltage is measured in decibels above 1.0 microvolt where 0 db is equivalent to 1.0 microvolt. Two limits are shown, the selection of class 1 or 2 being left to the designer/installer although guidance is given in the Standard as follows:

'The more stringent limit, class 1, will apply to equipment to be used where additional screening is not provided, for example, in a wood or glass fibre ship, above decks on a steel ship where cables or equipment are not screened, in a non-metallic superstructure on a steel hull, or where there is close coupling between the electrical wiring and the radio and navigation equipment. The less stringent limit, class 2, will be employed for electrical and electronic equipment intended to be fitted within the bonded metallic structure of a ship or where screening is provided deliberately.'

It should be noted that the limits quoted apply primarily to the protection of radio and similar types of equipment but they can also be applied and used for the protection of almost any type of equipment which is susceptible to interference.

Equipments which are known or considered to be susceptible to interference should comply with the ideas previously outlined under 'Susceptible equipments'. It is beyond the scope of this chapter to go into the many details that need to be considered as this particular aspect of the science is still developing.

Shipboard installation control starts with the siting of equipments and cable runs and ends with adoption of correct bonding and earthing procedures and proper maintenance during the working life of the ship. it is almost a maxim that if suppressors have to be added in any numbers after the completion of a ship, then the electro-magnetic compatibility study design has not been adequately considered.

The golden rule for electromagnetic compatibility control is physical separation, even to the extent of isolation. Equipments likely to cause interference and those likely to suffer from interference should be kept as far apart as possible, and this includes their connecting cables and all associated circuits. It is, of course, impracticable to give much separation in the average ship and the question then arises, how much?

An answer can only be given in general terms, e.g. that the closer together equipments are, the more likely they are to be incompatible. Screening can be used instead of separation, but it is difficult to assign any figure of merit as the variables are too numerous. In fact some experts even contend that a screen on a radio room is unnecessary; the money saved can be put to a much better use by the provision of more effective local screening for sensitive equipments and the use of various forms of double and superscreened cable.

Precautions

Precautions may be considered under three headings:

1. Spacing/screening
2. Suppressors
3. Cabling

Spacing/screening

Receiving equipments and transmitting equipments of all sorts should be separated from each other and where separation cannot be obtained, then screening should be adopted.

This means radio receivers and transmitters should be constructed so that their cases form complete electromagnetic screens with properly screened connectors to receive their respective aerial feeders and other interconnections.

Suppressors

Ideally, all equipment in a ship should be suppressed to the standards laid down in BS 1597 but there may be occasions when this standard is inadequate or only unsuppressed equipment is available. In such cases external suppressors must be fitted.

There are many types of suppressors available commercially and they should be selected for their suitability for marine conditions and of course for the voltage/current on which they will be used. Suppressors may be simply capacitors or combinations of capacitors and chokes and the values normally used vary between 0.001 and 2.0 microfarads whilst the chokes are usually 0.5 to 1.0 millihenry. (Some guidance on these points is contained in BS 1597).

In the majority of cases suppressors are sited in the power supply lines to equipments and serve to prevent the conduction of interference energy along the lines. Such suppressors should be installed as close as possible to the equipment being protected; preferably not more than 150 mm away. The frame of the suppressor must be bonded efficiently to the case of the relevant equipment and should not be separately connected to earth.

CABLING

Cables should be separated into two groups:

1. Cables connected to sensitive parts of equipments such as amplifier inputs, aerial inputs to radio receivers, etc, and
2. Cables connected to non-sensitive parts of equipments such as power supplies, etc.

Cables in group 1 should not be bunched with those in group 2 and the two groups should be separated by the maximum possible distance.

Single core cables should be avoided; 'feed' and 'return' conductors should be contiguous or better still twisted together. The use of lead-sheathed cables as a means of controlling interference and in order to obtain compatibility is not recommended. The disadvantages of cost, weight and adequate sheath bonding outweigh any interference control advantage. However, in employing the grouping and segregation principles use should be made of any inherent screening offered by the ship's structural material such as ventilation trunking, bulkheads or even metallic cable trays. Such conducting materials should be interposed between groups of sensitive and non-sensitive cables.

A list of cables follows and although this does not pretend to be complete, the typical cases chosen will enable the reader to extrapolate for particular classes of installation.

Cable classification	*Precautions*
Feeders from aerials to radio receivers	These cables should be co-axial, tri-axial or screened balanced pairs. Their route should be as short and direct as possible. Switching in these circuits should be avoided. The screens of the cables, including the inner screen of the tri-axial should be connected to the receiver chassis and not to earth. The exterior screen of the tri-axial should be connected directly to earth. These cables may be grouped with other aerial/receiver feeders and should be isolated from all other cables.
Feeders from radio transmitters to aerials	Similar precautions as for radio receiver feeders but in addition, feeders from high power transmitters should be isolated from all other cables of any kind
Feeders from aerials to transceivers	As for receiver feeders, but in addition these feeders should be isolated from all other cables.
Microphone cables	These should be anti-microphonic, screened twisted pairs. The use of ordinary co-axial type cable is not recommended. Separate these cables from all types of power supplies, fluorescent lighting circuits and digital circuits.

Signal input to computers input	Use twisted pairs or multi-cored cables made up of twisted pairs. Screening is not usually required but avoid the use of 'common returns'. Isolate from any cables carrying high energies.
Sonar transducer feeders	These cables should be installed in galvanised, screwed ferrous conduit. This conduit should enter the metallic framework of the transducer at one end and the framework of the input amplifier at the other.
Ship's rigging	The cables forming the ship's rigging are often a source of unsuspected 'noise'. This is due to the presence of induced currents in metallic conducting cables and the erratic, intermittent connections made by the terminations of such cables. The remedy is to either isolate such cables electrically or bond them efficiently to earth.

MAINTENANCE

Meticulous maintenance of equipment and cabling is essential to preserve electromagnetic compatibility standards and the following points should be considered:

(a) Replace all metallic covers carefully using *all* the fasteners provided.
(b) Ensure good connections between cable screens and their terminating connectors.
(c) Ensure that all bonding and earthing arrangements are clean and tight.
(d) Do not instal temporary wiring in such a way that separation rules are violated.
(e) Avoid loose connections/contacts of any sort.

BIBLIOGRAPHY

BS 1597 : 1975. *Radio interference suppression on marine installations.*

BS 2135 : 1966. *Capacitors for radio interference suppression.*

BS 5260 : 1975. *Code of practice for radio interference suppression on marine installations.*

IEC Publication No 533. *Electromagnetic compatibility of electrical and electronic installations in ships*

21 Insulation testing

Apart from the fact that good insulation resistance is an essential condition for maintaining service, the regular recording of insulation resistance values is undoubtedly the best method of detecting deterioration and of indicating when remedial action is desirable, or perhaps essential, in order to prevent complete failure.

Insulation resistance (IR) should accordingly be measured and recorded at regular intervals, the recording being preferably on a separate log-sheet for each important machine or circuit, so that each fresh reading can be compared with previous values and any downward trend immediately observed.

It cannot be too strongly emphasised that, subject of course to reasonable minimum values being maintained, trends are more important than actual values, a single value is of comparatively little significance. The intelligent interpretation of results is therefore of great importance and a general appreciation of the factors involved is essential.

Measuring insulation resistance

There are several methods of measuring insulation resistance, but the instrument universally used for ship's installations comprises a combined hand-driven generator and an ohmmeter giving direct readings in ohms and megohms. The principles of design of pre-1968 Series 3 Mk 3 Evershed and Vignoles Wee Megger Tester are shown in Figure 22.1. Details of construction are shown in Figure 22.2.

This construction was superseded and discontinued in 1968 by the Series 3 Mk 4 design. This embodies a brushless a.c. generator as shown in Figures 21.3 and 21.4. Outwardly the appearance is unaltered. The Mk 4 still has a d.c. output with the generated a.c. rectified.

In principle this instrument consists of a permanent magnet in the field of which is a voltage and a current coil fixed at an angle to one another with a pointer pivoted at the centre of rotation of the coils.

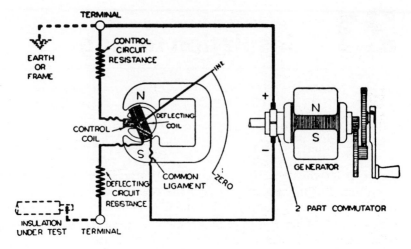

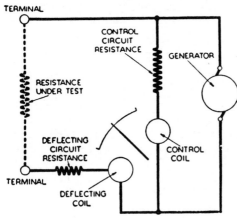

Figure 21.1 Arrangement and typical circuit of pre-1968 Series 3 Mk. 3 'Wee Megger' insulation tester

The needle deflection is a function of the ratio of the current in the coils and provides a direct reading of insulation resistance. The hand-driven generator has a permanent magnet and provides the test voltage. For general use a 500-V set is recommended. The open-circuit voltage (i.e. when the IR is infinity) is generally about 5% above the rated voltage and with zero resistance the voltage will be practically zero. The voltage characteristic curve of this generator rises steeply and reaches its rated value at about the mid point of the scale.

When using the miniature types of instrument where approximate readings are sufficient, the question of which terminal to connect to

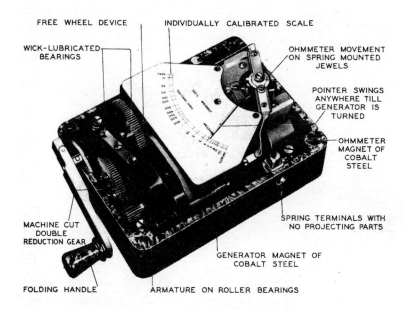

FREE WHEEL DEVICE

INDIVIDUALLY CALIBRATED SCALE

WICK–LUBRICATED BEARINGS

OHMMETER MOVEMENT ON SPRING MOUNTED JEWELS

POINTER SWINGS ANYWHERE TILL GENERATOR IS TURNED

OHMMETER MAGNET OF COBALT STEEL

MACHINE CUT DOUBLE REDUCTION GEAR

SPRING TERMINALS WITH NO PROJECTING PARTS

GENERATOR MAGNET OF COBALT STEEL

FOLDING HANDLE

ARMATURE ON ROLLER BEARINGS

Figure 21.2 'Wee Megger' Tester Series 3 Mk. 3 with cover removed showing arrangement of generator and ohmmeter (Evershed & Vignoles Ltd.)

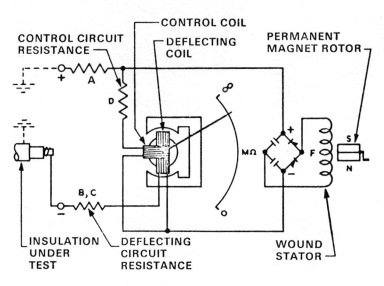

CONTROL COIL

CONTROL CIRCUIT RESISTANCE

DEFLECTING COIL

PERMANENT MAGNET ROTOR

INSULATION UNDER TEST

DEFLECTING CIRCUIT RESISTANCE

WOUND STATOR

Figure 21.3 Principles of design of the Series 3 Mk. 4 'Wee Megger' insulation tester (Evershed & Vignoles Ltd.)

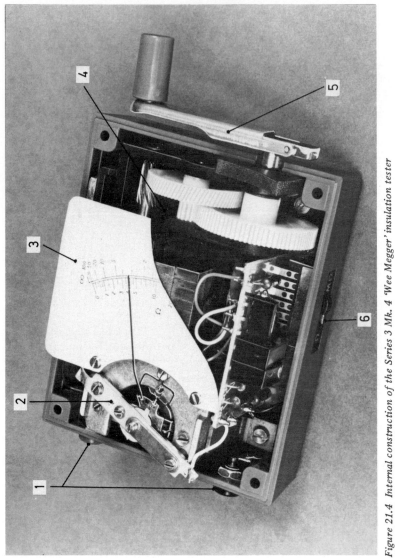

Figure 21.4 Internal construction of the Series 3 Mk. 4 'Wee Megger' insulation tester (Evershed & Vignoles Ltd.)

1. Standard 4 mm sockets
2. Evershed cross-coils movement
3. Individually calibrated scales
4. Brushless a.c. generator
5. Foldaway handle
6. Range switch

earth is relatively unimportant but for more accurate results using the larger instruments it is important that the terminal marked 'earth', which is the positive pole, should be the one connected to earth. It is also important in all cases to turn the handle at a steady constant speed of about 160 rev/min.

Factors affecting insulation resistance

Insulation materials are not perfect and when a voltage is applied a leakage current will flow, although with a good insulator the current will be extremely small. It is the passage of this current which enables the insulation resistance to be measured.

Dust, moisture, oily or saline deposits and other foreign matter deposited on end windings and connections of machines or on cable terminations will result in low readings, and periodical cleaning is therefore important. Solvents left in the varnishes on coils and windings also affect the result, and as the solvents disperse the insulation resistance may increase with age if the machine is kept clean and dry.

Temperature has a considerable effect as the resistance varies inversely with temperatures. At 75–80°C. (the normal working temperature of a machine in the tropics) the resistance may be one-tenth of the value when cold, at say 20°C. Humidity and conditions which lead to the deposit of condensation on the insulation will also produce low readings.

The type of insulation also affects the results. For example, a machine insulated solely with Class A insulation will generally give lower readings than one insulated with mica, and if it is not vacuum-dried and impregnated it will have a lower IR than one so treated. The current flow through the insulation combined with the leakage current along the surface determines the insulation resistance, and the use of mica between the windings and earth limits the current flow and thereby reduces the risk of failure.

A machine which runs continuously will have a better IR than one which runs only intermittently, not only will it dry itself out but the machine which runs intermittently will breathe because of the alternate heating and cooling.

It will be apparent from what has been said that the IR is very much dependent on climatic conditions and the temperature and conditions of the machine or apparatus, e.g. whether it has recently been cleaned or re-varnished. It is therefore important to include a reference to these circumstances in the log. A typical log-sheet is shown on the next page.

Apparatus or circuit			
....			
....			
Date and place	Insulation Resistance Megohms	Weather Conditions	Time of test and other remarks

N.B.—When the test is on a machine, state in the "Remarks" column whether the machine is hot or cold.

The date and place are an indication of the time of year and geographical location and therefore give some idea of the climatic conditions. Under the heading of 'Weather' such entries as fine and bright, cold, very cold, rainy, misty, dry, humid, etc are appropriate.

Where the number of items is too large to warrant a separate log-sheet for each an alternative log as indicated below might be used.

Apparatus or circuit	Date...............		Date...............		Date...............	
	IR	Remarks	IR	Remarks	IR	Remarks
Weather Conditions						

Satisfactory IR values

A formula previously quoted in various regulations for the IR of motors and generators, based on rated voltage and output has now been discarded as being unrealistic. The formula did not take into account the type of machine, e.g. a d.c. motor, an induction motor, and an a.c. generator all of the same voltage and kVA rating, according to the formula would have equal IR, but in practice it will not be the same as due to their different construction the ratio of insulation thickness and insulation area will be radically different, and the construction and insulation will also differ. Also a slow-speed machine will have a lower IR than a high-speed machine of equal rating.

Lloyd's Register requires that for new installations the IR for power and lighting circuits between all insulated poles and earth and, where practicable, between poles should be not less than one megohm. In practice much better results are attainable. At periodical surveys, i.e. after the installation has been in service, the minimum IR acceptable for any circuit is 100 000 ohms.

Whenever possible IR should be measured while machines are hot, i.e. immediately after shut-down. The insulation resistance is then probably at its lowest value and if satisfactory under this condition it will be even better when cold, provided it does not stand idle too long in a humid atmosphere. For machines it is recommended that periodical readings should be taken and the climatic and temperature conditions recorded. Trends in IR values under similar conditions are more important than the actual values.

Works test

A test which is applied in the factory to *new* machines and apparatus is a high voltage (a.c.) between separate windings and between all windings and earth. For machines above 3 h.p. (or kVA) per 1000 rev/min and, with certain exceptions for other apparatus, the test voltage is 100 + twice the rated voltage with a minimum of 2000 V. However, this type of test must not be applied to machines which have been in service or permanent damage may result. It can however be applied to machines or windings which have been completely renewed and reinsulated. Also, when such a test has been applied it is undesirable to repeat it. The duration of the test is usually one minute, and before apply the test the windings must if necessary be dried out.

If in special cases it should become necessary to repeat the works test after a new machine is installed, the test voltage should be not more than 85 per cent of that quoted, but such tests are rarely applied to installations in ships.

Drying-out electrical machines

It frequently becomes necessary to dry out electrical machinery either because it has been exposed to the weather prior to commissioning or has been accidentally immersed. In the latter case if the immersion is in sea water all salt deposits should first be washed out with plain water. In many cases also it may be advisable to dismantle and rebuild the commutator as water deposited inside the commutator cannot be got rid of by drying processes and even though an acceptable insulation resistance may be obtained subsequent failure may occur.

Machines may be dried out by either external or internal heating. If the former method is adopted the machine should be enclosed or covered up so as to retain the heat but in such a manner that moisture can escape either continuously or by periodically lifting the covers. Tarpaulins should not be used. Electric heaters are most suitable, taking care that the hottest part of the machine does not exceed 90°C. Coke, coal, gas or oil stoves should not be used. Internal heating is preferable if it can be arranged and before it is applied the insulation surfaces should be cleaned and surface moisture removed, for field coils not more than half the normal voltage or field current is suitable and if supplied from the busbars a suitable series resistance will be necessary. For load circuits about half full load current can be used. If the current is passed through brushes it is important to rotate the commutator or rotor at frequent intervals. In the case of d.c. machines it is preferable to run them slowly at a low voltage and for a.c. rotors to clamp copper bands around the collector rings and attach the supply leads to these. Winding temperatures should be taken periodically and should not exceed 80°C. Care must be taken not to melt the grease in bearings or to allow grease to run into the machine or along the shaft.

Whichever method is used regular readings or insulation resistance and temperature should be taken and recorded. If the insulation readings are plotted against time it will generally be found that initially there is a steady improvement but after a short while they will steadily drop and may remain low for some time. Eventually a steady recovery should occur until a constant value is reached, but drying-out should be continued, if possible, for several hours more.

Minimum insulation resistance values cannot be stated categorically and it may in some circumstances be necessary to put a machine back into service with a lower value than would normally be acceptable in which case it should be carefully watched until it is found to be operating satisfactorily. For normal ship's voltages a minimum of 1.0 megohms for machines up to 100 kW or b.h.p. and about 0.75 ohms for larger machines might be considered safe.

22 Graphical symbols

The following schedule includes a selection of those symbols which will normally appear in diagrams of ship's installations and is in accordance with British Standards. Those requiring more complete information on this subject might refer to BS 3939.

Description	*Symbol*
Systems symbols	
Earth.	
Alternating current, general symbol.	
Alternating current, single-phase.	
Alternating current, 3-phase.	
Alternating current, 3-phase 50 Hz	
Types of winding	
3-phase delta connected.	
3-phase 3-wire star connected.	
3-phase 4-wire star connected.	

Batteries

Battery of primary or secondary cells. The long thin line is the positive pole.

Alternative symbol.

Battery with tappings.

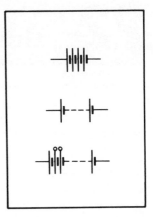

Conductors

Conductor or group of conductors, general symbol.

Two conductors: single-line representation.

Two conductors: multi-line representation.

Three conductors: single-line representation.

Three conductors: multi-line representation.

Single-line representation of n conductors
  Note. The stroke may be omitted if there is no risk of confusion.

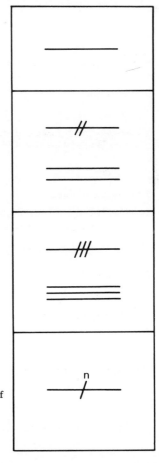

Changing from single-line representation to multi-line
representation.
Example: Four conductors

Crossings and connections of conductors

Crossing of conductor symbols (no electrical connection).

Junction of conductors.

Double junction of conductors.

Common point: A junction where the reduction
of common impedance is of overriding importance.

Terminals and links

Open circles represent readily separable contacts.

Solid circles represent hinged or bolted contacts.

Link normally closed with 2 readily separable contacts.

With two bolted contacts.

Example: Hinged link normally open

Warning and indicating devices

Signal lamp , general symbol.

Electric bell, general symbol.

Electric bell: single stroke.

Electric buzzer, general symbol.

Siren.

Horn.

Fuses

Fuse, general symbol.

   The supply side may be indicated by a thick line thus

Alternative general symbol.

   With bolted contacts.

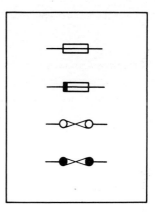

Resistors

Fixed resistor.

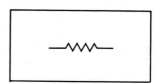

Fixed resistor: specially non-reactive.

Alternative symbol.

Resistor with inherent non-linear variability.

Capacitors

Capacitor, general symbol.
  Note: The clearance between the plates should
  be between one fifth and one third of the length
  of the plate.

Variable capacitor, general symbol.

Lamps and illumination

Filament lamp.

Cold cathode discharge lamp (e.g. neon lamp).

Discharge lamp, general symbol.

Hot cathode tubular fluorescent lamp.

Instrument transformers

Current transformer.

Single-phase voltage transformer, wound type.

3 phase voltage transformer connection star-star.

Transductors

Transductor core, general symbol.

Alternative symbol.

Self-exciting transductor with two control circuits.

Symbols for installation diagrams

Wiring in conduit.

Wiring in duct or trunking.

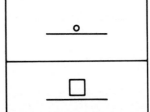

Wiring going upwards.	
Wiring going downwards.	
Lighting point or lamp, general symbol.	
Emergency (safety) lighting point.	
Single fluorescent lamp.	
Group of three fluorescent lamps.	
Signal lamp.	
Single-pole one-way switch.	
Three-pole one way switch.	
Push button.	

Socket outlet (mains), general symbol.

In UK practice this general symbol normally implies the presence of an earthing contact. Exceptions to this rule should be indicated by a note, e.g. shaver outlet.

Switched socket outlet.

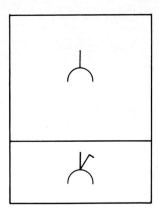

Switchgear and control

Make contact (normally open), general symbols.

Break contact (normally closed), general symbols.

Circuit breaker (four variants)

Alternative symbol for use on diagrams drawn in single-line representation.

Make contactor.

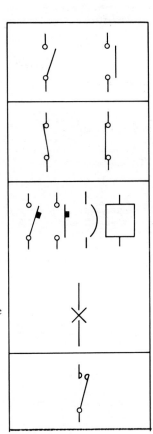

Break contactor.

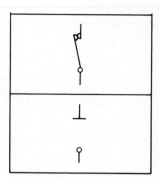

Isolator, not switching load.

Drum-type controllers

Note. The position of the rectangle represents the position(s) in which the circuit is completed between the associated terminals.
Example.
   3 position 4 circuit drum type controller.

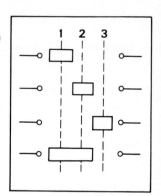

Transformers

Winding (i.e. of an inductor, coil choke coil, inductive reactor or transformer.

Alternative general symbols.

   non-preferred.

   non-preferred.

If it is desired to indicate that the winding has a core it may be shown thus

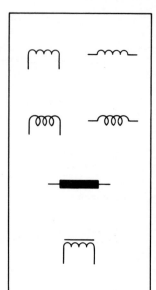

Transformer, general symbols

    Simplified form.

    Complete form.

    Variometer.

    Alternative symbol.

Induction regulators

    General symbols:

        Simplified form.

        Complete form.

A.C. machines

    A.C. generator, general symbol.

A.C. motor: general symbol.	(M ~)
Synchronous generator, general symbol.	(GS)
Synchronous motor, general symbol.	(MS)
Permanent magnet synchronous generator, 3-phase.	(GS 3~)
Induction motor, cage rotor, general symbol.	(M ~)
Induction motor, wound rotor, general symbol.	(M ~)
Induction motor, wound rotor, 3-phase.	(M 3~)

Diode devices

Note 1. The triangle points in the direction of conventional
current flow.

Note 2. In the objective symbol for diodes and thyristors, the
triangle is unfilled and to simplify drawing, the line
representing the connections passes through the centre.
Alternatively the triangle may be filled in.

pn diode, general symbol.

Alternative symbol.

Tunnel diode.

Thyristor, general symbol.

pnp transistor.

23 Regulations and regulating organisations

The following is a schedule of organisations concerned with shipping and shipbuilding, and references to regulations affecting electrical installations.

Classification Societies

Lloyd's Register of Shipping, 71 Fenchurch St., London EC3M 4BS

American Bureau of Shipping, 65 Broadway, New York 4, N.Y., and Winchester House, 77 London Wall, E.C.2.

Bureau Veritas, 31 rue Henri-Rochefort, Paris, and Ocean House, Great Tower Street, London, E.C.3.

Germanischer Lloyd, Neuer Wall 86, 2000 Hamburg 36, Germany. and c/o Stelp and Leighton, Ltd., St. Ives House, 99 Roseberg Avenue, London E.C.1.

Nippon Kaiji Kyokai, 1 Akasaka-Fukuzoshi-cho, Minato-kn, Tokyo, Japan, and Europe House, St. Katherines Way, London, E.C.1.

Det Norske Veritas, PO Box 6060, Etherstad. Oslo 6, Norway, and Cathedral Buildings, Dean St., Newcastle.

Registro Italiano Navale, via Corsica 12, 16128 Genoa, Italy.

USSR Register of Shipping, Corky St 11, Moscow K9, USSR.

Regulations and Standards

Regulations for the Electrical and Electronic Equipment of Ships with recommended practice for their implementation.

Published by The Institution of Electrical Engineers, Stevenage SG1 1HQ.
(As these Regulations are quoted in Statutory Instruments SI 1103–1965 and SI 1104–1965 they are obligatory for British Registered Ships)

Recommended Practice for Electrical Installations on Shipboard, IEEE Std 45
Published by The Institute of Electrical and Electronics Engineers, Inc. 345 East 47th St., New York N.Y. 10017. U.S.A.

Governmental and Official Publications

The following publications can be obtained from HM Stationery Office unless otherwise stated.

Cmnd 2812. International Convention for the Safety of Life at Sea 1960 (SOLAS 1960).
Treaty Series No 65 (1965).

SI 1103–1965. The Merchant Shipping (Passenger Ship Construction) Rules 1965.

SI 1104–1965. The Merchant Shipping (Cargo Ship Construction and Survey) Rules 1965.
(*Note:* SI 1103 and SI 1104 give effect to SOLAS 1960 *inter alia*).

SOLAS 1974. International Conference on Safety of Life at Sea 1974.
(Obtainable from the Inter-Governmental Maritime Consultative Organisation (IMCO), 101-1-4 Piccadilly, London W1V OAE)

SI 1105–1965. The Merchant Shipping (Life-Saving Appliances) Rules 1965. (Includes requirements for Electric Lighting and Signals).

SI 1106–1965. The Merchant Shipping (Fire Appliances) Rules 1965. (Includes requirements for fire detection systems and their sources of supply. Remote stopping of fans).

SI 1036–1953. The Merchant Shipping (Crew Accommodation) Regulations 1953. (Includes requirements for electric lighting standards and spare gear for fan motors).

SI 1660–1954. Amendments to SI 1036–1953.

British Standards

Published by British Standards Institution, British Standards House, 2, Park St., London, W1A 2BS
(Obtainable from BSI, 101 Pentonville Road, London N19ND)

BS 229: 1957. Flameproof enclosure of electrical apparatus.

BS 350. Conversion factors and tables.

    Part 1: 1974. Basis of tables. Conversion factors.

    Part 2: 1962. Detailed conversion tables.

    Supplement No. 1: 1967 Additional tables for SI conversions.

BS 1259: 1958. Intrinsically safe electrical apparatus and circuits for use in explosive atmospheres.

BS 1597: 1975. Radio interference suppression on marine installations.

BS 1991. Letter symbols, signs and abbreviations.

    Part 1: 1976. General.

    Part 2: 1961. Chemical Engineering, nuclear science and applied chemistry.

    Part 3: 1961. Fluid mechanics.

    Part 4: 1961. Structures, materials & soil mechanics.

    Part 5: 1961. Applied thermodynamics.

    Part 6: 1975. Electrical science & engineering.

    Supplement No. 1: 1973. List of subscripts for electrical technology.

BS 2757: 1956. Classification of insulating materials for electrical machinery and apparatus on the basis of thermal stability in service.

BS 2949: 1960. Rotating electrical machines for use in ships.

BS 3399: 1961. Transformers for use in ships.

BS 3763: 1976. The International System of Units (SI).

International Electrotechnical Commission

(Published by International Electrotechnical Commission 1 rue de Varembe, Geneva, Switzerland.)

(Also obtainable from British Standards Institution)

Electrical Installations in Ships

92–1 Part 1. General requirements.

92–2 Part 2. Graphical symbols.

92–3 Part 3. Cables (construction, testing and installation).

92–4 Part 4. Switchgear, electrical protection and control-gear.

92–5 Part 5. Transformers; semi-conductor rectifiers; generators (with associated prime movers) and motors; electric propulsion plant, tankers.

92–6 Part 6. Accessories; lighting; accumulator (storage) batteries; heating and cooking appliances; internal communications; lightning conductors.

Japan Marine Standards Association (JMSA)

Somitomo Bank Building, 6—12 Ichome Toranomon, Minato-ku, Tokyo 105, Japan.

24 Units and conversions

International Regulations will in future adopt SI units throughout. This applies also to TACS (International Association of Classification Societies). A selection of SI units is given below. Abbreviations for the names of units are the same in the singular and in the plural; they should not carry a full stop (as the mark of an abbreviation)

Base units

Quantity	Unit	Symbol
length	metre	m
mass	kilogram	kg
time	second	S
electric current	ampere	A
temperature	kelvin	K

Multiples and sub-multiples

Multiplying factor	Prefix	Symbol
$1\,000\,000\,000\,000 = 10^{12}$	tera	T
$1\,000\,000\,000 = 10^{9}$	giga	G
$1\,000\,000 = 10^{6}$	mega	M
$1\,000 = 10^{3}$	kilo	k
$100 = 10^{2}$	histo	h
$10 = 10^{1}$	deca	da
$0.1 = 10^{-1}$	deci	d
$0.001 = 10^{-3}$	milli	m
$0\,000\,001 = 10^{-6}$	micro	μ
$0\,000\,000\,001 = 10^{-9}$	nano	n
$0\,000\,000\,000\,001 = 10^{-12}$	pico	p

(*Note.* For a complete schedule of letter symbols, signs and abbreviations together with guidance on general principles for their use in engineering, see BS 1991.)

Derived SI units

Quantity	SI Unit	Symbol	Derived unit
frequency	hertz	Hz	$1\ Hz = s^{-1}$
force	newton	N	$1\ N = 1\ kgn/s^{2}$
pressure, stress	pascal	Pa	$1\ Pa = 1\ N/m^{2}$

quantity of heat, work, energy	joule	J	1 J = 1 NM
power	watt	W	1 W = 1 J/s
electric potential	volt	V	1 V = 1 W/A
electric capacitance	farad	F	1 F = 1 AS/V
electric resistance	ohm	Ω	1 Ω = 1 V/A
electric inductance	henry	H	1 H = Vs/A

Other units

Quantity	*Symbol*
square metre	m²
cubic metre	m³
square millimetre	mm²
minute (time)	min
hour	h
Celsius temperature	°C
International nautical mile (n mile)	1 n mile = 1852 m
	(1 fathom = 1.83 m)
velocity (knot)	kn
	(1 kn = 1 n mile/h)
root-mean-square	r.m.s.
maximum continuous rating	m.c.r.
volt-ampere	VA
revolution per minute	rev/min

Useful formulae

$$kW = kVA \times \text{power factor}$$

$$kVA = \frac{kW}{\text{power factor}}$$

$$kW = \frac{h.p. \times 746}{1000 \times \text{efficiency}}$$

$$kW \text{ (three-phase)} = \frac{\text{line amps} \times \text{line volts} \times 1.732 \times \text{power factor}}{1000}$$

$$kVA \text{ (three-phase)} = \frac{\text{line amps} \times \text{line volts} \times 1.732}{1000}$$

Values of some UK units in terms of SI units

Area	in.²	645.16 mm²
Volume	UK gal	4.546 dm³ *

Velocity	ft/s	0.3048 m/s
	mile/h	0.447 m/s
Mass	lb.	0.45359237 kg
Force	lbf	4.44822 N
Pressure	lbf/in.^{2}	6.89476 kN/m^2
Energy	cal	4.1868 J
(work, heat)	Bru	1.05506 kJ
Power	h.p.	745.700 W

(*The word 'litre' is now recognised as a special name for the cubic decimetre 1 UK gal. = 4.546 litres)

Table 24.1 Conversion factors

To convert	British to Metric Multiply by	Metric to British Multiply by
Inches—Millimetres	25.4	0.0394
Feet—Metres	0.305	3.281
Yards—Metres	0.914	1.094
Miles—Kilometres	1.609	0.621
Sq. Inches—Sq. Centimetres	6.452	0.155
Cu. Inches—Cu. Centimetres	16.387	0.061
Cu. Feet—Cu. Metres	0.028	35.315
Ocean Tons—Cu. Metres	1.132	0.883
Pounds—Kilogrammes	0.454	2.205
Tons—Tonnes	1.016	0.984
Gallons—Litres	4.546	0.220
British h.p. (746 watts)—Metric h.p. (736 watts)	1.014	0.986
p.s.i.—Kg. per sq. cm.	0.070	14.223
Tons per sq. in.—Kg. per sq. mm.	1.575	6.635
Gal. per min.—Cu. Metres per hr.	0.273	3.666

Table 24.2 Approximate full load currents of 3-phase motors of average efficiency

Motor size		Approx full load current (amps)		
kW	n.p. (approx)	380 V	415 V	440 V
1	1.3	2.2	2.1	2.0
2	2.7	4.7	4.2	4.0
3	4	6.7	6.0	5.7
5	6.7	10.8	10.0	9.6
7.5	10	15.4	13.7	13.0
10	13	20.1	17.8	16.8
20	27	41.0	37.5	34.5
30	40	60.0	54.1	51.0
40	54	81.0	74.0	71.0
50	67	98.0	91.0	84.0
75	101	146	134	126
100	134	213	176	166
300	402	570	519	489
450	603	835	778	733

Relative susceptibility of metals to galvanic action

Metals in electrical contact with other dissimilar metals in the presence of an electrolyte will corrode, the wastage occurring at the metal which is anodic in relation to the other. In the table below which is based on experience with corrosion and on laboratory measurement, the common metals are arranged in a galvanic series.

The further any two metals are from each other in this series the greater will be the tendency to corrode, but those grouped together will have only slight action on one another. Each metal will be anodic or positive in relation to those shown lower in the table and if in electrical contact therewith will corrode. Voltage figures are omitted as these vary according to conditions such as small changes in composition or the degree of salinity or the temperature of the electrolyte, and furthermore metals shown in the same group may also change their relative positions. Appreciable differences are found between steels of different qualities and even between steels ostensibly of the same specification. Generally however the positions shown are correct where the electrolyte is sea water.

Corroded end (anodic)	Magnesium
	Aluminium
	Duralumin
	Zinc
	Cadmium
	Iron
	Soft solder
	Tin
	Lead
	Nickel
	Brass
	Bronze
	Copper Nickel
	Copper
	Silver solder
Protected end (cathodic)	Silver

(Ref.—McKay and Worthington, *Corrosion Resistance of Metals and Alloys* (Reinhold 1936).)

Index